STANDING TO ENFORCE EUROPEAN UNION LAW BEFORE NATIONAL COURTS

Access to court has long been recognised as an essential element of a Union based on the rule of law. This book asks, how can Member States ensure that their rules on standing guarantee that right? The book answers this question by analysing the requirements of EU law from two angles: first, the effective protection of Union rights; second, the effectiveness of Union law per se. With detailed case law examination, the book formulates an autonomous Union law doctrine of standing based on the principle of effective judicial protection. It then goes further, setting out an effectiveness test of Member States' enforcement mechanisms, to ensure that EU law is rendered operative in practice. This is a rigorous study on a question of immense importance.

Volume 104 in the Series Modern Studies in European Law

Modern Studies in European Law

Recent titles in this series:

The Rise and Decline of Fundamental Rights in EU Citizenship
Adrienne Yong

The Court of Justice and European Criminal Law: Leading Cases in a Contextual Analysis
Edited by Valsamis Mitsilegas, Alberto di Martino and Leandro Mancano

The EU as a Global Regulator for Environmental Protection: A Legitimacy Perspective
Ioanna Hadjiyianni

Citizenship, Crime and Community in the European Union
Stephen Coutts

Critical Reflections on Constitutional Democracy in the European Union
Edited by Sacha Garben and Inge Govaere

Constitutional Law of the EU's Common Foreign and Security Policy: Competence and Institutions in External Relations
Graham Butler

The Juridification of Individual Sanctions and the Politics of EU Law
Eva Nanopoulos

Sixty Years of European Integration and Global Power Shifts: Perceptions, Interactions and Lessons
Edited by Julien Chaisse

Fundamental Rights and Mutual Recognition in the Area of Freedom, Security and Justice: A Role for Proportionality?
Ermioni Xanthopoulou

Law and Judicial Dialogue on the Return of Irregular Migrants from the European Union
Edited by Madalina Moraru, Galina Cornelisse and Philippe De Bruycker

Framing Convergence with the Global Legal Order: The EU and the World
Edited by Elaine Fahey

EU Citizenship at the Edges of Freedom of Movement
Katarina Hyltén-Cavallius

The Internal Market 2.0
Edited by Sacha Garben and Inge Govaere

New Directions in European Private Law
Edited by Mateja Durovic and Takis Tridimas

For the complete list of titles in this series, see 'Modern Studies in European Law' link at www.bloomsburyprofessional.com/uk/series/modern-studies-in-european-law

Standing to Enforce European Union Law before National Courts

Hilde K Ellingsen

• HART •
OXFORD • LONDON • NEW YORK • NEW DELHI • SYDNEY

HART PUBLISHING
Bloomsbury Publishing Plc
Kemp House, Chawley Park, Cumnor Hill, Oxford, OX2 9PH, UK
1385 Broadway, New York, NY 10018, USA
29 Earlsfort Terrace, Dublin 2, Ireland

HART PUBLISHING, the Hart/Stag logo, BLOOMSBURY and the Diana logo are trademarks of Bloomsbury Publishing Plc

First published in Great Britain 2021

A catalogue record for this book is available from the British Library.

Library of Congress Cataloging-in-Publication data

Names: Ellingsen, Hilde K, author.

Title: Standing to enforce European Union law before national courts / Hilde K Ellingsen.

Description: Oxford, UK ; New York, NY : Hart Publishing, an imprint of Bloomsbury Publishing, 2021. | Series: Modern studies in European law ; volume 104 | Based on author's thesis (doctoral - Universitetet i Oslo, 2018). | Includes bibliographical references and index.

Identifiers: LCCN 2020056201 (print) | LCCN 2020056202 (ebook) | ISBN 9781509937141 (hardback) | ISBN 9781509947454 (paperback) | ISBN 9781509937165 (pdf) | ISBN 9781509937158 (Epub)

Subjects: LCSH: International and municipal law—European Union countries. | Locus standi—European Union countries.

Classification: LCC KJE971.5 .E45 2021 (print) | LCC KJE971.5 (ebook) | DDC 347.4/052—dc23

LC record available at https://lccn.loc.gov/2020056201

LC ebook record available at https://lccn.loc.gov/2020056202

ISBN: HB: 978-1-50993-714-1
ePDF: 978-1-50993-716-5
ePub: 978-1-50993-715-8

Typeset by Compuscript Ltd, Shannon

ACKNOWLEDGEMENTS

This book is the product of four years of doctoral research at the University of Oslo. There are many people to whom I owe a debt of gratitude.

First, I am immensely grateful to my supervisors, Professors Finn Arnesen, Hans Petter Graver and Tarjei Bekkedal for their generosity and commitment every step of the way. I must also express my gratitude to former colleagues Bjarte Thorson, Stian Øby Johansen, Siri Venemyr, Anna Andersson and Sofie Høgestøl for reading and commenting on my work, and having confidence in the project.

This book has greatly benefited from constructive comments and words of encouragement offered by the members of the adjudication committee. I express my gratitude to Professors Niamh Nic Shuibhne, Ole-Andreas Rognstad and Michael Dougan, and to the expert assessor at the midway assessment, Professor Peter-Christian Müller-Graff.

I have received generous support from the administration at the University of Oslo. Special thanks go to Senior librarian Inger Hamre, who has gone beyond the call of duty to assist me over the years.

I am also grateful for the generous assistance given by copyeditors Chris Saunders and Catherine Minahan, and by the production team at Hart Publishing.

Lastly, many heartfelt thanks to my family for putting up with me when I was not at my best, and for allowing me to be selfish during the final stages of the project.

CONTENTS

TABLE OF CASES

European Court of Justice

General Court and the Court of First Instance

European Court and Commission of Human Rights

Domestic Courts

United Kingdom

United States

Advocate General Opinions

TABLE OF LEGISLATION

Treaties

Regulations

Directives

Other Documents

1

Introduction

I. The Topic of this Book

The Court of Justice of the European Union[1] has recognised that access to court is an essential element of a Union based on the rule of law.[2] National rules on *locus standi* act as important 'filters of access to justice'[3] in the Member States, since they can prevent a claimant from enforcing the law and obtaining a remedy. This book provides a theory on how European Union (EU) law shapes domestic standing rules.[4] The requirements Union law sets for national standing rules can be seen from various angles. One could, for example, ask how Union law influences national standing rules, or what requirements under Union law national laws governing standing must meet. Alternatively one could ask whether (and under what conditions) a private party must be afforded standing as a matter of Union law. These different angles are, nevertheless, variations of the same question: *Which standing rules must a Member State apply to live up to the demands of EU law?*

The enforcement of the substantive norms created at EU level lies largely in the hands of the Member States.[5] Domestic enforcement of Union law is primarily governed by national procedural and remedial rules. The Court has nevertheless expressed certain requirements with which the enforcement provisions of the Member States must comply in order to ensure that individual rights are protected and the effectiveness of Union law is guaranteed. These requirements are based on, first, the principles of equivalence and effectiveness – which require that domestic enforcement rules are no less favourable than those governing similar domestic actions, and do not render practically impossible

[1] The Court of Justice of the European Union comprises the Court of Justice, the General Court and specialised courts, see Art 19(1) of the Treaty on European Union (TEU). It is primarily the case law of the Court of Justice that will be addressed in this contribution, and I use the terms 'ECJ', 'Court' and 'Court of Justice' interchangeably.

[2] See, inter alia, Case 294/83 *Les Verts* [1986] para 23.

[3] AG Cruz Villalón in Case C-510/13 *E.ON* [2014] para 43.

[4] The terms 'European Union law', 'Union law' and 'EU law' will be used interchangeably in the following.

[5] The division of competences was designed to follow the logic of a system of 'executive federalism', where the EU lays down the rules, and the Member States implement, apply and enforce them: see AH Türk, 'Judicial Review of Integrated Administration in the EU' in HCH Hofmann and AH Türk (eds), *Legal Challenges in EU Administrative Law: towards an integrated administration* (Edward Elgar 2009) 218, 218; and H-W Micklitz, 'The ECJ Between the Individual Citizen and the Member States – A Plea for a Judge-Made European Law on Remedies' in H-W Micklitz and B de Witte (eds), *The European Court of Justice and the Autonomy of the Member States* (Intersentia 2012) 347, 367.

or excessively difficult the exercise of rights conferred by Union law[6] – and, second, the principle of effective judicial protection.

These principles are developed by the Court on a case-by-case basis, which provides for a rather incoherent legal framework.[7] Accordingly, identifying the division of competences between the EU and the Member States regarding procedures and remedies is by no means straightforward. This does not mean that we should call off the 'search [for] the dividing line between national and European law'.[8] This book aims to spell out the dividing line between Union law and domestic law in relation to standing. It addresses what EU law requires of the Member States in the context of (alleged) infringements of Union law committed by Member States and private parties.[9]

The impact of Union law on access to court will depend on the legal framework in the Member State concerned. It is a widely shared procedural principle that proceedings are initiated by the parties rather than the judge.[10] Still, the rules on legal standing vary considerably between the Member States.[11] The idea that every person should have the right to bring an action in the public interest – an *actio popularis* – is not fully recognised in any of the Member States. The Member States apply different doctrines to limit the scope of persons with standing. While natural or legal persons of full capacity are generally eligible to sue, most Member States require the claimant to demonstrate either a right or an interest in order to be granted access to court.[12] What this implies, more precisely, varies between the legal systems, and it may also vary depending on the type of proceeding. In the public law context, for instance, there may be 'good reasons for extending standing to a relatively large section of the population … such as protecting the rule of law by permitting concerned citizens to challenge the improper exercise of power by a public authority'.[13]

That being said, there are both practical and political reasons that militate against open standing. Standing rules can serve to exclude meddlesome 'busybodies'[14] with no

[6] Case C-13/01 *Safalero* [2003] para 49.

[7] In the words of Tridimas, '[t]his is an area where casuistry prevails'; see T Tridimas, *The General Principles of EU Law*, 2nd edn (Oxford University Press 2006) 422. The legal framework governing private enforcement is 'complex, opaque, and has been based (controversially) on a range of legal bases'; see S Drake, 'More Effective Private Enforcement of EU Law Post-Lisbon: Aligning Regulatory Goals and Constitutional Values' in S Drake and M Smith (eds), *New Directions in the Effective Enforcement of EU Law and Policy* (Edward Elgar 2016) 12, 13.

[8] The term is borrowed from JH Jans, 'State Liability: In Search of a Dividing Line between National and European Law' in D Obradovic and N Lavranos (eds), *Interface between EU Law and National Law* (Europa Law Publishing 2007).

[9] Standing relative to bringing cases before the Union courts and the ability to challenge Union acts collaterally through Art 267 of the Treaty on the Functioning of the European Union (TFEU) will not be the object of this contribution. See, however, ch 5, section III for an overview of standing rules before the Union courts.

[10] J Zekoll, 'Comparative Civil Procedure' in *The Oxford Handbook of Comparative Law* 2nd edn (Oxford University Press 2019) 1313.

[11] On the distinction between, and advantages of, 'open' and 'closed' systems, see K Schiemann, 'Locus Standi' (1990) 35 *Public Law* 342.

[12] S Beljin, 'Rights in EU Law' in S Prechal and B van Roermund (eds), *The Coherence of EU Law. The Search for Unity in Divergent Concepts* (Oxford University Press 2008) 91, 105.

[13] M Dougan, 'Who Exactly Benefits from the Treaties? The Murky Interaction Between Union and National Competence over the Capacity to Enforce EU Law' (2009) 12 *Cambridge Yearbook of European Legal Studies* 73, 76–77.

[14] See Lord Scarman in *R v Inland Revenue Commissioners, ex parte National Federation of Self-Employed and Small Businesses Ltd* [1981] UKHL 2, [1982] AC 617, speaking of the need to prevent 'abuse by busybodies, cranks and other mischief-makers'.

stake in the outcome of the case, ensure the appropriate use of scarce judicial resources and avoid the court being flooded with claims, overloading their dockets. Circumscribed standing rules may also serve to ensure a degree of 'concrete adverseness which sharpens the presentation of the issues' before the court, and prevent the court from having to address abstract questions of law.[15] Moreover, circumscribed standing rules can be a means of preserving the separation of powers, by preventing the court from being converted into a political arena.[16] These may well in and of themselves be legitimate considerations. The crux of the matter is what happens when these considerations clash with the rationale of ensuring the effective protection of Union rights and the effectiveness of Union law.

The influence of Union law on domestic standing doctrines cannot be analysed with reference to established theories of constitutional and administrative law. In the Union law context, the issue of standing is tainted by the fact that we are dealing with a *shared legal order*,[17] where the substantive norms are formulated at the Union level but given effect at the domestic level.[18] It will be argued that EU law primarily exerts its influence on national standing rules through the principle of effective judicial protection.[19] Hence, the Union law doctrine of standing is first and foremost predicated on the notion that the Union legal order grants rights that must be protected through legal proceedings before domestic courts.[20] The principle of effective judicial protection is now enshrined in Article 47(1) of the Charter of Fundamental Rights, requiring that '[e]veryone whose rights and freedoms guaranteed by the Union are violated has the right to an effective remedy', and Article 19(1) TEU, requiring the Member States to 'provide remedies sufficient to ensure effective legal protection in the fields covered by Union law'.

Based on the mentioned principle, I submit that an autonomous *Union approach to standing* can be formulated. The constitutive conditions are determined by EU law, and ultimately fall to be defined by the Court. Pursuant to the principle of supremacy, national rules incompatible with this standing doctrine have to yield. Member States are only competent to regulate standing in accordance with and in extension of the Union standard.[21] This Union doctrine of standing, it will be argued, is one of the many

[15] The citation is from *Baker v Carr*, 369 US 186 (1962), but the rationale is also of relevance in the European context.

[16] For a comparison of standing rules within the framework of the separation of powers, see T Zwart, 'Comparing Standing Regimes from a Separation of Powers Perspective' (2002) 53 *Northern Ireland Legal Quarterly* 391.

[17] The term is borrowed from JH Jans, 'On Inuit and Judicial Protection in a Shared Legal Order' (2002) 21 *European Energy and Environmental Law Review* 188.

[18] In the words of Godt, '[t]he main conflict inherent in the direct effect doctrine is the conflict between the EC and its Member States, *not* that between the individual and the state': see C Godt, 'Enforcement of Environmental Law by Individuals and Interest Groups: Reconceptualizing Standing' (2000) 23 *Journal of Consumer Policy* 79, 92.

[19] See, inter alia, Case C-510/13 *E.ON Földgaz* [2015] and Case C-104/13 *Olainfarm* [2014]. See further chs 4 and 5.

[20] In the words of Cappelletti and Garth, 'the possession of rights is meaningless without mechanisms for their effective vindication'; see B Garth and M Cappelletti, 'Access to Justice: The Newest Wave in the World-wide Movement to Make Rights Effective' (1978) 27 *Buffalo Law Review* 181, 185.

[21] See P van Cleynenbreugel, 'Judge-Made Standards of National Procedure in the Post-Lisbon Constitutional Framework' (2012) 37 *EL Rev* 90, 94, who makes this point in relation to EU-wide procedural standards more generally.

pieces of the 'judge-made jigsaw of [judicial] protection'.[22] It adds an extra layer to the procedural arrangements existing in the Member States. It may also entail modifying or adding elements to the domestic regime.

Allowing private parties to pursue their Union rights in court does not necessarily, in and of itself, render EU law effective in the Member States. This means that the influence of EU law on domestic standing rules cannot be analysed solely with reference to the principle of effective judicial protection. If individual rights are not at stake, there will be a need to examine the extent to which standing must be provided with a view to ensuring that Union law is rendered effective in the Member State concerned. This second question merits a shift in perspective. Rather than focusing on the claimant, focus should be on the effectiveness of EU law per se. The relevant question to ask is whether legal action initiated by the claimant is required to ensure effective enforcement. When answering this question, regard must be had to the overall enforcement regime in place in the Member State concerned. This means that public enforcement mechanisms must also be taken into account.[23] The principle of loyal cooperation enshrined in Article 4(3) TEU requires Member States to ensure an effective enforcement regime, which may entail opening up for private enforcement where this is required in order to avoid an enforcement deficit.

The two rationales underlying interference in domestic standing doctrines – the need to ensure the effective protection of Union rights and the need to render Union law effective in the Member States – are closely intertwined. A claimant initiating legal proceedings also contributes to vindicating the public interest for which the legal instrument was enacted. Private enforcement may thus, at the same time, serve both the private interest of the individual claimant and the public policies embodied in the Union law provision in question. One can say that the 'private interest contributes to safeguarding the public interest'.[24] The intertwinement of the rationale of ensuring effective judicial protection and that of rendering Union law effective in the Member State is reinforced by the EU's particular regulatory style. The Union legislature tends to enact detailed legal norms benefiting individuals, with a view to enlisting private parties as enforcers of Union law.[25] Acknowledging the (partly) instrumental nature of Union rights means accepting that considerations of *effet utile* influence the requirements stemming from Union law in the field of procedures and remedies.

The Court held in its Opinion 1/09 *Patent Court Agreement* that together with the Court itself, the Member States are the 'guardians of [the] legal order and the judicial system of the European Union', and they need to ensure 'the full application of European Union law in all Member States and to ensure judicial protection of an individual's rights under that law'.[26] This twofold standard – ensuring the effectiveness of EU law, on the one hand, and effective rights protection on the other – will be a recurrent theme throughout the book. We shall see how these requirements differ and interact, and how together they might impact the domestic standing regimes in the Member States.

[22] M Ross, 'Beyond Francovich' (1993) 56 *MLR* 55, 55.
[23] See further ch 13 on the interplay between various modes of enforcement.
[24] AP Komninos, 'Public and Private Antitrust Enforcement in Europe: Complement? Overlap?' (2006) 3 *The Competition Law Review* 5, 15.
[25] On this distinct regulatory style, see ch 2, section IV.
[26] Opinion 1/09 *Patent Court Agreement* [2011] paras 66 and 68.

The importance of standing rules for the effective functioning of Union law in the Member States can hardly be overstated. National courts are, together with the ECJ, the guardians of that legal order and the judicial system of the European Union.[27] The ability to accomplish this mandate is dependent on appropriate cases being let in. It is only once access to court has been granted that the breach of a duty or the violation of a right can be established by the court, and a sanction imposed or a remedy awarded. Without an available legal avenue, Union rights 'become no more than empty guarantees'.[28] It also merits emphasis that strict standing rules can jeopardise the adequate functioning of the preliminary reference procedure. The particular features of this procedure was highlighted in *Commission v Poland*:

> [I]n order to ensure that the specific characteristics and the autonomy of the EU legal order are preserved, the Treaties have established a judicial system intended to ensure consistency and uniformity in the interpretation of EU law … In particular, the judicial system as thus conceived has as its keystone the preliminary ruling procedure provided for in Article 267 TFEU, which, by setting up a dialogue between one court and another, specifically between the Court of Justice and the courts and tribunals of the Member States, has the object of ensuring that consistency and that uniformity in the interpretation of EU law, thereby serving to ensure its full effect and its autonomy as well as, ultimately, the particular nature of the law established by the Treaties.[29]

National courts serve as 'the gatekeepers' of the preliminary reference procedure.[30] If an action is rejected already at the admissibility stage, any possibility of involving the Court in the interpretation of Union law is ruled out.[31] This may hamper the ability of the Court to build up a coherent and uniform practice concerning the interpretation of Union law.[32]

The Court has looked unfavourably upon domestic rules closing the 'channel of communication' between the domestic and Union courts.[33] The aim of the preliminary

[27] ibid para 66.

[28] R Craufurd Smith, 'Remedies for Breaches of EC Law in National Courts Legal Variation and Selection' in P Craig and G De Búrca (eds), *The Evolution of EU Law* (Oxford University Press 1999) 296.

[29] Case C-619/18 *Commission v Poland* [2019] paras 44–45.

[30] T Tridimas, 'Bifurcated Justice: The Dual Character of Judicial Protection in EU Law' in A Rosas, E Levits and Y Bot (eds), *The Court of Justice and the Construction of Europe: Analyses and Perspectives on Sixty Years of Case-law* (TMC Asser Press 2013) 367, 375.

[31] Whereas lower courts have discretion as to whether to make a preliminary reference, domestic courts adjudicating at last instance are obliged to make a reference when a question on the interpretation of EU law arises, unless the Court has already provided an interpretation (*acte éclairé*) or the answer is 'so obvious as to leave no scope for any reasonable doubt' (*acte clair*); see Case 283/81 *CILFIT* [1982] paras 14 and 16. The obligation to refer does not arise if 'the answer to that question, whatever it may be, cannot have any effect on the outcome of the case'; see Case C-3/16 *Aquino* [2017] para 43.

[32] N Fenger, *Forvaltning og fællesskab: Om EU-rettens betydning for den almindelige forvaltningsret: Konfrontation og frugtbar sameksistens* (DJØF 2004) 698. He argues that for this reason, there is a greater need for Union law interference with respect to domestic standing rules than other enforcement provisions.

[33] The expression is borrowed from M Dougan, *National Remedies Before the Court of Justice: Issues of Harmonisation and Differentiation* (Hart Publishing 2004) 48. The Court's strict stance in Case C-312/93 *Peterbroeck* [1995] (concerning the raising of Union law arguments *ex officio*) can arguably be explained by the fact that the rule prevented domestic courts from making a preliminary reference; see further Dougan, *National Remedies Before the Court of Justice* 48–49. Case C-284/16 *Achmea* [2018] (where the Court found arbitration clauses under bilateral investment treaties between Member States to violate EU law) can also be seen as an expression of this stance.

ruling procedure is first and foremost to assist domestic courts in their function as Union courts, and to ensure the full effect of Union law in the Member States.[34] As the Court stated in *CILFIT*, (now) Article 267 TFEU 'does not constitute a means of redress available to the parties'.[35] But although this procedure was not meant to be a means of private enforcement, it has, on occasion, been used as such.[36] The European Court of Human Rights (ECtHR) has, moreover, ruled that that a refusal to refer without providing proper explanation can constitute a violation of Article 6(1) of the European Convention on Human Rights (ECHR).[37] Private parties are not, as a matter of EU law, entitled to challenge a national court's decision on whether to seek a preliminary ruling.[38] Nevertheless, in legal scholarship it has been suggested that denial to refer a preliminary question could constitute an infringement of the right to effective judicial protection enshrined in Article 47 of the Charter, and consequently that such a refusal should be susceptible to challenge.[39] It remains to be seen whether the Court will follow this route in years to come. Should that turn out to be the case, one may conclude that strict standing rules jeopardise not only individuals' right of access to domestic courts but their right to (indirect) access to the ECJ through the preliminary reference procedure, too.[40]

II. Clarification and Elaboration of Core Concepts

A. Private Enforcement

The term 'private enforcement' is elusive, and the relevant literature rarely spells out its exact meaning. The term has certain connotations, leading the reader to think of proceedings taken for the purpose of general law enforcement – compelling observance of the law – rather than for the protection of the interests of individuals or groups.[41] In the Union law context, this distinction cannot be upheld. Although private parties mostly litigate to protect their own rights or interests, at the same time, 'the vigilance of individuals concerned to protect their rights amounts to an effective supervision'

[34] R Barents, 'EU Procedural Law and Effective Legal Protection' (2014) 51 *CML Rev* 1437, 1456.

[35] Case 283/81 *CILFIT* [1982] para 9.

[36] See further, M Broberg, 'Privates håndhævelse af EU-retten gennem præjudicielle forelæggelser' (2015) 128 *Tidsskrift for Rettsvitenskap* 455.

[37] See *Dhahbi v Italy* App no 17120/09 (ECtHR, 2014) and *Schipani v Italy* App no 38369/09 (ECtHR, 2015).

[38] See, inter alia, Joined Cases C-72/14 and C-197/14 *X and TA van Dijk* [2015] paras 57–59. A legal avenue may, however, be available under domestic law, see further Z Varga, 'National Remedies in the Case of Violation of EU Law by Member State Courts' (2017) 54 *CML Rev* 51, 64–66.

[39] See C Lacchi, 'Multilevel Judicial Protection in the EU and Preliminary References' (2016) 53 *CML Rev* 679. She largely draws on the parallel between Art 6 ECHR and Art 47(2) of the Charter, see ibid 701–03. Krommendijk also argues that the preliminary reference procedure should be examined in light of the principle of effective judicial protection; see J Krommendijk, '"Open Sesame": Improving Access to the ECJ by Requiring National Courts to Reason Their Refusals to Refer' (2007) 42 *EL Rev* 46, 56–59.

[40] Krommendijk holds that 'the ECJ has not completely ignored the effective judicial protection dimensions of the preliminary reference procedure'; see Krommendijk '"Open Sesame"' (n 39) 52, with reference to Case C-50/00 P *UPA* [2002], Case C-263/02 P *Jégo-Quéré* [2004] and Art 19(1) TEU.

[41] P Nebbia, 'Damages Actions for the Infringement of EC Competition Law: Compensation or Deterrence?' (2008) 33 *El Rev* 23, 24.

of Member States.[42] For the purpose of this book, the term 'private enforcement' will be used to cover litigation initiated by private parties to pursue (prospective) infringements of Union law. This encompasses the power of individuals to enforce the fulfilment of Union law duties placed upon both public and private entities.[43] Private enforcement should, however, be kept apart from 'privately triggered public enforcement', where private parties seek to protect their interests by attempting to induce national public authorities to pursue a Union law infringement.[44] In the latter context, the private party is merely considered a source of information, and does not enjoy party status.

Union law rules can be used both positively as a 'sword', that is as a basis for a claim (such as damages, restitution, injunction or interim measures), or as a 'shield' against actual or potential claims from others ('Euro-defence').[45] Since standing issues only arise when a private party initiates legal action, the term 'private enforcement' will be reserved for situations in which Union law is used as a 'sword', providing the basis for a lawsuit.

Both natural and legal persons can initiate private enforcement proceedings. The subjects of protection under Article 47 of the Charter are 'everyone', comprising both individuals and undertakings to the extent they are bearers of Union law rights.[46] The terms 'individual' and 'private party' will be used interchangeably to cover this category of claimants. Depending on the field, I may also use more specific terms, such as 'consumer' or 'competitor'. Non-governmental organisations (NGOs) and other bodies representing public or collective interests will also be considered 'private parties' in the following, both when they seek to protect their own rights under the Treaties *and* when they litigate with a view to protecting the interests they are set up to pursue.[47]

B. Standing

A lawsuit must be initiated by a party which satisfies the requirements for standing. The term 'standing' is used interchangeably with terms like '*locus standi*' or 'title to sue'. Standing is 'essentially concerned with the entitlement of particular individuals to move the court to make a substantive decision'.[48] Provisions on standing are normally part

[42] Case 26/62 *Van Gend en Loos* [1963].

[43] Similarly N Póltorak, *European Union Rights in National Courts* (Wolters Kluwer 2015) 44.

[44] FG Jacobs and T Deisenhofer, 'Procedural Aspects of the Effective Private Enforcement of EC Competition Rules: A Community Perspective' in CD Ehlermann and I Atanasiu (eds), *European Competition Law Annual 2001: Effective Private Enforcement of EC Antitrust Law* (Hart Publishing 2003) 187, 197.

[45] ibid 189. Odudu defines the 'Euro-defence' as 'the use of any provision of EU law to defeat any claim based on national law'; see O Odudu, 'Competition Law and Contract: The Euro-Defence' in D Leczykiewicz and S Weatherill (eds), *The Involvement of EU Law in Private Law Relationships* (Hart Publishing 2013) 395, 396.

[46] See Case C-279/09 *DEB* [2010] para 59, where the Court held that 'the principle of effective judicial protection, as enshrined in Article 47 of the Charter, must be interpreted as meaning that it is not impossible for legal persons to rely on that principle'. The relevant Union law provision must be interpreted to determine the extent to which individual or corporate interests are protected.

[47] See, however, F Wilman, *Private Enforcement of EU Law Before National Courts: The EU Legislative Framework* (Edward Elgar 2015) 491, who questions whether 'such "general interest litigation" amounts to private enforcement at all' given that the claimants do not seek to defend a strictly individual interest.

[48] J Miles, 'Standing under the Human Rights Act 1998: Theories of Rights Enforcement & the Nature of Public Law Adjudication' (2000) 59 *CLJ* 133, 148.

of domestic rules on admissibility, and serve to ensure that the claimant has sufficient connection to the subject matter of the litigation. Standing is mostly a preliminary issue, and therefore distinct from the merits of the case (although the court may have to inspect the substance of the pleas to determine whether the claimant has standing).

When dealing with Union law requirements relating to standing, a caveat is in place: every legal system has its own approach when it comes to restrictions on access to court, and these restrictions may be given different qualifications.[49] It is not always evident whether the rule hampering the court from exercising jurisdiction results from limitations on *locus standi* or some other domestic procedural or substantive bar.[50] Particularly in civil proceedings, some Member States treat access to court partly as a matter of substance.[51] Considering the great variations in the Member States' respective legislative frameworks, it must be emphasised that the term 'standing' in the following should not be equated with any particular domestic doctrine.[52] This means that although this book crafts a Union law theory on standing, it may well have an impact on admissibility doctrines that in certain jurisdictions may be dealt with under other headings, such as ripeness, mootness and dismissal for failure to state a claim.

In the following, the term 'standing' should be taken to encompass questions as to *who is entitled to initiate proceedings in which circumstances*. The concept is broader than that used in relation to annulment proceedings under Article 263(4) TFEU. In its jurisprudence under the latter provision, the Court has drawn a distinction between '*locus standi*' and 'interest' in bringing proceedings, and held that these are distinct conditions, which must be satisfied cumulatively by a natural or legal person in order to initiate proceedings.[53] The Court has also distinguished the two aspects when addressing Union law requirements on national standing doctrines. For instance, in *Mono Car Styling*, the Court held that it is in principle for national law to determine an individual's 'standing and legal interest' in bringing proceedings.[54] Whether legal interest is treated as a separate requirement or rather as a condition for *locus standi* is simply a matter of structure, and does not bear on the substantive findings of this book. For reasons of structural clarity, the latter option has been chosen. As will be seen, the interest requirement is so closely related to the other standing conditions that they are on occasion difficult to keep apart.

The issue of standing is usually governed by the law of the court that has *jurisdiction*.[55] In the context of judicial review proceedings, the issue of jurisdiction does not pose any

[49] The term '*locus standi*' or 'standing' is not necessarily used in proceedings before civil courts, see M Eliantonio et al, *Standing Up for Your Right(s) in Europe – A Comparative Study on Legal Standing (Locus Standi) before the EU and Member States' Courts* (Intersentia 2013) 49.

[50] Półtorak, *European Union Rights in National Courts* (n 43) 239.

[51] In the common law jurisdictions, for instance, the claimant must demonstrate a cause of action, and concepts such as the 'duty of care' in tort law serve as gatekeepers, limiting the litigants that may seize the court. On the common law notion of a 'cause of action', see further ch 4, section II.

[52] This means, for instance, that it will cut across the German distinction between '*Aktivlegitimation*' and '*Klagebefugnis*' and the French distinction between '*intérêt à agir*' and '*qualité pour agir en justice*'.

[53] See, inter alia, Case C-33/14 P *Mory, Mory Team and Superga Invest* [2015] para 62. The interest requirement entails that the action must be liable, if successful, to procure an advantage for the party who has brought it, and the interest must be actual and current; see Case C-524/14 P *Hansestadt Lübeck* [2016] para 26.

[54] Case C-12/08 *Mono Car Styling* [2009] para 49.

[55] See Case C-396/13 *Sähköalojen ammattiliitto* [2015] para 20. In the context of international private law, this conclusion is based on the premise that standing is a procedural issue falling under the *lex fori*. Yet a

difficulties. As national courts only control the authorities of their own Member State, it is the national court of the state that issued the decision that has jurisdiction to settle disputes concerning this decision.[56] In civil proceedings, on the other hand, the dispute can have a link to more than one Member State, which actuates the need to determine the appropriate forum to settle the dispute. Such a jurisdictional regime is contained, inter alia, in Regulation (EU) No 1215/2012 (Brussels I). Issues of jurisdiction will not, however, be addressed further in this book.

This book deals with the right to initiate proceedings, and *locus standi* on appeal is not addressed separately.[57] Neither will issues pertaining to who should be sued (sometimes referred to as *passive locus standi*) be given a thorough assessment in the following. It is presumed that the action is brought against the violator – that being a state or another private party.[58] Third party intervention before the court, for example through *amicus curiae*, also falls outside the ambit of this book.

C. Remedies and Procedures

Since the concepts 'procedure' and 'remedy' are central to this book, there is a need to address them in some detail. Procedures and remedies are distinct parts of a legal claim, but the Court has not been explicit as to how or where exactly the line should be drawn. The reason for this deference may be the great divergence in the Member States' respective legal systems on these matters.

The term 'remedy' is used in a variety of senses in case law and legal discourse. It is used synonymously with and by way of contrast to a range of different terms:

> It is used synonymously with action, response, redress and relief. It is used in contradiction to wrong, injury, cause of action, liability substance, institution and doctrine. Most confusingly, it is used both as a synonym of right and in opposition to it.[59]

Generally speaking, 'remedy' can mean either the means provided by law to recover rights or obtain redress or relief, or the form of relief or redress given by a court.[60] In other words, the term can cover the judicial process in its entirety, or be restricted to refer to the relief a court can award to a successful claimant.[61] The Court has adopted a fairly wide definition of what counts as a 'remedy', encompassing access to the court, temporary protection through interim relief and redress for rights infringements.[62]

'uniform approach at the EU level as to the classification of standing and right to sue can hardly be read in the Rome I or Rome II Regulation'; see D-P Tzakas, 'Effective Collective Redress in Antitrust and Consumer Protection Matters: A Panacea or a Chimera?' (2011) 48 *CML Rev* 1125, 1171.

[56] AM Keessen, *European Administrative Decisions: How the EU Regulates Products on the Internal Market* (Europa Law Publishing 2009) 185.

[57] The principle of effective judicial protection does not afford a right of access to a number of levels of jurisdiction, see Case C-69/10 *Samba Diouf* [2011] para 69 and Case C-169/14 *Sánchez Morcillo* [2014] para 36.

[58] Determining which body of the state will be the proper defendant is as a starting point a matter for natioanl law, see Case C-302/97 *Konle* [1999] para 62.

[59] R Zakrzewski, *Remedies Reclassified* (Oxford University Press 2005) 2.

[60] S Prechal, *Directives in EC Law* (Oxford University Press 2005) 145, fn 99.

[61] C Harlow, 'A Common European Law of Remedies?" in C Kilpatrick, T Novitz and P Skidmore (eds), *The Future of Remedies in Europe* (Hart Publishing 2000) 69, 73.

[62] ibid 73–74.

Moreover, in Article 19(1) TEU the term 'remedy' is used in a broad sense, referring to the means provided by the law to recover rights or obtain redress or relief.[63] The concept thus has both a procedural and a substantive dimension. This is also how the term 'remedy' is used in the ECJ's case law, where the essential point is that a legal avenue should be available to the claimant.[64]

Given that this contribution addresses the issue of standing, it is of importance to distinguish *access* to judicial proceedings from the *outcome* of judicial proceedings. I will therefore use the term 'remedy' in the narrow sense, referring to the form of redress an individual can obtain. This will allow for a separate treatment of the right to *pursue remedies in court*, which is the overarching theme of this book. Depending on the circumstances, remedies may entail, inter alia, restitution, compensation, injunctions or declarations. The purpose of such a remedy is to prevent or terminate a breach, and to undo its detrimental effects.[65]

The term 'sanction' is sometimes used in lieu of 'remedy'.[66] It is submitted that these terms have different meanings and should thus be kept apart. Whereas a remedy is afforded in the interest of a private party whose rights or interests are adversely affected by an infringement, a sanction aims at ensuring compliance with the substantive norms and deterring unlawful behaviour. Consequently, the term 'remedy' will be used in the context of private enforcement, whereas the term 'sanction' will be used in the context of public enforcement (hence meriting the distinction between *private* remedies and *public* sanctions).[67]

Defining 'remedy' narrowly to cover only substantive redress allows for a distinction between such substantive remedies and the procedural rules that make these remedies operational. 'Procedural rules' will in the following be taken to mean the rules governing the enforcement of claims based on EU law.[68] The term will cover not only procedural rules *sensu stricto* (such as rules about the role of judges in the proceedings, third party intervention and costs), but also matters such as burden of proof and the granting of legal aid.[69] The entire legal framework concerning the judicial enforcement

[63] S Prechal and R Widdershoven, 'Redefining the Relationship between "Rewe-Effectiveness" and Effective Judicial Protection' (2011) 4 *Review of European Administrative Law* 31, 37, fn 33. The terms '*voies de recours*' and '*Rechtsbehelfe*' are used in French and German law, respectively, to denote this wider use of the term.

[64] See, inter alia, Case C-432/05 *Unibet* [2007].

[65] Tridimas, *The General Principles of EU Law* (n 7) 422.

[66] As several commentators have noted, the requirements pertaining to remedies are on occasion treated as virtually interchangeable with those pertaining to public sanctions: see, inter alia, Wilman, *Private Enforcement of EU Law before National Courts* (n 47) 47; and KE Sørensen, 'Member States' Implementation of Penalties to Enforce EU Law: Balancing the Avoidance of Enforcement Deficits and the Protection of Individuals' (2015) 40 *EL Rev* 811, 818. Private remedies and public sanctions are, however, guided by two separate strands of case law. These should not be conflated, as they concern individual rights protection and enforcement in the general interest respectively; see further ch 13, section V.B.

[67] In the context of competition law, it is appropriate to speak about public remedies; see further I Lianos, 'Competition Law Remedies in Europe' in D Geradin and I Lianos (eds), *Handbook on European Competition Law: Enforcement and Procedure* (Edward Elgar 2013) 362.

[68] In the context of domestic enforcement of Union law, it is often challenging to draw a clear distinction between rules of substance and procedure. For an illustration, see Case C-8/08 *T-Mobile Netherlands* [2009], where the Court held that rules on burden of proof were to be determined by Union law, since these rules were intrinsic to the concept of concerted practice in (now) Art 102 TFEU; see ibid paras 51–53.

[69] Conversely see Van Gerven, who distinguishes between 'procedural rules *sensu stricto*' and 'remedial rules', the latter meaning rules governing the 'conditions and restrictions, under which individuals are enabled

of Union law may also be placed under the shorthand of 'enforcement rules', and this term will be employed where the distinction between procedures and remedies is of limited importance.[70]

D. The Defendant: States and Private Parties

The requirements relating to standing may vary according to who is responsible for the breach and the nature of the infringement. Still, as we shall see, neither the (not so clear-cut) public–private law distinction found in domestic law, nor the distinction between vertical and horizontal proceedings decisive for the direct effect of Union law is suitable for categorising the Union law requirements on *locus standi*. The distinction drawn in this book will rather be between proceedings brought against a state and proceedings brought against private parties.

In the Member States, it is often the case that standing requirements differ depending on whether the claim is of a public law or private law nature.[71] Union law, however, 'calls into question the fundamental, if always contested, contrast between public law and private law'.[72] The EU legislator has never paid great regard to the public–private divide, and it may be difficult to assign any given provision of Union law either to the public or private law realm,[73] since EU law has an ambiguous character:

> It is not 'public law' in the orthodox sense(s) understood at national level, nor is it private law. It is both and it is neither. In fact, EU law operates without any such anchor, which makes it fluid and which makes it at the same time unstable. EU law challenges and sometimes transforms orthodox categories within national legal orders.[74]

The Union adopts a functional approach to the law, in which the law is instrumental to the political aims the Union is meant to achieve.[75] It is left to the Member States to determine how to implement the obligations stemming from EU law in light of their own national conceptions of the public–private divide.[76]

to bring and maintain actions before courts of law in order to safeguard their rights, whilst the former category refers to practical rules according to which the remedy is to be pursued in a court', see: W Van Gerven, 'Of Rights, Remedies and Procedures' (2000) 37 *CML Rev* 501, 524.

[70] The term is borrowed from J Engström, 'The Europeanisation of Remedies and Procedures Through Judge-Made Law: Can a Trojan Horse Achieve Effectiveness? Experiences of the Swedish Judiciary' (PhD thesis, European University Institute 2009) 11.

[71] When seeking to classify the proper domains of public and private law, one can adopt either an institutional approach (focusing on the actor carrying out the activities) or a functional approach (focusing on the nature of the activity carried out); see further P Cane, 'Accountability and the Public/Private Distinction' in N Bamforth and P Leyland (eds), *Public Law in a Multi-Layered Constitution* (Hart Publishing 2003) 247.

[72] H Collins, 'The Hybrid Quality of European Private Law' in R Brownsword et al (eds), *The Foundations of European Private Law* (Hart Publishing 2011) 253, 454.

[73] Dougan has argued that the lack of a clear public–private divide in EU law can constitute an obstacle to the development of a truly autonomous Union approach to standing; see Dougan, 'Who Exactly Benefits from the Treaties? (n 13) 76–77.

[74] D Leczykiewicz and S Weatherill, 'Private Law Relationships and EU Law' in Leczykiewicz and Weatherill (eds), *The Involvement of EU Law in Private Law Relationships* (n 45) 1, 2.

[75] MW Hesselink, *The New European Private Law: Essays on the Future of Private Law in Europe* (Kluwer Law International 2002) 229.

[76] C Semmelmann, 'The Public–Private Divide in European Union Law' in U Neergaard and R Nielsen (eds), *European Legal Method: in a multi-level EU legal order* (DJØF 2012) 183, 197.

Given the hybrid nature of Union law, a possibility would be to fall back on the 'basic grammar' of EU law, namely vertical and horizontal relations.[77] However, such a distinction conceals aspects of importance when mapping out the EU's private enforcement regime. I therefore align myself with Dougan when he remarks, '[a] mature system of effective judicial protection needs to reach beyond our enduring tendency to see the entire Community landscape in terms of the vertical and the horizontal'.[78] The vertical–horizontal distinction is primarily relevant when discussing the direct effect of Union law, and also in this contribution the terms 'vertical' and 'horizontal' proceedings will be used when discussing matters pertaining to direct effect. In its direct effect jurisprudence, the Court has adopted an institutional approach, where the decisive factor is whether we are dealing with an organ of the state.[79] It is immaterial in what capacity the Member State is acting; an unimplemented directive can be applied against an organ of the state, also when that organ acts in a 'private law' capacity.[80]

It will be submitted here that this approach – focusing on the *specifics of the organ* – is not suitable when it comes to outlining the criteria for standing. The Court's case law lends support to the view that it is not necessarily the specifics of the organ that is of importance, but rather the *nature of the activity carried out*.[81] A central tenet of the rule of law is that the exercise of public power must take place according to and within the limting framework of the law.[82] Decisive in the following will therefore be whether the state (or exceptionally a private party) has exercised public powers, meaning 'powers derogating from the rules of law applicable to relations between private individuals'.[83] For the sake of structural clarity I talk about proceedings brought *against a state* and proceedings brought against *private parties*. Still, in situations where private parties exercise public powers in the general interest, they will be treated interchangeably with the state.[84] Conversely, where public authorities do not act in a public capacity, but rather as market participants, they will be perceived as 'private parties' in the following.[85]

[77] The term is borrowed from M Claes, 'The European Union, Its Member States and Their Citizens' in Leczykiewicz and Weatherill (eds), *The Involvement of EU Law in Private Law Relationships* (n 45) 29, 33.

[78] M Dougan, 'What Is the Point of Francovich?' in T Tridimas and P Nebbia (eds), *European Union Law for the Twenty-first Century*, vol 1: *Rethinking the New Legal Order* (Hart Pubishing 2004) 239, 255.

[79] The leading case is *Foster*, where the Court held that unimplemented directives can be relied on against organisations or bodies that were 'subject to the authority or control of the State or had special powers beyond those which result from the normal rules applicable to relations between individuals'; see Case C-188/89 *Foster* [1990] para 18. The Court has confirmed that these are alternative criteria, see Case C-413/15 *Farrell* [2017] paras 24–29.

[80] See Case 152/84 *Marshall* [1986] para 49.

[81] As will be seen, the Court has mostly elaborated on what the principle of effective judicial protection requires in the context of judicial review proceedings, where the legality of public (administrative and legislative) measures has been challenged (see in particular chs 8 and 9).

[82] For a further account of the 'rule of law' concept, see ch 2, section II.

[83] Case C-167/00 *Henkel* para 30. See also M Dougan, 'Addressing Issues of Protective Scope within the *Francovich* Right to Reparation' (2017) 13 *European Constitutional Law Review* 124, 155–57. He argues (ibid 155) that '[j]udicial protection under EU law is characterized … by a division between public law and private law situations'.

[84] For instance, where a private company has been entrusted with the task of levying tolls, it will be treated interchangeably with the state when undertaking this duty. For an illustration, see Case C-157/02 *Rieser* [2004].

[85] For instance, in the area of competition law, an undertaking is defined as an 'entity engaged in economic activity, regardless of the legal status of the entity and the way in which it is financed'; see Case C-41/90 *Höfner* [1991] para 21. Wilman also uses the term 'private parties' so that it includes public authorities where they do not act in a public capacity; see Wilman, *Private Enforcement of EU Law before National Courts* (n 47) 4, fn 8.

III. The Structure of the Book

Three important distinctions inform the structure of this book. First, a distinction is made between, on the one hand, requirements stemming from the principle of effective judicial protection and, on the other, the principle of effectiveness (*effet utile*); second, a distinction is made between proceedings against states and proceedings against private parties; and, third, a distinction is made based on the type of proceeding initiated.

The first distinction is presented in chapter 2 and further elaborated on in chapter 3. It bears emphasising that approaching the Union law requirements on domestic standing doctrines from the angle of effective judicial protection differs markedly from an approach from the angle of effectiveness per se. In chapter 5 I examine which standing rules a Member State must apply to ensure the protection of individual Union rights, while in chapter 13 I examine the standing rules a state must apply in order to render Union law effective within its jurisdiction.

The second distinction – separating proceedings brought against states from proceedings brought against private parties – has already been presented in section II.D. The main reason for making this distinction is that the *principle of effective judicial protection* does not apply with the same force in private disputes due to the need to protect the autonomy of the defendant.[86] In chapters 8 to 10 I address how the principle of effective judicial protection operates in proceedings against states, whereas in chapter 11 I look at the principle as used in proceedings against private parties. Distinguishing between enforcement against states and against other private parties is also important when discussing how the *effectiveness principle* frames domestic standing rules. The crux of the matter is that the added value of private suits depends on the enforcement mechanisms already in place. Where private parties seek to enforce Union law provisions against the Member State, they are first and foremost supplementing the enforcement conducted by the Commission. Conversely, where they seek to enforce the obligations of other private parties, they are primarily aiding the Member States' public authorities in their enforcement efforts (see chapter 13).

The third distinction – based on the *type of action* initiated – is what informs the approach in chapters 8 to 11, where standing will be addressed in relation to various types of action. It is not possible, however, to account for all the procedural variations existing in the Member States. The national courts' obligation to protect individual rights and to ensure the effective enforcement of EU law in the Member States can arise in a variety of procedural settings, depending on the different types of actions that are available under national law. The categories addressed in this contribution are broad enough to cover the bulk of national variations, although I do not attempt to be exhaustive.[87]

This book is not structured according to sectors of substantive law but will cover the enforcement of Union law more broadly. Private enforcement is often

[86] Along the same lines, Leczykiewicz holds that '[t]he insistence of a division between the public and private law of remedies performs the function of protecting private actors, from subjecting them to standards that bind public actors, and thus protect the autonomy of private actors'; see D Leczykiewicz, 'The Constitutional Dimension of Private Law Liability Rules in the EU' in Leczykiewicz and Weatherill (eds), *The Involvement of EU Law in Private Law Relationships* (n 45) 199, 214.

[87] Depending on national procedural law, other types of legal action may be possible. For instance, where the exercise of public power takes the form of an agreement – which is often the case in the context of state aid – the claimant may have to utilise a procedure that differs from that of judicial review of administrative decisions.

discussed in the context of competition law, and this field clearly enjoys a special status due to the importance of ensuring a well-functioning internal market. As will be seen, the Court has adopted a distinct approach to the question of standing in this field.[88] Private enforcement may, however, have a strong role to play in other fields of Union law too, such as financial services and environmental protection.[89] The reason for eschewing a sectoral approach is first and foremost that the method of precedent applied by the Court does not provide for it. As Leczykiewicz explains:

> While in the common law system the case has to be significantly similar on facts to be relevant for deciding another case, the Court of Justice makes connections between cases at a much higher level of abstraction [that] enables the Court to move freely between formal sources of law and sectors of Union law.[90]

It should also be added that it can be challenging to identify with sufficient precision a particular sector of Union law activity, given that they are not 'marked off … by clear ascertainable boundaries'.[91] With these caveats in place, it must be emphasised that the proper role of the individual is not the same in relation to all fields of EU policy. First, the Union deploys various modes of regulation, and the scope for private enforcement is greatest when it comes to legislation containing detailed legal norms susceptible to direct judicial application. Consequently, the degree of discretion afforded to Member States has a bearing on the matter. Second, the extent of the duty of Member States to ensure effective judicial protection and effective enforcement – and consequently the requirements imposed on domestic standing rules – may differ, depending on the objective of the infringed Union law provision.[92] Alongside the central objective of establishing and facilitating a well-functioning internal market, the Union also contains a social dimension encompassing, inter alia, consumer protection, labour policy and environmental protection.[93] This means that the interests at stake in the case of Union law infringements are various. As will be seen, there are valid arguments for aligning the enforcement mechanisms to the regulatory goals and the underlying interests of the substantive law. In particular, whether the provisions aim at protecting individuals' interests – or rather collective or public interests – is of importance when determining the remedial tools the Member States have to employ as a matter of EU law. Since the required balance between private and public enforcement may vary depending on the sector, I provide examples along the way to illustrate how the legal domain can shape the scope and character of private enforcement, and consequently influence the conditions for standing.[94]

[88] See ch 3, section IV.C.

[89] A-M Van den Bossche, 'Private Enforcement, Procedural Autonomy and Article 19(1) TEU: Two's Company, Three's a Crowd' (2014) 33 *Yearbook of European Law* 41, 44.

[90] D Leczykiewicz, 'Effectiveness of EU Law Before National Courts: Direct Effect, Consistent Interpretation and Member State Liability' in A Arnull and D Chalmers (eds), *Oxford Handbook of European Union Law* (Oxford University Press 2015) 212, 213. Along the same lines, A Arnull, 'Remedies before National Courts' in R Schütze and T Tridimas (eds), *Oxford Principles of European Union Law*, vol I: *The European Union Legal Order* (Oxford University Press 2018) 1011, 1018.

[91] Dougan, *National Remedies Before the Court of Justice* (n 33) 213.

[92] M Brealey and M Hoskins, *Remedies in EC Law: Law and Practice in English and EC Courts* (Sweet & Maxwell 1998) 100.

[93] See, inter alia, Art 4 TFEU.

[94] See, in particular, ch 8, sections III (environmental law) and IV (telecommunications law).

2

Normative Underpinnings in the Court's Case Law

I. Introduction

The Court has a brief and formal way of reasoning, and is rarely explicit as to the normative rationale on which it bases its judgments.[1] It would therefore be useful, before spelling out the requirements set by EU law for domestic standing rules, to look into the underlying norms and values guiding the Court's approach to access to judicial process. The aim of this chapter is to explore the normative underpinnings of the Court's case law on standing in the abstract. The 'rule of law' concept is addressed in section II, and effective judicial protection and effectiveness *per se* are addressed in sections III and IV. How these norms and values find expression in the legal framework used by the Court to outline the Union law requirements pertaining to procedures and remedies will be addressed in chapter 3.

It will be argued that whereas the Court has stressed that access to court is essential in a legal system based on the rule of law, the reference to this abstract ideal is of limited aid when seeking to dissect the Court's jurisprudence on standing. The reason is that this ideal does not help us answer the question of *who* should be afforded access to court. The overarching question that has to be answered is rather whether the Court's emphasis is on the protection of individual rights or on the effective enforcement of Union law per se. These rationales are closely linked, and they often pull in the same direction and reinforce each other.[2] This does not mean, however, that the distinction is without relevance. Telling these two aspects apart is of vital importance when analysing the Court's standing jurisprudence, since – as will be seen – it will have a direct bearing on the range of persons that must be granted access to judicial process.

[1] M Beijer, *The Limits of Fundamental Rights Protections by the EU: The Scope for the Development of Positive Obligations* (Intersentia 2017) 142.

[2] F Wilman, *Private Enforcement of EU Law Before National Courts: The EU Legislative Framework* (Edward Elgar 2015) 457–58. The rationale of effective rights protection and effective enforcement may also pull in opposite directions, requiring a balancing of these competing considerations; see for instance Case C-360/09 *Pfleiderer* [2011] (concerning access to documents contained in an application for leniency from a cartel participant).

II. The Rule of Law (as an 'Essentially Contested Concept')

Standing is a necessary prerequisite for gaining access to court, and the Court has stressed that access to court constitutes an essential element of a Union based on the rule of law.[3] Yet what this means more precisely is difficult to pin down, since we are dealing with an elusive concept. The 'rule of law' can in fact be considered an 'essentially contested concept', insofar as disagreement about this notion extends to its core.[4] Although there is clearly some overlap, a common distinction is made between *formal* and *substantive* conceptions of the rule of law.[5] The distinction consists in substantive accounts, as opposed to formal accounts, also addressing the content of the law, including components such as respect for private property and individual rights.[6]

Some formalists concentrate primarily on the more formal nature of law;[7] others also stress the importance of courts and judicial procedures.[8] It bears emphasising that an independent judiciary is material for upholding the rule of law, in the sense that 'it is an important means for holding government officials to the law (vertical), and for resolving disputes between citizens in accordance with the law (horizontal)'.[9] The importance of an independent judiciary was stressed by the ECJ in *Associação Sindical dos Juízes Portugueses (ASJP)* and *LM*.[10] The Court underlined that the independence of national courts and tribunals serves as a guarantee that EU rights will be protected and that 'the values common to the Member States set out in Article 2 TEU, in particular the value of the rule of law, will be safeguarded'.[11] The Court's rationale seems to be that in order to function within the Union's judicial system, national courts need to meet certain fundamental requirements.

What the 'rule of law' means more precisely in the context of EU law is subject to debate, and scholars disagree as to whether we are dealing with a formal or substantive notion. To illustrate, Arnull subscribes to a formal conception, and argues that the rule

[3] Case C-294/83 *Les Verts* [1986] para 23. See also Case C-64/16 *ASJP* [2018] para 36, where the Court stated that 'The very existence of effective judicial review designed to ensure compliance with EU law is of the essence of the rule of law.' See also Case C-619/18, *Commission v Poland* [2019] para 46.

[4] J Waldron, 'Is the Rule of Law an Essentially Contested Concept (In Florida)?' (2002) 21 *Law and Philosophy* 137. The term 'essentially contested concept' was introduced by Gallie in his seminal article WB Gallie, 'Essentially Contested Concepts' (1955) 56 *Proceedings of the Aristotelian Society* 167.

[5] See further PP Craig, 'Formal and Substantive Conceptions of the Rule of Law: An Analytical Framework' [1997] *Public Law* 467; and BZ Tamanaha, *On the Rule of Law: History, Politics, Theory* (Cambridge University Press 2004) 91–113.

[6] Dworkin includes individual rights within the rule of law, see R Dworkin, *A Matter of Principle* (Harvard University Press 1985). He presents two different conceptions of the rule of law, what he calls the 'rule-book conception' and the 'rights conception' respectively, and argues in favour of the latter (see in particular ibid 9–33).

[7] These characteristics are often variations of Fuller's lists of different traits that together constitute the 'inner morality' of law: rules should be general, publicised, prospective, understandable, practicable, stable and congruent. See LL Fuller, *The Morality of Law* (Yale University Press 1965) 46–94.

[8] Amongst others, Raz emphasises the need for an independent judiciary and access to court; see J Raz, *The Authority of Law: Essays on Law and Morality* (Clarendon Press 1979) 216–17.

[9] BZ Tamanaha, 'A Concise Guide to the Rule of Law' in G Palombella and N Walker (eds), *Relocating the Rule of Law* (Hart Publishing 2009) 3, 11.

[10] Case C-64/16 *ASJP* [2018] and Case C-216/18 PPU *LM* [2018].

[11] Case C-216/18 PPU *LM* [2018] para 48. The Court stressed national courts' role in ensuring 'the full application of EU law in all Member States and judicial protection of the rights of individuals under that law' (ibid para 50).

of law should be regarded as a 'particular set of requirements about the form of the law and the mechanics of the legal system of the Union and its Member States'.[12] Pech, on the other hand, holds that the rule of law in the context of Union law is an 'umbrella principle with formal and substantive components'.[13] For the purposes of this book, there is no need to engage in this debate. At the very least, the rule of law in the Union law context means that access to court must be guaranteed.[14] To borrow the words of Fuller, '[t]he essence of the rule of law consists in being assured of your day in court'.[15]

The ECJ has made clear that the right to effective judicial protection and to an effective remedy, enshrined in Article 47 of the Charter and foreseen in Article 19(1) TEU, is a concretisation of the rule of law.[16] Since national courts are bound to uphold Union law, the Court has also stressed that 'the very existence of effective judicial review designed to ensure compliance with provisions of EU law is of the essence of the rule of law'.[17] Moreover, the Court has explicitly linked rule of law to the *effet utile* of Union law, by stating that the 'effective application of EU law' constitutes 'an essential component of the rule of law'.[18]

Although the case law of the Court can certainly be seen as reflecting rule of law considerations, in and of itself the rule of law concept is too vague to serve as a yardstick for assessing domestic standing doctrines for conformity with Union law.[19] Reference to this ideal does not establish which category of persons must be granted standing. As Pech puts it:

> Although access to justice is universally seen as a basic right and one of the rule of law's core components, it is rare to see scholars deducing from the rule of law, an individual right to initiate proceedings in any court, or a right to *actio popularis* in any situation, against any type of legal measure, merely on the basis of a general interest in the observance of the law.[20]

Strand has similarly pointed out that it is clearly not possible 'to bring any kind of claim before the courts of the … Member States and invoke the fundamental right of access to court as a *carte blanche* to litigate'.[21] There is therefore a need to move beyond abstract ideals and look at the reasoning of the Court. More specifically, it must be determined whether the Court places emphasis on rights protection or on effectiveness per se.

[12] A Arnull, 'The Rule of Law in the European Union' in A Arnull and D Wincott (eds), *Accountability and Legitimacy in the European Union* (Oxford University Press 2002) 241, 254.

[13] L Pech, '"A Union Founded on the Rule of Law": Meaning and Reality of the Rule of Law as a Constitutional Principle of EU Law' (2010) 6 *European Constitutional Law Review* 359, 369.

[14] See, inter alia, Case 294/83 *Les Verts* [1986] para 23; Case C-15/00 *Commission v European Investment Bank* [2003] para 75; Case C-50/00 *UPA v Council* [2003] para 38; Case C-229/05 P *PKK and KNK v Council* [2007] para 109; Joined Cases C-402/05 P and C-415/05 P *Kadi* [2008] para 281 and Case C-274/12 P *Telefónica* [2013] para 56.

[15] L Fuller, 'The Forms and Limits of Adjudication' (1978) 92 *Harvard Law Review* 353, 372.

[16] Case C-216/18 PPU, *LM* [2018] para 50.

[17] Case C-72/15 *Rosneft* [2017] para 73. See also AG Bobek in Case C-556/17 *Torubarov* [2019] para 49, who defines effective judicial review as 'the bedrock of the rule of law on which … the European Union is based'.

[18] Case C-441/17 R *Commission v Poland* [2017] para 102.

[19] This is, however, not the case with the principle of effective judicial protection, which can be seen as a 'rule of law principle'; see M Bonelli, 'Effective Judicial Protection in EU Law: an Evolving Principle of a Constitutional Nature' (2019) 2 *Review of European Administrative Law* 35, 45.

[20] Pech, '"A Union Founded on the Rule of Law"' (n 13) 387.

[21] M Strand, *The Passing-On Problem in Damages and Restitution under EU Law* (Edward Elgar 2017) 26.

III. The Need for (and Difficulties Associated with) Distinguishing Rights Protection from Effectiveness Per Se

In order to induce general requirements from the available case law, it must be determined whether the Court's primary focus is on the protection of individuals, or whether it is rather about private parties policing Member States' and private parties' Union law compliance. If the emphasis is on the possibility for individuals to enforce their rights emanating from Union law, it will provide little scope to extend standing beyond right holders. On the other hand, the more claimants are required to demonstrate the impairment of a right in order to obtain standing, the less they can contribute to the overall effectiveness of Union law by ensuring that the state and private parties act in accordance with Union law.[22] From an effectiveness point of view, it would be desirable to confer the right to pursue infringements on a wide range of 'private attorney generals' to serve as guardians of the Union interest, regardless of the detriment to their own individual situation, and of their specific interest in the outcome of a case. Actions for injunctions and judicial review are particularly suited to furthering the public interest. As these remedies prevent or put an end to illegal conduct, they have ramifications beyond the parties to the dispute.[23]

The rationale of the *public enforcement* of Union law is to ensure observance of the law. The centralised enforcement conducted (primarily) by the Commission is geared towards controlling behaviour and ensuring the effectiveness of Union law in the Member States. As the Court held in *Firma Molkerei*, 'intervention by the Community authorities has as its object the general and uniform observance of Community law'.[24] The Commission plays the role of a public prosecutor vis-à-vis Member States, and may initiate infringement proceedings in order to ensure Union law is respected.[25] Similarly, the decentralised enforcement conducted by the organs of the Member States is also a means of rendering Union law effective at the domestic level, by terminating illegal conduct and preventing and sanctioning violations. Public enforcement bodies first and foremost enforce the law in the public interest, and they are not required to pursue individual claims. This was made evident by the Court in *Ruijssenaars*.[26] The Court was asked whether Article 16 of Regulation No 261/2004 (Denied Boarding Compensation) should be interpreted as meaning that the body designated by each Member State is required to take enforcement action with a view to ensuring compensation to individual passengers as provided for by the Regulation. The Court found that the organ is to ensure *general compliance* with the Regulation and is not required to

[22] Boch has pointed out that if private enforcement 'is about individuals keeping the member states in line … then questions regarding title and interest must be approached differently. The primary focus of judicial review is not about private law rights, but rather about public law wrongs …': see C Boch, 'The Iroquois at the Kirchberg; Or, Some Naïve Remarks on the Status and Relevance of Direct Effect' in JA Usher (ed), *The State of the European Union: Structure, enlargement and economic union* (Longman 2000) 37.

[23] See AG Geelhoed in Case C-253/00 *Muñoz* [2001] para 67.

[24] Case 28/67 *Firma Molkerei* [1968].

[25] N Reich, 'Public Interest Litigation Before European Jurisdictions' in H-W Micklitz and N Reich (eds), *Public Interest Litigation before European Courts* (Nomos 1996) 3, 17.

[26] Joined Cases C-145/15 and C-146/15 *Ruijssenaars* [2016].

act on individual complaints in order to guarantee each individual passenger's right to obtain compensation.[27]

The scarce resources of public enforcement authorities are not used for the main purpose of vindicating private rights, which means that public enforcement will rarely provide adequate remedies to affected individuals.[28] While individuals may well benefit from public supervision and enforcement, the obligation of Member States to enforce Union law is not owed to individuals.[29] One could also add that the Member States' competent authorities are not obliged to commence enforcement proceedings in every single case of infringement but have a degree of 'prosecutorial discretion', which excludes a right for individuals to demand they take action.[30]

The Court has been more equivocal when it comes to defining the *rationale underlying the private enforcement* of Union law. In *Firma Molkerei*, the Court stated that, in contrast to enforcement actions initiated by the Commission, whose object is to ensure the observance of Union law, individual proceedings 'are intended to protect individual rights in a specific case'.[31] Aspects of rights protection and effectiveness become intertwined, however, due to the way the policy making works in the Union.

Private parties are largely granted rights with a view to enlisting them as enforcers of Union law. This instrumentalisation of individuals is highlighted by several scholars. Caranta has argued that effective judicial protection is 'used more to exact obedience from Member States than to protect citizens'.[32] Similarly, Prechal has held that the Court 'benefits from the language of individual rights in order to ensure that the requirements which it formulates in relation to the full effectiveness of Community law are more readily accepted in national legal orders and by national courts'.[33] Mendes has held that 'Individuals are endowed with substantive rights and remedies that enable them to be a vehicle for ensuring Member States' compliance, by resorting, if necessary, to national courts'.[34] Jacobs has stated that, historically, the approach of the Court

> has not been to promote the rights of individuals for their own sake or as a matter of ideology; its approach has been essentially pragmatic and the recognition of individual rights has been almost instrumental, being seen as necessary to ensure the effectiveness of the legal order.[35]

As these scholars all stress, private parties serve the general Union interest when they enforce their own rights.

The argument is not that protecting individuals is merely a means to the end of ensuring *effet utile*.[36] But private lawsuits *also* serve a role beyond protecting the individual,

[27] ibid paras 29–32.

[28] There is, however, nothing to *prevent* a public enforcement regime from paying regard to the harmed interests of private parties, and to require the violator to grant compensation.

[29] See Case C-222/02 *Peter Paul* [2004].

[30] See further ch 13, section V.E.

[31] Case 28/67 *Firma Molkerei* [1968].

[32] R Caranta, 'Judicial Protection against Member States: A New Jus Commune Takes Shape' (1995) 32 *CML Rev* 703, 725.

[33] S Prechal, 'Protection of Rights: How Far?' in S Prechal and B van Roermund (eds), *The Coherence of EU Law. The Search for Unity in divergent Concepts* (Oxford University Press 2008) 155, 155.

[34] J Mendes, *Participation in EU Rule-Making: A Rights-Based Approach* (Oxford University Press 2011) 153.

[35] FG Jacobs, 'The Evolution of the European Legal Order' (2004) 41 *CML Rev* 303, 308.

[36] Ensuring the effective enforcement of the rights that private parties derive from Union law must be seen as an objective in and of itself; see Wilman, *Private Enforcement of EU Law Before National Courts* (n 2) 552.

since by initiating legal proceedings private parties become 'part of the implementation process'.[37] To provide a conceptual background to the Court's approach to standing, and to grasp the role of private parties in the decentralised enforcement regime, there is first a need to look into the particularities of the dominating mode of regulation in the EU. The particularities of this mode of regulation are well captured in Kelemen's notion of 'eurolegalism'.[38] This notion denotes a regulatory style 'distinguished by an emphasis on strict, judicialised enforcement of detailed legal norms through a combination of public enforcement and the broad empowerment of private actors to assert their legal rights'.[39] A brief survey of Kelemen's account will be undertaken in section IV. This survey will provide a backround against which to understand the Court's case law pertaining to standing.

IV. 'Eurolegalism': The Particularities of the Union Mode of Regulation

The term 'eurolegalism' seeks to capture the adoption by EU Member States of features of the United States' legal system, where greater reliance is placed on private enforcement for policy implementation. Although historically there have been widely different legal traditions in Europe and the US when it comes to enforcement – the former relying primarily on public enforcement through competent authorities, the latter largely on private enforcement – we are seeing signs of convergence.[40]

Private enforcement in the EU context is often called a model of 'private attorney generals', a label borrowed from the American system.[41] There is no legal definition identifying who is to be perceived as a private attorney general, and since scholars and judges have utilised the concept in a variety of contexts, its meaning has become both vague and undifferentiated.[42] On occasion, the term is used broadly to cover anyone

Similarly Dougan, who holds that the principle of effective judicial protection 'fulfils the Union's binding obligation to safeguard respect for human rights on behalf of those individuals who derive legal entitlements from the Treaty'; see M Dougan, 'The Vicissitudes of Life at the Coalface: Remedies and Procedures for Enforcing Union Law before the National Courts' in P Craig and G de Búrca (eds), *The Evolution of EU Law* (Oxford University Press 2011) 407, 431.

[37] M Ruffert, 'Rights and Remedies in European Community Law: A Comparative View' (1997) 34 *CML Rev* 307, 316. He uses the term 'functional subjectivation'. Along the same lines, Galetta has stressed that 'the citizen of the EU becomes an instrument in the process of implementation of EU law and the pursuit of its *effet utile*'; see D-U Galetta, *Procedural Autonomy of EU Member States: Paradise Lost?* (Springer 2010) 21.

[38] RD Kelemen, *Eurolegalism: The Transformation of Law and Regulation in the European Union* (Harvard University Press 2011).

[39] RD Kelemen, 'The Impact of the Court of Justice on the European Law Enforcement Architecture' in H-W Micklitz and A Wechsler (eds), *The Transformation of Enforcement. European Economic Law in a Global Perspective* (Hart Publishing 2016) 163, 164.

[40] J Rathod and S Vaheesan, 'The Arc and Architecture of Private Enforcement Regimes in the United States and Europe: A View Across the Atlantic' (2016) 14 *University of New Hampshire Law Review* 303, 306.

[41] C Kilpatrick, 'The Future of Remedies in Europe' in C Kilpatrick, T Novitz and P Skidmore (eds), *The Future of Remedies in Europe* (Hart Publishing 2000) 1, 2; and CA Ball, 'The Making of a Transnational Capitalist Society: The Court of Justice, Social Policy, and Individual Rights under the European Community's Legal Order' (1996) 37 *Harvard International Law Journal* 307, 337.

[42] WB Rubenstein, 'On What a "Private Attorney General" Is – And Why It Matters' (2004) 57 *Vanderbilt Law Review* 2129, 2171.

who brings a lawsuit that may benefit third parties, which means that almost any litigant may qualify.[43] For present purposes the term will be taken to mean 'any person who mixes private and public features in the adjudicative arena'.[44]

The role of the private attorney general in the American enforcement landscape must be seen against the backdrop of the American regulatory style, which has been labelled 'adversarial legalism' by Kagan.[45] This style has several characteristics, most notably detailed and prescriptive norms; adversarial and legalistic enforcement and dispute resolution; limited discretion and frequent judicial review of administrative decisions, use of sanctions to deal with infractions and the involvement of private parties in policy implementation.[46] The reasons for this regulatory style are complex, but the style is partly due to a distrust of government and bureaucracy. This distrust is also what lies behind the delegation of enforcement to private parties and courts.[47]

There are, Kelemen argues, 'increasing indications that a European variant of American regulatory style is spreading across the European Union'.[48] The pace of the spread and the precise form this shift takes varies across policy areas.[49] Moreover, not every policy undertaken by the EU fits the characteristics of adversarial legalism, since '[t]he EU has a wide range of instruments and approaches in its regulatory repertoire and certainly does occasionally deploy flexible, informal approaches to regulation'.[50] One such example is the open method of coordination (OMC), which is characterised by (non-binding) guidelines, monitoring and cooperation.[51] Another trend pulling in the direction of less litigation is the various forms of alternative dispute resolution that are on the rise, particularly in the field of consumer law. Concrete manifestations of this tendency can be found in Directive 2013/11/EU (Consumer ADR) and Regulation (EU) No 524/2013 (Consumer Online Dispute Resolution). These extra-judicial mechanisms have the effect of sidelining domestic courts.[52] Even so, Kelemen insists that these alternative approaches are 'red herrings';[53] the tendency to resort to 'adversarial legalism' is evident in various regulatory domains – indeed it is emerging as its dominant mode of governance.[54]

[43] JA Rabkin, 'The Secret Life of the Private Attorney General' (1998) 61 *Law and Contemporary Problems* 204, 195.

[44] Rubenstein, 'On What a "Private Attorney General" Is – And Why It Matters' (n 42) 2131.

[45] RA Kagan, *Adversarial Legalism: The American Way of Law* (Harvard University Press 2001). He uses the term 'adversarial legalism' with reference to a mode of policy implementation and dispute resolution that encourages lawyer-dominated litigation.

[46] ibid 7. This mode of governance is distinguished from methods that rely on 'bureaucratic administration, or on discretionary judgment by experts or political authorities, or on the judge-dominated style of litigation' (ibid 3).

[47] For an overview of the role of civil litigation in the American regulatory landscape, see S Farhang, *The Litigation State: Public Regulation and Private Lawsuits in the US* (Princeton University Press 2010).

[48] Kelemen, *Eurolegalism* (n 38) 5.

[49] Kelemen, 'The Impact of the Court of Justice on the European Law Enforcement Architecture' (n 39) 169.

[50] Kelemen, *Eurolegalism* (n 38) 11.

[51] See further D Hodson and I Maher, 'The Open Method as a New Mode of Governance: The Case of Soft Economic Policy Co-Ordination' (2001) 39 *Journal of Common Market Studies* 719.

[52] H Eidenmüller and M Fries, 'Against False Settlement: Designing Efficient Consumer Rights Enforcement Systems in Europe' in Micklitz and Wechsler (eds), *The Transformation of Enforcement European* (n 39) 87, 88.

[53] T Idema and RD Kelemen, 'New Modes of Governance, the Open Method of Co-Ordination and Other Fashionable Red Herring' (2006) 7 *Perspectives on European Politics and Society* 108, 109.

[54] Kelemen, *Eurolegalism* (n 38) 12.

Importantly, though, Kelemen is not arguing that Europe has adopted a full-fledged US model; rather, that what we find is a more restrained and sedate version, due to the 'moderating influence of entrenched national legal institutions and norms'.[55] Hence the term 'eurolegalism' – it is a distinct European version we are dealing with. The crux of the argument is that as a consequence of European integration, traditional approaches to regulation at the national level – generally rather operative, informal and opaque – have been undermined, ceding position to EU-level regulatory regimes characterised by formal, detailed, transparent legal norms, backed by the threat of public and private enforcement through the courts.[56]

The spread of eurolegalism as a mode of governance is primarily caused by two closely interlinked mechanisms, Kelemen explains: *economic liberalisation* and *political fragmentation*.[57] As to the first, in the pursuit of establishing a single market, deregulation at the national level has been coupled with a re-regulation at the EU level. But comparing EU regulation with the national regulatory regimes it replaces, it is seen that the former tends to be more formal, inflexible and juridified. This is a consequence of the demand from both market participants and governments to ensure a 'level playing field'.[58]

As to the second, in the EU system, political power is fragmented, with power divided both between the Union institutions (horizontal division) and between the Union institutions and Member State governments (vertical division). This fragmentation leads to principal–agent problems, since the principals (the EU legislature) cannot control the agents to whom they grant authority (the Commission and national administrations). Consequently, lawmakers have an incentive to limit and control the discretion of their agents, and for that reason enact detailed laws that specify what their agents must do, and empower the courts to enforce these norms. Given the detailed and enforceable provisions, the Commission can bring enforcement action before the ECJ. Yet due to the limited enforcement bureaucracy of the Union, the primary responsibility for enforcement is entrusted to the Member States. By framing policies as rights, and by encouraging enforcement before the courts, private parties 'serve as the eyes, ears, and long arm of Brussels'.[59] As Kelemen points out:

> Policy makers have framed policies in the language of individual rights even where rights-based approaches were clearly not the norm at the national level in the EU Member States. This can be seen … in fields ranging from competition policy, to securities regulation, to consumer protection, to environmental policy, to employment discrimination regulation, to Eurozone governance.[60]

Kelemen points to two trends that reflect the spread of eurolegalism as a mode of governance: First, the increase in the number and scope of EU rights and judicially

[55] ibid 8.
[56] RD Kelemen, 'Eurolegalism and Democracy' (2012) 50 *Journal of Common Market Studies* 55, 56.
[57] Kelemen, *Eurolegalism* (n 38) 8–9.
[58] ibid 8.
[59] RD Kelemen, 'Suing for Europe Adversarial Legalism and European Governance' (2006) 39 *Comparative Political Studies* 101, 121.
[60] Kelemen, 'The Impact of the Court of Justice on the European Law Enforcement Architecture' (n 39) 167.

enforceable legal norms and, second, the Union's efforts to expand access to justice to enable private parties to enforce Union law in domestic courts. These two trends are clearly intertwined. It is not sufficient to craft detailed and justiciable legal norms and establish individual rights for a system based on adversarial legalism to operate adequately; private parties must also be ensured effective access to court.[61] Although the legislative organs of the Union are not competent to eliminate or eradicate all procedural and substantive barriers existing in the Member States, there have been various initiatives to increase access to justice with a view to facilitating private enforcement.[62]

The Union institutions have worked in concert to advance the spread of eurolegalism, and the ECJ has also played an active role. The Court has favoured an expansive interpretation of EU rights – both substantive and procedural – and also promoted private enforcement before national courts with reference to effectiveness and effective judicial protection.[63] Outlining the regulatory style dominating in the US and its spread to Europe does not, however, tell us the full story about enforcement. In order for private parties to play a role in policy implementation, they must be granted access to court. Standing doctrines are important – one could even say one of the most important – impediments to access to justice. Restrictive standing rules may hamper their ability to serve as private attorney generals, whereas liberal standing rules will enhance that ability.[64]

The particular mode of regulation in the EU – the 'eurolegalism' – provides a background against which to understand the Court's case law on standing. This intertwinement of effective judicial protection and effectiveness must be kept in mind now that we turn to see how the ECJ has contributed to shaping domestic standing rules in the name of effective judicial protection and effectiveness. The private enforcement model 'seeks to build on the parallelism between the general interest and the individual interest of the parties concerned [and the] concept of a "right" constitutes the crucial link between the two'.[65] By initiating proceedings, the private party contributes to furthering the Union interest in the proper implementation, application and enforcement of Union law.

[61] ibid 168.

[62] See Kelemen, *Eurolegalism* (n 38) 63–79, addressing, inter alia, issues of legal aid and collective actions.

[63] Kelemen, 'The Impact of the Court of Justice on the European Law Enforcement Architecture' (n 39) 175.

[64] In the US context, a restrictive standing doctrine has diminished the role of the 'private attorney general'. Although Congress has enacted provisions authorising private parties to challenge government and private action in the public interest, the Supreme Court has adopted a restrictive standing regime. Standing in federal court has, based on an interpretation of the 'case or controversy' requirement in Art III of the Constitution, been confined to those who can demonstrate 'injury in fact', which excludes claimants without a personal injury; see, inter alia, *Lujan v Defenders of Wildlife*, 504 US 555 (1992).

[65] Wilman, *Private Enforcement of EU Law Before National Courts* (n 2) 556.

3

The Union Law Principles at Play

I. Introduction

Having explored in the abstract the normative underpinnings in the Court's case law, I take a closer look at the legal framework governing Union interference in domestic procedures and remedies. The general Union law principles of equivalence, effectiveness and effective judicial protection are at the heart of this survey. The content and scope of their application will be presented in sections III to IV. Before embarking on this presentation, however, I provide a historical background to the system of private enforcement of Union law in the Member States (section II).

II. The Evolvement of Private Enforcement

The possibility of private enforcement before national courts does not follow explicitly from the Treaties. Pursuant to the wording of the Treaties, the only mechanisms geared at ensuring compliance of the Member States with their EU law obligations are infringement proceedings under (now) Article 258 TFEU or, alternatively, proceedings by a Member State against another under (now) Article 259 TFEU. Such actions are brought before the ECJ, and therefore deserve the label 'centralised' enforcement. Centralised enforcement is not necessarily sufficient to ensure the effective implementation of and compliance with Member States' Union law obligations. States tend to resolve their differences (if at all) through diplomatic channels rather than by legal means, and the Commission has limited resources to pursue infringements.[1] Moreover, from the perspective of private parties affected by an infringement committed by a Member State or a private party, centralised enforcement is not an option, since private parties cannot challenge such acts or measures before the Union courts.[2]

[1] F Wilman, 'The End of the Absence? The Growing Body of EU Legislation on Private Enforcement and the Main Remedies It Provides For' (2016) 53 *CML Rev* 887, 888.

[2] M Dougan, *National Remedies Before the Court of Justice: Issues of Harmonisation and Differentiation* (Hart Publishing 2004) 2.

These shortcomings led the Court to establish the system of dual vigilance in *Van Gend en Loos*, paving the way for private enforcement before the Member States' courts. The Court explicitly rejected the argument of several Member States that the centralised, public enforcement mechanisms laid down by the Treaty were exclusive, and held that

> the vigilance of individuals concerned to protect their rights amounts to an effective supervision in addition to the supervision entrusted by [now Articles 258 and 259] to the diligence of the Commission and of the Member States.[3]

As a result of the system of decentralised private enforcement, national courts have, in effect, become Union courts.[4] Whenever they are seized of a dispute governed by rules of EU law, they therefore have a duty to operate as functional Union courts.[5] This means that 'the entire judiciary of Europe from the lowliest tribunal to the most venerable court of appeal has (at least in theory) been harnessed to the service of the Community, all under the guidance of the Court of Justice'.[6] The system of private enforcement crafted by the ECJ must be understood against this background of decentralised enforcement before domestic courts.

Since there is no common procedural framework applicable in the case of decentralised enforcement of Union law, domestic courts essentially apply their own national enforcement provisions. Union law can impact domestic procedural and remedial rules in three different ways, however: first, through the substantive rules in the TFEU; second, through explicit rules in secondary legislation; and, third, through general Union law principles.

As to the first of these, national remedial rules must comply with the substantive rules contained in the TFEU. This means, for example, that Member States are prohibited from sanctioning infringements of domestic measures found to be incompatible with the provisions on free movement.[7] Moreover, the principle of non-discrimination on grounds of nationality enshrined in Article 18(1) TFEU implies that the same procedural and remedial rules must apply without regard to nationality or residence.[8] It is only exceptionally that national enforcement rules will constitute a breach of the substantive Treaty rules, and this situation will not be addressed further in this book.[9]

[3] Case 26/62 *Van Gend en Loos* [1963].

[4] Opinion 1/09 *Patent Court Agreement* [2011] paras 66 and 68. See also AG Cosmas in Case C-83/98 P *France v Ladbroke Racing and Commission* [2000] para 92, who refers to the national courts as the 'ordinary courts of Community law'.

[5] V Trstenjak and E Beysen, 'European Consumer Protection Law: Curia Semper Dabit Remedium?' (2011) 48 *CML Rev* 95, 97.

[6] Dougan, *National Remedies Before the Court of Justice* (n 2) 3.

[7] See, inter alia, Case 269/80 *Tymen* [1981]; and Case C-13/01 *Safalero* [2003]. See further Dougan, *National Remedies Before the Court of Justice* (n 2) 20.

[8] See, inter alia, Case C-398/92 *Mund & Fester* [1994]; and Case C-29/95 *Pastoors v Belgium* [1997]. As Ebbesson points out, this means that the criteria for distinguishing persons with standing in domestic cases must also apply to transboundary cases; see J Ebbesson, *Access to Justice in Environmental Matters in the EU* (Kluwer Law International 2002) 63.

[9] For a more detailed account, see Dougan, *National Remedies Before the Court of Justice* (n 2) 20–23.

As to the second, the legislative organs of the Union have adopted secondary legislation governing procedures and remedies applicable in domestic proceedings. The EU legislature is gradually expanding the EU legislative framework with a view to facilitating private enforcement of EU law before domestic courts.[10] There is a growing number of directives and regulations that contain explicit provisions concerning the enforcement of the substantive provisions laid down therein, and there are also instruments that deal only with aspects of enforcement.[11] We see an increased tendency both to specify the national remedies available for breaches of Union law and also to list the range of persons who must be granted standing. Examples of such enforcement rules can be found, inter alia, in the field of consumer protection,[12] public procurement,[13] data protection,[14] asylum law[15] and intellectual property.[16] To the extent that a directive expressly regulates the issue of standing, the Member States must provide a legal avenue to the persons covered. Conflicting national provisions have to yield because of the principle of supremacy.[17] Standing provisions contained in secondary legislation are not, however, the object of this book.[18]

Despite fragementary harmonisation efforts by the Union legislature, it is still the case that most secondary legislation is silent on the range of persons to be granted standing. This means that Union law primarily exerts it influence in the third way listed, through general principles of Union law. General Union law principles – *in casu* the principles of equivalence, effectiveness and effective judicial protection – apply in the context of decentralised enforcement of Union law.[19] These principles will be presented in the following.

[10] For a thorough account of procedural regulation in secondary legislation, see F Wilman, *Private Enforcement of EU Law Before National Courts: The EU Legislative Framework* (Edward Elgar 2015). For a general overview of harmonisation in the field of civil procedure, see E Storskrubb, *Civil Procedure and EU Law: A Policy Area Uncovered* (Oxford University Press 2008). In the 1990s, a body composed of academics examined the possibility of drafting a model 'EU Code of Civil Procedure', but the attempt stalled because members of the group were unable to reach a consensus: see M Storme, *Approximation of Judiciary Law in the European Union* (Nijhoff 2004).

[11] See, inter alia, Directive 2014/54/EU (Free Movement of Workers Enforcement Directive).

[12] Directive 85/374/EEC (Product Liability); Directive 2009/22/EC (Consumer Injunctions) and Directive 2011/83/EU (Consumer Rights).

[13] Directive 92/13/EEC (Procurement Remedies Directive for the utilities sector) and Directive 89/665/ EC (Procurement Remedies Directive for the public sector).

[14] Regulation (EU) 2016/679 (General Data Protection Regulation).

[15] Directive 2013/32/EU (International Protection).

[16] Directive 2004/48/EC (IPR Enforcement Directive).

[17] Case C-462/99 *Connect Austria* [2003] para 40. Explicit provisions on standing laid down in secondary law must be given a broad interpretation as to their personal scope, due to the importance of subjecting administrative decisions to judicial review; see Case C-459/99 *MRAX* [2002] para 101.

[18] Provisions contained in secondary legislation are, however, often read in light of the principle of effective judicial protection; see, for instance, Case C-69/10 *Samba Diouf* [2011] and Joined Cases C-439/12 and C-488/14 *Star Storage* [2016].

[19] See, inter alia, Case C-432/05 *Unibet* [2007] and Case C-418/11 *Texdata* [2013]. They apply to 'national choices about the imposition of sanctions for breaching Union law; over the provision of remedies to right-holders benefiting from the Treaties; and concerning the procedural rules that govern claims seeking to assert rights derived from Union law', see M Dougan, 'Judicial Review of Member State Action under the General Principles and the Charter: Defining the Scope of Union Law' (2015) 52 *CML Rev* 1201, 1213.

III. Equivalence, Effectiveness and Effective Judicial Protection

A. Introduction

The division of competence between the Union and the Member States in determining who has access to the court for the enforcement of Union law provisions was spelled out in *Mono Car Styling*.[20] The Court held:

> Whilst it is, in principle, for national law to determine an individual's standing and legal interest in bringing proceedings, Community law nevertheless requires, in addition to observance of the principles of equivalence and effectiveness, that the national legislation does not undermine the right to effective judicial protection.[21]

Based on the principles of equivalence, effectiveness and effective judicial protection, the Court has made substantial inroads into the procedural autonomy of the Member States.[22] The standard procedure applicable in proceedings of a wholly domestic character will not necessarily be applicable where the proceedings engage issues of EU law. Classifying a claim as a Union claim, rather than as a strictly national one, is therefore decisive for the application of the Union requirements pertaining to procedures and remedies.[23]

B. Equivalence and Effectiveness

The reference to national procedural rules in *Mono Car Styling* was in line with the Court's earlier jurisprudence. The Court had already held in *Rewe* that

> in the absence of Community rules on this subject it is for the domestic legal system of each Member State to designate the courts having jurisdiction and to determine the procedural conditions governing actions at law intended to ensure the protection of the rights which citizens have from the direct effect of Community law.[24]

The Member State's liberty to designate the courts competent to handle cases involving Union law is a feature of their *institutional autonomy*. This implies that Member States

[20] See Case C-12/08 *Mono Car Styling* [2009].

[21] ibid para 49.

[22] Particularly the principle of effective judicial protection 'seems to have established itself as hierarchically superior to that of national procedural autonomy'; see A Arnull, 'The Principle of Effective Judicial Protection in EU Law: An Unruly Horse?' (2011) 36 *EL Rev* 51, 68.

[23] N Póltorak, *European Union Rights in National Courts* (Wolters Kluwer 2015) 116. A case brought before the court is not necessarily strictly of Union law origin. Union law may be invoked as one of many arguments, which is often the case in relation to, for instance, Union law directives that have been implemented in the domestic legal order.

[24] Case 33/76 *Rewe* [1976] para 5. See also Case 45/76 *Comet* [1976] para 13. As stated by AG Jacobs in Joined Cases C-430/93 and C-431/93 *Van Schijndel* [1995] para 30, 'The underlying premise is that States based on the rule of law will organize their national legal systems in such a way as to ensure proper application of the law and adequate legal protection for their subjects.'

are free to designate the public institutions responsible for performing tasks resulting from Union law.[25] The freedom to determine the procedural conditions governing actions involving Union law is often referred to as the principle of *national procedural autonomy*.[26] The term conceals the fact that the autonomy also covers remedial rules.[27] Moreover, the appropriateness of the term has been questioned, as the determination of procedural rules is not a domain reserved for the Member States.[28] The term 'procedural autonomy' has, however, been incorporated into the vocabulary of legal scholars, and will be employed in the following.

Differences in procedural and institutional frameworks may lead to differences in substantive outcomes. An unfettered procedural autonomy could therefore jeopardise the uniform and effective application of Union law and undermine the protection of Union rights. As Kelemen points out, the notion that one level could establish and guarantee substantive rights while another level could have exclusive control over procedures and remedies was 'implausible from the outset [since if] national procedures governing the exercise of EU rights or national remedies for breach of those rights were inadequate, this could render EU rights dead letters'.[29] Procedural autonomy is therefore not absolute: the Court required as early as *Rewe* that 'such conditions cannot be less favorable than those relating to similar actions of a domestic nature … [and must not make it] impossible in practice to exercise the rights which the national courts are obliged to protect'.[30] These two conditions – the principle of equivalence and effectiveness, respectively – are cumulative, in the sense that both need to be fulfilled in order for national procedural law to live up to the demands of EU law. The principles of effectiveness and equivalence are derived from the duty of loyal cooperation laid down in Article 4(3) TEU, requiring the Member States to 'facilitate the achievement of the Union tasks and refrain from any measure which could jeopardise the attainment of the Union's objectives'.[31]

The principle of equivalence requires the national rule at issue to be applied without distinction, whether the infringement alleged is of Union law or national law, where the purpose and cause of action are similar.[32] It is, in essence, a non-discrimination principle. As the Court held in *Pasquini*, it is 'simply the expression of the principle of

[25] Póltorak, *European Union Rights in National Courts* (n 23) 23. Institutional autonomy also encompasses *administrative autonomy*, meaning that the vast majority of Union law is implemented by national authorities in accordance with national administrative rules.

[26] See Case C-201/02 *Wells* [2004] paras 65 and 67; and Case C-93/12 *ET Agrokonsulting* [2013] para 35.

[27] See, inter alia, Case 130/79 *Express Diary Foods* [1980] para 11. In this context, the term 'remedial autonomy' can be used, see AG Trstenjak in Case C-591/10 *Littlewoods Retail* [2012] para 24.

[28] See CM Kakouris, 'Do the Member States Possess Judicial Procedural "Autonomy"?' (1997) 34 *CML Rev* 1389, 1406. To the same effect, see M Bobek, 'Why There Is No Principle of "Procedural Autonomy" of the Member States' in H-W Micklitz and B de Witte (eds), *The European Court of Justice and the Autonomy of the Member States* (Intersentia 2012) 305. Van Gerven proposes abandoning the term, speaking instead of the 'procedural competence' of the Member States, see W Van Gerven, 'Of Rights, Remedies and Procedures' (2000) 37 *CML Rev* 501, 502. Póltorak uses the term 'principle of national procedures', see Póltorak, *European Union Rights in National Courts* (n 23) 38.

[29] RD Kelemen, 'American-Style Adversarial Legalism and the European Union' (European University Institute) *EUI Working Papers RSCAS 2008/37*, 8.

[30] Case 33/76 *Rewe* [1976] para 5. See also Case 45/76 *Comet* [1976] paras 13 and 16.

[31] See, *inter alia*, Case C-93/12 *ET Agroconsulting* [2013] para 36.

[32] Case C-326/96 *Levez* [1998] para 41; and Case C-63/08 *Pontin* [2009] para 45.

equal treatment, which is one of the fundamental principles of Community law'.[33] The principle of equivalence ensures that EU law can benefit fully from the procedural and remedial structures in place in the Member States.[34]

It is for the national court, which alone has direct knowledge of the procedural rules governing domestic actions, to determine whether the procedural rules in place comply with the principle of equivalence.[35] For that purpose, the national court must consider whether the actions concerned are similar as regards their purpose and essential characteristics.[36] In order to determine whether the procedural rules are equally favourable, the national court must decide, in the abstract, whether the relevant rules are similar, taking into account the role played by those rules in the procedure as a whole, the conduct of that procedure and any special features of those rules.[37] Although the Court tends to leave it to the national courts to determine equivalence, on occasion it has sufficient information on the content of potentially comparable domestic law to provide detailed guidance as to the equivalence of the actions concerned.[38]

The Court tends to pay relatively little attention to the principle of equivalence in comparison to the twin principle of effectiveness. Since the application of the principle of equivalence depends on the comparable legal framework in the Member State concerned, there is only so much one can say about the principle in the abstract. This principle will therefore play a minor role in the present book.[39]

More attention will be devoted to the principle of effectiveness. The original formula applied by the Court in *Rewe*, that procedural rules should not render the enforcement of EU law rights 'impossible in practice', has been extended to cover situations where national procedural rules would make the enforcement of such rights 'virtually impossible or excessively difficult',[40] thereby extending the scope of the Court's ability to scrutinise domestic enforcement rules. While impossibility refers to situations where the enforcement of Union law is completely barred due to the lack of an appropriate remedy, excessive difficulty 'relies more on subjective visions of the appropriate level of "difficulty" claimants ought (not) to be facing when vindicating their rights under EU law'.[41] The ECJ has applied the effectiveness principle as a means to scrutinise a

[33] Case C-34/02 *Pasquini* [2003] para 70.

[34] D Leczykiewicz, 'The Constitutional Dimension of Private Law Liability Rules in the EU' in D Leczykiewicz and S Weatherill (eds), *The Involvement of EU Law in Private Law Relationships* (Hart Publishing 2013) 199, 213.

[35] Case C-326/96 *Levez* [1998] paras 39 and 43; and Case C-63/08 *Pontin* [2009] para 45.

[36] Case C-78/98 *Preston* [2000] para 57; and Case C-63/08 *Pontin* [2009] para 45.

[37] Case C-78/98 *Preston* [2000] paras 61–63; and Case C-63/08 *Pontin* [2009] para 46.

[38] See, eg, Case C-261/95 *Palmisani* [1997] paras 38–39; and Case C-147/01 *Weber's Wine World* [2003] paras 104–08 and Case C-234/17 *XC* [2018] paras 35–48.

[39] For a detailed account of the principle of equivalence, see Póltorak, *European Union Rights in National Courts* (n 23) 72–82.

[40] Case 199/82 *San Giorgio* [1983] para 14; and Joined Cases C-6/90 and C-9/90 *Francovich* [1991] para 43.

[41] M Bobek, 'The Effects of EU Law in the National Legal Systems' in C Barnard and S Peers (eds), *European Union Law* 3rd edn (Oxford University Press 2020) 154, 183. This change in the effectiveness test gives the Court greater discretion to take into account the particularities of national legal systems, because '[u]nlike the question whether the exercise of a right conferred by EU law is made "impossible" in general, which only allows for a very straightforward answer, the question of whether the exercise of such a right is made "excessively difficult" requires a comprehensive review, in which all the particularities of national legal systems must be taken into consideration'; see Trstenjak and Beysen, 'European Consumer Protection Law: Curia Semper Dabit Remedium?' (n 5) 102.

wide range of domestic enforcement rules concerning both access to court (such as time limits[42] and res judicata[43]) and rules applicable during the proceedings (such as rules on evidence and the obligation to raise matters of Union law *ex officio*).[44]

The Court elaborated on the principle of effectiveness in *Van Schijndel* and *Peterbroeck*, both addressing the *ex officio* application of Union law. The Court reiterated its classic formula from *Rewe*, but went on to state that

> each case which raises the question whether a national procedural provision renders application of Community law impossible or excessively difficult must be analysed by reference to the role of that provision in the procedures, its progress and its special features, viewed as a whole, before the various national instances. In the light of that analysis the basic principles of the domestic judicial system, such as protection of the rights of the defence, the principle of legal certainty and the proper conduct of procedure, must, where appropriate, be taken into consideration.[45]

In order to establish whether a domestic enforcement provision renders the application of Union law impossible or excessively difficult, one must examine whether the limitation finds its justification in a fundamental principle of the relevant legal system.[46] Rules on legal procedure express the legal tradition in the state, and should not always be sacrificed at the altar of effectiveness. If the provision is found to serve a legitimate interest, and the procedural limitation is proportionate to the objectives served, the exercise of EU rights may be limited in individual cases.[47] This balancing approach can be seen as a procedural equivalent to the 'rule of reason' test, well known from the area of free movement.[48] When assessing domestic procedural rules for conformity with the effectiveness principle, one therefore needs to understand the rationale underlying the rule at issue.

National rules cannot be assessed in the abstract; whether the principle of effectiveness has been complied with will depend on the particularities of each case. Procedural restrictions that might be justified in principle may yet infringe on the effectiveness principle given the particular circumstances of the case.[49] When addressing the effectiveness principle, the Court often restricts its ruling to the case at hand, finding that a

[42] See, inter alia, Case C-208/90 *Emmott* [1991]; Case C-255/00 *Grundig Italiana* [2002]; and Case C-2/06 *Kempter* [2008].

[43] See, inter alia, Case C-234/17 *XC* [2018].

[44] See Case C-228/98 *Dounias* [2000] (evidence) and Case C-312/93 *Peterbroeck* [1995]; and Joined Cases C-430/93 and C-431/93 *Van Schijndel* [1995] (*ex officio* application of Union law).

[45] Joined Cases C-430/93 and C-431/93 *Van Schijndel* [1995] para 19; and Case C-312/93 *Peterbroeck* [1995] para 14. This has been repeated in several subsequent rulings: see, inter alia, Case C-2/08 *Fallimento Olimpiclub* [2009] para 27; Case C-618/10 *Banco Español de Crédito* [2012] para 49; and Case C-169/14 *Sánches Morcillo* [2014] para 34.

[46] S Prechal, 'Community Law in National Courts: The Lessons from van Schijndel' (1998) 35 *CML Rev* 681, 690. It has been questioned whether these cases really represent a new approach to the effectiveness test: see Dougan, *National Remedies Before the Court of Justice* (n 2) 31; and L Flynn, 'When National Procedural Autonomy Meets the Effectiveness of Community Law, Can It Survive the Impact?' (2008) 9 *ERA Forum* 245, 249.

[47] M Accetto and S Zleptnig, 'The Principle of Effectiveness: Rethinking Its Role in Community Law' (2005) 11 *European Public Law* 375, 402–03.

[48] See further, Prechal, 'Community Law in National Courts: The Lessons from van Schijndel' (n 46) 690–91.

[49] See, for instance, Case C-327/00 *Santex* [2003] para 57. On the factors to be taken into consideration in this balancing approach, see Van Gerven, 'Of Rights, Remedies and Procedures' (n 28) 531.

procedural rule renders the enforcement of Union law impossible or excessively difficult in the particular circumstances of the case.[50] On occasion, however, the Court frames the conflict as having broader and more general scope, and thefore dictates the disapplication of the national procedural rule in potential future disputes too.[51] Where this is the case, the legislature or executive should step in and amend the incompatible domestic provision so as to comply with Union law.

C. Effective Judicial Protection

i. Introduction

The procedural autonomy of the Member States is also restricted by the right to effective judicial protection enshrined in Article 47 of the Charter of Fundamental Rights. Originally, the Charter was primarily of a declaratory nature, expressing the EU's commitment to observe fundamental rights, but on the entry into force of the Treaty of Lisbon, the Charter acquired the status of primary law within the Union legal order.[52] According to Article 6(1) TEU, the Charter shall have 'the same legal value as the Treaties'.

Article 47(1) of the Charter reads that '[e]veryone whose rights and freedoms guaranteed by the Union are violated has the right to an effective remedy before a tribunal'. This right to an effective remedy comprises the right to a fair trial (see Article 47(2)), but this aspect will not be addressed in detail in this book. The Charter applies, pursuant to Article 51(1), to the Member States when they are 'implementing EU law', which has been interpreted broadly. In *Åkerberg Fransson*, the Court stated that the requirement to respect fundamental rights is binding on the Member States only when they act within the scope of Union law. It elaborated further:

> Since the fundamental rights guaranteed by the Charter must therefore be complied with where national legislation falls within the scope of European Union law, situations cannot exist which are covered in that way by European Union law without those fundamental rights being applicable. The applicability of European Union law entails applicability of the fundamental rights guaranteed by the Charter.[53]

The responsibility for providing effective judicial protection is shared between the Union and the Member States. The Member States' duty to provide effective judicial protection is explicitly laid down in Article 19(1) TEU, which requires them to 'provide

[50] This means that judgments 'cannot be applied mechanically in fields other than those in which they were made'; see Case C-473/00 *Codifis* [2002] para 37.

[51] P Van Cleynenbreugel, 'National Procedural Choices before the Court of Justice of the European Union' in L Gruszczynski and W Werner (eds), *Deference in International Courts and Tribunals: Standard of Review and Margin of Appreciation* (Oxford University Press 2014) 175, 182–83. Such 'facial review' was conducted by the Court, inter alia, in Case 106/77 *Simmenthal* [1978], addressed further in ch 6, section III.C.

[52] AG Trstenjak in Case C-282/10 *Dominguez* [2011] para 72.

[53] Case C-617/10 *Åkerberg Fransson* [2013] para 21. The scope of application of the Charter corresponds in essence with the application of the general principles of Union law: Case C-206/13 *Siragusa* [2014] para 35. See further Dougan, 'Judicial Review of Member State Action under the General Principles and the Charter' (n 19).

remedies sufficient to ensure effective legal protection in the fields covered by Union law'.[54] This provision 'turns the subjective right into an objective obligation for Member States to ensure that their judicial systems provide effective judicial protection'.[55]

ii. *The Evolvement from a Union Principle to a Charter Right*

The principle of effective judicial protection has long been perceived as a general principle of Union law.[56] With the enactment of the Charter of Fundamental Rights, the general principle of effective judicial protection was given expression in Article 47. This prompts the question whether this change in status has implications for the content and evolvement of the right to judicial protection.

The Court has made clear that the Charter 'reaffirms the rights, freedoms and principles recognised in the Union and makes those rights more visible, but does not create new rights or principles'.[57] That Article 47 of the Charter is a codification of the principle of effective judicial protection is clearly stated in *ET Agroconsulting*, where the Court held that

> it is apparent from the Court's case-law that that provision [Article 47 of the Charter] constitutes a reaffirmation of the principle of effective judicial protection, a general principle of European Union law stemming from the constitutional traditions common to the Member States, which has been enshrined in Articles 6 and 13 of the European Convention for the Protection of Human Rights and Fundamental Freedoms.[58]

The Court also builds on its prior case law on effective judicial protection when interpreting Article 47 of the Charter.[59] It seems safe to conclude that we are not so much dealing with the transformation of a principle to a Charter right, but rather a *codification* of an already existing right to effective judicial protection, which the Member States were already bound to respect. Therefore, the terms 'principle of effective judicial protection' and 'right to effective judicial protection' will be used interchangeably in the following.[60]

[54] The terms 'legal protection' and 'judicial protection' are used interchangeably by the Court, and in the following 'effective judicial protection' will be taken to encompass both the right to court and the scope of protection afforded. See, however, Półtorak, *European Union Rights in National Courts* (n 23) 47, who is of the opinion that the former concept is broader than the latter.

[55] V Roeben, 'Judicial Protection as the Meta-norm in the EU Judicial Architecture' (2020) 12 *Hague Journal on the Rule of Law* 29, 31. Art 19(1) TEU has a wider scope of application than the Charter. The provision refers to 'the fields covered by Union law', and the provision applies irrespective of whether the Member States are implementing Union law within the meaning of Art 51(1) of the Charter; see Case C-64/16, *ASJP* [2018] para 29.

[56] See Case C-432/05 *Unibet* [2007] para 37.

[57] Joined Cases C-411/10 and C-493/10 *NS* [2011] para 119. Prior to the enactment of the Charter, fundamental rights were perceived as part of the 'general principles of Community law', see Case 29/69 *Stauder v City of Ulm* [1969] para 7 and Case 4/73 *Nold* [1974] para 13.

[58] Case C-93/12 *ET Agroconsulting* [2013] para 59. See also Case C-386/10 P *Chalkor v Commission* [2011] para 52; Case C-583/13 P *Deutsche Bahn* [2015] para 47; and Case C-239/14 *Tall* [2015] para 51.

[59] See, eg, Case C-562/12 *Liivimaa Lihaveis* [2014], where the Court draws directly on Case C-97/91 *Borelli* [1992] and Case C-269/99 *Kühne* [2001], both of which were rendered before the entry into force of the Lisbon Treaty.

[60] On occasion, the Court mentions both the principle and the right to effective judicial protection; see, for instance, Case C-685/15 *Online Games* [2017] para 54.

A caveat is nevertheless in order. It may well be that the Court perceives it as more legitimate to elaborate on what the principle of effective judicial protection requires now that it has a firm legal mandate in the Treaties. As Drake has pointed out, Article 47 of the Charter constitutes a 'more visible and highly legitimate legal basis upon which the Court can develop its standards of fundamental rights protection in relation to the right to an effective remedy'.[61] For that reason, some scholars argue that the acquistion of binding force by the Charter marked the beginning of a new phase in the Court's case law on remedies and procedures before national courts.[62]

An explicit legal basis in the Treaties makes the Court more resilient to the accusations of judicial activism that are directed at the Court's jurisprudence in the field of procedures and remedies.[63] In recent times, the Court seems to have adopted a more elaborative style, giving more detail on what the principle of effective judicial protection requires. One example is *DEB*, where the Court held that it also had to be possible, in principle, for legal persons to obtain legal aid, another one is *Schrems*, where the Court invalidated the Safe Harbour decision of the Commission, due to a complete absence of a legal avenue for individuals alleging an infringement of their Union rights.[64] This is not, however, an unequivocal trend. There are also examples of the Court's adopting a more restrained approach, leaving the referring court considerable leeway to determine whether the procedural restrictions constitute a proportionate interference with the right to effective judicial protection.[65]

iii. The Formal and Substantive Aspects of Effective Judicial Protection

In order to comply with the principle of effective judicial protection, it is first necessary that individuals have access to a national court, in other words, a right to *judicial process*. Second, the national court should have at its disposal *effective remedies* with which to prevent and redress violations of Union law. That is to say, the principle of effective judicial protection has one aspect related to *access* to court and another related to the *outcome* of the court's proceedings.[66] These two aspects may be referred to as the *formal* and *substantive* aspects of judicial protection respectively.[67]

[61] S Drake, 'More Effective Private Enforcement of EU Law Post-Lisbon: Aligning Regulatory Goals and Constitutional Values' in S Drake and M Smith (eds), *New Directions in the Effective Enforcement of EU Law and Policy* (Edward Elgar 2016) 12, 35.

[62] A Arnull, 'Remedies before National Courts' in R Schütze and T Tridimas (eds), *Oxford Principles of European Union Law*, vol I: *The European Union Legal Order* (Oxford University Press 2018) 1011, 1026; and Drake, 'More Effective Private Enforcement of EU Law Post-Lisbon' (n 61) 27–28. Mak similarly suggests that Art 47 of the Charter may have an added value and 'support a judge-made European law on remedies'; see C Mak, 'Rights and Remedies: Article 47 EUCFR and Effective Judicial Protection in European Private Law Matters' in H-W Micklitz (ed), *Constitutionalization of European Private Law* (Oxford University Press 2014) 251.

[63] See further ch 5, section VII.

[64] Case C-279/09 *DEB* [2010]; and Case C-362/14 *Schrems* [2015] (further addressed in ch 5, section V).

[65] See, eg, Case C-73/16 *Puškár* [2017].

[66] It bears emphasis, however, that the principle of effective judicial protection comprises also other elements; such as the rights of the defence, the principle of equality of arms, and the right to be advised, defended and represented, cf. Case C-348/16 *Sacko* [2017] para 32.

[67] R Widdershoven, 'The Principle of Loyal Cooperation: Lawmaking by the European Court of Justice and the Dutch Courts' in FAM Stroink and ECHJ Linden (eds), *Judicial Lawmaking and Administrative Law* (Intersentia 2005) 3, 17–18.

The *substantive* aspect of the right to effective judicial protection consists of the right to an effective remedy, a matter addressed in detail in chapter 7. Member States are granted considerable discretion as to the form of remedy provided, yet the remedy chosen must be such as to guarantee real and effective judicial protection, and be deterrent and adequate.[68] Thus, while the Court has set out certain requirements regarding the remedies that need to be provided, it tends to stress the 'significance of the *functional nature* of [such] measures rather than the *juridical form* or *label*'.[69] It is largely left to the Member State to decide on the appropriate means to remedy a (prospective) breach of EU law, provided that it meets the requirement of judicial protection. So although the protection afforded to individuals stems essentially from the national legal system, national remedies may have to be 'upgraded', through consistent interpretation, to meet Union standards.[70] Union law may require not only the reshaping of existing remedies under national law; the Court has gone a long way in specifying the remedies the Member States need to provide, and also in setting out to some extent the conditions that need to be fulfilled in order to obtain a given remedy.[71] The principle of effective judicial protection is thus no longer merely an obligation of result – the Court has increasingly decided on the means to achieve this end.[72] As a result, the leeway granted to the Member States has been increasingly limited.

The *formal* aspect of the right to judicial protection, which is in focus in this book, consists of the right to judicial process. Access to judicial process is a necessary precondition for obtaining effective protection of Union rights. In *Johnston*, the Court ruled that a right of access to judicial control was mandatory when a breach of Union law was alleged.[73] The right to access to judicial process cannot be perceived in a strictly formal manner.[74] The Court seems to be concerned with ensuring rights that are 'practical

[68] Case 14/83 *Von Colson* [1984] para 23 (emphasis added). See also Case C-271/91 *Marshall II* [1993] para 26, where the Court held that a state opting for financial compensation must 'enable the loss and damage actually sustained – to be made good in full'; and Joined Cases C-46/93 and C-48/93 *Brasserie du Pêcheur* [1996] para 82, where the Court held that reparation for loss or damage must be 'commensurate with the loss or damage sustained'.

[69] C Harding, 'Member State Enforcement of European Community Measures: The Chimera of "Effective" Enforcement' (1997) 4 *Maastricht Journal of European and Comparative Law* 5, 9.

[70] Reich calls this the 'hybridisation of remedies', see N Reich, 'The Interrelation between Rights and Duties in EU Law: Reflections on the State of Liability Law in the Multilevel Governance System of the Union: Is There a Need for a More Coherent Approach in European Private Law?' (2010) 29 *Yearbook of European Law* 112, 124.

[71] On these 'Union law remedies', see further ch 7, section III. It has been argued that the Court through its case law is gradually moving towards a '*jus commune*' in the field of judicial protection: see R Caranta, 'Judicial Protection against Member States: A New Jus Commune Takes Shape' (1995) 32 *CML Rev* 703, 715.

[72] N Fenger, *Forvaltning og Fællesskab: Om EU-Rettens Betydning for den Almindelige Forvaltningsret: Konfrontation og Frugtbar Sameksistens* (DJØF 2004) 83.

[73] Case 222/84 *Johnston* [1986] paras 18–19. See also Case 222/86 *Heylens* [1987] para 14; Case C-185/97 *Coote* [1998] paras 20–21; Case C-1/99 *Kofisa* [2001] para 46; and Case C-340/89 *Vlassopoulou* [1991] para 22. As Ward has noted, the Court refers almost interchangeably to the requirement of 'judicial control', the obligation to allow individuals to 'pursue their claim by judicial process' and the right to 'obtain an effective remedy before a competent court'; see A Ward, *Judicial Review and the Rights of Private Parties in EC Law* (Oxford University Press 2000) 173.

[74] LM Ravo, 'The Role of the Principle of Effective Judicial Protection in the EU and Its Impact on National Jurisdictions' in Edizioni Università di Trieste (ed), *Sources of Law and Legal Protection* (Edizioni Università di Trieste 2012) 101, 105.

and effective' rather than 'theoretical and illusory'.[75] Therefore, the Court has scrutinised various forms of national (procedural) rules, such as, for instance, court fees[76] and schemes for legal aid for Union law compliance.[77]

In order to ensure effective judicial protection as required by Article 47 of the Charter, the body hearing a case and granting a remedy must be considered a 'tribunal'.[78] The latter is an autonomous concept, governed by Union law.[79] The Court's definition of a tribunal for the purposes of judicial protection corresponds to the definition laid down in relation to Article 267 TFEU, concerning the bodies entitled to make a preliminary reference.[80] In order to determine whether a body making a reference is a court or tribunal for the purposes of Article 267 TFEU, the Court takes account of several factors, such as whether the body is established by law, whether it is permanent, whether its jurisdiction is compulsory, whether its procedure is *inter partes*, whether it applies rules of law, whether it is independent and in what capacity it is acting.[81]

The Court has made clear that the right to effective judicial protection is not absolute; the exercise of the right can be subject to limitations, provided they respect the essence of the right, pursue a legitimate purpose and are proportionate with regard to the objectives pursued in accordance with Article 52(1) of the Charter.[82] This test resembles the 'procedural rule of reason' test applicable under the effectiveness principle.[83] Interestingly, though, there are no signs of such a balancing approach in the Court's case law pertaining to standing, a matter that will be futher examined in chapter 5.

D. *Effet Utile*

In addition to the principles of effectiveness and effective judicial protection, the Court has also referred in several cases to the '*full effect*' or the '*full effectiveness*' of EU law in cases where national enforcement rules were seen as hampering the application of Union law domestically.[84] This is a reference to the broader principle of

[75] This expression is borrowed from the ECtHR, see *Artico v Italy* App no 6694/74 (ECtHR, 1980) para 33.

[76] Case C-530/11 *Commission v the United Kingdom* [2014].

[77] Case C-279/09 *DEB* [2010]. Art 47(3) of the Charter prescribes that '[l]egal aid shall be made available to those who lack sufficient resources in so far as such aid is necessary to ensure effective access to justice'. The right to legal aid in cross-border civil cases is further regulated by Directive 2002/8/EC (Legal Aid in Cross-border Disputes).

[78] The existence of an administrative appeals system is not sufficient to comply with the Union standard; see Case C-424/99 *Commission v Austria* [2001] paras 42–47. The requirement of effective judicial protection is, however, satisfied provided that an administrative decision can be appealed to a court; see Case C-175/11 *D and A* [2013] paras 102–03.

[79] Case C-54/96 *Dorsch Consult* [1997] para 23.

[80] Case C-506/04 *Wilson* [2006] paras 47–48.

[81] See, inter alia, Case C-54/96 *Dorsch Consult* [1997] para 23; Case C-363/11 *Epitropos tou Elegktikou Sinedriou* [2012] para 18; and Case C-503/15 *Panicello* [2017] paras 27–28. The importance of independence was emphasised in Case C-64/16 *ASJP* [2018] para 41.

[82] Case C-300/11 *ZZ* [2013] para 51.

[83] The test may, however, be stricter when the right of judicial protection is at stake, see S Prechal and R Widdershoven, 'Redefining the Relationship between "Rewe-Effectiveness" and Effective Judicial Protection' (2011) 4 *Review of European Administrative Law* 31, 44.

[84] See, inter alia, Case C-213/89 *Factortame* [1990] para 21; Joined Cases C-6/90 and C-9/90 *Francovich* [1991] para 33; and Case C-253/00 *Muñoz* [2002] para 30.

effectiveness – *effet utile*. Effectiveness considerations are of paramount importance, due to the system of decentralised implementation and enforcement of Union law. The duty of loyal cooperation as enshrined in Article 4(3) TEU entails an obligation on Member States to 'take all the measures necessary to guarantee the application and effectiveness of [EU] law'.[85]

The principle of *effet utile* is not restricted to imposing limits on the Member States' procedural autonomy, but also pervades the whole field of Union law encompassing implementation, enforcement and compliance.[86] That law is rendered operative – that is, exists not only on paper – is a minimum in order for it to be fairly described as effective.[87] But there is more to it; the principle is result-orientated, in that it seeks to ensure the promotion of the underlying purpose of Union law. This implies ensuring that the policy behind a specific rule is fulfilled and that the legislature's intentions are realised.[88] The Court seems to use the term 'effectiveness' in both of these senses, and the effectiveness of EU law thus seems to have two dimensions: Union law must be applied fully (in the sense of formal compliance) and it must be applied in a manner that is consistent with its purpose in the Union's legal order.[89] In the following, I use the term *effet utile* to encompass both aspects.[90]

If taken literally, the requirement of 'full effect' and 'full effectiveness' leaves little room for considerations of the legitimate objectives pursued by national enforcement rules. The Court's jurisprudence can, however, hardly be taken to mean that Union law must be given full effect across the board, leaving no scope for national procedural autonomy. The principle of *effet utile* is often used in conjunction with the principles of equivalence effectiveness and effective judicial protection, and it guides the Court's interpretation. It is a value that underlies the Union legal order, and the principle can therefore be used as an interpreting device, guiding both the Court and the Member States. Yet it is submitted that the principle can also be used as a benchmark against which to assess domestic enforcement regimes. To ensure the effectiveness of Union law in the Member States, the Court has imposed certain requirements on the decentralised enforcement of Union law. Domestic enforcement regimes must be assessed against the

[85] Case C-339/00 *Ireland v Commission* [2003] para 71.

[86] F Snyder, 'The Effectiveness of European Community Law: Institutions, Processes, Tools and Techniques' (1993) 56 *MLR* 19, 26. The Court has adopted several mechanisms with a view to ensuring the effect of EU law in the Member States, and ground-breaking cases in the Court's history – such as Case 26/62 *Van Gend en Loos* [1963] and Case 6/64 *Costa v ENEL* [1964] on direct effect and supremacy, respectively – were grounded on *effet utile* arguments.

[87] Snyder writes that effectiveness 'is taken to mean the fact that "law matters": it has effects on political, economic and social life outside the law – that is apart from simply the elaboration of legal doctrine'; see Snyder, 'The Effectiveness of European Community Law' (n 86) 19.

[88] J Engström, 'The Europeanisation of Remedies and Procedures Through Judge-Made Law: Can a Trojan Horse Achieve Effectiveness? Experiences of the Swedish Judiciary' (PhD thesis, European University Institute 2009) 62 and 64. In the words of Leczykiewicz, '[i]t could … be argued that effectiveness is devoid of any normative content [and that its] normative potency stems only from the rule or policy which it makes effective'; see Leczykiewicz, 'The Constitutional Dimension of Private Law Liability Rules in the EU' (n 34) 212.

[89] V Milutinović, *The 'Right to Damages' under EU Competition Law: From Courage v Crehan to the White Paper and Beyond* (Kluwer Law International 2010) 236. He describes the two dimensions as *plein effet* (full effect) and *effet utile* (useful effect) respectively.

[90] To the same effect, see Komninos, who uses the term *effet utile* to cover the 'full and useful effectiveness of EU law'; see AP Komninos, 'Private Enforcement in the EU with Emphasis on Damages Actions' in D Geradin and I Lianos (eds), *Handbook on European Competition Law: Enforcement and Procedure* (Edward Elgar 2013) 228, 236.

enforcement requirements spelled out by the Court. The duty of loyal cooperation, now enshrined in Article 4(3), requires the Member States to take measures necessary to guarantee the application of Union law, and the Court has spelled out what this means in further detail.[91] As we shall see, private enforcement may play a role in fulfilling the Member States' obligation under Article 4(3) TEU to ensure the effective enforcement of EU law.[92]

E. Distinguishing (Rewe) Effectiveness from Effective Judicial Protection

Both the principles of *equivalence* and *effectiveness* and the principle of *effective judicial protection* are general principles of Union law. They have constitutional status[93] and are on a par with the Treaties.[94] How these principles interrelate is not entirely clear. The Court has held that the requirements of equivalence and effectiveness 'embody the general obligation on the Member States to ensure judicial protection of an individual's rights under Community law',[95] and that the principle of effectiveness 'implies a requirement of judicial protection, guaranteed by Article 47 of the Charter'.[96] Depending on the facts of the case and the questions presented by the domestic court, the Court occasionally limits itself to applying either the more modest principle of effectiveness or the more demanding principle of effective judicial protection.[97] Yet on other occasions the Court examines separately whether the requirements of effectiveness and the requirements of effective judicial protection are met, implying that these are different principles.[98]

Although the relationship between the principle of effectiveness and that of effective judicial protection 'may be described as blurry',[99] and although the two principles are similar in some respects, it is submitted that there are relevant differences that merit consideration.[100] First, they have different legal bases. Whereas the principle of effectiveness is derived from the duty of loyal cooperation enshrined in Article 4(3) TEU, the

[91] See, most notably, Case 68/88 *Greek Maize* [1989] paras 23–25.

[92] See ch 13.

[93] See, inter alia, Case C-174/08 *NCC Construction Denmark* [2009] para 42.

[94] For an overview of the general principles of Union law, see T Tridimas, *The General Principles of EU Law*, 2nd edn (Oxford University Press 2006).

[95] See, inter alia, Case C-63/08 *Pontin* [2009] para 44. Similarly, Case C-268/06 *Impact* [2008] para 47.

[96] Case C-61/14 *Orizzonte* [2015] para 48.

[97] Compare Joined Cases C-89/10 and C-96/10 *Q-Beef* [2011] (concentrating on 'Rewe' effectiveness) and Case C-562/12 *Liivima Lihaveis* [2014] (concentrating on effective judicial protection). Case C-483/16 *Sziber* [2018] is noteworthy, as the Court refers to the principle of equivalence and Art 47 of the Charter, leaving out any reference to the principle of effectiveness.

[98] See, inter alia, Case C-93/12 *ET Agroconsulting* [2013] paras 48–60; Joined Cases C-317/08 to 320/08 *Alassini* [2010]; and Case C-205/15 *Toma* [2016] paras 39–59.

[99] K Havu, 'EU Law in Member State Courts: "Adequate Judicial Protection" and Effective Application – Ambiguities and Nonsequiturs in Guidance by the Court of Justice' (2016) 8 *Contemporary Readings in Law & Social Justice* 158, 159.

[100] Conversely Engström, who holds that 'the principle of effectiveness has two main facets, one aiming at the protection of individual rights, the other mainly being concerned with effectiveness of the general interests that Community is set to promote, but that this should not be seen as two different principles'; see Engström, 'The Europeanisation of Remedies and Procedures Through Judge-Made Law' (n 88) 54.

principle of effective judicial protection was first derived from Articles 6 and 13 ECHR and the common constitutional traditions of the Member States,[101] and has now a firm legal basis in the Charter Article 47. Second, the rationales underlying the two principles are not the same. The principle of effective judicial protection seeks to ensure the protection of individual Union rights. The rationale underlying the principle of effective judicial protection is that in a Union based on the rule of law, everyone must have the opportunity to assert their rights before the courts, and obtain effective redress.[102] Conversely, the effectiveness principle is more geared towards ensuring that national rules do not impede the *effective application* of Union law.[103] The suggestion that the existence of a right is no precondition for the principle to come into play, finds support in the fact that is also utilised by the Court in cases where Union law is enforced against the individual.[104] Where Union rights are not at stake, it is rather the case that national enforcement rules should not make the *application of Union law* impossible or excessively difficult.[105] The principle of effectiveness can as such be regarded as an aspect of the wider principle of *effet utile*.[106] That we are dealing with two different principles is also reflected in the fact that the effectiveness principle – as a direct consequence of the decentralised enforcement of Union law – is only applicable at the Member State level, whereas the principle of effective judicial protection also binds the Union itself.[107] Since the scope of application of the two principles is guided by their underlying rationales, they should be kept apart.

The Court has not adopted a fully coherent approach when it comes to delineating the demarcation lines between the principle of effectiveness and that of effective judicial protection. It has been argued in legal scholarship that a distinction must be drawn between, on the one hand, procedural rules that obstruct *access* to judicial process (covering rules on, inter alia, legal costs and jurisdiction) and, on the other, rules that do not hinder access but rather pose difficulties in subsequent legal proceedings (such as rules on evidence and limitation periods).[108] In relation to the first category of rules,

[101] Case 222/84 *Johnston* [1986] para 18 and Case 222/86 *Heylens* [1987] para 14.

[102] S Prechal, *Directives in EC Law* (Oxford University Press 2005) 143–44; and Prechal and Widdershoven, 'Redefining the Relationship' (n 83) 46.

[103] To the same effect, see, inter alia, Engström, 'The Europeanisation of Remedies and Procedures Through Judge-Made Law' (n 88) 69; and Półtorak, *European Union Rights in National Courts* (n 23) 71. Conversely Wilman, *Private Enforcement of EU Law before National Courts* (n 10) 39, who holds that '[b]oth principles generally appear to fulfil the same function in ensuring that rights of private parties vested in EU law can be sufficiently enforced'.

[104] See, inter alia, Case C-74/14 *Eturas* [2016] paras 34–35 (evidence and standard of proof in competition law proceedings); and Case C-24/95 *Alcan* [1997] para 24 (recovery of unlawfully received funds).

[105] See Joined Cases C-430/93 and C-431/93 *Van Schijndel* [1995] para 19; and Case C-312/93 *Peterbroeck* [1995] para 14.

[106] To the same effect, C Görisch, 'Effective Legal Protection in the European Legal Order' in Z Szente and K Lachmayer (eds), *The Principle of Effective Legal Protection in Administrative Law: A European Perspective* (Routledge 2016) 29, 34–35.

[107] B Thorson, *Individual Rights in EU Law* (Springer 2016) 19. On the relationship between the two principles, see further Prechal, *Directives in EC Law* (n 102) 144–45; and Prechal and Widdershoven, 'Redefining the Relationship' (n 83).

[108] J Krommendijk, 'Is There Light on the Horizon? The Distinction between "Rewe Effectiveness" and the Principle of Effective Judicial Protection in Article 47 of the Charter after Orizzonte' (2016) 53 *CML Rev* 1395, 1413.

it is argued, the principle of effective judicial protection applies, whereas the latter category is to be assessed against the *Rewe* requirement of effectiveness.[109] Prechal and Widdershoven have similarly argued that

> issues that relate to the access to a court should, in line with ECtHR case law, be approached as a matter of effective judicial protection [and this] includes the 'appealability' of certain acts, questions of standing, time limits for bringing action, the right to legal aid and the requirement that at least one of the courts hearing a case have full jurisdiction.[110]

Support for the position that the Court in fact has adopted such a view can be found in *DEB*, where the Court was asked whether a company was entitled to legal aid under the Charter, which is an aspect of access to court. The Court found it necessary to 'recast the question referred [as to the principle of effectiveness] so that it relates to the interpretation of the principle of effective judicial protection as enshrined in Article 47 of the Charter'.[111] Yet there are also rulings that do not fit this pattern; questions pertaining to time limits for taking legal action, for instance, tend to be examined for compliance with the principle of effectiveness.[112] The overall impression is nevertheless that the growing importance of the principle of effective judicial protection 'leads to a decrease of the importance of the *Rewe* principles'.[113]

When it comes to assessing domestic standing rules, the Court has showed a clear tendency to approach the matter from the angle of effective judicial protection.[114] It seems that, at least with respect to standing, the principle of effective judicial protection overshadows the effectiveness principle as laid down in *Rewe*.[115] The principle of effective judicial protection has a 'more encompassing nature', entailing not only negative but also positive procedural obligations.[116] A denial of standing for the protection of Union rights renders the enforcement of Union rights 'impossible or excessively difficult' by definition, and can hardly be seen as providing effective judicial protection. The principle of effectiveness is, moreover, ill-fitted to deal with the issue of standing. There is a 'conceptual tautology' inherent in the Court's case law pertaining to the principle of effectiveness, namely, that 'the very act of applying the principle of effectiveness seems to presuppose that, as a matter of Union law the claimant is already recognised as having rights or interests capable and deserving of being judicially protected within the

[109] ibid. Similarly Engström, 'The principle of effective judicial protection after the Lison Treaty' (2011) 4 *REAL* 63.

[110] Prechal and Widdershoven, 'Redefining the Relationship' (n 83) 47. According to Widdershoven, 'it seems a rule of thumb that the Court assesses procedural issues in the light of Article 47 CFR if the ECtHR would assess the same issue in the light of Article 6 ECHR'; see R Widdershoven, 'National Procedural Autonomy and General EU Law Limits' (2019) 2 *Review of European Administrative Law* 5, 22.

[111] Case C-279/09 *DEB* [2010] para 33.

[112] See, inter alia, Case C-177/10 *Rosado Santana* [2011] paras 92–96; and Joined Cases C-89/10 and C-96/10 *Q-Beef* [2011] paras 34–37. See, however, Case C-664/15 *Protect* [2017], where the Court examines domestic time limits for compliance with the principle of effective judicial protection.

[113] Widdershoven, 'National Procedural Autonomy and General EU Law Limits' (n 110) 33.

[114] Case C-104/13 *Olainfarm* [2014] and Case C-510/13 *E.ON Földgaz* [2015]; and (by implication) Case C-432/05 *Unibet* [2007] para 44. For a detailed account, see ch 5, section IV.

[115] Arnull argues that 'it seems only a matter of time before the principle of effectiveness becomes redundant: it is almost a tautology to say that the principle of effective judicial protection is infringed where national law makes it excessively difficult to pursue a claim'; see Arnull, 'Remedies before National Courts' (n 62) 1026.

[116] Krommendijk, 'Is There Light on the Horizon?' (n 108) 1408.

national legal system'.[117] The tautology pointed to above can be overcome if we separate two distinct (but closely related) questions: first, the extent to which standing must be provided in order for the state to comply with the principle of effective judicial protection; and, second, the extent to which standing must be provided in order to ensure that EU law is rendered effective in the Member States. Having concluded that the claimant is entitled to enforce Union law, the principles of equivalence and effectiveness can thereafter be used as yardsticks against which to assess the domestic procedural rules on aspects such as time limits and evidence.

IV. Effective Judicial Protection as the Leading Principle and Rationale in Relation to Standing

A. Introduction

It has been argued that when it comes to *locus standi*, the Court's case law is primarily based on the principle of effective judicial protection, now codified in Article 47 of the Charter.

The issue of standing came up for the first time in *Rewe- Handelsgesellschaft*.[118] The case concerned the Union law compatibility of so-called 'butter-buying cruises', where goods (such as butter, liquor and tobacco) purchased outside of Germany's territorial waters were exempt from custom duties, indirect taxes and any other charges. The claimants were competitors of the shipping companies organising these cruises, whose economic interests were adversely affected by the Member State's failure to apply Union law to prevent such tax-free sales. They sought an injunction, restraining the customs authorities from applying incompatible internal provisions, or requiring them to comply with the relevant Union law provisions. The case is mostly known for the statement that the Treaty did not intend to create new remedies that national courts would be bound to apply to ensure observance of Union law. Despite that categorical statement – which was later abandoned by the Court[119] – the Court did not have to address the principles of effectiveness or effective judicial protection in depth, as the principle of equivalence was applicable to the case: since the claimants would have been entitled to a legal avenue under domestic law in comparable circumstances, the Member State had to grant standing.

Advocate General Capotorti was more elaborate on the issue of standing. He argued in favour of a strict approach, suggesting that only the holders of individual Union rights should be afforded *locus standi* – even if liberal standing rules would further the

[117] M Dougan, 'Who Exactly Benefits from the Treaties? The Murky Interaction Between Union and National Competence over the Capacity to Enforce EU Law' (2009) 12 *Cambridge Yearbook of European Legal Studies* 73, 104. He suggests that such a circular reasoning can be broken if one accepts that the 'procedural autonomy' is activated 'only having already ascertained that the claimant falls within the scope of the relevant Union acts as construed by the Court of Justice itself; and that the Member State's true margin of discretion is thereby limited to regulating, rather than actually determining or denying the claimant's right of access to the courts'.

[118] Case 158/80 *Rewe- Handelsgesellschaft* [1981].

[119] See Case C-432/05 *Unibet* [2007].

effectiveness of Union law.[120] A mere interest in the application of the rule was deemed insufficient:

> In order to be entitled to institute proceedings before the courts (for example for an injunction requiring another person to fulfil certain obligations) the plaintiff must be personally entitled to the right which the proceedings are specifically intended to uphold. In fact, court proceedings are not employed to provide general and hypothetical confirmation of the content of a rule but to apply within the framework of a particular legal relationship. Accordingly, a person who merely has an interest in the enforcement of a rule, or more precisely, a person who does not stand in a specific legal relationship based upon that rule, is not entitled to [institute proceedings].[121]

He went on to state that the opposite would entail 'allowing a kind of *azione populare* … contrary to the legal traditions common to the Member States', and would also 'threaten to give rise to serious practical difficulties in the administration of justice'.[122]

It is submitted that the approach suggested by Advocate General Capotorti decades ago has found resonance in the Court's jurisprudence. A mere (factual) interest in the enforcement of Union law is not sufficient to ground standing, despite the fact that liberal standing rules would certainly serve the effectiveness of Union law. It is first and foremost individuals whose rights are violated, who needs to be granted standing before domestic courts, pursuant to the principle of effective judicial protection enshrined in Article 47 of the Charter.

B. No Standing Based on Effectiveness Considerations Alone

There are several rulings in which the Court has stressed the importance of private parties in ensuring the effectiveness of Union law in the Member States. The extent to which effectiveness concerns are highlighted in the Court's jurisprudence varies depending on the field. Particularly in the area of competition law, the Court has been eager to stress the importance of safeguarding the public interest in maintaining free and undistorted competition.[123] Ensuring compliance with these rules is of importance for ensuring a well-functioning internal market, and the Court has perceived private enforcement as a useful supplement to the public enforcement regimes in place in the Member States. As the Court held in *Skanska*:

> [A]ctions for damages for infringement of EU competition rules are an integral part of the system for enforcement of those rules, which are intended to punish anticompetitive behaviour on the part of undertakings and to deter them from engaging in such conduct.[124]

[120] Engström, 'The Europeanisation of Remedies and Procedures Through Judge-Made Law' (n 88) 143.
[121] AG Capotorti in Case 158/80 *Rewe-Handelsgesellschaft* [1981].
[122] ibid.
[123] See, inter alia, Case C-360/09 *Pfleiderer* [2011] para 25; and Case C-536/11 *Donau Chemie* [2013] para 33.
[124] Case C-724/17 *Skanska* [2019] para 45. In this ruling, the Court held that the determination of the entity that is required to provide compensation for damage caused by an infringement of Art 101 TFEU is directly governed by EU law, and stated that economic successors can be held liable for damages resulting from such infringements. The 'twofold function of of private actions for antitrust damages' was also stressed by AG Wahl in his Opinion in Case C-724/17 *Skanska* [2019] at para 31.

This emphasis in case law on effectiveness per se raises the question of whether the Court has required Member States to provide standing based on effectiveness considerations alone. Within the field of competition law, the question must be answered in the affirmative (see section IV.C). The Court has repeatedly held that *any person* has the right to claim damages for harm suffered as a consequence of anti-competitive agreements, and found this remedy to be rooted directly in Article 101 TFEU. Beyond the field of competition law, there is, however, scarce support for the position that standing extends beyond individuals whose rights are adversely affected by a breach of Union law. The fact that the Court has stressed that private lawsuits contribute to the full effect of Union law does not mean the Court disregards the existence of rights.

The value of private enforcement in ensuring the effectiveness of Union law in the Member States was emphasised by the Court in *Muñoz*. The case concerned a suit brought by Muñoz against his competitor, Frumar, for its failure to comply with the labelling standards for table grapes enshrined in Regulations (EEC) No 1035/72 and (EC) No 2200/96. The action was dismissed in the British courts, as the relevant Regulation could not be enforced by way of a civil action. The Regulations obliged the Member States to set up a specific public authority to monitor and enforce the rules laid down, and a supervisory authority was appointed in the United Kingdom. The Court was asked whether the rules laid down in the Regulation still had to be enforceable in civil proceedings initiated by a competitor, and answered in the affirmative. The Court made reference to the purpose of applying common quality standards, which is to keep products of unsatisfactory quality off the market, to guide production to meet consumers' requirements and to facilitate trade relations based on fair competition. The Court went on to state that the full effectiveness of the quality standards implies that it must be possible to enforce the obligations by means of civil proceedings instituted by a trader against a competitor:

> The possibility of bringing such proceedings strengthens the practical working of the Community rules on quality standards. As a supplement to the action of the authorities designated by the Member States to make the checks required by those rules it helps to discourage practices, often difficult to detect, which distort competition. In that context, actions brought before the national courts by competing operators are particularly suited to contributing substantially to ensuring fair trading and transparency of markets in the Community.[125]

The Court was not clear as to why Muñoz should be allowed to bring a civil action, and there are two ways of reading the Court's ruling. Either the claimant was entitled to initiate proceedings in order to pursue the public interest in the proper functioning of the market, or he was entitled to pursue his own right under the Regulations.[126] Put differently, the ruling can be read either through the lens of effective application of Union law, or through the lens of individual rights protection. Supporting the first reading is the fact that the Court emphasised both the added value in terms of detection and

[125] Case C-253/00 *Muñoz* [2002], para 31.

[126] As Dougan asks, '[D]id its direct commercial concern confer a right of standing upon the claimant in *Muñoz*, but only so far as to protect the public interest in a system of fair competition; or was the claimant endowed with the capacity to enforce its own individual right to fair competition against the predations of its market rivals?': see Dougan, 'Who Exactly Benefits from the Treaties?' (n 117) 96.

the deterrent effect of private enforcement. But although it is possible to read *Muñoz* as pertaining to effectiveness per se, and some scholars do just that,[127] it is submitted that the Court's ruling should rather be seen as pertaining to rights protection. Although the Court admittedly placed emphasis on effectiveness, there are indications in the ruling pointing in the direction of the protection of rights. The Court examined the protective scope of the provisions infringed, and arguably this was to see whether the interests of the claimant were covered.

The need to examine the protective scope of the quality standards for fruit and vegetables was made explicit by Advocate General Geelhoed in his Opinion to the judgment. He found that the interests of competing undertakings were covered, and consequently that the Regulation conferred rights on Muñoz. The Court seems to have implicitly endorsed the position of the Advocate General.[128] The Court looked into the objective of the provisions on quality standards, and found that they also serve to protect traders operating on the market for fruit and vegetables.[129] This indicates that it is the claimant's own rights that are being vindicated in the proceedings, rather than (merely) the wider market interest.[130] The Court's emphasis on the contribution of private enforcers in detecting and preventing infringements does not inhibit a reading of the ruling in the light of rights protection; rather, this is a case where rights protection and effectiveness pull in the same direction.

The clearest expression to the effect that standing is dependent on the violation of a Union right is found in the Court's ruling in *Züchtverband für Ponys*. The question that arose in this case was whether a breeding association was entitled to demand the refusal of the recognition of a new association, and whether it had standing to contest before the court the administrative decision recognising the new association. The criteria for the approval of associations that maintain or establish stud-books for registered equidae were laid down in Commission Decision 92/353. In order to be officially approved, an association had to meet certain conditions, such as having a 'sufficient number of equidae to carry out an improvement or selection programme or to preserve the breed where this is considered necessary'.[131] According to Article 2(2), the Member State could refuse to recognise a new organisation if it 'endangers the preservation of the breed or jeopardises the operation or the improvement or selection programme of an existing organisation or association'. With reference to the discretion possessed by the competent authority, the Court held that Union law could not be interpreted as creating a right for existing associations to have the recognition of the new association

[127] See, inter alia, S Prechal, 'Protection of Rights: How Far?' in S Prechal and B van Roermund (eds), *The Coherence of EU Law. The Search for Unity in Divergent Concepts* (Oxford University Press 2008) 155, 181; Havu, 'EU Law in Member State Courts' (n 99) 166–67; and R Nazzini, 'Potency and Act of the Principle of Effectiveness: The Development of Competition Law Remedies and Procedures in Community Law' in C Barnard and O Odudu (eds), *The Outer Limits of European Union Law* (Hart Publishing 2009) 401, 412–13.

[128] To the same effect, G Betlem, 'Torts, A European Ius Commune and the Private Enforcement of Community Law' (2005) 64 *CLJ* 126, 138.

[129] Similarly W Van Gerven, 'Bringing (Private) Laws Closer to Each Other at the European Level' in F Cafaggi (ed), *The Institutional Framework of European Private Law* (Oxford University Press 2006) 37, 55–56.

[130] To the same effect, see A Biondi, 'Case C-253/00, Antonio Muñoz y Cia, Superior Fruiticola SA v Frumar Ltd, Redbridge Produce Marketing Ltd' (2003) 40 *CML Rev* 1241, 1246; and Engström, 'The Europeanisation of Remedies and Procedures Through Judge-Made Law' (n 88) 145.

[131] See Art 2(1) and point 2(d) of the Annex to the decision.

refused. Consequently, the Court held that the Member State was not required to grant the claimant standing in order to contest the decision.

This would arguably have been different if the competent authority had been obliged to refuse recognition in the circumstances mentioned in Article 2(2). The finding that the claimant had no right to demand that recognition should be refused was a natural consequence of the discretion granted to the competent authority. As Dougan points out, it is more surprising

> that the Court did not even address the obvious next question of whether the claimant could nevertheless enjoy a right of standing, directly as a matter of Union law, to challenge the decision to grant such approval, if not on the grounds that it simply disagreed with the outcome, then at least on the grounds that the competent national authorities had exceeded the boundaries of their discretion under the applicable Union legislation.[132]

The Court did not address whether the claimant was factually concerned, or whether the association should be allowed to enforce the law in the public interest. As pointed out by Engström, if the Court had wanted to ensure the effectiveness of EU law, it could have allowed the organisation to initiate proceedings to ensure the administration had complied with the conditions laid down in the Annex. The consequence of the ruling is that no one can bring proceedings to control whether the administration complies with these criteria.[133] The ruling supports the view that the Court is more attuned to rights protection, and that Member States are generally entitled to restrict standing to those seeking to protect their individual rights. Although this was a case concerning judicial review of an administrative decision, it is submitted that the case is useful for shedding light on the Court's broader approach to standing, since – as we shall see – the rationale underlying the enforcement case law seems to be the same, regardless of whether a private party seeks to challenge the acts of a Member State or of a private party.

The notable exception is found within the area of competition law, where the Court has adopted a somewhat different approach. The Court has perceived effectiveness concerns as having particular importance in this field, and stressed the essential role played by these rules in facilitating a well-functioning internal market, a matter that will be addressed in the following. Beyond the field of competition law, however, the Court seems to focus on the protection of individual Union rights.

C. The Court's Distinct Approach to Standing in the Field of Competition Law

In *Courage*, the Court established the right to claim damages in national courts for losses caused by breach of Article 101 TFEU, prohibiting agreements the object or effect of which is to restrict competition.[134] Although the right to compensation is now codified

[132] Dougan, 'Who Exactly Benefits from the Treaties?' (n 117) 99.
[133] J Engström, 'Rättsskyddsprincipens krav på talerätt i nationell domstol i ljuset av RÅ 2006 Ref 9 och C-216/02' 2006 *Europarättslig tidsskrift* 511, 525–26.
[134] Case C-453/99 *Courage* [2001].

in Directive 2014/104/EU (Competition Damages),[135] the case still sheds light on the Court's approach to *locus standi*. When the Court stated in *Courage* that 'any individual' who has suffered loss because of a breach may claim compensation, it laid down a rule on standing.[136]

Mr Crehan leased two pubs, agreeing to a contract obliging him to buy most of his beer from Courage (a 'beer tie'). When sued for unpaid debts, his defence and counterclaim rested on the allegation that the beer tie was contrary to (now) Article 101 TFEU, and that he had suffered loss as a result of the infringement. The Court was asked whether the well-established British rule whereby a party to an illegal agreement cannot claim damages arising from that agreement (the *in pari delicto* defence) was compatible with Union law. The Court referred to the Member States' duty to ensure the full effect of Union law and provide effective protection of individual rights, and held:

> The full effectiveness of Article 85 [now Article 101] of the Treaty and, in particular, the practical effect of the prohibition laid down in Article 85(1) [now Article 101(1)] would be put at risk if it were not open to any individual to claim damages for the loss caused to him by a contract or by conduct liable to restrict or distort competition. Indeed, the existence of such a right strengthens the working of the Community competition rules and discourages agreements and practices, which are frequently covert, which are liable to restrict and distort competition. From that point of view, actions for damages before the national courts can make a significant contribution to the maintenance of effective competition in the Community.[137]

On that basis, the Court found that the parties to an anti-competitive agreement must not be barred from bringing an action for damages against an infringing party.

The right to damages for competition law infringements was confirmed and further elaborated in *Manfredi*.[138] The case arose from a follow-on action after the Italian competition authority had found an agreement between insurance companies to be in violation of the competition rules. Manfredi and the other claimants had allegedly suffered loss due to an unlawful exchange of information, resulting in the rise of premiums charged to consumers. The Court reiterated its statement of principle from *Courage*, that the full effectiveness of Article 101 TFEU would be put at risk if it were not open to any individual to claim damages for loss suffered. The Court went on to state that it follows that 'any individual can claim compensation for the harm suffered where there is a causal relationship between the harm and an agreement and practice prohibited under [Article 101(1)].'[139]

In *Courage* and *Manfredi*, the Court did not explicitly examine whether the claimants were the holders of Union rights, and the term 'any individual' could indicate that the issue of rights was not of importance. There were strong voices supporting a literal reading of these rulings. Eilmansberger held that the doubt as to the 'irrelevance of the *Schutzzweck* doctrine in EC torts … was finally and conclusively eliminated in

[135] According to Art 3(1), Member States shall ensure that any natural or legal person who suffered harm caused by an infringement of competition law is able to claim and obtain compensation for that harm.

[136] Milutinović, *The 'Right to Damages' under EU Competition Law* (n 89) 221.

[137] Case C-453/99 *Courage* [2001] paras 26–27.

[138] Joined Cases C-295/04 to C-298/04 *Manfredi* [2006].

[139] ibid para 61. See also Case C-421/05 *City Motors* [2007] para 33; and Case C-360/09 *Pfleiderer* [2011] para 28.

Courage',[140] and similarly Komninos stated that 'irrespective of the protective scope of the competition law provisions, all private parties who have been harmed by an anti-competitive practice enjoy *a Community law-based right* in damages'.[141] This was, however, not the only possible reading of these rulings. As Thorson pointed out, there was no indication that the Court, by taking effectiveness into account, meant to exclude the need to assess the protective purpose of the infringed provision.[142]

Reich argued strongly against the view that any individual had unfettered access to bring an action, and took the position that the category of enforcers entitled to damages should be determined based on considerations of the protective scope of the competition law provisions: '"Any individual" is not "every individual", but only the persons specifically protected against the type of antitrust injury.'[143]

In *Otis II*, the Court provided much needed clarification concerning the persons entitled to claim damages for loss caused by a competition law infringement.[144] The case in the main proceedings concerned a damages action initiated by, inter alia, the Province of Upper Austria against members of an elevator cartel. The claimant granted low-interest loans for the purpose of realising social housing projects, and the price of the elevators installed in the supported housing construction increased as a result of the anti-competitive agreement. The amount of the loans was therefore significantly higher than it would have been if the price formation had taken place in a situation of free competition. The claimant sought compensation for loss resulting from the increase in construction costs, since it had been deprived of the opportunity to make more profitable investments. Under Austrian tort law, the Province of Upper Austria could not claim compensation, since the loss incurred did not fall within the protective scope of Article 101 TFEU. The Supreme Court of Austria decided to ask the Court whether this restrictive definition of the group of beneficiaries was compatible with the requirements of EU competition law. It was clear that the right to claim compensation for losses from members of a cartel had to be construed broadly so as to cover indirect purchasers[145] and umbrella customers.[146] The Supreme Court enquired whether such compensation might also be claimed 'by persons who are not active as suppliers or consumers on the relevant product and geographic market affected by a cartel, but who grant loans to buyers' of products from the cartelists.

[140] T Eilmansberger, 'The Relationship between Rights and Remedies in EC Law: In Search of the Missing Link' (2004) 41 *CML Rev* 1199, 1226.

[141] AP Komninos, 'Civil Antitrust Remedies Between Community and National Law' in Barnard and Odudu (eds), *The Outer Limits of European Union Law* (n 127) 363, 393 (emphasis in original).

[142] Thorson, *Individual Rights in EU Law* (n 107) 310.

[143] N Reich, 'The Courage Doctrine: Encouraging or Discouraging Compensation for Antitrust Injuries' (2005) 42 *CML Rev* 35, 61. He holds that '[a] claim of compensation always depends on whom competition law wants to protect, more precisely, what persons come into the protective ambit of a certain anti-competitive practice'; see N Reich, 'Horizontal Liability in EC Law: Hybridization of Remedies for Compensation in Case of Breaches of EC Rights' (2007) 44 *CML Rev* 705, 722. A parallel can be found in the notion of 'antitrust injury' in US law, where an injury is only perceived as legally relevant if it is of the type the antitrust laws were intended to prevent and that flows from that which makes the defendants' acts unlawful: see the US Supreme Court in *Brunswick Corp v Pueblo Bowl-o-mat, Inc*, 429 US 477 (1977).

[144] Case C-435/18 *Otis II* [2019].

[145] Directive 2014/104/EU (Competition Damages), Art 14.

[146] Case C-557/12 *Kone* [2014].

The ECJ held that one does not have to be active on the market affected by the cartel to have a right to claim damages. Rather, the Court stated that any loss that is causally linked to an infringement of Article 101 TFEU must be capable of giving rise to compensation in order to ensure the effective application of Article 101 TFEU and to guarantee the effectiveness of that provision. It then went on to state that

> [s]ubject to the possibility of the participants to a cartel not being held liable to compensate for all the loss that they could have caused, it is not necessary … that the loss suffered by the person concerned present, in addition, a specific connection with the 'objective of protection' pursued by Article 101 TFEU.

It could, perhaps, be feasible to fit the Court's ruling in *Otis II* in with the Court's general rights–remedies approach, by arguing that the protective scope of Article 101 covers any loss causally linked with the anti-competitive conduct.[147] Not much is gained, however, from trying to shoehorn this decision into the Court's general case law based on the principle of effective judicial protection. Rather, it seems fair to conclude that the 'irrelevance of the *Schutzzweck* doctrine' in competition damages claims was finally and conclusively eliminated in in *Otis II*.[148]

The right of any person to claim damages caused by anti-competitive agreements is, however, a Union law remedy *sui generis*, rooted directly in Article 101 TFEU.[149] The Court has been eager to stress the particular features of EU competition law, and thus seems to have confined this line of reasoning to this particular field. In his opinion in *Banks*, Advocate General Van Gerven argued in favour of a general principle of private party liability in damages, but the Court refrained from addressing the matter explicitly.[150] As I see it, it is unlikely that the right to damages extends beyond the field of competition law. The Court has placed emphasis on the fundamental importance of the provisions breached.[151] Moreover, the rulings are 'carefully constructed around the particular context of competition law', not drafted in a style apt for generalisation of an EU principle of private party liability.[152] It is therefore submitted that this particular remedy, and also the Court's strong *effet utile* focus, should be confined to the area of competition law.

[147] The Court did not merely refer to the effectiveness of Art 101 TFEU, but also stated that the 'effective protection against the adverse effects of an infringement of competition law would be seriously undermined' if the possibility of claiming compensation for loss caused by a cartel were limited to suppliers and customers of the market affected by the cartel: see ibid para 27.

[148] This is a paraphrasing of Eilmansberger (n 140).

[149] Opinion of AG Kokott in Case C-435/18 *Otis II* [2019] para 40.

[150] Case C-128/92 *Banks* [1994]. AG Van Gerven argued that an action in damages against private individuals was 'based on the Community legal order itself': see his Opinion in Case C-128/92 *Banks* [1993] para 45. In legal scholarship there is also some support for the position that private party liability is inherent in the system of the Treaties; see, eg, Wilman, *Private Enforcement of EU Law before National Courts* (n 10) 58 and Milutinović, *The 'Right to Damages' under EU Competition Law* (n 89) 83–88.

[151] Case C-453/99 *Courage* [2001] para 20. The special status of Art 101 TFEU has also been stressed by the Court in Case C-126/97 *Eco Swiss* [1999] para 37, where the Court perceived it as equivalent to national rules on public policy.

[152] S Weatherill, 'The Elusive Character of Private Autonomy in EU Law' in Leczykiewicz and Weatherill (eds), *The Involvement of EU Law in Private Law Relationships* (n 34) 9, 26. As Leczykiewicz points out, if the principle of private party liability is to be given general application, the criteria for liability outlined in the *Courage* jurisprudence – breach, damage and causation – would have to be circumscribed to avoid an excessive burden on individuals; see Leczykiewicz, 'The Constitutional Dimension of Private Law Liability Rules in the EU' (n 34) 218.

V. A Twofold Approach to Dissecting Union Law Requirements on Standing

It has been argued that the Court generally seems to focus its attention on whether the provision invoked creates individual rights that needs to be protected before domestic courts.

Where the ECJ has established that a provision creates rights, the Member States are required to give effect to those findings at the domestic level and grant standing.[153] In the absence of specific provisions in secondary law to that effect, the Court has not required the Member States to provide standing where the sole purpose is to vindicate the public interest. Nevertheless, effectiveness concerns have led the Court to adopt a fairly liberal approach to what constitutes a right under Union law.[154]

Tying standing closely to the protection of individual rights may leave a lacuna in the enforcement of Union law norms. Duties that are not enforced can easily turn into toothless paper tigers. Prechal and Hancher have warned against the 'tunnel of individual rights', arguing that it excluded pressure groups, NGOs and public-spirited individuals seeking to vindicate the general interest.[155] Writing in the context of environmental law, they hold that the diffuse interests often represented in this area cannot easily be captured in the language of individual rights:

> The underlying problem remains that any thinking in terms of individual rights remains inextricably linked to the protection of individual interests. … [T]he individual rights approach should not divert attention from the possibilities and need to develop realistic alternatives for the sake of effective environmental protection.[156]

They propose shifting the perspective from protecting rights to responding to wrongs, which will have implications for the range of persons granted standing.[157] Although their arguments pertain to environmental protection, they are of broader relevance. While the Union legal system is generous in granting rights, there are still norms that do not have the character of rights and yet which require effective enforcement. Moreover, it may also be the case that Union law does create individual rights but that these rights, for various reasons, are not likely to be enforced by the right holders.[158] In these cases, access to court cannot find its justification in the principle of effective judicial protection.

Since only those seeking protection for their Union rights can rely on the principle of effective judicial protection, the principle of effectiveness (*effet utile*) may therefore have a role to play where private parties are not seeking to vindicate their own rights but rather act in the interest of the general public.[159] A public-spirited individual or NGO

[153] Prechal, 'Protection of Rights: How Far?' (n 127) 178.
[154] See ch 4, section III on the concept of Union rights.
[155] S Prechal and L Hancher, 'Individual Environmental Rights: Conceptual Pollution in EU Environmental Law?' [2002] *The Yearbook of European Environmental Law* 89, 105–09.
[156] ibid 109.
[157] ibid 110–11.
[158] See further ch 13, section V.D on the reasons for such underenforcement.
[159] Similarly, Prechal and Widdershoven argue that the principles of equivalence and effectiveness primarily apply in areas that are not covered by the principle of effective judicial protection. Yet they are open to the possibility that the principles of equivalence and effectiveness could 'develop into an additional and more

seeking to pursue infringements of environmental norms, for instance, cannot invoke the principle of effective judicial protection; rather, attempts to be granted standing will have to be founded on the argument of effective enforcement of Union law. Whether a private party needs to be granted access to court in the capacity of a 'private attorney general' pursuing the public interest will be addressed in chapter 13.

Thorson has argued that Union law appears as a two-tier system, where right holders have access to court by virtue of the right to judicial protection, whereas others may also on occasion have access to court by way of the principle of effectiveness.[160] The public interest underlying Union law is generally vindicated through a public enforcement regime. There may nevertheless be shortcomings in the public enforcement regime that may potentially result in an enforcement deficit. It is therefore necessary to explore the extent to which private enforcement is called for to render Union law effective in the Member States – and what that may mean in terms of standing.[161] What has been said above means that the requirements stemming from Union law on domestic standing doctrines will have to be analysed from two different angles: first, from the angle of effective judicial protection of Union rights (chapters 5 and 8 to 11); second, from the angle of effectiveness per se (chapter 13).

stringent standard' that may go beyond the requirements stemming from the ECHR; see Prechal and Widdershoven, 'Redefining the Relationship' (n 83) 49.

[160] Thorson, *Individual Rights in EU Law* (n 107) 124.

[161] See ch 13.

4

Invoking the Principle of Effective Judicial Protection

I. Introduction

Standing pursuant to Union law is primarily about ensuring protection of individual Union rights. In this chapter, I examine the relationship between rights and judicial protection, and take a closer look at the concept of Union rights (sections II and III respectively). I then move on to examine more closely when the prinicple of effective judicial protection can be relied on in order to obtain standing (section IV).

II. The Relationship between Rights and Judicial Protection in EU Law

In order to understand the Court's approach to the issue of standing, there is a need to grasp the relationship between rights and judicial protection in the Union legal order. In the Member States, the relationship between rights, on the one hand, and judicial protection, on the other, varies. Whereas the Continental legal systems have a long tradition of distinguishing between substantive rights and their enforcement, the common law system has traditionally considered rights and remedies to be interdependent. In the words of Dedek:

> If a comparative lawyer were asked to boil down the complexities to a single catchphrase the answer would probably look something like this: in the common law the remedy is said to precede the rights, *ubi remedium, ibi ius*; whereas in the civil law the right is said to precede the remedy, *ubi ius, ibi remedium*.[1]

The common law approach has traditionally required that an individual demonstrate a *cause of action* – encompassing both the substantive and procedural aspects of a claim – in order to seize the court of a matter.[2] In other words, the focus has not been directed

[1] H Dedek, 'From Norms to Facts: The Realization of Rights in Common and Civil Private Law' (2010) 56 *McGill Law Journal* 77, 79–80.

[2] A cause of action is, roughly speaking, 'the facts that entitle a person to sue'; see S Prechal and L Hancher, 'Individual Environmental Rights: Conceptual Pollution in EU Environmental Law?' [2002] *The Yearbook of European Environmental Law* 89, 97. The 'common law approach' is further addressed in S Prechal, *Directives in EC Law* (Oxford University Press 2005) 104.

upon the specific interpretation of the provision at issue to establish whether an individual right has been granted, rather the emphasis has been placed on remedies.[3] In the civil law tradition rights are often separated from procedure, procedure being regarded as the 'servant' of substantive law.[4]

The relationship between rights and judicial protection is of particular importance when enforcing Union law, since the rights are granted at Union level, while enforcement – and, consequently, judicial protection – takes place before the domestic courts in the Member States. The question, in the words of Eilmansberger,

> as to whether rights determine remedies or remedies determine rights … appears to translate into the question of which legal order assumes the commanding position, and thus ultimately determines the fate of individual Community rights.[5]

Union law resembles the civil law model, since 'the existence of a right and the ways in which it is protected are two separate issues'.[6] The ECJ tends to take rights as the starting point, requiring Member States to provide effective protection.[7] Hence in the Union law context,

> one cannot … make the existence of the right depend on whether or not the right is protected in the court. In other words, in Community law it is not '*ubi remedium ibi ius*' but '*ubi ius ibi remedium*'.[8]

If Union rights are not to be rendered illusory, Member States need to provide an adequate legal framework for the enforcement of these rights, and that entails securing access to court and effective remedies.[9] Within the context of EU law, the maxim *ubi ius ibi remedium* means that where EU law provides for a right, Member States need to ensure the necessary procedural and remedial frameworks are in place within their own legal systems.[10] This maxim is now clearly reflected in Article 47(1) of the Charter, which states that '[e]veryone whose rights and freedoms guaranteed by the law of the Union are violated has the right to an effective remedy'.

[3] S Prechal, 'Does Direct Effect Still Matter?' (2000) 37 *CML Rev* 1047, 1053. Today it is, however, possible to make a distinction between the creation of rights and the judicial protection of rights in both Continental European and in common law states, see S Beljin, 'Rights in EU Law' in S Prechal and B van Roermund (eds), *The Coherence of EU Law. The Search for Unity in Divergent Concepts* (Oxford University Press 2008) 91, 95.

[4] Dedek, 'From Norms to Facts' (n 1) 89–91.

[5] T Eilmansberger, 'The Relationship between Rights and Remedies in EC Law: In Search of the Missing Link' (2004) 41 *CML Rev* 1199, 1237.

[6] Prechal, *Directives in EC Law* (n 2) 106. As Beljin explains, 'EU rights are a substantive notion and not purely procedural because their relevance is not limited to their judicial enforceability'; see Beljin, 'Rights in EU Law' (n 3) 121.

[7] See, inter alia, Case 222/84 *Johnston* [1986]; and Case 222/86 *Heylens* [1987].

[8] Prechal, *Directives in EC Law* (n 2) 130. Similarly Van Gerven, who holds that 'rights and remedies are closely linked to each other because the adage *ubi ius, ibi remedium* reflects the Community law principle of access to court'; see W Van Gerven, 'Substantive Remedies for the Private Enforcement of EC Antitrust Rules before National Courts' in CD Ehlermann and I Atanasiu (eds), *European Competition Law Annual 2001: Effective Private Enforcement of EC Antitrust Law* (Hart Publishing 2003) 53, 53.

[9] In the words of AG Cosmas, 'if persons enjoying the protection of certain rules of law are completely debarred by procedural rules from obtaining judicial protection, the legal order is simply abdicating its function'; see AG Cosmas in Case C-321/95 P *Greenpeace* [1997], fn 115.

[10] In the words of Beljin, '[w]hen an EU provision grants a right, the Member State must warrant the enforceability'; see Beljin, 'Rights in EU Law' (n 3) 104.

III. The Concept of Union Rights

A. Introduction

The right to effective judicial protection is triggered when Union rights are at stake. It expressly follows from the wording of Article 47(1) that the claimants must claim that they have suffered a violation of their 'rights and freedoms guaranteed by the law of the Union'.[11] As Roeben points out, 'The animating idea of this fundamental right [to effective judicial protection] is to enforce individual rights and only rights.'[12]

Having a clear idea of what a Union law right is and how to determine whether it is granted is therefore central to an understanding of how Union law and national law interact in the context of decentralised enforcement. The aim of this section is to take a closer look at the concept of rights in Union law, and set out the criteria that help us determine whether a right is granted.

The Court has not been explicit as to what it means when speaking of a 'right', and the term seems to have been used rather indiscriminately.[13] The concept is described as 'vague' and surrounded by 'considerable uncertainty'.[14] Thorson points to the confusion surrounding the issue of rights: 'We seem then to be faced with incoherent terminology draped over an obscure notion – an EU law right – the consequences of which remain unclear.'[15]

The uncertainty surrounding the concept of rights has led some scholars to reject its usefulness as a tool for legal analysis.[16] Although it may well be that the Court's rights-talk is lacking in coherence, and that this body of case law is difficult to rationalise into a unified whole, it is nevertheless a key concept when it comes to judicial protection and cannot be left unaddressed. It is also possible to find guidance in the case law to help us dissect the *Union concept of rights.*

There is a wide variety of rights models in use in the Member States. The Union concept of rights is, however, autonomous and therefore conceptually distinct from its

[11] The right to effective judicial protection does not derive from the mere applicability of the Charter. AG Wahl has suggested that Art 47 of the Charter should be seen as a self-standing principle, independent of any other Union rights; see his Opinion in Case C-33/17 *Čepelnik* [2018]. This far-reaching stance does not, however, find support in the case law of the Court.

[12] V Roeben, 'Judicial Protection as the Meta-norm in the EU Judicial Architecture' (2020) 12 *Hague Journal on the Rule of Law* 29, 31. AG Wathelet raised the question 'whether the applicability of [Art 47] is conditional upon the alleged violation of a right or freedom guaranteed by the law of the Union' in his Opinion in Case C-682/15 *Berlioz* [2017] para 51. The Court (implicitly) answered in the affirmative, stating that the right at stake was the right to 'protection against arbitrary or disproportionate intervention by public authorities in the sphere of the private activities of any natural or legal person', which constitutes a general principle of EU law; see Case C-682/15 *Berlioz* [2017] para 51.

[13] Prechal, 'Does Direct Effect Still Matter?' (n 3) 1057.

[14] See J Engström, 'The Europeanisation of Remedies and Procedures Through Judge-Made Law: Can a Trojan Horse Achieve Effectiveness? Experiences of the Swedish Judiciary' (PhD thesis, European University Institute 2009) 212; and Prechal, *Directives in EC Law* (n 2) 111, respectively. Eilmansberger has called the notion of rights the 'missing link' in the Court's jurisprudence relating to national remedies and procedures; see T Eilmansberger, 'The Relationship between Rights and Remedies in EC Law: In Search of the Missing Link' (2004) 41 *CML Rev* 1199.

[15] B Thorson, *Individual Rights in EU Law* (Springer 2016) 4.

[16] Prechal and Hancher, 'Individual Environmental Rights' (n 2) 105.

domestic namesakes. National concepts cannot, therefore, serve as more than a starting point when looking into the concept at Union level.[17] With this caveat in place, it must be stressed that national legal concepts may have influenced the jurisprudence of the Court. After all, the Court consists of judges from the Member States who necessarily carry with them their own preconceptions of how similar issues are dealt with in their own legal systems.[18]

B. The Panopoly of Rights

Union rights can be inferred from various sources. There are rights established in the Treaties, such as the rights to free movement, equal treatment regardless of gender and EU citizenship rights; there are fundamental rights that are now enshrined in the Charter; and there are 'statutory rights' created in EU secondary legislation, most notably directives and regulations.[19] Provisions of a directive can also be *read in light of* a Treaty provision so as to confer rights.[20] There is also the possibility of what Robin-Olivier calls 'normative combination', whereby a general principle or a fundamental right is coupled with a provision of secondary legislation, to derive rights when the norms taken separately could not produce such effects.[21]

Rights arise in various sectors covered by Union law. European integration has a 'double aim, which is at once economic and social'.[22] This means that private parties are not merely granted economic rights, but also social rights, such as consumer and environmental rights. These two categories of rights may at time clash, which makes it necessary to strike an (often controversial) balance between the economic and social aspects of the Treaties.[23]

There are, of course, rights against the state, but Union law also confers rights against other private parties.[24] Rights can be negative (entitling the right holder to be free from interference) or positive (entitling the right holder to active measures).[25] One and the

[17] Beljin, 'Rights in EU Law' (n 3) 109.

[18] Similarly Prechal and Hancher, 'Individual Environmental Rights' (n 2) 93.

[19] RD Kelemen, 'American-Style Adversarial Legalism and the European Union' (European University Institute) *Working Paper EUI Working Paper RSCAS 2008/37*, 6.

[20] See Case C-445/06 *Danske Slagterier* [2009] para 23, where provisions in Directives 64/433/EEC and 89/662/EEC (governing, inter alia, health controls for, and certification of, fresh meat produced in one Member State and exported to another) were seen as defining and giving 'concrete expression' to the right laid down in (now) Art 34 TFEU.

[21] S Robin-Olivier, 'The Evolution of Direct Effect in the EU: Stocktaking, Problems, Projections' (2014) 12 *International Journal of Constitutional Law* 165, 170–71. She makes reference to, inter alia, Case C-149/10 *Chatzi* [2010], where the Court read Directive 96/34/EC (Parental Leave) in light of the general principle of equal treatment (affirmed in Art 20 of the Charter), and found that the national legislature had to establish a parental leave regime that took due account of the particular needs of parents with twins.

[22] Case 43/75 *Defrenne v SABENA* [1976] para 12.

[23] The Court's rulings in Case C-438/05 *Viking* [2007] and Case C-341/05 *Laval* [2007] exemplified the tension between the EU's market imperatives and its social aspirations, and fuelled the critics. See further D Leczykiewicz, 'Conceptualising Conflict between the Economic and the Social in EU Law after Viking and Laval' in M Freedland and J Prassl (eds), *Viking, Laval and Beyond* (Bloomsbury 2015) 307.

[24] See further ch 11, section II.

[25] Some scholars have sought to rationalise the Court's case law using Hohfeld's framework of legal correlatives: see C Hilson and T Downes, 'Making Sense of Rights: Community Rights in EC Law' (1999) 24

same Union law provision may, however, give rise to both negative and positive rights.[26] The Union legal order grants *substantive* as well as *procedural* rights.[27]

Rights can come into being as a result of direct effect, or they can be created by means of the transposition of provisions of a directive into domestic law.[28] Directives can be regarded as 'indirect sources of rights and obligations', since they can be 'the origin of rights and obligations laid down in national legislation [which] reaches the individuals through implementing measures adopted by the Member States'.[29] In both cases, however, I will speak of a Union law right as it originates from the Union legal order.

C. Not Necessarily a Uniform Rights Concept in Union Law

It is not necessarily the case that the term 'rights' has the same content regardless of the context in which it is used. The Court has primarily discussed the issue of whether a provision confers rights in three different contexts: first, in the context of correct implementation of Union acts (hereinafter 'implementation case law'); second, as one of the conditions for Member State liability under its *Francovich* case law; and, third, in relation to direct effect. The last strand of case law will not be addressed in the following. Although the issue of rights has figured in the debate on direct effect, it is now widely agreed that rights are no precondition for direct effect.[30]

Several scholars have pointed out that there may not be a uniform rights concept in Union law, and that the Court's finding may be tailored to the specific demands in each field. Prechal, for example, has held that although

> from the point of view of coherence of Community law, a differentiation in relation to the concept of rights does not seem to be beneficial, in particular as it causes confusion … from a functional point of view, such a differentiation might be unavoidable.[31]

EL Rev 121; and J Bengoetxea and N Jääskinen, 'Rights and Diverse Effects in EU Law: A Hohfeldian Approach to the Doctrine of Direct Effect of Directives' in R Banakar (ed), *Rights in Context: Law and Justice in Late Modern Society* (Ashgate 2010) 277, drawing on WN Hohfeld, *Fundamental Legal Conceptions as Applied in Judicial Reasoning*, ed W Wheeler Cook (Yale University Press 1964). This legal framework will not be used in the following, since, it is submitted, the Court's case law cannot easily be captured in Hohfeldian terms, and moreover, the added value of resorting to this framework seems limited.

[26] By way of illustration, in Case C-112/00 *Schmidtberger* [2003] the Court ruled that the failure of Austrian authorities to prohibit a demonstration blocking the transport of goods constituted a prima facie violation of (now) Art 34 TFEU. The latter provision, coupled with the duty of loyal cooperation enshrined in Art 4(3) TEU, implies that the Member States are under a positive obligation to adopt adequate measures to ensure that private parties do not impede the free movement of goods.

[27] A Union right must, however, be distinguished from a mere 'right to rely' or 'invocation right', see further ch 6, section III. On occasion it may nevertheless be challenging to determine whether the Court has acknowledged the one or the other; see, eg, Case C-350/96 *Clean Car Autoservice* [1998] paras 19–20 and Case C-208/05 *ITC Innovative Technology Center* [2007] para 23.

[28] See M Ruffert, 'Rights and Remedies in European Community Law: A Comparative View' (1997) 34 *CML Rev* 307, 328.

[29] Prechal, *Directives in EC Law* (n 2) 96.

[30] See ch 6, section II.

[31] Prechal, *Directives in EC Law* (n 2) 119. Similarly, Jans and Duijkersloot have suggested that 'even though the case law is not entirely clear on the matter, it must be assumed that the Court of Justice does not always apply the concept "rights for individuals" consistently'; see JH Jans and AP Duijkersloot, 'State Liability' in JH Jans, S Prechal and RJGM Widdershoven (eds), *Europeanisation of Public Law*, 2nd edn (Europa Law Publishing 2015) 435, 453. Thorson leaves the question open; see Thorson, *Individual Rights in EU Law* (n 15) 50–56.

When it comes to the implementation case law, the finding of a Union right has implications for how these provisions are to be implemented in national law. Provisions intended to grant rights to individuals need to be implemented so they can be relied on in the courts. When individual rights are at stake, Member States must ensure that the legal situation at the national level is 'sufficiently precise and clear and that the person concerned are put in a position to know the full extent of their rights and, where appropriate, to be able to rely on them before the national courts'.[32]

It has been suggested that when the Court uses the term 'right' in its implementation case law 'it has nothing specific in mind'[33] and that 'no particular significance should be afforded to the concept',[34] and that consequently one cannot automatically apply the Court's findings in infringement proceedings in the context of state liability.[35] Particularly in relation to the rulings in the field of environmental law, scholars have expressed doubts as to their relevance to state liability. Prechal warns that 'A more or less automatic transplant of a "right" labelled as such in infringement proceedings to, for instance, the area of State liability would seem a perilous undertaking.'[36] Thorson, on the other hand, acknowledges the particular policy considerations underlying the implementation case law, yet he predicts that the Court would build upon this line of jurisprudence were it to be faced with the question of Member State liability.[37]

It can be suspected that resistance to acknowledging a uniform rights concept derives from the fear that it would open the floodgates to Member State liability claims, including in the case of environmental infringements. This fear should not be exaggerated, since liability can be limited by construing the other criteria (sufficiently serious breach, causality and *not least* relevant harm) restrictively.[38] There are valid arguments for arguing that there is, in fact a uniform rights concept. First, the Court has used the term 'right' without ever indicating that the term is tailored to the specific context. Second, both in its implementation case law and in its case law on state liability, the Court's underlying rationale seems to be *the protection of individuals*. In its implementation case law, the Court has stressed that the persons concerned must be able to rely on mandatory rules before domestic courts.[39] The binding nature of the implementing measure is important for individuals not only from the perspective of legal certainty (by allowing them to ascertain the extent of their rights and duties), but also from the perspective of

[32] See, inter alia, Case C-456/03 *Commission v Italy* [2005] para 51.

[33] Prechal, *Directives in EC Law* (n 2) 110. She holds that 'the main concern of the Court seems to be that the legal position of the individual must be safeguarded and, perhaps even more importantly, that Community law is simply applied'.

[34] Prechal and Hancher, 'Individual Environmental Rights' (n 2) 103–04.

[35] Jurgens holds that with regard to the 'rights' that can be assumed within the framework of liability proceedings, the Court seems to 'seek more concrete provisions which can provide an entitlement for individuals to pursue a certain course of conduct with a view to their own interests', see G Jurgens, 'Introduction of a Relativity-Related Requirement in Dutch Administrative Law' (2007) 4 *Journal for European Environmental & Planning Law* 260, 267. For a thorough discussion, see Thorson, *Individual Rights in EU Law* (n 15) 50–57.

[36] Prechal, *Directives in EC Law* (n 2) 110.

[37] Thorson, *Individual Rights in EU Law* (n 15) 56–57.

[38] See further ch 10, section III.

[39] See, inter alia, Case C-361/88 *Commission v Germany* [1991] para 16, where the Court held that private parties concerned must 'be in a position to rely on mandatory rules in order to be able to assert their rights'.

effective judicial protection (by defining a legal position subject to enforcement by the courts).[40] In its liability case law, the Court has placed emphasis on the need to make good the harm inflicted on individuals.[41] Third, the approach adopted by the Court to see whether a right is granted seems to be the same regardless of context. As will be seen, the Court places emphasis on the *protective scope* of the norm, to see whether it aims at the protection of individual, as opposed to merely public, interests.[42] These arguments point in the direction of a uniform rights concept. The Court seems, however, to move in the direction of a rather expansive interpretation of the concept of 'right' under Article 47 of the Charter, and it remains to be seen whether the same stance will be adopted in the area of state liability.[43]

For present purposes, there is no need to conclude on this matter. The concept of rights is a broad one under Article 47 of the Charter, and the case law relating both to implementation of Union law and Member State liability will be utilised in order to shed light on the right to effective judicial protection in the following.

D. Parameters for Determining the Existence of a Right

The Court has not so far articulated a test enabling us to identify when Union law provisions give rise (or intend to give rise) to rights. Rights can be granted both explicitly and implicitly. Numerous provisions of EU law contain explicit rights. Parental leave, for instance, is defined as an individual entitlement in Directive 2010/18/EU (Parental Leave).[44] Where a right is not explicitly granted in the Union law provision, a right may still be implied as a 'reflex' of a precise and unconditional Union law obligation.[45] The Court held, for example, in *Parliament v Council*, that Article 4(1) of Directive 2003/86/EC (Family Reunification) imposes precise positive obligations, 'with corresponding clearly defined individual rights, on the Member States, since it requires them, in the cases determined by the Directive, to authorise family reunification of certain members of the sponsor's family, without being left a margin of appreciation'.[46]

The two aforementioned categories of rights can be labelled *directly* and *indirectly* conferred rights, respectively.[47] This distinction may be useful for thinking clearly about the issue, although there is no watershed between the two categories. As regards indirectly conferred rights, there is a need to interpret the norm to determine whether – and

[40] See Joined Cases C-178/94, C-179/94, C-188/94, C-189/94 and C-190/94 *Dillenkofer* [1996] para 48 (legal certainty); and Case C-340/96 *Commission v United Kingdom* [1999] para 37 (judicial protection).

[41] Case C-470/03 *A.G.M-COS.MET* [2007] para 88.

[42] Beljin has therefore defined EU rights as the 'normatively protected position of an individual'; see Beljin, 'Rights in EU Law' (n 3) 110.

[43] See, in particular, Case C-682/15 *Berlioz* [2017], which relevance to state liability may be questioned.

[44] Section II, cl 2 in the annexed Framework Agreement.

[45] As the Court held already in *Van Gend en Loos*, rights arise 'not only where they are expressly granted by the Treaty, but also by reason of obligations which the Treaty imposes in a clearly defined way upon individuals as well as upon the Member States and upon the Institutions of the Community', see Case 26/62 *Van Gend en Loos* [1963].

[46] Case C-540/03 *Parliament v Council* [2006] para 60.

[47] Eilmansberger, 'The Relationship between Rights and Remedies in EC Law' (n 14) 1238–43.

if so, to whom – a right is granted.[48] The Union law provision must be interpreted in light of its wording, object and purpose. The Court seems primarily to apply two criteria to determine whether a right is granted by the provision invoked: first, whether the norm in question aims at protecting individuals; and, second, whether the content of the right can be inferred from the said provision.[49]

As to the first criterion, the protective scope of the relevant norm must be examined to determine whether it exists to protect individual, as opposed to merely public, interests.[50] The protective scope of Union law must be defined autonomously by Union law itself, rather than by reference to national standards.[51] The Court has in several cases stressed the protective scope of the norm at issue. In *Dillenkofer*, the Court found that obligations imposed on the operator by Directive 90/314/EEC (Package Travel) amounted to a conferral of rights on consumers, as 'The purpose of Article 7 [of the Directive] is … to protect consumers, who thus have the right to be reimbursed or repatriated in the event of the insolvency of the organizer from whom they purchased the package travel.'[52] Similarly, in *E.ON Földgaz*, the Court stressed the protective orientation of the Regulation No 1775/2005 (Conditions for access to the natural gas transmission networks) and held that

> the principles set out in Article 5 of that regulation, read in conjunction with the Annexes thereto, must be interpreted as constituting protective measures adopted in the interest of users wishing to gain access to the network and therefore capable of conferring rights on them.[53]

When locating rights, one should not focus strictly on the wording of the provision in question. Rights can on occasion be inferred from what Thorson calls 'a contrario reasoning': if the Union measure allows for restrictive measures towards individuals, the individual may have a 'right not to be subject to measures falling outside what is expressly lawful'.[54] The Court's ruling in *Braathens*, concerning the levying of an unlawful tax, can illustrate this category of rights.[55] Taxation on petroleum products was

[48] Whereas the personal scope of a piece of legislation (its *ratione personae*) identifies those to which such legislation applies, the material scope (*ratione materiae*) relates to the situations to which the legislation applies; see E Spaventa, 'Seeing the Wood Despite the Trees – On the Scope of Union Citizenship and Its Constitutional Effects' (2008) 45 *CML Rev* 13, 14. These two aspects are, however, closely related. As Derlén and Lindholm have noted, the question of scope can often be phrased in either personal terms ('does this person enjoy this right?') or material terms ('is this situation covered by the rule?'); see M Derlén and J Lindholm, 'Three Ideas: The Scope of EU Law Protecing against Discrimination' in M Derlén and J Lindholm (eds), *Volume in Honor of Pär Hallström* (Iustus 2012) 77, 80.

[49] Similarly, Prechal, *Directives in EC Law* (n 2) 118–29.

[50] S Prechal, 'Protection of Rights: How Far?' in Prechal and van Roermund (eds), *The Coherence of EU Law* (n 3) 155, 164. For illustration, see Case C-380/87 *Enichem Base* [1989] para 23, where the Court found that Art 3(2) of Directive 75/442/EEC (Waste), requiring the Member States to notify national measures to the Commission, did not protect individual interests and thus did not confer rights.

[51] M Dougan, 'Who Exactly Benefits from the Treaties? The Murky Interaction Between Union and National Competence over the Capacity to Enforce EU Law' (2009) 12 *Cambridge Yearbook of European Legal Studies* 73, 76.

[52] Joined Cases C-178/94, C-179/94, C-188/94, C-189/94 and C-190/94 *Dillenkofer* [1996] para 36. The directive has been replaced by Directive (EU) 2015/2302.

[53] Case C-510/13 *E.ON Földgaz* [2015] para 46.

[54] Thorson, *Individual Rights in EU Law* (n 15) 231.

[55] Case C-346/97 *Braathens* [1999].

harmonised in Directive 92/81/EEC (Duties on Mineral Oils), and under Article 1 of the Directive, Member States were obliged to impose a harmonised excise duty on mineral oils. Nevertheless, pursuant to Article 8(1)(b), Member States were exempt from the obligation to levy duties on 'mineral oils supplied for use as fuels for the purpose of air navigation other than private pleasure flying'. The Court found that the provision could be invoked by a private party who had been subjected to excise duties. Since the tax levied did not fall within the scope of the harmonising directive, the private party had a right not to be subjected to such a tax.[56]

How strict the requirement of an individual interest is in Union law is not fully clear.[57] The individual interest must be juxtaposed with the 'public interest', but the distinction is not easily drawn. Moreover, it may also be useful to distinguish the public interest in the narrow sense from 'collective' or 'diffuse' interests. The difference is spelled out by Godt:

> The public interest is the result of a policy decision by the state weighing different concerns; collective interests are the aligned, identical interests of many people; diffuse interests are defined by their indivisible nature and their attribution to an indeterminate number of people.[58]

The Court has not required that the duty must be imposed for the protection of a limited class of persons. The clearest illustration of the stance that the category of beneficiaries must not necessarily be limited is found in the field of environmental law, where the Court has held that environmental directives that aim at the protection of public health grant rights to individuals.[59]

Although the Court's jurisprudence supports the position that protection of an individual interest is a condition for recognising a Union right, it is not required that the provision is enacted with the sole aim of protecting the individual.[60] For instance, in *Rampion*, the Court found that Directive 87/102/EEC (Consumer Credit) granted rights although the purpose of the Directive was not only the protection of consumers, but also the creation of a common consumer credit market.[61] A different approach would hardly be conceivable in Union law. The competence of the Union 'is defined by its goals, so as a consequence all laws it enacts must by necessity be instrumentalist

[56] See ibid paras 29–31. This 'a contrario' reasoning was made explicit by the Court in Case T-341/07 *Sison* [2007] para 51.

[57] Prechal, 'Protection of Rights: How Far?' (n 50) 164.

[58] C Godt, 'Enforcement of Environmental Law by Individuals and Interest Groups: Reconceptualizing Standing' (2000) 23 *Journal of Consumer Policy* 79, 81. Hence, she perceives the consumer interest as primarily a collective interest, whereas the environmental interest is regarded as a diffuse interest, see ibid 86.

[59] See Cases C-361/88 *Commission v Germany* [1991]; Case C-58/89 *Commission v Germany* [1991]; Case C-59/89 *Commission v Germany* [1991]; Case C-13/90 *Commission v France* [1991]; and Case C-14/90 *Commission v France* [1991]. These cases all concerned water- and air-quality legislation, see further ch 8, section III.B. Conversely, environmental directives that merely seek to protect the environment as such are found not to confer rights; see, eg, Case C-115/09 *Bund für Umwelt und Naturschutz Deutschland* [2011] concerning Art 6 of Directive 92/43/EC (Habitats).

[60] The General Court made this explicit in *Sison*, where it held that the infringed provision can be seen as granting a right if the provision 'while in the main concerning interests of a general nature, also protects the individual interests of the persons concerned', see Case T-341/07 *Sison* [2011] para 47. The ECJ has not been this explicit, but it is evident from the case law that it has adopted the same position.

[61] Case C-429/05 *Rampion* [2007] para 59.

in nature'.[62] Union measures often explicitly state that their purpose is to further both public and private interests. For instance, Regulation (EU) No 596/2014 (Market Abuse) aims 'to ensure the integrity of financial markets in the Union and to enhance investor protection and confidence in those markets'.[63]

From the foregoing, it can be inferred that the type of interest pursued by a Union law provision is important in order to determine whether a right is granted. It has been pointed out in legal scholarship that this method bears a clear resemblance to the German *Schutzzweck* doctrine, according to which the protective scope of the norm is decisive for determining rights.[64] While there is a resemblance, this stems primarily from the fact that both legal systems are based on the 'interest theory' of rights, rather than the 'will theory'. Whereas the first theory places emphasis on the individual right holder, the latter emphasises individual autonomy.[65] Pursuant to the interest theory,

> whether a right exists depends on the reasons why, or the intention with which, the correlative duty was imposed. Understanding whether a particular right exists, entails understanding the purposes, or reasons behind, the imposition of the duty. Thus determining whether a right exists depends upon understanding a process of justification.[66]

Despite this common theoretical foundation – in that both EU law and German law are based on the interest theory of rights – one should be cautious not to draw the parallel too far. Effectiveness concerns are of the utmost importance in the Union law context, since we are dealing with a shared legal order, which means that 'considerations on the usefulness of allowing private enforcement are often centre-stage when discussing the rights issue'.[67] When the Court relies upon effectiveness arguments, the conferral of rights is a way of making sure that Union law is rendered effective and that the purpose of the provision is promoted.[68] Union rights are granted generously, and this is largely a consequence of how the Union legal order works. This mode of governance – captured

[62] R Michaels, 'Of Islands and the Ocean: The Two Rationalities of European Private Law' in R Brownsword et al (eds), *The Foundations of European Private Law* (Hart Pubishing 2011) 139, 142. Distinguishing instrumental from non-instrumental rights, however, is not straightforward. Art 157 TFEU was, for example, initially enacted with a view to levelling the playing field by equalising labour costs in the Member States, but protection against discrimination has evolved into a self-standing aim, see Case C-50/95 *Schröder* [2000] paras 51–57.

[63] See Art 1.

[64] Reich is of the opinion that the Court has taken over a 'modified German *Schutznorm*- or *Normweck-theorie* which, however, is interpreted in a strictly objective sense depending on the need for protection', see N Reich, 'The Interrelation between Rights and Duties in EU Law: Reflections on the State of Liability Law in the Multilevel Governance System of the Union: Is There a Need for a More Coherent Approach in European Private Law?' (2010) 29 *Yearbook of European Law* 112, 127. Conversely N Poltorak, *European Union Rights in National Courts* (Wolters Kluwer 2015) 115, rejects such a parallel.

[65] The interest theory is associated with Joseph Raz (see, inter alia, J Raz, *The Morality of Freedom* (Oxford University Press 1988) ch 7; and N MacCormick, 'Rights in Legislation' in PMS Hacker and J Raz (eds), *Law, Morality and Society* (Clarendon Press 1977) 189) and the 'will theory' with HLA Hart (see HLA Hart, *Essays on Bentham* (Clarendon Press 1982) 183–88).

[66] JE Penner, 'The Analysis of Rights' (1997) 10 *Ratio Juris* 300, 303–04.

[67] Thorson, *Individual Rights in EU Law* (n 15) 350. I agree with Prechal, who advises against dismissing effectiveness as a basis for determining the protective scope; it is necessary rather to 'get a clear picture of how much weight should be given to the various elements – control and protection – that characterize the role of the courts in the context of Community law', see Prechal, 'Protection of Rights: How Far?' (n 50) 181.

[68] The idea that individual rights may be granted also with a view to furthering the public interest is not specific to Union law. One of the main proponents of the interest theory, Raz, has held that 'the weight given

in Kelemen's notion of 'eurolegalism' (see chapter 2, section IV), largely relies on private parties to ensure compliance with the relevant substantive norms. Thus, the EU is pursuing policy objectives through the creation of individual rights and 'pursues rights-based approaches to policy in a striking diverse range of policy areas, including areas where rights-based approaches were by no means the norm at the national level'.[69]

At the beginning of this section it was held that the Court seems to apply two criteria to determine whether a right is granted by the provision invoked; whether the relevant norm aims at protecting individuals; and whether the content of the right can be inferred from said provision. So far I have addressed the first criterion relating to the protection of individual interests; in the following I examine the second criterion pertaining to the ascertainability of the scope of the right. As pointed out in legal scholarship,

> the Court seems to pursue a general line of thinking, which also prevails in national law, namely that the ascertainability of the scope of the right is a criterion which helps us decide whether a provision confers rights as such.[70]

For a Union right to be acknowledged, its content must be susceptible to being identified based on the provision invoked: 'one must know *what* one is claiming *in concreto* and, accordingly, the other party must know *to what* it is obliged *in concreto*'.[71] This was listed as a separate requirement in *Francovich*, for the state to incur liability, but it has later been seen as an element of the condition that the provision infringed must entail the grant of a right.[72] While this condition is of particular importance where the legal basis invoked for a right is a directive, the condition must also be satisfied where the claimant relies on a different legal basis. The issue of 'identifiability' or 'ascertainability' is, for example, also what underlies the distinction between rights and principles in the Charter.[73]

The requirement of 'identifiability' should not be conflated with the requirements for direct effect, and a Union law provision may grant rights without being directly effective.[74] A right is 'a thick concept, focused on the legislatively intended entitlement rather than the completeness of the rule it is based on'.[75] As the Court held in *Dillenkofer*:

> The fact that States may choose between a wide variety of means for achieving the result prescribed by a directive is of no importance [for determining whether a right is granted] if the purpose of the directive is to grant to individuals rights whose content is determinable with sufficient precision.[76]

to the interests of the rightholder in determining whether his interest is protected by a right, and how extensive that protection is, reflects not only our concerns for the individual, but also our concern for the public interest that will be served by protecting the interest of the rightholder', see J Raz, 'Rights and Politics' (1995) 71 *Indiana Law Journal* 27, 39.

[69] Kelemen, 'American-Style Adversarial Legalism and the European Union' (n 19) 6.

[70] Prechal and Hancher, 'Individual Environmental Rights' (n 2) 102.

[71] Prechal, *Directives in EC Law* (n 2) 125 (emphasis in original).

[72] See Joined Cases C-6/90 and C-9/90 *Francovich* [1991] para 40, where the Court held that 'it should be possible to identify the content of those rights on the basis of the provisions of the directive'.

[73] The principles enshrined in the Charter 'may be implemented through legislative or executive acts … accordingly, they become significant for the Courts only when such acts are interpreted or reviewed'; see Explanations Relating to the Charter of Fundamental Rights [2007] OJ C303/17, 35.

[74] Prechal, *Directives in EC Law* (n 2) 126–27. Direct effect is merely 'one of several ways of enforcing [the right]', cf Roeben, 'Judicial Protection as the Meta-norm in the EU Judicial Architecture' (n 12) 34.

[75] Roeben, 'Judicial Protection as the Meta-norm in the EU Judicial Architecture' (n 12) 32.

[76] Joined Cases C-178/94, C-179/94, C-188/94, C-189/94 and C-190/94 *Dillenkofer* [1996] para 45.

For instance, although the concrete identity of the holder of the duties enshrined in a directive is not entirely clear, its provisions may still be intended to grant rights.[77] The Court's ruling in *Gharehveran* may serve to illustrate the distinction between direct effect and the granting of rights.[78] Sweden had transposed Directive 80/987/EEC (Employer Insolvency) into its national law, but excluded certain categories of employees from the wage payment guarantee in breach of the Directive. The Court was asked whether such employees could still rely directly on the Directive and claim pay. In *Francovich*, the Court had ruled out this possibility, due to the lack of direct effect of the Directive. This case was distinguished from *Francovich*, however, due to the fact that Sweden had implemented the Directive and designated public authorities responsible for guaranteeing employees' wage claims. Consequently, the Directive could be relied on before the domestic court.

The ruling illustrates that 'although it is the State which is free to decide the liable subject, the individual has a Union law right against that subject once the decision has been taken'.[79] When determining the degree of clarity and precision needed in order for a provision to be seen as granting rights, the case law pertaining to direct effect may consequently provide guidance. The decisive aspect is whether the *content* of the right is sufficiently identifiable.

The requirement that the content of the alleged right must be sufficiently concrete and delineated means that provisions involving discretion may not give rise to rights at all.[80] That being said, elements of discretion do not necessarily rule out the granting of rights, which means that rights can be violated when a state exceeds its discretionary powers. This may, for instance, be the case in relation to rights to be free from various kinds of discrimination.[81] The Court's ruling in *Maïstrellis*[82] serves to illustrate this point. The case concerned a father who sought parental leave from his employer pursuant to Directive 96/34/EC (Parental Leave). According to Greek law, a father could not obtain such leave if the mother was at home, unless she was unable to take care of the child. For mothers there was no equivalent requirement relating to the employment status of the husband. When the Court was asked whether this requirement contravened EU law, it answered in the affirmative. The Directive leaves it to the Member States (by way of legislation or collective agreements) to craft the detailed rules on parental leave, provided that the minimum requirements laid down in the Directive are complied with. Still, the Court found that the condition constituted discrimination based on gender, contrary to Directive 2006/54/EC (Equal treatment of men and

[77] Prechal, *Directives in EC Law* (n 2) 127. In the words of Anagnostaras, 'one can possibly talk about the absence of a technical direct effect relating not to the quality of a given legal norm but rather to the status of the person against which the measure needs to be relied upon'; see G Anagnostaras, 'State Liability and Alternative Courses of Action: How Independent Can an Autonomous Remedy Be?' (2001) 21 *Yearbook of European Law* 355, 357.

[78] Case C-441/99 *Gharehveran* [2001].

[79] Thorson, *Individual Rights in EU Law* (n 15) 222.

[80] Prechal and Hancher, 'Individual Environmental Rights' (n 2) 102. 'Discretion' is used in several different meanings, but for present purposes we refer to the space left unregulated by Union law, what Dworkin compares to the 'hole in the doughnut': it 'does not exist except as an area left open by a surrounding belt of restriction [and it] is therefore a relative concept'; see R Dworkin, *Taking Rights Seriously* (Duckworth 1977) 31.

[81] Thorson, *Individual Rights in EU Law* (n 15) 223.

[82] Case C-222/14 *Maïstrellis* [2015].

women in matters of employment and occupation). Consequently, although states are given considerable leeway in crafting their parental leave schemes, the right to parental leave cannot be subject to conditions that discriminate based on gender.

To sum up, the requirement of 'ascertainability' means that the content of the alleged right must be identifiable from the provision invoked. How strictly this requirement is to be interpreted is not clear, however, and the Court's *ad hoc* approach does not give much guidance. Having concluded that the Union law provision grants a right, there is still a need to determine who can draw on that right for the purposes of being granted standing. This issue will be addressed in chapter 5, section IV.

IV. Requirement of an Arguable Claim

The principle of effective judicial protection accrues to those holding a Union law right. In the preceding section, I elaborated on the content of the concept of Union law rights, and how one goes about determining whether such a right exists. In the following, I look more closely at the question of when the principle of effective judicial protection can be invoked with a view to obtaining standing. It will be argued that it is not sufficient for the claimant to allege that his rights have been infringed; he must have an *arguable claim* to that effect.

If one adopts a literal reading of Article 47 of the Charter, it would only guarantee access to court and an effective remedy if the violation of a right set forth has already been established. Such a narrow reading must, however, be rejected from the outset, since it is only once access to court has been granted that the case can be argued. The Court has not addressed this issue explicitly, although Advocate General Szpunar did so in his Opinion in *T-Mobile*.[83] One must not, he warned, 'disregard the differences between the right to bring an action and the subject-matter of that action. The right to bring an action cannot be dependent on the outcome of that action, that is to say, on a finding that the claimant has certain rights,' and '[o]nly the authority hearing the merits of the case may decide whether individual rights have been infringed'.[84]

Standing is a preliminary issue that the courts must examine before going to the merits. This raises the question whether Member States must grant access to court for any alleged breach of Union law, or may impose limits in this regard. Are they, for example, permitted to have rules in place to verify whether the claimant actually falls within the scope of protection of the relevant Union legislation, or to make a preliminary assessment of the merits of the case without encroaching upon the principle of effective judicial protection? Answering such questions may be of importance for Member States with certain types of rules in place to screen cases at the admissibility stage. In Germany, for instance, standing is only granted where there is the possibility of a right's being violated (the 'possibility theory').[85]

[83] AG Szpunar in Case C-282/13 *T-Mobile Austria* [2014].
[84] ibid paras 62 and 86.
[85] M Eliantonio et al, *Standing Up for Your Right(s) in Europe – A Comparative Study on Legal Standing (Locus Standi) before the EU and Member States' Courts* (Intersentia 2013) 132.

Given the lack of guidance from the Court, the case law of the ECtHR under Article 13 may provide guidance as to the scope of the right to effective judicial protection.[86] Article 47(1) of the Charter corresponds in essence to Article 13 ECHR, providing for the 'right to an effective remedy before a national authority'.[87] The relationship between the ECHR and the Charter is regulated in Article 52(3) of the Charter, which states that, insofar as the Charter contains rights that correspond to rights guaranteed by the ECHR, the meaning and scope of those rights shall be the same as those laid down by the said Convention. There is no complete correspondence between Article 47 of the Charter and Article 13 ECHR.[88] First, Article 47 of the Charter covers the protection of all Union rights, as opposed to Article 13 ECHR, which merely covers the other Convention rights. Second, the protection offered in Article 47 is more extensive, since it guarantees the right to an effective remedy *before a court*.[89] It must also be taken into account that the ECJ and the ECtHR operate in different contexts and seek to accomplish different objectives.[90] In particular, the (partly) instrumental nature of Union rights and the need to ensure effective application of Union law in the Member States may influence the interpretation of the Charter.[91] Nevertheless, the autonomy of EU law is mainly grounded in the principle of the 'more extensive protection', which means that the guarantees enshrined in Article 13 ECHR constitute a floor below which the Union must not go.[92] Hence, when mapping the requirements stemming from Article 47(1) of the Charter, we can draw on Article 13 and the case law stemming from the ECtHR.[93]

The ECtHR held in *Klass and others v Germany* that

> it cannot be a prerequisite for the application of Article 13 … that the Convention be in fact violated [and the provision] requires that where an individual considers himself to have been prejudiced by a measure allegedly in breach of the Convention, he should have a remedy before a national authority in order both to have his claim decided and, if appropriate, to obtain redress.[94]

[86] On the parallelism between Art 47 of the Charter and Art 13 ECHR, see ch 3, section III.C.

[87] See Explanations Relating to the Charter of Fundamental Rights (n 73) and Case C-239/14 *Tall* [2015] para 52. The State Parties to the Convention must provide redress for violations of the Convention. The Court has held that as far as Convention wrongs are concerned, it is not under Art 6(1) but rather 'under Article 13 that the applicants' right to a remedy should be examined and, if appropriate, vindicated', see *Z and others v the United Kingdom* App no 29392/95 (ECtHR, 2001) para 103. Similarly *Vladimir Polishchuk and Svetlana Polishchuk v Ukraine* App no 12451/04 (ECtHR, 2010) para 50. Art 13 is less strict than Art 6(1) ECHR, see *Airey v Ireland* App no 6289/73 (ECtHR, 1979) para 35 and *Sporrong and Lönnroth v Sweden* App nos 7151/75, 7152/75 (ECtHR, 1982) para 88.

[88] As AG Cruz Villalón stated in his Opinion in C-69/10 *Samba Diouf* [2011] para 39, Art 47 of the Charter has 'aquired a separate identity and substance'.

[89] Explanations Relating to the Charter of Fundamental Rights (n 73) 29.

[90] The Court placed great emphasis on the autonomy of EU law in Opinion 2/13 *Accession of the European Union to the ECHR* [2014]; see in particular ibid paras 155–77.

[91] It should be noted that the ECHR also has a certain 'objective' aspect, meaning that human rights observance is beneficial to other private persons and society in general; see M Emberland, *The Human Rights of Companies* (Oxford University Press 2006) 58–59. This wider objective finds its expression, inter alia, in Art 37(1), which states that the Court may pursue a case in the public interest, even if the applicant withdraws his application 'if respect for human rights … so requires'.

[92] K Lenaerts, 'Exploring the Limits of the EU Charter of Fundamental Rights' (2012) 8 *European Constitutional Law Review* 375, 394. The Court stated this expressly in Case C-400/10 PPU, *J McB v LE* [2010] para 53. See Joined Cases C-585/18, C-624/18 and C-625/18 *A.K.* [2019] paras 117–18.

[93] See in particular ch 4, section IV (arguable claim) and ch 5, section IV.C (the 'victim test').

[94] *Klass and others v Germany* App no 5029/71 (ECtHR, 1978) para 64.

The Court therefore concluded that Article 13 must be interpreted as guaranteeing an effective remedy before a national authority to everyone 'who claims that his rights and freedoms under the Convention have been violated'.[95] In its later case law the ECtHR has made it clear that Article 13 is not applicable just because an applicant alleges that his Convention rights are infringed; he must have an 'arguable claim' of a violation. As the Court held in *Boyle v Rice*, the provision

> cannot reasonably be interpreted so as to require a remedy in domestic law in respect of any supposed grievance under the Convention that an individual may have, no matter how unmeritorious his complaint may be: the grievance must be an arguable one in terms of the Convention.[96]

The Court did not want to 'give an abstract definition of the notion of arguability'.[97] It has, however, held that the criterion of arguability in Article 13 has similarities with the criterion 'manifestly ill-founded' under Article 35(3) ECHR, and 'it is difficult to conceive how a claim that is "manifestly ill-founded" can nevertheless be "arguable" and vice versa'.[98] This implies that the applicant must present his claim with some degree of certainty, meaning that 'he must present a *prima facie* case that substantive rights have been violated'.[99] A complaint may be considered manifestly ill-founded if, for instance, the applicant has made wholly unsubstantiated allegations, or where the allegations, even if substantiated, would not suffice to establish a violation.[100]

Returning to the principle of effective judicial protection in EU law, presumably the principle is triggered where the claimant has a prima facie case of a violation, meaning that a claimant cannot obtain standing by merely alleging his Union rights are infringed; rather, the determination of standing must depend on a preliminary assessment of the pleas brought forward. Hence, the standing inquiry involves a 'preliminary look at the merits – a sort of nibble at the apple before [taking] a real bite'.[101] First, the claimant must demonstrate that he arguably falls within the scope of application of the provision invoked; second, he must demonstrate that the relevant Union provision has arguably been breached.

As to the first, the claimant must fall within the personal scope of the legislation (its *ratione personae*), and the situation must fall within its material scope (its *ratione materiae*).[102] For instance, in relation to Art 56 TFEU (freedom to provide services), the

[95] ibid.

[96] *Boyle and Rice v United Kingdom* App no 9659/82 (ECtHR, 1988) para 52. The requirement that the claim must be 'arguable' has been reiterated in subsequent rulings, see, for example, *Kudla v Poland* App no 30210/96 (ECtHR, 2000) para 157.

[97] *Boyle and Rice v United Kingdom* (n 96) para 55.

[98] ibid para 54. After all, these two provisions are concerned with the availability of remedies for the enforcement of the same Convention rights and freedoms, albeit at the domestic and international level respectively, see *Powell and Rayner v United Kingdom* App no 9310/81 (ECtHR, 1990) para 33, where it is pointed out that 'the coherence of this dual enforcement is at risk of being undermined' by such a discrepancy.

[99] M Reiertsen, 'The European Convention on Human Rights Article 13: Past, Present and Future' (PhD thesis, University of Oslo 2017) 185.

[100] DJ Harris et al, *Harris, O'Boyle & Warbrick: Law of the European Convention on Human Rights*, 4th edn (Oxford University Press 2018) 75.

[101] W Fletcher, 'The Structure of Standing' (1988) 98 *Yale Law Journal* 221, 234. He writes about standing under Art III of the American Constitution, but I argue that this is the approach that needs to be adopted for the purposes of determining standing in the context of Union law.

[102] Spaventa, 'Seeing the Wood Despite the Trees' (n 48) 14.

claimant must first prove he is a service provider (or service recipient), and then must demonstrate, inter alia, that the issue has a cross-border character.[103] Although 'certain national rules might be permitted or required for the purposes of verifying that this particular claimant does actually fall within the class of intended beneficiaries envisaged by the relevant Union legislation', Member States can arguably not impose too strict requirements in this regard.[104] In *Tele2*, the Court found that standing had to be granted to 'potential beneficiaries' of the rights in question, which can indicate that the claimant does not have to demonstrate with certainty that he is protected by the provision in question.[105] If the Court has doubts as to whether the claimant is covered by the provision invoked, the case should be declared admissible, and the question of interpretation should be referred to the ECJ for a preliminary ruling. Rejecting an action at the admissibility stage in effect rules out the Court's involvement in the process of interpretation.

As to the second – the arguability of a breach – it is submitted that Member States cannot be required to provide access to court pursuant to the principle of effective judicial protection regardless of how unmeritorious a claim may be.[106] Presumably, in order for Article 47 of the Charter to be triggered, the claim must be sufficiently tenable. Hence, the Member States must be allowed to deny standing where there clearly has not been a violation of Union law. In order to determine whether the claimant should be able to proceed, the domestic court needs to glance at the merits of the case. However, the court must avoid an in-depth examination of the merits when deciding whether to grant standing. Requiring the claimant at the preliminary stage to provide evidence to support that he has a well-founded claim may be perceived as rendering the enforcement of Union law excessively difficult, contrary to the principle of effectiveness.

When deciding where the threshold for arguability lies, the case law of the ECtHR may provide guidance, although this line of jurisprudence should not be applied mechanically. Whereas the protection afforded by Article 13 ECHR constitutes a floor beyond which the Member States cannot go, it does not constitute a ceiling.[107] There are valid arguments for affording a higher level of protection in the context of Union law. The main reason is that the threshold for considering a claim manifestly ill-founded under Article 35(3) ECHR – which has spilled over to Article 13 – has been influenced by the backlog of cases in the ECtHR's dockets. The need to prevent the ECtHR from being loaded down has resulted in a low threshold for considering a case to be 'manifestly ill-founded' (and conversely a high threshold for 'arguability'). This consideration is not as relevant in the Union law context, as it is hardly conceivable that a formal right of action will result in a flood of cases before domestic courts (and hence a flood of preliminary references to the Court).[108] Considering the important role granted

[103] For an illustration of a situation where this element was found lacking, see Case C-17/94 *Gervais* [1995].

[104] Dougan, 'Who Exactly Benefits from the Treaties?' (n 51) 102.

[105] Case C-426/05 *Tele2* [2008] para 36.

[106] That wholly unmeritorious cases are not worthy of protection under Union law finds support, inter alia, in Directive 2002/8/EC (Legal Aid in Cross-border Disputes) Art 6(1), stating that Member States may provide that 'legal aid applications for actions which appear to be manifestly unfounded may be rejected by the competent authorities'. See also Commission Recommendation on Collective Redress (2013/396/EU), which in Art 8 states that the Member States should provide for verification at the earliest possible stage of litigation that 'manifestly unfounded cases … are not continued'.

[107] See further ch 4, section IV.

[108] On this matter, see further ch 14, section II.

domestic courts in protecting Union rights, the threshold for arguability should not be set too high; and, particularly if the case presents complex legal issues, a case should not be easily dismissed at too early a stage of the procedure. In the Union context, the requirement of arguability should primarily serve to exclude cases that are clearly without merits, or where Union rights are clearly not at stake. It is therefore submitted that the domestic court is entitled to hold inadmissible an application only if it appears to be prima facie wholly unjustified.

5

EU Law Requirements on National Standing Rules

I. Introduction

In the following, I take a closer look at the interface between Union law requirements on standing and domestic standing doctrines. I first examine the extent to which the Court has harmonised domestic standing rules (section II), before turning to examine whether the standing criteria relative to bringing cases before the Union courts under Article 263(4) TFEU, is apt to shed light on what the principle of effective judicial protection requires from domestic courts (section III). Since it is submitted that the Court has moved in the direction of a rather extensive harmonisation in order to ensure the effective protection of Union rights, I take a closer look at the criteria that must be fulfilled in order to be afforded standing as a matter of Union law. That the infringement of a right requires a remedy may seem obvious, but, as will be seen, the issue of standing has many facets. Since Union rights tend to be rather fuzzy around the edges, determining who can draw on these rights by initiating judicial proceedings raises challenges.[1] The criteria that together constitute the Union doctrine of standing will therefore be addressed in detail (section IV). I ask whether the Union right to standing is an absolute right (section V); thereafter, I look into how the Union standard is given effect in a concrete case before the court (section VI) and end the chapter with an assessment of the legality and legitimacay of a court made doctrine of standing (section VII).

II. Harmonised Standing Rules Based on the Principle of Effective Judicial Protection?

The question raised and answered in the following is whether the Court merely indicates that particular domestic rules on standing are inconsistent with Union law, and hence need to be set aside, or whether the Court rather gives a positive indication as to which rules the Member States need to apply.

[1] Similarly J Engström, 'The Europeanisation of Remedies and Procedures Through Judge-Made Law: Can a Trojan Horse Achieve Effectiveness? Experiences of the Swedish Judiciary' (PhD thesis, European University Institute 2009) 7.

This is closely connected to the question of what *standard of review* the Court applies when scrutinising national enforcement rules.[2] The case law is by no means coherent, and the Court has used varying levels of scrutiny in assessing domestic procedural and remedial rules. Several scholars have sought to explain the different standards of review by deducing historical periods in the Court's jurisprudence.[3] The Court seems, however, to apply various standards of review simultaneously, and it is not easy to predict which approach the Court will adopt in a given case.[4] Although the Court rarely articulates which review standard it uses, looking at the Court's jurisprudence, van Cleynenbreugel has managed to identify various implicit standards of review. He places these categories on a sliding scale from an abstract and deferential form of scrutiny to the superimposing of an EU-wide standard of adequate national procedures.[5] The argument in the following is that when it comes to national standing rules, the Court is using this latter method, spelling out for itself what Union law requires in terms of standing for the protection of Union rights. The principle of effective judicial protection therefore gives rise to a *positive obligation* binding on the Member States.

To provide a conceptual background, it would be usedful to look at the dichotomy between negative and positive obligations:

> [A] 'negative obligation' means that national provisions which fail to satisfy the requirements of the principles of effectiveness or effective judicial protection must be set aside. In other words, they are eliminated. The positive obligation, on the other hand, is that new national powers and remedies have to be created.[6]

The distinction between negative and positive obligations is not clear-cut, and the line between the two can on occastion be rather fine.[7] Nevertheless, distinguishing between negative and positive obligations is of importance, since it determines the division of competences between the EU and the Member States.[8] In the case of negative obligations, the Court would merely declare that EU law precludes certain procedural rules, whereas in the case of positive obligations, the Court would itself define the measures that must be taken.[9]

[2] The Court itself does not refer to the 'standard of review' concept, but an alaysis of its jurisprudence reveals that there, the margin of discretion left to the Member States varies greatly; see P van Cleynenbreugel, 'National Procedural Choices before the Court of Justice of the European Union' in L Gruszczynski and W Werner (eds), *Deference in International Courts and Tribunals: Standard of Review and Margin of Appreciation* (Oxford University Press 2014) 175, 179.

[3] See, inter alia, M Dougan, *National Remedies Before the Court of Justice: Issues of Harmonisation and Differentiation* (Hart Publishing 2004) 227–33; and A Arnull, 'The Principle of Effective Judicial Protection in EU Law: An Unruly Horse?' (2011) 36 *EL Rev* 51. Conversely, Półtorak finds no grounds for differentiating between generations of the Court's case law, but rather distinguishes between negative and positive harmonisation, see N Poltorak, *European Union Rights in National Courts* (Wolters Kluwer 2015) 65–66.

[4] To the same effect, see van Cleynenbreugel, 'National Procedural Choices' (n 2) 186, who holds that the different review standards 'have not operated in distinctive and clearly demarcated timeframes'.

[5] ibid 186.

[6] S Prechal and R Widdershoven, 'Redefining the Relationship between "Rewe-Effectiveness" and Effective Judicial Protection' (2011) 4 *Review of European Administrative Law* 31, 41.

[7] The setting aside of national rules that make the claim may create a legal gap, 'and quite some creativity might be needed on the part of the national court to fill this gap: ibid 41, fn 54.

[8] M Beijer, *The Limits of Fundamental Rights Protections by the EU: The Scope for the Development of Positive Obligations* (Intersentia 2017) 266.

[9] P van Cleynenbreugel, 'The Confusing Constitutional Status of Positive Procedural Obligations in EU Law' (2012) 5 *Review of European Administrative Law* 81, 89–91.

The principle of effectiveness lays down negative requirements, which can be seen already from the negative formulation that national procedural rules should not make the enforcement of claims based on EU law 'virtually impossible or excessively difficult'.[10] As Lenaerts puts it, the principle of effectiveness merely seeks to 'neutralize the effect of national rules of procedure which hamper the proper enforcement of EU law, but are incapable of guaranteeing an effective protection of EU rights where national law does not provide sufficient … relief'.[11] In other words, the principle merely dictates that domestic provisions rendering the enforcement of Union law 'impossible or excessively difficult' must be set aside, and it will then be left to the Member States to provide an adequate solution.[12] This is different with respect to the principle of effective judicial protection, which implies not only negative but also positive obligations, thereby prescribing a Union standard of protection that needs to be applied in the Member States.[13] In *DEB*, for example, the Court held that it had to be possible, in principle, for legal persons, too, to rely on the principle of effective judicial protection enshrined in Article 47 of the Charter to obtain legal aid.[14] The case law suggests that the Court has demonstrated its willingness to 'rely on the Charter to develop directly applicable judicial standards of national procedure'.[15] The Court thereby 'concretises the requirements of judicial protection by balancing optimal rights protection with any countervailing objectives of an orderly judicial procedure [and the] outcomes of this balancing crystallise into doctrine'.[16]

As Póltorak has pointed out, the Court is very reluctant to speak of positive obligations in a direct manner, even though such obligations are clearly present in its case law.[17] She particularly mentions the duty to provide *locus standi*, referring to the Court's ruling in *Connect Austria*,[18] where the Court ordered a national court to refrain from applying a national measure precluding a third party from challenging a decision issued by a regulatory authority. This entails a positive obligation on the Member States:

> Such extension of *locus standi*, as compared with the one provided for in national law, in fact does not consist in the non-application of the provisions restricting this *locus standi*, as held by the Court, but in extending its scope beyond what has been provided for in the said provision. Therefore, it means application of a measure that does not exist in national laws.[19]

It is submitted that a *positive obligation to provide standing* for the protection of rights can be based on an interpretation of the right to effective judicial protection

[10] Prechal and Widdershoven, 'Redefining the Relationship' (n 6) 40.

[11] K Lenaerts, 'The Court's Outer and Inner Selves: Exploring the External and Internal Legitimacy of the European Court of Justice' in M Adams et al (eds), *Judging Europe's Judges: The Legitimacy of the Case Law of the European Court of Justice* (Hart Publishing 2009) 13, 15.

[12] van Cleynenbreugel, 'The Confusing Constitutional Status' (n 9) 89.

[13] van Cleynenbreugel, 'National Procedural Choices' (n 2) 178; and Prechal and Widdershoven, 'Redefining the Relationship' (n 6) 41–42.

[14] Case C-279/09 *DEB* [2010] para 59.

[15] P van Cleynenbreugel, 'Judge-Made Standards of National Procedure in the Post-Lisbon Constitutional Framework' (2012) 37 *EL Rev* 90, 94.

[16] V Roeben, Judicial Protection as the Meta-norm in the EU Judicial Architecture' (2020) 12 *Hague Journal on the Rule of Law* 29, 32.

[17] Poltorak, *European Union Rights in National Courts* (n 3) 97.

[18] Case C-462/99 *Connect Austria* [2003].

[19] Poltorak, *European Union Rights in National Courts* (n 3) 97.

enshrined in Article 47 of the Charter, read in conjunction with the obligation of the Member States to provide remedies enshrined in Article 19(1) TEU.[20] Consequently, when individual rights are at stake, it is not a matter of testing national standing doctrines against the principles of equivalence and effectiveness, but of applying a standing doctrine that is determined at the Union level.[21] Within the ambit of this doctrine, the principle of procedural autonomy does not apply. The argument is that,

> [a]s an extension of EU law itself, 'effective judicial protection' necessarily *precedes* any discussion on national procedural autonomy and mitigating conditions of equivalence and effectiveness. The Court establishes a particular obligation that needs to be translated into national legal orders as a matter of effective judicial protection.[22]

Signs of this approach are evident in the standing jurisprudence of the Court. The ruling in *Connect Austria* has been mentioned, yet this ruling concerned the interpretation of an explicit provision in secondary legislation, namely Article 5a(3) of Directive 90/387/EEC (Telecommunication Services), which stated that users and undertakings 'affected' by a decision of a regulatory authority have the right to appeal a decision. In its judgments in *Olainfarm* and *E.ON Földgaz*, on the other hand, the Court explicitly answered the question of standing with reference to Article 47 of the Charter.[23] In *Olainfarm*, the Court was asked whether the holder of an original marketing authorisation for a medical product had the right to bring an action challenging the decision of a competent authority authorising the registration of a generic medicinal product of another manufacturer, using his product as the reference product. Referring to Article 47 of the Charter, the Court held that the claimant had the right to challenge the decision of the competent authority that granted the approval of the generic, provided he was seeking judicial protection of a right conferred on him by Article 10 of Directive 2001/83/EC (Medicines Directive).[24]

In *E.ON Földgaz*, the Court was called upon to address the *locus standi* of a company to challenge a decision of a regulatory authority amending the criteria for deciding on applications for long-term reserve capacity in a gas pipeline. The Court held that Article 5 of Regulation (EC) No 1775/2005 – setting out the principles a regulatory authority is required to respect to ensure that access to the transmission network takes place under non-discriminatory and transparent conditions – was a protective measure conferring rights on users wishing to gain access to the network. Moreover, the claimant in the main proceedings must be regarded as potentially having its rights infringed

[20] Conversely, B Thorson, *Individual Rights in EU Law* (Springer 2016) 106.

[21] Similarly S Prechal, *Directives in EC Law* (Oxford University Press 2005) 150, who holds that '[t]he question of who should be considered as "persons concerned" by Community law provisions and, thus, what degree of interest is necessary and what is the appropriate test for standing is a matter to be decided under Community law'.

[22] P van Cleynenbreugel, 'The Confusing Constitutional Status' (n 9) 91. AG Szpunar argued along the same lines in his Opinion in Case C-282/13 *T-Mobile Austria* [2014] para 42, holding that the principle of procedural autonomy 'should not apply … to the actual possibility of bringing an action in order to protect rights that individuals derive from EU law'.

[23] Case C-104/13 *Olainfarm* [2014]; and Case C-510/13 *E.ON Földgaz* [2015].

[24] The ruling will be further analysed in section IV.C.

by the decision. Under these circumstances, the Court held that Article 47 of the Charter precluded national rules denying the claimant *locus standi* for the purpose of challenging the decision in question.[25] Although the Court expressed itself in negative terms – holding that Union law *precludes* domestic provisions denying the claimant standing – the Court was in fact saying that standing must be provided.

These rulings indicate that the Member State must provide for standing as a matter of Union law, to allow individuals to protect their Union rights. In other words, it is submitted that a positive obligation to provide standing can be inferred from Article 47 of the Charter.

One could ask what difference it makes whether the Union impact on standing consists of negative or positive requirements. Whether the Court starts off from the premise of national autonomy, or rather seeks a uniform solution to the question of sufficient interest, it might end up at the same place anyway. If the Court strictly scrutinises domestic solutions for compliance with the effectiveness test, hence imposing tight limits on the acceptability of national law, it would largely amount to the same as dictating the condition itself. There is, however, an important difference between these two approaches. The setting aside of incompatible domestic provisions will not necessarily provide adequate protection for individuals, and may indeed result in the 'creation of a legal void' where no legal avenue remains for the claimant.[26] This void can only be filled by the positive application of a Union standard of effective judicial protection.[27]

It is the *content* of this positive obligation that is the main object of this book. It is argued that the Member States must grant standing when three criteria are met: the claimant must be the holder of a Union right; this right must be adversely affected by the alleged infringement; and the claimant must demonstrate that he has a vested and present interest in the proceedings. Together these criteria constitute the *Union law doctrine on standing*.[28]

It is for the Court – as the final interpreter of Union law – to spell out what the principle of effective judicial protection requires with regard to standing. The case law of the Court governing the EU's private enforcement system is *ad hoc* and fragmented, since the Court can only respond to the questions that have been brought before it.[29] Moreover, in hard cases of constitutional importance, the Court limits its answers to what is necessary to resolve the case at hand:

> [T]he ECJ does not take 'long jumps' when expounding the rationale underpinning the solution given to novel questions of constitutional importance. On the contrary, the persuasiveness of its argumentative discourse is built up progressively, ie, 'stone-by-stone'.[30]

[25] Case C-510/13 *E.ON Földgaz* [2015] paras 45–51. The ruling is further analysed in ch 8, section IV.B.
[26] Poltorak, *European Union Rights in National Courts* (n 3) 95.
[27] The application of the principle of effective judicial protection 'may force the Member States and/or their courts to provide for access and remedies not existing in national law', cf R Widdershoven, 'National Procedural Autonomy and General EU Law Limits' (2019) 2 *Review of European Administrative Law* 5, 27.
[28] This doctrine will be fleshed out in ch 5, section IV.
[29] F Wilman, *Private Enforcement of EU Law Before National Courts: The EU Legislative Framework* (Edward Elgar 2015) 429.
[30] Lenaerts, 'The Court's Outer and Inner Selves' (n 11) 46.

There is clearly a need to examine a wider array of rulings handed down over time to get the broader picture. The Court has not (yet) adopted the approach well known from its state liability jurisprudence, explicitly setting out the conditions for standing more broadly.[31] What we have seen is rather a piecemeal elaboration of what the right to effective judicial protection entails. Consequently, this doctrine is – as of now – only embryonic in form. Moreover, as Aalto has warned, it is 'daring if not rash to attempt to construe perfect systems out of cases' as the ECJ builds up its case law 'incrementally, little by little'.[32] This is a result of the need to reach consensus, which explains the Court's tendency to limit the argumentative discourse to the essential.[33]

Only those invoking a Union right can benefit from the principle of effective judicial protection. Those who seek to enforce Union law without themselves being considered right holders must instead invoke the principle of *effet utile* or 'full effect'. The Court has used the latter principle in exceptional cases as the basis for imposing procedural obligations on the Member States. Perhaps the most well-known case is *Simmenthal*, where the Court held that every national court must set aside provisions of national law conflicting with Union law.[34] Another, more recent case is *VEBIC*, in which the Court derived from the effectiveness of Articles 101 and 102 TFEU an obligation to allow for the participation of competition authorities in appellate proceedings against their decisions.[35] The right to claim damages for competition law infringements, established in *Courage* (see chapter 3, section IV.C), also needs mention.[36]

In chapter 13, it will be argued, however, that the principle of *effet utile* cannot form the basis of a coherent Union doctrine of standing. Clearly, EU law needs to have effect in the domestic legal orders, yet the Member States are granted considerable leeway in determining how this should be achieved. The Court cannot be 'left with the formidable task of developing from scratch' principles applicable to claims brought in the public interest in the national courts.[37] Rather, the principle of *effet utile* is primarily of use in assessing whether a Member State has fulfilled its obligations, and for striking down domestic rules or enforcement regimes that unduly undermine the effectiveness of Union law.

[31] Joined Cases C-46/93 and C-48/93 *Brasserie du Pêcheur* [1996]. The Court's assertive stance in its state liability jurisprudence can be explained by the direct parallel to the liability of the Union organs. The Court held (ibid para 42) that '[t]he protection the rights which individuals derive from Community law cannot vary depending on whether a national authority or a [Union] authority is responsible for the damage'.

[32] P Aalto, *Public Liability in EU Law: Brasserie, Bergaderm and Beyond* (Hart Publishing 2011) 65.

[33] Lenaerts, 'The Court's Outer and Inner Selves' (n 11) 46.

[34] Case 106/77 *Simmenthal* [1978] paras 21–22.

[35] Case C-439/08 *VEBIC* [2010]. This is, however, not a 'pure' *effet utile* case, since effectiveness arguments were used for the purpose of interpreting Art 35 of Regulation (EC) No 1/2003 (Competition Enforcement). For an analysis of the case, see P van Cleynenbreugel, 'Transforming Shields into Swords: The Vebic Judgment, Adequate Judicial Protection Standards and the Emergence of Procedural Heteronomy in EU Law' (2011) 18 *Maastricht Journal of European and Comparative Law* 513.

[36] Case C-453/99 *Courage* [2001].

[37] A Afilalo, 'Towards A "Common Law" of Europe: Effective Judicial Protection, National Procedural Autonomy, and Standing to Litigate Diffuse Interests in the European Union' (1999) 22 *Suffolk Transnational Law Review* 349, 354.

III. Standing Before the Union Courts – A Useful Guideline?

A. Introduction

The obligation to provide effective judicial protection of Union rights is not only binding on the Member States, it is also binding on the Union itself.[38] The question is therefore whether the standing criteria relative to bringing cases before the Union courts, particularly under Article 263(4) TFEU, may give an indication as to what the principle of effective judicial protection also requires from domestic courts. In order to answer this question, I shall explore the case law from the Union courts.[39] I will argue that there are relevant differences between the two types of proceedings, and that the Court has partly justified the narrow standing conditions before the Union Courts by the complementary role of national courts in ensuring judicial protection. The value of this line of jurisprudence is therefore limited in the determining the procedural leeway granted domestic courts.

B. Strict Rules on Standing for Private Parties

The requirements of standing before the Union courts vary depending on the type of action brought. The Treaty provides for action for annulment (Article 263 TFEU); action for failure to act (Article 265 TFEU); and action for damages (Articles 268 and 340 TFEU). As regards action for damages, any natural or legal person who claims to have been injured by acts or the conduct of an EU institution or its officials may initiate proceedings for the purpose of seeking compensation for the damage allegedly suffered. The standing criteria pertaining to the other two types of action are not as straightforward. Judicial review of acts adopted by the institutions, bodies, offices or agencies of the Union is provided for in Article 263 TFEU, and actions for failure to act are governed by Article 265 TFEU. The Court has, however, held that the two provisions prescribe one and the same remedy.[40] The standing requirements for individuals are therefore identical under the two forms of action. Since the case law has primarily developed in relation to the former provision, this will be the focus of the following.

Standing of natural or legal persons is regulated by the fourth paragraph of Article 263 TFEU. A claimant can challenge acts addressed to him without having to fulfil any further conditions for standing. In order to challenge a decision addressed to another person or an act of a legislative nature, the claimant must establish both 'direct and individual concern'. With the Lisbon Treaty, the standing conditions were somewhat relaxed with respect to regulatory acts that do not require implementing

[38] See M Safjan and D Düsterhaus, 'A Union of Effective Judicial Protection: Addressing a Multi-Level Challenge through the Lens of Article 47 CFREU' (2014) 33 *Yearbook of European Law* 3, 4, who speak of this responsibility's being 'shared between the Union and its Member States'.

[39] Actions for judicial review are brought before the General Court (formerly the Court of First Instance), but may be appealed to the Court of Justice as regards points of law, cf Art 256(1) TFEU.

[40] Case 15/70 *Chevalley v Commission* [1970] para 6; Case T-395/04 *Air One v Commission* [2006] para 25; Case T-167/04 *Asklepios Kliniken v Commission* [2007] para 45.

measures, and a claimant seeking to challenge such an act only has to satisfy the condition of 'direct concern', not the more demanding condition of 'individual concern'. The reasoning behind this relaxation of the standing criteria was spelled out in *European Union Copper Task Force*:

> Where a regulatory act directly affects the legal situation of a natural or legal person without requiring implementing measures, that person could be denied effective judicial protection if he did not have a legal remedy before the European Union judicature for the purpose of challenging the legality of the regulatory act. In the absence of implementing measures, natural or legal persons, although directly concerned by the act in question, would be able to obtain a judicial review of that act only after having infringed its provisions, by pleading that those provisions are unlawful in proceedings initiated against them before the national courts.[41]

The Court has, however, given the third limb in Article 263(4) a narrow understanding, in particular in interpreting the term 'regulatory act' so as to exclude legislative acts, hence limiting the practical relevance of this more liberal standing test.[42]

The requirement of 'direct concern' entails that the measure must directly affect the claimant's legal situation and leave no discretion to the addressee of the measure who is entrusted with the task of implementing it.[43] However, it is the requirement of 'individual concern' that tends to constitute the bottle-neck of standing. The Court has adopted a strict test as to what constitutes 'individual concern'. The requirement that a measure must concern a claimant individually is usually not fulfilled if the measure applies to objectively defined situations and produces legal effects on categories of persons determined in a general and abstract manner.[44] The Court held in *Plaumann* that persons other than those to whom a decision is addressed may only claim to be individually concerned if that decision

> affects them by reasons of certain attributes which are peculiar to them or by reason of circumstances in which they are differentiated from all other persons and by virtue of these factors distinguishes them individually just as in the case of the person addressed.[45]

Plaumann, himself an importer of clementines, sought to challenge a Commission decision addressed to Germany, denying authorisation to reduce customs duties on clementines imported into the Union. The Court held that the decision was not of individual concern to Plaumann, as this type of commercial activity – clementine

[41] Case C-384/16 P, *European Union Copper Task Force* [2018] para 35.

[42] See Case C-583/11 P *Inuit* [2013] and Case T-262/10 *Microban* [2011]. Moreover, in Case C-456/13 P *T & L Sugars* [2015], the Court held that a regulatory act requiring any form of implementing measure under national law, although this is merely an issue of rubber-stamping, does not fall under the third limb of Art 263(4).

[43] Joined Cases 41/70 to 44/70 *International Fruit Company* [1971] and Case C-404/96 P *Glencore Grain* [1998] para 41 and Case C-486/01 P *Front National* [2004] para 34. The Court has exceptionally considered the claimants to be directly concerned, although the challenged measure leaves those entrusted with its implementation some degree of discretion. This has been the case, for example, where it was certain how this discretion would be exercised; see Case 11/82 *Piraiki-Patraiki v Commission* [1985]. See also Case T-435/93 *ASPEC* [1995].

[44] Joined Cases 789/79 and 790/79 *Calpack* [1980] para 9. A legislative measure may, however, exceptionally be of individual concern to some individuals, see Case C-309/89 *Codorníu* [1994].

[45] Case 25/62, *Plaumann* [1963]. See also Case C-583/11 P *Inuit* [2013] para 72; Case C-274/12 P *Telefónica* para 46; and Joined Cases C-408/15 P and C-409/15 P *Ackermann Saatzucht* [2016] para 30.

import – could be taken up by anyone. The *Plaumann* test is therefore often referred to as a 'closed category' test, implying that the claimant must belong to a class that is fixed and ascertainable at the date the measure enters into force.[46]

The strictness of the test has given rise to widespread criticism in legal scholarship.[47] However, the Court of Justice has not succumbed to attempts to relax the criteria for standing. In his Opinion in *UPA*, Advocate General Jacobs argued that the current test for standing did not afford individuals sufficient judicial protection.[48] In light of this Opinion, the Court of First Instance, in its ruling in *Jégo-Quéré*, adopted a new test, whereby an individual should be regarded as individually concerned by a regulation if it 'affects his legal position in a manner which is both definite and immediate, by restricting his rights or by imposing obligations on him'.[49] The ECJ did not, however, follow the Opinion of Advocate General Jacobs in *UPA*, and *Jégo-Quéré* was overturned on appeal; instead the Court upheld the strict *Plaumann* test.[50]

The Court did not find this problematic from the perspective of effective judicial protection, and drew attention to the 'complete system' of remedies and procedures established by the Treaty with a view to ensuring judicial review of the legality of acts of the institutions. It pointed out that where a private party cannot directly challenge Union measures of general application, they may be able to do so before national courts and ask them to make a reference to the Court for a preliminary ruling on the validity of the measure.[51] The Court went on to state that

> it is for the Member States to establish a system of legal remedies and procedures which ensure respect for the right to effective judicial protection [and] in accordance with the principle of sincere cooperation laid down in [now Article 4(3)] of the Treaty, national courts are required, so far as possible, to interpret and apply national procedural rules governing the exercise of rights of action in a way that enables natural and legal persons to challenge before the courts the legality of any decision or other national measure relative to the application to them of a Community act of general application, by pleading the invalidity of such an act.[52]

The Court's strict approach to standing has largely 'shut the door for private enforcement in direct actions' at Union level.[53] Rather, pursuant to Article 19(1) TEU, domestic courts are obliged to provide remedies sufficient to ensure effective legal protection of

[46] See, inter alia, A Albors-Llorens, 'Judicial Protection before the Court of Justice of the European Union' in C Barnard and S Peers (eds), *European Union Law*, 3rd edn (Oxford University Press 2020) 283. There is some flexibility built into this test, and the Court has on occasion adopted a generous interpretation of what constitutes 'individual concern'; see, eg, Case C-358/89 *Extramet* [1992] (stressing the economic impact on the claimant). For an overview of the various areas where the Court has applied *Plaumann* in a more liberal fashion, see AH Türk, *Judicial Review in EU Law* (Edward Elgar 2009) 74–95.

[47] See, among others, A Albors-Llorens, 'The Standing of Private Parties to Challenge Community Measures: Has the European Court Missed the Boat?' (2003) 62 *CLJ* 72.

[48] AG Jabocs in Case C-50/00 P, UPA [2002]. He proposed a new and more lenient test for 'individual concern', requiring only that the measure 'has, or is liable to have, a substantial adverse effect on [the claimant's] interests', see ibid para 60.

[49] Case T-177/01 *Jégo-Quére* [2002] para 51.

[50] See respectively Case C-50/00 P *UPA* [2002] and Case C-263/02 P *Jégo-Quére* [2004].

[51] Case C-50/00 P *UPA* [2002] para 40.

[52] ibid paras 41–42. See also Case T-600/15 *Pan Europe* [2016] para 51, where the Court explicitly held that Art 47 of the Charter could not be used to reinterpret the standing criteria laid down in Art 263(4) TFEU.

[53] P Wennerås, *The Enforcement of EC Environmental Law* (Oxford University Press 2007) 249.

individual rights stemming from Union law.[54] The limited access to the ECJ by private parties does not necessarily constitute a gap in the Union system of effective judicial protection, 'provided that the second subparagraph of Article 19(1) TEU essentially "picks up the slack" at the national level'.[55]

In practice domestic courts play a valuable complementary role in offering judicial protection against decisions issued by the Union institutions. Individuals may gain access to the ECJ indirectly through the preliminary ruling procedure, as the Court made clear in *European Union Copper Task Force*:

> [I]f, owing to the conditions for admissibility laid down in the fourth paragraph of Article 263 TFEU, the appellant cannot directly attack the regulation at issue before the European Union judicature, it can, by contrast, in the context of an action brought before a national court against an act by a Member State which is an implementing measure of the regulation, plead the invalidity of the latter and cause that court to refer questions to the Court of Justice pursuant to Article 267 TFEU …[56]

Whether this 'remedial complementarity'[57] is sufficient to ensure the effective judicial protection of individuals can, however, be questioned.[58] The indirect route to judicial review through domestic courts has several weaknesses, which were pointed out by Advocate General Jacobs in his opinion in *UPA*. A claimant is not entitled to require that the national court refer the case to the ECJ for a ruling on the validity of a measure, and such a procedure is in any event costly and time-consuming. Most importantly, however, where the contested measure does not require any acts of implementation by national authorities, there may be no national measure to challenge.[59]

The modest relaxation of the standing critera that took place with the Lisbon Treaty – with respect to regulatory acts that do not require implementing measures – did not adequately cure the problem of lack of standing, since legislative acts are excluded from its scope. The indirect route may well turn out to be a dead end, since 'it appears that the ECJ does not require Member States to ensure that individuals do actually have access to a court so as to be able to raise their concerns on the validity of EU acts'.[60] And, as

[54] See Case C-384/16 P, *European Union Copper Task Force* [2018] paras 116–17. For an account of the role of national courts in securing the judicial protection of individuals, see S Bogojević, 'Judicial Protection of Individual Applicants Revisited: Access to Justice through the Prism of Judicial Subsidiarity' (2015) 34 *Yearbook of European Law* 5.

[55] K Gutman, The Essence of the Fundamental Right to an Effective Remedy and to a Fair Trial in the Case-Law of the Court of Justice of the European Union: The Best Is Yet to Come?' (2019) 20 *German Law Journal* 884, 898.

[56] Case C-384/16 P, *European Union Copper Task Force* [2018] para 119. See also Joined Cases C-408/15 P and C-409/15 P *Ackermann Saatzucht* [2016] para 52. Domestic courts are obliged to refer the question of the validity of the Union measure to the Court, see Case 314/85 *Foto-Frost* [1987].

[57] Safjan and Düsterhaus, 'A Union of Effective Judicial Protection' (n 38) 6.

[58] There are still examples of individuals breaking the law in order to gain access to the Union Court; see, eg, Case C-616/17 *Blaise* [2019].

[59] See AG Jacobs in Case C-50/00 P *UPA* [2002] paras 41–44.

[60] C Lacchi, 'Multilevel Judicial Protection in the EU and Preliminary References' (2016) 53 *CML Rev* 679, 688, fn 55. Where an individual lacks standing, his only means of gaining access to court is by breaching the rules in question and challenging the validity of the Union law measure in subsequent judicial proceedings. This solution is problematic from the perspective of effective judicial protection, see C Koch, 'Locus Standi of Private Applicants under the EU Constitution: Preserving Gaps in the Protection of Individuals Right to an Effective Remedy' (2005) 30 *EL Rev* 511, 515; and Albors-Llorens, 'The Standing of Private Parties to Challenge Community Measures' (n 47) 87.

Ward rhetorically asks, 'In practice, how easy is it to persuade national judges to open up a channel for redress in the absence of a national implementing measure, and thus a lack of direct connection with the judge's own national jurisdiction?'[61]

C. A Divergence in Judicial Safeguards

The Court's general tendency to align the judicial safeguards operating at the Union and domestic levels does not seem to apply to standing rules.[62] On the contrary, there are clear signs that the Court is operating two different standards.[63] As will be seen (section IV.C), there are no indications that the Court requires a claimant to be affected in a way that distinguishes him from all others to be entitled to standing before domestic courts. In fact the Court seems to have rejected this strict approach in *Muñoz*, despite Advocate General Geelhoed's suggestion that domestic standing criteria should mirror those laid down in Article 263(4) TFEU.[64]

The Court's implicit rejection of parallel standing doctrines was sound, since there are good reasons for operating with different standards at the Union and domestic levels. First, a claimant adversely affected by a Union law infringement has a need for judicial protection, regardless of whether and how other private parties are affected.[65] It can even be argued that the need for judicial control increases when a measure affects a large number of people.[66] This militates against a requirement that a claimant be 'individually concerned' in the sense that his situation can be differentiated from that of all others. Second, since – as seen –private parties' access to the Union courts is severely restricted, the national courts are the primary venue for ensuring judicial protection of individual rights. Third, in legal scholarship it has been argued that the tasks of the domestic courts and Union courts differ: whereas proceedings before Union court are largely orientated towards objective legality control, the aim of domestic proceedings is first and foremost to protect Union rights.[67]

Taking into account the strictness of the standing requirements under Article 263(4), and its shortcomings when it comes to ensuring effective judicial protection, it is submitted that the provision gives limited guidance when determining the standards that national standing rules must respect.

[61] A Ward, 'National and EC Remedies under the EU Treaty: Limits and the Role of the ECHR' in C Barnard and O Odudu (eds), *The Outer Limits of European Union Law* (Hart Publishing 2009) 329, 346.

[62] This tendency is evident as regards liability in damages (see Joined Cases C-46/93 and C-48/93 *Brasserie du Pêcheur* [1996] para 42; and Case C-352/98 P *Bergaderm v Commission* [2000] para 41).

[63] To the same effect, see T Tridimas, *The General Principles of EU Law*, 2nd edn (Oxford University Press 2006) 454; and J Ebbesson, *Access to Justice in Environmental Matters in the EU* (Kluwer Law International 2002) 27.

[64] AG Geelhoed in Case C-253/00 *Muñoz* [2001] para 68. Case C-253/00 is addressed further in ch 3, section IV.B.

[65] N Fenger, *Forvaltning og Fællesskab: Om EU-Rettens Betydning for den Almindelige Forvaltningsret: Konfrontation og Frugtbar Sameksistens* (DJØF 2004) 694.

[66] ibid.

[67] R Barents, 'EU Procedural Law and Effective Legal Protection' (2014) 51 *CML Rev* 1437. The distinction is not, however, clear-cut, and alleging the impairment of rights is one possible way of fulfilling the requirement of 'direct and individual concern'; see further S Beljin, 'Rights in EU Law' in S Prechal and B van Roermund (eds), *The Coherence of EU Law. The Search for Unity in Divergent Concepts* (Oxford University Press 2008) 91, 104.

IV. The Union Doctrine of Standing: Fleshing Out the Criteria

A. Introduction

It was argued in section II that Union law requires Member States to furnish a claimant with standing when three criteria are met: first, the claimant is the holder of a Union right; second, this right is adversely affected by the (alleged) infringement; and, third, the claimant has a vested and present interest in the proceedings. Put differently, an individual whose rights are adversely affected cannot be denied standing if he has a personal stake in the outcome of the case. The aim of this section is to take a closer look at these three criteria, which together constitute the *Union law doctrine of standing*.

The right to have Union rights enforced could, if taken at face value, imply that the answer to the standing inquiry is to be found in the relevant Union law provision itself. In other words, one could perhaps assume that standing followed directly from the existence of a right.[68] Still, citing the existence of a Union right is not sufficient to be granted standing as a matter of Union law. The protective scope of a Union norm is determined in the abstract, yet nothing is gained from determining in the abstract who, for example, is entitled to clean air or a competitive market place (see chapter 8, sections III and IV respectively). Since Union rights are granted generously, there is an evident need – particularly when it comes to diffuse rights – to narrow down the category of persons who can draw on the right by initiating judicial proceedings. The issue of standing, it is submitted, concerns the question of whether a claimant is sufficiently affected by the breach's having taken place.[69] It is therefore the (threat of) violation of the abstract provision that merits consideration. In the words of Vitorelli, 'The entitlement of the right comes into existence from the violation. Therefore, one must define who the relevantly affected group is.'[70] Once a violation is (about to be) committed, it is possible to single out those entitled to draw on the right, and thus entitled to demand that the court intervene. It will be argued, to paraphrase Beljin, that the vaguer the definition of the protected group of people, the more the entitlement will depend on factual aspects of concern.[71]

That the Court has adopted such a twofold approach to the issue of standing – where, first, the protective scope of a norm must be examined to see whether the claimant's interest is covered and, second, it must be examined whether the claimant is sufficiently affected by the act or measure allegedly in contravention with this norm – was made

[68] Such an approach has been suggested in legal scholarship. Kadelbach holds that 'the concept of standing is inseparably intertwined with the scope of substantive rights [and that] standing before national courts follows the requirements of direct effect'; see S Kadelbach, 'European Administrative Law and the Law of a Europeanized Administration' in C Joerges and R Dehousse (eds), *Good Governance in Europe's Integrated Market* (Oxford University Press 2002) 167, 199.

[69] To the same effect, Fenger, *Forvaltning og Fællesskab* (n 65) 709.

[70] E Vitorelli, 'Collective Due Process of Law: Reconciling Representation and Participation' in L Cadiet, B Hess and M Requejo Isidro (eds), *Approaches to Procedural Law: The Pluralism of Methods* (Nomos 2017) 345, 367.

[71] Beljin, 'Rights in EU Law' (n 67) 118 and 122.

evident in the Court's ruling in *Tele2*.[72] When called upon to address the right of a third party to challenge an administrative decision rendered by a domestic regulatory authority in the telecoms sector, the Court stated that it was necessary to determine whether

> users and undertakings operating in competition with an undertaking (formerly) having significant power on the relevant market *may derive rights from the Community legal order* … and whether their *rights may be affected* by a decision taken by a national regulatory authority which is not addressed to them.[73]

In addition to these two criteria, it is also submitted that an interest requirement follows implicitly from the Court's jurisprudence. The concept of Union rights has been addressed in detail in chapter 4, section III. In the following, I take a closer look at the other two criteria forming part of the Union doctrine of standing (sections IV.C and IV.D respectively). But first, I shall attempt to substantiate the claim that right holders cannot *a priori* be excluded from the category of persons granted standing.

B. Right Holders Must in Principle be Entitled to Bring an Action

It seems safe to conclude from the case law of the Court that those falling within the protective scope of the norm infringed cannot be denied access to judicial process altogether. This follows, inter alia, from the Court's ruling in *Daihatsu Deutschland*, concerning the failure of a company to fulfil its obligation to disclose annual accounts under Directive 68/151/EEC (First Company Law Directive). Under German law, the courts could only impose fines in the form of a period penalty payment on companies failing to disclose their accounts, upon request of a member of the company, a creditor or the works council. The application of an association of German car dealers was therefore initially dismissed. The Court found this restriction unacceptable under the Directive, given that the fact that the Directive was intended to protect a wider class of people.[74]

That right holders must in principle be entitled to bring an action was also made evident by the Court in *Gruber*.[75] The ruling also serves to illustrate that standing does not follow directly from the fact that the claimant has a Union law right. The case concerned the right to judicial review in the environmental field. Directive 2011/92/EU (consolidated Environmental Impact Assessment (EIA) Directive) contains participatory rights of a group of individuals described as the 'public concerned'. The right to judicial review was laid down in Article 11(1) of the Directive, stating that Member States shall ensure that, in accordance with the relevant national legal system, members of the 'public concerned' having a sufficient interest, or alternatively maintaining the impairment of a right, where administrative procedural law of a Member State requires this as a precondition, have access to a judicial review procedure to challenge the substantive or procedural legality of decisions, acts or omissions subject to the public participation provisions of the Directive.

[72] Case C-426/05 *Tele2* [2008].
[73] ibid para 33 (emphasis added).
[74] Case C-97/96 *Daihatsu Deutschland* [1997] paras 22–23.
[75] Case C-570/13 *Gruber* [2015].

The Court was called upon to decide whether a decision of an administrative authority denying the necessity for an environmental impact assessment of a project, was binding upon neighbours, such as Ms Gruber, who were precluded from bringing an action against that administrative decision. The case arose in the context of a decision authorising the construction and operation of a retail park on land bordering property belonging to Ms Gruber. The Court held that not all persons coming within the notion of 'public concerned' must be entitled to a review procedure, but '*only those having a sufficient interest or, as the case may be, maintaining the impairment of a right*'.[76] However, it must 'in principle' be possible for individuals who are part of the 'public concerned' to bring an action, which means that the Member States cannot *a priori* exclude this category from the right to contest such a decision.[77]

The ruling demonstrates that having a Union right is not sufficient to trigger the principle of effective judicial protection, and hence being granted access to court as a matter of Union law. Although right holders must in principle be entitled to bring an action, a private party cannot derive a right to standing directly from the existence of a Union law right. It is submitted that in order to benefit from the principle of effective judicial protection, a claimant must also demonstrate that he is adversely affected by an infringement, and also that he has a vested and present interest in the proceedings. These two criteria will be addressed in sections IV.C and IV.D respectively.

C. Requirement of Being 'Directly Affected'

Determining whether a claimant is adversely affected by the challenged measure is often quite straightforward. As pointed out by Prechal, as a rule, persons falling within the personal scope of a Union law provision will be sufficiently affected by the misapplication or non-application of the provisions that give them some advantage or right; and since they will then have an interest in the judicial decision they are striving to obtain, they should be given standing.[78] For example, where a directive entitles an individual to an authorisation where the prescribed conditions are fulfilled, the right holder clearly has a right to challenge an administrative decision declining to acknowledge that right.[79]

The Court has on occasion presumed that such an interest exists, without further discussion. In *Olainfarm*, the Court found that the holder of a marketing authorisation for a medical product had standing to challenge the grant of a marketing authorisation for a generic product, where his product was used as a reference product.[80] Referring to Article 47 of the Charter, the Court held that the claimant had the right to a judicial remedy enabling him to challenge the decision of the competent authority that granted the approval of the generic, provided he was seeking judicial protection of a right conferred on him by Article 10 of Directive 2001/83/EC (Medicines Directive). This was the case because the holder demanded that his medicinal product not be used for

[76] ibid para 32.
[77] ibid para 45.
[78] Prechal, *Directives in EC Law* (n 21) 149.
[79] See for instance Case C-127/95 *Norbrook* [1998] para 108.
[80] Case C-104/13 *Olainfarm* [2014].

the purpose of obtaining a marketing authorisation for a product in relation to which his own product could not be regarded as a reference product within the meaning of the Directive. The Court did not address whether the undertaking was sufficiently affected by the alleged breach or what he stood to gain from the proceedings, as this was rather obvious from the circumstances of the case. Olainfarm would be put at a competitive disadvantage by placing a generic product on the market.[81]

While a sufficient interest in initiating proceedings may be presumed in the case of infringement of Union law provisions laying down individual entitlements, it cannot be presumed for Union law provisions protecting diffuse interests.[82] These types of rights accrue to wide category of people, and the need to delimit the range of enforcers is therefore particularly pressing. The Court has not been explicit as to the range of persons entitled to pursue infringements of provisions protecting diffuse interests. Boch argues individuals should be regarded as

> guardians of the [Union] interest, in so far as overseeing actions by member states, ensuring that member states comply with the [Union] obligations and fulfil their duties, in turn guarantees that individuals are not deprived of the benefits that would accrue to them [in the case of compliance].[83]

Support for such a liberal approach to standing cannot, however, be found in the Court's case law. The principle of effective judicial protection entitles private parties to vindicate their own rights, rather than the interests of the entire community involved. The general interest that individuals have in the government or private parties' duly observing Union law is, I submit, not sufficient to ground standing. There may well be Union law infringements that do not affect any private party such as to entitle him to sue. By way of illustration, an infringement of Article 101 TFEU, prohibiting agreements the object or effect of which is to restrict competition, does not necessarily affect the rights of customers or competitors so as to afford them standing.[84]

As to the magnitude of the adverse effects a private party must demonstrate in order to benefit from the right to judicial protection, the Court has been rather laconic. In *Kühne*, the Court held that the right to judicial control extended to administrative measures 'capable of *adversely affecting* the rights of third parties under Community law'.[85] Similarly, in *Tele2*, the Court held that the requirement to provide effective judicial protection applies to those deriving rights from the Union legal order and 'whose rights are *adversely affected*'

[81] AG Wahl explicitly stated that 'it seems justified to assume that the placing on the market of a generic will have an impact on sales of the reference product and competitive conditions in its regard'; see his Opinion in Case C-104/13 *Olainfarm* [2014] para 48.

[82] Similarly Prechal, *Directives in EC Law* (n 21) 149. Garth and Cappelletti define diffuse interests as 'collective and fragmented interests such as those in clean air and consumer protection'; see B Garth and M Cappelletti, 'Access to Justice: The Newest Wave in the Worldwide Movement to Make Rights Effective' (1978) 27 *Buffalo Law Review* 181, 194.

[83] See C Boch, 'The Iroquois at the Kirchberg; or, Some Naïve Remaks on the Status and Relevance of Direct Effect' in JA Usher (ed), *The State of the European Union. Structure, enlargement and economic union* (Longman 2000) 21, 32.

[84] The Court has, for instance, held that an agreement that has an anti-competitive object 'constitutes, by its nature and *independently of any concrete effect that it may have*, an appreciable restriction on competition'; see Case C-226/11 *Expedia* [2012] para 37 (emphasis added).

[85] Case C-269/99 *Kühne* [2001] para 58 (emphasis added).

by a decision taken by a national regulatory authority.[86] The Court has not been explicit as to whether the adverse effects on the claimant must reach a certain threshold in order to entitle the claimant to standing as a matter of Union law.[87] There are valid reaons for assuming that a *de minimis* threshold applies, since a claimant does not have an interest worthy of protection if the adverse effects on him are negligible.[88] At the same time, the threshold should not be set too high, because it would hamper the ability of private parties to serve as instruments in the process of implementation of Union law.

When spelling out the requirements for standing, guidance can be sought from the requirements under Article 13 ECHR. Article 47(1) of the Charter corresponds in essence to Article 13 ECHR, and we may recall that pursuant to Article 52(3) of the Charter, the meaning and scope of these rights shall largely be the same.[89] In order to be entitled to a remedy under Article 13, the individual must claim to be a 'victim' of a violation of one of the Convention rights. The victim test has primarily been developed in relation to the case law on admissibility under Article 34, which prescribes that the ECtHR may receive applications from any person, NGO or group of individuals 'claiming to be a victim of a violation by one of the High Contracting Parties of the rights set forth in the Convention or the protocols thereto'. There seems, however, to be a direct parallel between the victim test under Article 34 and the requirement of an arguable violation under Article 13 ECHR. The two provisions are concerned with the availability of remedies for the enforcement of the same Convention rights and freedoms, thus the coherence of the system supports the view that the victim requirement applies equally in relation to Article 13.[90] The Convention is premised on a principle of subsidiarity, and the ECtHR only deals with individual complaints when national remedies are exhausted (see Article 35(1) ECHR).[91] Support for such a parallelism can also be found in some rulings from the ECtHR. The Court stated, for instance, in *Monnat v Switzerland*, that

> it falls first to the national authorities to redress any alleged violation of the Convention. In this regard, the question whether the applicant can claim to be the victim of the violation alleged is relevant at all stages of the proceedings under the Convention.[92]

[86] Case C-426/05 *Tele2* [2008] para 48 (emphasis added).

[87] It seems that requiring the claimant to show actual damage will run counter to the principle of effective judicial protection, since the Court seems to be concerned with bringing infringements to an end, see Case C-237/07 *Janecek* [2008], further addressed in ch 8, section III.

[88] This question must be kept apart from the (related) question of whether there is a *de minimis* threshold for delimiting the scope of the relevant Union law provision. The Court has, for example, consistently held that Art 101 TFEU is not applicable where the impact of an agreement on competition is not appreciable; see, inter alia, Case C-238/05 *Asnef-Equifax and Administración del Estado* [2006] para 50. In the context of standing, the question would rather be whether the *impact on the competitor's position on the market* is appreciable.

[89] See Explanations Relating to the Charter of Fundamental Rights [2007] OJ C303/17.

[90] As the Court held in Kudla, the objective of Art 13 'is to provide a means whereby individuals can obtain appropriate relief at national level for violations of their Convention right before having to set in motion in the international machinery of complaint before the Court'; see *Kudla v Poland* App no 30210/96 (ECtHR, 2000) para 152 and *Öneryildiz v Turkey* App no 48939/99 (ECtHR, 2004) para 145.

[91] That the Convention States are granted the opportunity to redress violations at the domestic level is an 'important aspect of the principle that the machinery of protection established by the Convention is subsidiary to the national systems safeguarding human rights'; see *Akdivar and others v Turkey* App no 21893/93 (ECtHR, 1996) para 65.

[92] *Monnat v Switzerland* App no 73604/01 (ECtHR, 2006) para 30. See similarly *Karahalios v Greece* App no 62503/00 (ECtHR, 2003) para 21. See also *Tauira and 18 Others v France* App no 2804/95 (Commission decision 1995) para 3.

The concept of 'victim' is autonomous, and must be interpreted independently of domestic law concerning such matters as interest or capacity to initiate proceedings.[93] Pursuant to the case law of the ECtHR (and previously the Commission),[94] applications are only admissible if the applicant is able to substantiate that he is affected by the act or omission of the contracting state.[95] There is no right to have measures examined for compliance with the Convention rights in the abstract. As the Court held in *Asselbourg and 78 others*, the Convention

> does not allow an *actio popularis* but requires as a condition for exercise of the right of individual petition that an applicant must be able to claim on arguable grounds that he himself has been a direct or indirect victim of a violation of the Convention resulting from an act or omission which can be attributed to a contracting state.[96]

The notion of 'victim' is somewhat elastic, and there are 'uncertain and shifting boundaries between those directly affected by a particular measure and those remotely affected [and hence not covered by the notion of "victim"]'.[97] As a starting point, only persons *directly affected* by the conduct of the contracting state are granted victim status. However, in exceptional circumstances, also those affected by the infringement of another person's Convention rights are perceived as (indirect) victims (see further chapter 12, section III). Moreover, the Court has also accepted applications from potential victims (see further chapter 9, section IV). Exceptionally, the ECtHR has deviated from the requirement that claims must be brought by the actual victims of an infringement, and accepted applications from NGOs on behalf of a deceased victim.[98]

D. Requirement of a Vested and Present Interest

Member States are presumably not required to provide for standing unless the claimant has a *vested and present interest* in bringing a case to court. In other words, the claimant must have a personal stake in the outcome of the proceedings.

[93] *Gorraiz Lizarraga and others v Spain* App no 62543/00 (ECtHR 2004) para 35. See also *Scozzari and Giunta v Italy* App nos 39221/98 and 41963/98 (ECtHR, 2000) para 139; and *Zehentner v Austria* App no 20082/02 (ECtHR, 2009) para 39.

[94] Before the entry into force of Protocol 11 of the ECHR, individuals did not have direct access to the ECtHR; instead they had to apply to the Commission, who could initiate a case on behalf of the individual in the Court. The decisions of the Commission are therefore relevant in relation to the 'victim' criterion.

[95] The individual applicant should 'claim to have been actually affected by the violation he alleges', see *Klass and Others v Germany* App no 5029/71 (ECtHR, 1978) para 33. Although the person must be directly affected by the act or omission in issue, 'the existence of a violation of the Convention [is] conceivable even in the absence of prejudice'; see *Amuur v France* App no 19776/92 (ECtHR, 1996) para 36 and *Lüdi v Switzerland* App no 12433/86 (ECtHR, 1992) para 34.

[96] *Asselbourg and 78 others v Luxembourg* App no 29121/95 (ECtHR, 1999).

[97] DJ Harris, M O'Boyle and C Warbrick, *Law of the European Convention on Human Rights* (Butterworths 1995) 633. For an overview of the 'victim' test, see DJ Harris et al, *Harris, O'Boyle & Warbrick: Law of the European Convention on Human Rights* 4th edn (Oxford University Press 2018) 87, 92.

[98] See *Centre for Legal Resources on behalf of Valentin Câmpeanu v Romania* App no 47848/08 (ECtHR, 2014). The Court held (ibid para 105) that the Court's judgments 'serve not only to decide those cases brought before the Court but, more generally, to elucidate, safeguard and develop the rules instituted by the Convention, thereby contributing to the observance by the States of the engagements undertaken by them as Contracting Parties'.

As a rule, a claimant who can demonstrate that his Union rights are adversely affected by a breach of Union law will have an interest in initiating judicial proceedings. The Court has seldom addressed this issue explicitly, largely due to the fact that this criterion is most often satisfied. The interest requirement was, however, made evident in *Streekgewest*, where the Court was asked whether a breach of the standstill provision (now) enshrined in Article 108(3) TFEU may be relied on by a litigant who is not affected by distortion of competition arising from an aid measure. The Court stated that

> [a]n individual may have an interest in relying before the national court on the direct effect of the prohibition on implementation referred to in the last sentence of [Article 108(3)] of the Treaty not only in order to erase the negative effects of the distortion of competition created by the grant of unlawful aid, but also in order to obtain a refund of a tax levied in breach of that provision.[99]

In its case law pertaining to standing under Article 263(4) TFEU, the Court has repeatedly held that an action for annulment brought by a natural or legal person is not admissible unless the claimant has a vested and present interest in the proceedings, which means that the action must be capable of procuring him an advantage.[100] The interest must not only exist at the time when the application is lodged, but must also persist during the proceedings. If the interest upon which the claimant relies relates to a future legal situation, he must demonstrate that the prejudice to that situation is already certain.[101] We may recall from section III that one should be cautious when drawing parallels to Article 263(4) TFEU. Yet it is submitted that the requirement of a vested and present interest must also apply in the domestic context. As the Court held in *Mory, Mory Team and Superga Invest*, '[having an] interest in bringing proceedings is an essential and fundamental prerequisite for any legal proceedings'.[102]

While the interest criterion is closely linked to that of being directly affected, since the action *through its outcome* must be capable of procuring an advantage to the claimant, it is relevant what the claimant seeks to achieve with the proceedings. The interest requirement must be assessed with reference to the remedy sought. Private parties (allegedly) entitled to reimbursement of unlawfully levied charges or damages for Union law violations have, for example, a sufficient interest at stake to file a lawsuit. The outcome of the case – monetary substitution – will clearly serve to remedy the infringement at issue. The interest requirement may, however, merit further consideration in the context of proceedings for judicial review or declaratory or injunctive proceedings. Here it must be assessed what implications a favourable outcome has for the claimant. For instance, in relation to declaratory proceedings, the claimant will not have an interest in initiating proceedings if the defendant has never contested the rights at issue.

The requirement that the claimant's interest must be *vested and present* means that a claimant is generally not, as a matter of EU law, entitled to initiate preventive actions with a view to hindering future unlawful conduct or to challenge a decision before it is

[99] Case C-174/02 *Streekgewest* [2005] para 19.
[100] See, inter alia, Case C-133/12 P *Stichting Woonlinie* [2014] para 54.
[101] See, inter alia, Case T-138/89 *Nederlandse Bankiersvereniging* [1992] para 33.
[102] Case C-33/14 P *Mory, Mory Team and Superga Invest* [2015] para 58. See also case C-333/18 *Lombardi* [2019] with respect to Directive 89/665.

issued. It cannot be excluded, however, that a claimant in exceptional circumstances is entitled to initiate a preventive action. Advocate General Kokott stated in her Opinion in *Inuit*, with reference to Article 19(1) TEU, that 'conditions for admissibility of actions before national courts, including possible preventive actions for declarations and injunctions, may not be excessively restrictive'.[103] The Court did not, however, comment on the availability of preventive actions, and there are no indications in the Court's case law that Member States must provide for preventive actions. All the same time, a right of action to prevent a breach cannot necessarily be excluded, where the claimant can demonstrate that a breach is imminent and that the prejudice to his situation is already certain. In the context of competition law, an undertaking may, for instance, become aware that its competitor is about to commit an infringement that will adversely affect the undertaking's position on the market. If there are clear signs that such a practice will be implemented, the undertaking must arguably be entitled to initiate preventive action.[104] Such an action would normally take the form of declaratory proceedings.[105]

This would be in line with the jurisprudence of the ECtHR, which has left the door open for preventive actions in exceptional circumstances. The Court has held that normally the

> exercise of the right of individual petition cannot have the aim of preventing a violation of the Convention [and that it] is only in wholly exceptional circumstances that the risk of a future violation may nevertheless confer the status of 'victim' on an individual applicant, and only then if he or she produces reasonable and convincing evidence of the probability of the occurrence of a violation concerning him or her personally.[106]

To be able to initiate proceedings, it cannot be required that the *effects* of the Union law infringement have manifested themselves. For instance, if a state has already decided on a certain measure, the claimant does not have to await its implementation in order to challenge it.[107] In *CELF II*, the Court addressed the obligation of national courts to adopt safeguard measures in the form of interim relief with a view to enforcing the standstill provision in Article 108(3) TFEU. The Court held that there is an obligation to adopt safeguard measures provided, inter alia, the aid '*is about to be*, or has been, implemented'.[108] Generally speaking, it is preferable to prevent the adverse effects from occurring. To quote Advocate General Geelhoed in *British American Tobacco*, 'A system

[103] AG Kokott in Case C-583/11 P *Inuit* [2013] para 121.

[104] Hjelmeng addresses this situation from the perspective of domestic standing rules, and holds that the conditions for standing will 'most likely' be satisfied; see E Hjelmeng, 'Competition Law Remedies: Striving for Coherence or Finding New Ways?' (2013) 50 *CML Rev* 1007, 1016–17. For illustration he refers to Case 62/86 *AKZO Chemie BV v Commission* [1991], where an undertaking allegedly threatened to initiate measures contrary to (now) Art 102 TFEU (predatory pricing); see ibid paras 76–82.

[105] See AG Jacobs in Case C-195/98 *Österreichischer Gewerkschaftsbund* [2000] para 44. He spoke of declaratory judgments as 'an important element of developed procedural systems [since] they may prevent at an early stage potentially costly infringements of a contract or the law where the rights and obligations of the parties are uncertain'.

[106] *Asselbourg and 78 others v Luxembourg* App no 29121/95 (ECtHR, 1999). An example would be an expulsion or extradition case where the applicant may be able to provide that there is a prima facie risk of inhuman and degrading treatment; see *Tauira and 18 Others v France* App no 2804/95 (Commission decision 1995).

[107] This is also the case under Art 34 ECHR; see further Harris et al, *Harris, O'Boyle & Warbrick* (n 97) 85.

[108] Case C-1/09 *CELF II* [2010] para 36 (emphasis added).

of legal remedies should be established in such a way that it makes provision to prevent, so far as possible, damage arising or at least to limit the extent of the damage.'[109]

In relation to the non-contractual liability of Union institutions pursuant to Article 340(2) TFEU, the Court has also acknowledged the right to seek compensation for future harm in *Kampffmeyer Mühlenvereinigung*. The Court stated that (now) Article 340(2)

> does not prevent the Court from being asked to declare the Community liable for imminent damage foreseeable with sufficient certainty even if the damage cannot yet be precisely assessed. To prevent even greater damage it may prove necessary to bring the matter before the Court as soon as the cause of damage is certain.[110]

Given the close link between the liability of the Union institutions and that of Member States, this argument must be valid also for actions at the domestic level.[111]

A claimant will rarely have an interest in seeking review where the unlawful conduct has been terminated, a decision is no longer in force or where he has achieved what he sought prior to or in the course of the proceedings. But such an interest cannot be ruled out from the outset, and the assessment must be done on a case-by-case basis. Having an infringement recognised by a court may cause the defendant to change its course of conduct, which may benefit the claimant in the future.[112] The interest of the claimant can thus vary depending on whether he is a one one-shot player or a repeat player. Having a court recognise a breach can also be of relevance for later proceedings for monetary damages. In its case law relating to Article 263(4), the Court has also acknowledged that having the illegality of the contested act recognised can constitute a form of reparation for the non-material harm the claimant has suffered by reason of that illegality.[113] Considerations of moral redress can possibly – depending on the area – also be of relevance in relation to judicial protection before domestic courts.[114]

E. Judicial Protection of Procedural Rights

As seen in chapter 4, section III , the Union affords not only substantive, but also *procedural* rights.[115] While there is clearly a need to ensure judicial protection of procedural rights, these rights have special features that merit particular consideration.

[109] AG Geelhoed in Case C-491/01 *British American Tobacco* [2002] para 57. Although the case concerned whether the Court could rule on the validity and interpretation of a directive before the period for its implementation had expired, the argument is of broader relevance.

[110] Joined Cases 56 to 60/74 *Kampffmeyer Mühlenvereinigung* [1976] para 6. The Court's stance was confirmed in Case 281/84 *Zuckerfabrik Bedburg* [1987] para 14.

[111] On the convergence of these liability regimes, see Aalto, *Public Liability in EU Law* (n 32).

[112] By implication, Case C-432/05 *Unibet* [2007].

[113] See Case T-290/14 *Portnov* [2015] para 30.

[114] This would primarily be relevant where moral protection is an imperative aim of the provisions, such as for instance the right to non-discrimination under Directive 2000/43/EC (Equal Treatment Irrespective of Racial or Ethnic Origin).

[115] Differentiating between substantive and procedural rights can on occasion be difficult; see further Z Szente, 'Conceptualising the Principle of Effective Legal Protection in Administrative Law' in Z Szente and K Lachmayer (eds), *The Principle of Effective Legal Protection in Administrative Law: A European Perspective* (Routledge 2016) 5, giving an overview of the characteristics and particularities of procedural rights.

That access to judicial process also needs to be granted in the event of non-compliance with procedural provisions is clear from the Court's ruling in *Leth*.[116] The case concerned an individual who had purchased a house close to an airport, following which extensive works were carried out at the airport, resulting in increased noise. Many of these works were carried out without prior environmental impact assessments having been conducted. Ms Leth brought proceedings against Austria and claimed damages to compensate for the devaluation of her property and a declaration as to future losses. For present purposes it is interesting to note what the Court said about the nature of the obligations in Directive 85/337/EEC (former EIA Directive).[117] The Court held that the Directive confers on individuals a right to have environmental effects assessed.[118] The obligation of the government to carry out an environmental impact assessment thus has as its corollary a right vested in 'individuals concerned'.[119]

Importantly, though, the successful invocation of a procedural right will not necessarily result in the substantive result the claimant wants. Put differently, despite the procedural error, the Member State could have reached, and may still reach, the same substantive decision. When determining the conditions under which standing should be granted, one needs to take into account this special feature of procedural rights.

The criterion of being adversely affected by an infringement raises particular challenges in the event of procedural infringements, since not every procedural defect affects the content of the decision. *Altrip* lends support to the view that standing need not be granted where the procedural error has not affected the decision subject to challenge.[120] The claimant in the main proceedings sought the annulment of a decision by the Rheinland-Pfalz region, approving plans to construct a flood retention scheme, claiming that the environmental impact assessment carried out was inadequate. The Court stated that it would be permissible for national law not to recognise *locus standi* if it is established that it is conceivable that the contested decision would not have been different without the procedural defect.[121] Where that is the case, the claimant's rights are not impaired by the illegality. However, shifting the burden of proof on to the claimant could make the exercise of the rights conferred by the Directive excessively difficult.[122] Hence, the claimant cannot be required to demonstrate that the agency certainly or probably would have reached a different result in the absence of the procedural defect.

When it comes to procedural infringements, the requirement of a vested and present interest is also challenging, since it is not always easily determined whether the claimant will benefit if the court grants relief. Making the decision subject to all the right procedures, the government may still decide not to change its substantive decision. Building on the same line of thought as in *Altrip*, requiring the claimant to establish that the contested decision *will be altered* following the annulment would render the

[116] Case C-420/11 *Leth* [2013].
[117] Now Directive 2011/92/EU.
[118] Case C-420/11 *Leth* [2013] para 32.
[119] See also Case C-75/08 *Christopher Mellor* [2009] para 58, where the Court stressed the right to seek judicial protection of the rights under the EIA Directive, 'if necessary through legal action'.
[120] Case C-72/12 *Altrip* [2013].
[121] This was reiterated in Case C-535/18, *Land Nordrhein-Westfalen* [2020] paras 58–60.
[122] See Case C-72/12 *Altrip* [2013] paras 49–53.

enforcement of such rights 'virtually impossible or excessively difficult'. Standing should rather be granted, provided there is a *real possibility* that the state will reconsider the decision.

The infringement of procedural rules also poses challenges for claimants seeking compensation pursuant to the *Francovich* case law. Particularly the requirement of a causal connection between the infringement and the damage sustained can be hard to satisfy. Of course, the infringement of a procedural provision may result in a substantive provision's being breached. If that is the case, the procedural infringement is not necessarily of decisive importance in determining the issue of state liability. The Court's ruling in *A.G.M.-COS.MET* may serve as illustration.[123] A Finnish state official stated publicly on several occasions that a vehicle lift certified as conforming to Directive 98/37/EC (Machinery) was dangerous, causing the sales to drop. The Court found that the statement could be attributed to the Finnish state, since it gave the impression of reflecting official opinions. It found that the Member State had failed to comply with Article 7(1) of the Directive, which required the state to take all appropriate measures to withdraw from the market machinery liable to endanger the safety of persons or property, and to inform the Commission immediately of any such measure. Hence, the Court found that the state had violated Article 4(1), obliging the Member State not to 'prohibit, restrict or impede the placing on the market and putting into service in their territory of machinery and safety components which comply with [the Directive]'. If the Finnish authorities had informed the Commission of their plans to warn the public, there would have been no infringement of Article 4 of the Directive. Hence, a violation of this procedural rule led to an infringement of the substantive right to free movement of goods.[124]

F. Judicial Protection of Collective Rights

Some of the rights enshrined in EU law have a collective aspect, which justifies the use of the term 'collective rights'.[125] Where collective rights are infringed, Member States are not required to allow for individual actions. As pointed out by Dougan, Union law operates on the basis of a principle of parallelism or symmetry: an individual right requires an individual remedy, whereas a collective right may be enforced by way of a collective remedy.[126]

Collective rights are commonly found in – but not restricted to – the area of labour law. In *Mono Car Styling*, the ECJ held that the right to information and consultation provided for in Directive 98/59/EC (Collective Redundancies) was intended to

[123] Case C-470/03 *A.G.M.-COS.MET* [2007].

[124] HH Fredriksen, *Offentligrettslig erstatningsansvar ved brudd på EØS-avtalen* (Fagbokforlaget 2013) 208.

[125] The label 'collective rights' is used to describe both the rights of collective agents and rights to collective goods. Whereas the first form of collective rights focuses on the nature of the right holder, the second distinguishes according to the nature of the interests under consideration; see L Green, 'Two Views of Collective Rights' (1991) 4 *Canadian Journal of Law and Jurisprudence* 315. Here the term 'collective rights' is used in the first sense.

[126] M Dougan, 'Who Exactly Benefits from the Treaties? The Murky Interaction Between Union and National Competence over the Capacity to Enforce EU Law' (2009) 12 *Cambridge Yearbook of European Legal Studies* 73, 101.

benefit workers as a collective group, and the right was hence of a collective nature.[127] Consequently, Belgian rules that limited and placed conditions on individuals' right of action were found not to infringe the principle of effective judicial protection.[128] Collective rights are also found, for instance, in Directive 2001/23/EC (Transfer of Undertakings) and Directive 2009/38/EC (European Works Council). These collective rights are, however, the exception rather than the rule. Secondary EU law primarily contains labour law that grants rights to individual workers.[129] Rules that protect individual workers are found, inter alia, in Directive 2003/88/EC (Working Time). In *Pfeiffer*, the Court ruled that the maximum 48-hour-week laid down in the precursor directive[130] should be perceived as an individual right, and consequently that it could not be deviated from in a collective agreement.[131] Acknowledging the individual nature of these rights also means that they must be subject to enforcement by the individual right holder.[132]

The possibility of limiting individual claims has also been addressed by the Court in the context of public procurement law. In *Club Hotel Loutriaki*,[133] the Court was asked about a national rule whereby individual members of a tendering consortium were deprived of the possibility of having an allegedly illegal decision annulled, and also of the possibility of seeking compensation for individual damage suffered as a result of the irregularities in the contract award procedure. The Court had previously accepted that the interest in obtaining the contract rested with the consortium as a whole rather than the single members individually, and that this collective right was adequately protected by the availability of a collective legal recourse.[134] This case was distinguished, however, due to the fact that the claimant had claimed compensation for damage suffered individually. Under Greek law, the jurisdiction to annul or find the invalidity of an administrative act and, on the other hand, the jurisdiction to award compensation for the loss suffered were held by two different courts. Since the award of damages under Greek law was subject to the prior annulment of the allegedly unlawful act (and the legality of the act could not be reviewed as an incidental matter), the individual member of the consortium was in practice precluded from seeking compensation. The Court concluded that 'such a tenderer is thus deprived of effective judicial protection of the rights in that area of the law which it has under European Union law'.[135]

This ruling illustrates the parallelism previously addressed: whereas an individual right requires an individual right of action, a collective recourse is sufficient for the

[127] Case C-12/08 *Mono Car Styling* [2009] para 38.

[128] Restricting the *locus standi* of individual employees to exercise this right did not infringe the principle of effective judicial protection, because the beneficiaries of this right are representatives of employees, not individual employees; see Poltorak, *European Union Rights in National Courts* (n 3) 244.

[129] H Collins, 'Social Dumping, Multi-Level Governance and Private Law in Employment Relationships' in S Weatherill and D Leczykiewicz (eds), *The Involvement of EU Law in Private Law Relationships* (Hart Publishing 2013) 223, 239.

[130] Directive 93/104/EC (Working Time).

[131] Joined Cases C-397/01 to C-403/01 *Pfeiffer* [2004].

[132] As Collins explains, 'the individual worker can insist upon his or her legal rights regardless of whether the working conditions have been settled through collective bargaining', see Collins, 'Social Dumping, Multi-Level Governance and Private Law in Employment Relationships' (n 129) 251.

[133] Joined Cases C-145/08 and C-149/08 *Club Hotel Loutraki* [2010].

[134] Case C-129/04 *Espace Trianon* [2005] para 22.

[135] Joined Cases C-145/08 and C-149/08 *Club Hotel Loutraki* [2010] para 78.

enforcement of a collective right.[136] It therefore needs to be determined whether the provision infringed protects the collective entity, rather than the individual, in which case a collective legal recourse would be sufficient to ensure judicial protection.

G. Collective Redress Mechanisms

In the following, I examine whether the Member States are required to provide for collective redress mechanisms as a matter of EU law. For present purposes collective redress can be defined as 'a procedural mechanism that allows, for reasons of procedural economy and/or efficiency of enforcement, many similar legal claims to be bundled into a single court action'.[137] The terms used to describe the phenomenon of combining multiple parties' claims are various, including class action, multiparty action and collective action.[138] This is different from an *actio popularis*, where concerned citizens or certain organisations pursue litigation in the public interest.[139]

Individual actions are the usual tools used in order to prevent harm and claim compensation for harm suffered as a result of a rights infringement.[140] Yet the low stakes involved and the costs associated with losing the case may cause a rational sense of apathy, or the private party may lack the time or motivation to engage in lengthy proceedings.[141] The availability of collective redress mechanisms may reduce the burdens on the individual claimant and thus enhance effective access to justice. Collective actions may also serve a function beyond the protection of individuals, since they may deter potential infringers by having them internalise the cost of infringements. One could also add that the aggregation of claims can relieve the courts of the burdens of having to deal with several parallel proceedings.[142] Hence, while collective redress mechanisms facilitate effective judicial protection by transforming paper tigers into real Union rights, they also further the public interest in the effective and efficient enforcement of Union law.

As of yet, there is no secondary legislation providing for the harmonisation of national procedures on collective redress in the Member States. This may change with

[136] This distinction between collective and individual rights finds its parallel in the ECHR. Although the rights recognised in the Convention are first and foremost individual rights, the Court has stressed the collective aspect of Art 9 (freedom of religion). In *Hasan and Chaush v Bulgaria* App no 30985/96 (ECtHR, 2000), the ECtHR accepted that the state's obligation under Art 13 could be discharged by the provision of remedies accessible to representatives of the religious community affected, see paras 98–99.

[137] Commission Communication, 'Towards a European Horizontal Framework for Collective Redress', COM (2013) 401, 4.

[138] In focus is the aggregation of individual claims; litigation in the public or general interest will be addressed in ch 13. As Micklitz has pointed out, if the group of affected individuals is not identifiable then the 'boundaries between the collective and the public interest are swept away'; see H-W Micklitz, 'Administrative Enforcement of European Private Law' in R Brownsword et al (eds), *The Foundations of European Private Law* (Hart Publishing 2011) 263, 568.

[139] SB Lahuerta, 'Enforcing EU Equality Law Through Collective Redress: Lagging Behind?' (2018) 55 *CML Rev* 783, 787–88.

[140] Recommendation 2013/396 (Collective Redress), Recital 8.

[141] S Wrbka, *European Consumer Access to Justice Revisited* (Cambridge University Press 2014) 38.

[142] V Trstenjak and P Weingerl, 'Collective Actions in the European Union – American or European Model?' (2014) 5 *Beijing Law Review* 155, 156.

the introduction of new EU-wide legislative measures. In its 'New Deal for Consumers', the Commission has proposed the introduction of rules on collective redress for the protection of the collective interests of consumers, to enable qualified entities to bring representative actions on behalf of groups of consumers before civil courts or administrative authorities.[143]

The European Commission issued a non-binding Recommendation on collective redress in 2013, calling on Member States to implement collective procedures for the vindication of Union rights.[144] The Recommendation is not limited to specific sectors but covers all rights enjoyed by private parties under EU law. The instrument calls on Member States to provide for both compensatory and injunctive collective redress mechanisms.[145] The purpose of the recommendation is 'to facilitate access to justice, stop illegal practices and enable injured parties to obtain compensation in mass harm situations caused by violations of rights granted under Union law' while avoiding abusive litigation.[146] This formulation suggests a dual rationale covering both rights protection and behaviour control. Yet the rather particular terminology used in the Union law context – collective *redress* – indicates that the instrument is orientated towards judicial protection.[147] Moreover, if one takes a closer look at the specific provisions of the Recommendation, it is evident that the emphasis is on rights protection, behaviour control serving as merely a beneficial side-effect.[148] This primarily has to do with the fact that the Recommendation advocates an *opt-in* solution, where the express consent of the affected individuals is required.[149] Since the incentives to take action depend on the amount at stake, an opt-in solution is likely to result in the pursuit of mass damages, while scattered damages remain unpursued.[150] The first category comprises low- and lowest-value damages, which occur in multiple cases, whereas the latter category consists of cases in which relatively higher amounts are at stake.[151]

The Recommendation is not legally binding on the Member States. Temple Lang has suggested that the principle of loyal cooperation enshrined in (now) Article 4(3) TEU

[143] The proposed rules will permit qualified representative entities to pursue breaches of Union law in areas such as consumer rights, data protection, financial services, energy and telecommunications, and to seek compensation on behalf of consumers for losses sustained as a result of infringements.

[144] See Commission Recommendation of 11 June 2013 on common principles for injunctive and compensatory collective redress mechanisms in the Member States concerning violations of rights granted under Union Law. The Recommendation was adopted pursuant to Art 292 TFEU.

[145] Art 2 of the Recommendation.

[146] Art 1 of the Recommendation.

[147] See also C Hodges, 'Collective Redress: A Breakthrough or a Damp Sqibb?' (2014) 37 *Journal of Consumer Policy* 67, 72, who points out that the terminology also bears signs of the Commission's desire to distinguish the Union model from the 'class action' model found in the United States.

[148] This also finds support in Recital 10, where it is stated that the aim of the Recommendation is to 'facilitate access to justice in relation to violations of rights under Union law'.

[149] Art 21. Exceptions are, however, allowed, provided they are 'duly justified by reasons of sound administration of justice'.

[150] See Wrbka, *European Consumer Access to Justice Revisited* (n 141) 38.

[151] S Wrbka, 'European Consumer Protection Law: Quo Vadis? Thoughts on the Compensatory Collective Redress Debate' in S Wrbka, S Van Uytsel and M Siems (eds), *Collective Actions: Enhancing Access to Justice and Reconciling Multilayer Interests?* (Cambridge University Press 2015) 23, 42–43. As Wrbka makes clear, the rationale for not pursuing low-value scattered damages claims is a 'rational disinterest' or 'rational apathy', since the possible gain from proceedings is not worth the time and effort. In the case of high-value claims, it is rather the financial risk inherent in the loser-pays principle that may prevent right holders from suing.

obliges national courts to facilitate collective actions by large numbers of individuals with small individual claims.[152] There is, however, nothing in the Court's case law to indicate that this is in fact so. Clearly, if a Member State allows for collective actions for claims based on national law, it must also allow this for similar claims pursuant to the principle of equivalence.[153] Outside the ambit of the aforementioned principle, the finding of an obligation on the national legislature or the courts to provide effective collective redress mechanisms seems to be based on a far-reaching view of loyalty and effectiveness.[154]

As argued in section II, the principle of effectiveness – requiring that national procedural provisions do not make the enforcement of Union law 'virtually impossible or excessively difficult' – is merely a *negative* standard, providing a yardstick against which domestic provisions must be tested (and set aside if found to be incompatible). *Positive* obligations can only be derived from the principle of effective judicial protection enshrined in Article 47 of the Charter of Fundamental Rights. It is, however, highly doubtful whether an obligation to provide collective redress mechanisms can be derived from the aforementioned provision. Core elements of such an obligation (such as the qualified entities, form and conditions of the action, and representation requirements) cannot be clearly established, which indicates that legislative action is called for.[155] In the words of Warin:

> [A]ggregating a number of individual interests into a single action is not a natural feature of EU law; the Court sticks to the default setting, which is that an individual interest activates an individual right – unless additional legislation fosters the development of a new mechanism.[156]

Since collective redress is currently not required as a matter of EU law, this matter will not be explored further in the following.

V. The Union Right to Standing: The Scope for Balancing Countervailing Considerations

In the following, I examine whether the Union right to standing is an absolute right, or whether Member States can impose restrictions in this regard. One should perhaps

[152] JT Lang, 'Article 10 EC: The Most Important "General Principle" of Community Law' in U Bernitz, J Nergelius and C Cardner (eds), *General Principles of EC Law in a Process Of Development* (Wolters Kluwer 2008) 75, 101. Along the same lines, Nazzini has argued that 'the unavailability or the specific features of collective redress mechanisms in the Member States may be subject to scrutiny under the doctrine of effectiveness', see R Nazzini, 'Potency and Act of the Principle of Effectiveness: The Development of Competition Law Remedies and Procedures in Community Law' in Barnard and Odudu (eds), *The Outer Limits of European Union Law* (n 61) 401, 424.

[153] N Reich, 'Horizontal Liability in EC Law: Hybridization of Remedies for Compensation in Case of Breaches of EC Rights' (2007) 44 *CML Rev* 705, 739.

[154] To the same effect, D-P Tzakas, 'International Litigation and Competition Law: The Case of Collective Redress' in J Basedow, S Francq and L Idot (eds), *International Antitrust Litigation: Conflict of Laws and Coordination* (Hart Publishing 2012) 421, 421.

[155] D-P Tzakas, 'Effective Collective Redress in Antitrust and Consumer Protection Matters: A Panacea or a Chimera?' (2011) 48 *CML Rev* 1125, 1132.

[156] C Warin, 'Individual Rights and Collective Interests in EU Law: Three Approaches to a Still Volatile Relationship' (2019) 56 *CML Rev* 463, 477, with reference to Case C-498/16, *Schrems II* [2018] para 44.

assume that such restrictions were possible, given that Article 52(1) of the Charter allows for limitations on the exercise of the Charter rights insofar as they are

> provided for by law and respect the essence of those rights and freedoms [and subject] to the principle of proportionality [are] made only if they are necessary and genuinely meet objectives of general interest recognised by the Union or the need to protect the rights and freedoms of others.

The provision contains three elements: first, limitations must be provided for by law; second, any limitation must respect the essence of the right; and, third, any limitation must be proportionate. The last element means that the limitation must be suitable and necessary for the attainment of the objectives pursued, and that the measure must be proportionate *stricto sensu*.[157] Generally speaking, this exception also applies to Article 47 of the Charter, laying down the right to effective judicial protection, and it is clear from the case law of the Court that the Member States are allowed to impose restrictions provided these criteria are met.[158] In *Alassini*the Court found a mandatory out-of-court settlement procedure compliant with the right to effective judicial protection. The Court emphasised that the national provisions pursued a legitimate objective in the general interest, as the aim was the quicker and less expensive settlement of the relevant types of disputes and a lightening of the burden on the court system; nor was it evident that any disadvantages caused by the mandatory nature of the out-of-court settlement procedure were disproportionate to those objectives.[159]

There are both practical and political rationales underlying national standing rules, and these considerations may well in and of themselves be legitimate.[160] Moreover, national standing rules operate within a broader constitutional and cultural context.[161] The Court tends to be respectful of the constitutional traditions of the Member States, and generally seeks to balance legitimate domestic interests against the Union interest. Interestingly, though, in the Court's case law pertaining to *locus standi* there are no signs of the Court's resorting to its traditional legitimate justification test. The Court's view seems to be that claimants who derive rights from Union law and whose rights are adversely affected, should be granted standing to pursue a remedy.[162] The right to standing pursuant to the principle of effective judicial protection is therefore construed as an *absolute right*.

Although such a rigid approach may seem striking at first sight, this is arguably not the case if we take a closer look at what the obligation to grant standing actually entails. The reason why the Court does not, and should not, resort to this 'legitimate justification' approach in its case law on standing can be explained by the fact that a

[157] M Strand, *The Passing-On Problem in Damages and Restitution under EU Law* (Edward Elgar 2017) 45–46. See also Case C-205/15 *Toma* [2016] paras 45–46, where the Court speaks of a 'disproportionate' hindrance of access to court.

[158] Case C-279/09 *DEB* [2010] para 60.

[159] Joined Cases C-317 to C-320/08 *Alassini* [2010] paras 63–65. Similarly, Case C-75/16, *Menini* [2017] paras 53–60. See also Joined Cases C-439/13 and C-488/13 *Star Storage* [2016] paras 49–63, where the Court found that a requirement of a 'good conduct guarantee' in order to challenge public procurement decisions could be justified under Art 52(1) of the Charter.

[160] For an overview of these rationales, see ch 1, section I.

[161] Dougan, 'Who Exactly Benefits from the Treaties?' (n 126) 78.

[162] See, inter alia, Case C-426/05 *Tele 2* [2008] paras 32–33; and see further ch 8, section IV.

denial of *locus standi* would easily undermine the *very essence* of the right to effective judicial protection, since it would constitute an absolute obstacle to enforcement.[163]

Such a reading can be supported by the Court's ruling in *Schrems*, which concerned the validity of the Commission decision on the adequacy of the Safe Harbour agreement, pursuant to which data were transferred from the EU to the US. The measure did not provide for judicial review of compliance with the data subjects' rights, and the Court thus found the essence of Article 47 of the Charter to be violated. The Court held that

> legislation not providing for any possibility for an individual to pursue legal remedies in order to have access to personal data relating to him, or to obtain the rectification or erasure of such data, does not respect the essence of the fundamental right to effective judicial protection, as enshrined in Article 47 of the Charter.[164]

The crux lies in the phrase 'any possibility'. The Court seems to stress that the complete absence of a legal avenue for individuals alleging an infringement of their Union rights, impinges upon the very core of the right to effective judicial protection. In contrast, the Court held in *Puškár* that an obligation to exhaust available administrative remedies before seizing the court, respects the essence of the right to judicial protection, since such an obligation does not 'call into question that right as such', it merely imposes '[a]n additional procedural step … in order to exercise it'.[165]

As Gutman rightly points out, the essence of the fundamental right to an effective remedy appears to be underdeveloped in the case law of the ECJ as compared to other aspects concerning the Charter.[166] Yet the Court's reasoning indicates that a measure that does not afford any judicial remedy undermines the essence of Article 47 of the Charter, and thus will not be justified.[167] This aspect was also highlighted by Advocate General Bobek in his Opinion in *El Hassani*:

> [T]he duty of the Member States under the first paragraph of Article 47 of the Charter is to guarantee the very core or essence of the right enshrined therein, namely access to the courts. To preserve that core, judicial review of decisions cannot be excluded when an EU right or freedom has been infringed.[168]

This line of reasoning is readily transferrable to the matter of standing. After all, without legal standing a private party is completely barred from bringing an action to enforce his rights. Allowing the state to bar enforcement of Union rights through restrictive rules on standing would effectively render these rights nugatory.

[163] The essence of a right 'represents the untouchable core or inner circle of a fundamental right that cannot be diminished, restricted or interfered with'; see M Brkan, 'The Concept of Essence of Fundamental Rights in the EU Legal Order: Peeling the Onion to its Core' (2018) 14 *European Constitutional Law Review* 332, 333.

[164] Case C-362/14 *Schrems* [2015] para 95.

[165] Case C-73/16, *Puškár* [2017]. Similarly Joined Cases C-317 to C-320/08 *Alassini* [2010]. For a further discussion on this matter, see H Ellingsen, 'Effective judicial protection of individual data protection rights: Puškár' (2018) 55 *CML Rev* 1879, 1892.

[166] K Gutman, 'The Essence of the Fundamental Right to an Effective Remedy and to a Fair Trial in the Case-Law of the Court of Justice of the European Union: The Best Is Yet to Come?' (2019) 20 *German Law Journal* 884, 885.

[167] ibid 894. The essence of the right to a remedy would moreover be infringed if a Member State's legal system were to allow a final binding judicial decision to remain ineffective to the detriment of a private party, see Case C-752/18 *Deutsche Umwelthilfe* [2019] paras 35–36.

[168] Opinion of AG Bobek in Case C-403/16 *El Hassani* [2017] para 110.

Another reason for arguing that we are dealing with an absolute right can be found in the fact that we are dealing with a positive – as opposed to a merely negative – obligation. It has been argued that the obligation to provide private parties with standing is a *positive* obligation, requiring the state to take active measures.[169] Such positive obligations have certain features that set them apart from negative obligations, which require the state to *abstain* from taking certain measures. It may well be that the Court has been influenced by the way the ECtHR goes about determining the existence of positive obligations. The approach of the Strasbourg Court involves striking a balance between the general interest of the community and the interest of the individual.[170] When determining whether a state is under a positive obligation to act, the ECtHR also considers arguments militating against the imposition of such an obligation.[171] This entails a 'merging of the two stages of review' that in relation to negative obligations are normally kept apart, namely, first, whether a right exists and, second, whether a restriction can be objectively justified.[172] This is arguably also the approach adopted by the Court. The argument is that when the Court has taken upon itself to specify the criteria for standing, it has also taken into account countervailing considerations, and found that these have to yield for the sake of protecting Union rights. The Member States are consequently prevented from objectively justifying restrictions to the right to standing within the bounds of the Court's doctrine.

Where the three conditions spelled out above are met – the claimant is the holder of a Union right, this right is adversely affected, and the claimant has a vested and present interest in the proceedings – standing must be provided as a matter of EU law, and there is no scope left for procedural autonomy. Member States cannot impose supplementary conditions, as this would call into question the very right to standing. This standing doctrine is, however, merely a minimum standard, and Member States are free to adopt more liberal standing rules.[173] As will be seen in chapter 13, on occasion they may also be *obliged* to afford standing in order to ensure the effective enforcement of Union law in the Member State.

Although it has been argued that the states are under an obligation to grant standing where Union law criteria are met, a caveat is nevertheless in order. Article 54 of the Charter prohibits the abuse of Charter rights, and reads that nothing in the Charter shall be interpreted as implying a right to 'engage in any activity or to perform any act aimed at the destruction of any of the rights and freedoms recognized in this Charter or at their limitation to a greater extent than is provided for herein'. The right of access to court therefore cannot be relied on to engage in abusive litigation.[174]

[169] See ch 5, section II.

[170] This 'fair balance test' is spelled out, inter alia, in *Velosa Barreto v Portugal* App no 18072/91 (ECtHR, 1995) para 23 and *Rees v the United Kingdom* App no 9532/81 (ECtHR, 1986) para 37.

[171] Hence, 'there are limits to positive obligations resulting from the necessity of balancing interests'; see H-J Cremer, *Human Rights and the Protection of Privacy in Tort Law: A Comparison between English and German Law* (Routledge-Cavendish 2010) 125.

[172] Beijer, *The Limits of Fundamental Rights Protections by the EU* (n 8) 53. See further J Gerards and H Senden, 'The Structure of Fundamental Rights and the European Court of Human Rights' (2009) 7 *International Journal of Constitutional Law* 619, 634–36.

[173] See, eg, Case C-54/07 *Feryn* [2008], addressed further in ch 13, section III.

[174] Litigation can be seen as abusive 'when it is intentionally targeted against law-abiding businesses to cause reputational damage or to influct an undue financial burden on them'; see Commission Communication, 'Towards a European Horizontal Framework for Collective Redress', COM(2013) 401, 7.

The Court has consistently held that Union law cannot be relied on for abusive or fraudulent ends.[175] What this means more specifically with regard to Article 47 of the Charter remains to be clarified. It must be clear that a legal action can be harmful to a defendant – both in terms of costs and reputation – even if the action is unlikely to succeed.[176] The right to access to court cannot reasonably be read to cover the right to engage in vexatious litigation with the aim of harassing the defendant. But litigation that is not meant to harass can also be contrary to the aim of the Union law provisions invoked. For instance in the field of competition law, competitors may use allegations of competition law infringements strategically to chill competition. As pointed out by Hjelmeng, 'In this respect, competitors' incentives do not fit well with the goals of competition law; competitors generally complain about too much and not too little competition.'[177] How the carve out in Article 54 – on abuse of rights – should be interpreted with respect to the right to court is too soon to tell, due to the lack of relevant case law.[178]

The Court has also held that the initiation of a legal action may, in highly exceptional circumstances, constitute an abuse of dominant position contrary to Article 102 TFEU.[179] That recourse to litigation may amount to a competition law infringement was made clear by the Court in *Huawei*.[180] The case concerned proceedings initiated by Huawei, the owner of a patent that is essential to a standard established by a standardisation body ('standard-essential patent'). The company sought an injunction against a company that used the patent without a licence, after unsuccessful attempts to negotiate a licence agreement for that patent on fair, reasonable and non-discriminatory terms. The Court held that although the proprietor of the essential patent at issue had the right to bring an action for the protection of that right, the fact that a standard essential patent was indispensable to the competitors' manufacture of their products meant that the proprietor could prevent competitors' products from appearing or remaining on the market. In order to prevent an action from being regarded as abusive, the Court held that the proprietor must comply with specific requirements to ensure a fair balance between the interests concerned. The case confirms the possibility that the initiation of a legal action may constitute an abuse of dominant position contrary to Article 102. Yet given the importance of ensuring access to court for the vindication of Union rights, it is only in wholly exceptional circumstances that the institution of legal proceedings is capable of constituting such a breach.[181]

[175] See, inter alia, Case 39/86 *Lair* [1988] para 43 and Case C-206/94 *Brennet* [1996] para 24. The Court has, however, held that reliance on domestic provisions on abuse of rights must not prejudice the full effect and uniform application of Union law in the Member States, see Case C-367/96 *Kefalas* [1998] para 22.

[176] Wilman, *Private Enforcement of EU Law Before National Courts* (n 29) 487–88.

[177] Hjelmeng, 'Competition Law Remedies: Striving for Coherence or Finding New Ways?' (n 104) 1032.

[178] See, however, Case C-373/97 *Diamantis* [2000], which indicates that the remedy chosen may be of relevance in determining whether there is an abuse of rights.

[179] See Case T-111/96 *Promedia* [1998] para 60.

[180] Case C-170/13 *Huawei* [2015]. See further N Banasevic, 'The Implications of the Court of Justice's Huawei/ZTE Judgment' (2015) 6 *Journal of European Competition Law & Practice* 463.

[181] Case T-111/96 *Promedia* [1998] para 60.

VI. The Effects of the Doctrine in a Concrete Case

A. Introduction

In the following, I explore how the principle of effective judicial protection operates in a *concrete case before the court*. The principle is clearly binding on the Member States' legislatures and executives, in the sense that they have to establish a system of legal remedies and procedures that ensures respect for the right to effective judicial protection of individuals' rights under EU law.[182] In the words of Roeben, the right to effective judicial protection 'is also the right to a state of affairs, beyond a specific omission or action [and it] generates requirements and standards for general organization and procedure as well for individual judicial decisions'.[183] Any provision incompatible with these Union law requirements must be removed from the domestic legal order.[184] Moreover, if no procedure is available that will ensure the effective protection of Union law rights in the Member State, it may prove necessary to introduce into the national legal system a separate procedure for ascertaining the compliance of national law with Union law.[185] The focus in the following is on how these principles operate in the context of judicial proceedings. The principle of effective judicial protection can take effect indirectly through the interpretation of domestic law (section VI.B), but the principle can also have direct effect (see section VI.C).

The case law relating to effective judicial protection has primarily developed in the realm of administrative law. The Court has, however, 'transplanted' this principle to horizontal relations without questioning whether there are relevant differences that would merit a distinction.[186] It is now undisputed that the aforementioned principle also applies when the claimant's Union law rights have been breached by another private party.[187] The Court seems, however, to be less vigorous and intrusive when it comes to horizontal enforcement.[188] Particularly as regards the remedies that must be made

[182] The autonomy granted to legislators in procedural matters is arguably greater than that of the courts, see A Wallerman, 'Towards an EU Law Doctrine on the Exercise of Discretion in National Courts? The Member States' Self-Imposed Limits on National Procedural Autonomy' (2016) 53 *CML Rev* 339. She argues that, pursuant to the principle of loyal cooperation enshrined in Art 4(3) TEU, 'EU law places demands on national courts even if they act within their competence according to national law and even if the national rule itself is not to be set aside' (ibid 359).

[183] Roeben, 'Judicial Protection as the Meta-norm' (n 16) 40.

[184] See Case 104/86 *Commission v Italy* [1988] para 12.

[185] Poltorak, *European Union Rights in National Courts* (n 3) 152. In order to ensure effective judicial protection, the Member State must, of course, not only make such a procedure available, but also provide standing in relation to it; see Engström, 'The Europeanisation of Remedies and Procedures Through Judge-Made Law' (n 1) 127–28.

[186] Leczykiewicz is critical, pointing out that employment of the principle of effective judicial protection may lead to an 'unwarranted extension' of a public law doctrine to a private law context, see D Leczykiewicz, 'The Constitutional Dimension of Private Law Liability Rules in the EU' in Leczykiewicz and Weatherill (eds), *The Involvement of EU Law in Private Law Relationships* (n 129) 199, 216.

[187] See, *inter alia*, Case C-177/88 *Dekker* [1990]; Case C-180/95 *Draehmpaehl* [1997]; Case C-169/14 *Sánchez Morcillo* [2014].

[188] H-W Micklitz, 'The ECJ Between the Individual Citizen and the Member States – A Plea for a Judge-Made European Law on Remedies' in H-W Micklitz and B de Witte (eds), *The European Court of Justice and the Autonomy of the Member States* (Intersentia 2012) 347, 373.

available, the Court has been more prescriptive in the context of infringements committed by the state.[189]

It should be stressed at the outset that the principle of effective judicial protection cannot be construed so as to impose obligations directly on individuals. It is the *Member States'* duty to grant effective judicial protection, even if the claim in its substantive aspects is directed against a private party. Article 51(1) of the Charter makes it clear that the Charter, here Article 47, is not addressed to individuals. It is therefore incumbent on Member States to guarantee access to court and effective remedies for those whose rights have been infringed by another private party. The argument is that disputes involving private parties *inter se* should be understood as 'triangular in nature', meaning that the right holder's right to effective judicial protection is binding upon the national court deciding the case, rather than the other private party.[190] Put differently, proceedings between individuals involve public law considerations since it is the domestic court that is required to afford such protection.[191]

B. Indirect Effect: Duty of Consistent Interpretation

When a private party initiates proceedings with a view to enforcing Union law, national courts must strive first of all to interpret national standing rules such as to comply with the principle of effective judicial protection. As the Court held in *Unibet*:

> [I]t is for the national courts to interpret the procedural rules governing actions brought before them … in such a way as to enable those rules, wherever possible, to be implemented in such a manner as to contribute to the attainment of the objective … of ensuring effective judicial protection of an individual's rights under Community law.[192]

The courts of the Member States must do whatever lies within their jurisdiction so as to render these principles operative in a concrete case. This means that the domestic court will have to interpret domestic standing rules so as to comply with Union law requirements to the greatest extent possible. National courts must, however, apply the interpretative methods recognised by domestic law, and the courts are not obliged to resort to a *contra legem* interpretation.[193] The possibility of successfully invoking the principle of consistent interpretation therefore depends on how national standing doctrines are formulated. In jurisdictions operating with vaguely formulated interest requirements, the individual will be well served by an interpretation compatible with Union law, whereas courts in states operating with more rigid requirements may resist such interpretation.[194]

[189] The field of competition law constitutes an exception in this respect, see ch 3, section IV.C.

[190] Dougan, *National Remedies Before the Court of Justice* (n 3) 60.

[191] R Gordon and R Moffatt, *EU Law in Judicial Review*, 2nd edn (Oxford University Press 2014) 152. Along the same lines, C Mak, 'Rights and Remedies: Article 47 EUCFR and Effective Judicial Protection in European Private Law Matters' in H-W Micklitz (ed), *Constitutionalization of European Private Law* (Oxford University Press 2014) 236, 242–43.

[192] See Case C-432/05 *Unibet* [2007] para 44.

[193] Case C-268/06 *Impact* [2008] para 100; Case C-282/10 *Dominguez* [2012] para 25; Case C-176/12 *AMS* [2014] para 39; and Case C-441/14 *Dansk Industri* [2016] para 32.

[194] On various forms of standing doctrines, see, in particular, ch 8, section II.

Nevertheless, the obligation of national courts is not exhausted by using Union law as an interpretive device; the obligation extends even further. As the Court held in *Deutsche Umwelthilfe*:

> [W]here it is unable to interpret national law in compliance with the requirements of EU law, the national court, hearing a case within its jurisdiction, has, as an organ of a Member State, the obligation to disapply any provision of national law which is contrary to a provision of EU law with direct effect in the case pending before it.[195]

As will be seen in the next section, domestic courts are also obliged to afford standing directly on the basis of Article 47 of the Charter.

C. Direct Effect

Article 47 of the Charter, prescribing the right to effective judicial protection, must be seen as sufficiently unconditional and precise to be relied upon before domestic courts without further implementing legislation. As the Court held in *Egenberger*, the provision is 'sufficient in itself and does not need to be made more specific by provisions of EU or national law to confer on individuals a right which they may rely on as such'.[196] The Court has in several rulings required national courts to admit an action seeking to protect a Union right, irrespective of domestic procedural rules.

The first case where the Court expressed itself in such assertive terms was *Borelli*, where the Court was asked about the right to challenge a preparatory measure rendered in the course of a composite decision-making procedure. The Court held that it is

> for the national courts … to rule on the lawfulness of the national measure in issue on the same terms on which they review any definitive measure adopted by the same national authority which is capable of adversely affecting third parties and, consequently, to regard an action brought for that purpose as admissible even if the domestic rules on procedure do not provide for this in such a case.[197]

The Court used similar formulations in *Kühne* and *Liivimaas Lihaveis*.[198] Admittedly, these cases did not directly concern restrictive rules on standing but rather limitations as to the type of act susceptible to judicial review. Still, by requiring the Member States to review measures capable of adversely affecting the rights of third parties, the Court is at the same time opening up the right of such third parties *to seek judicial review*,

[195] Case C-752/18, *Deutsche Umwelthilfe* [2019] para 42. The Court included the caveat that the principle of effective judicial protection does not oblige the national court to disapply a provision of national law if, in doing so, it would infringe another fundamental right guaranteed by EU law. In such a case, the fundamental rights at issue must be weighed against one another (see paras 43–45).

[196] Case C-414/16 *Egenberger* [2018] para 78. This was reiterated in Joined Cases C-585/18, C-624/18 and C-625/18, *A.K.*, [2019] para 162.

[197] Case C-97/91 *Borelli* [1992] para 13. See, however, Case C-219/17 *Berlusconi* [2018], where the Court made it clear that national courts are prohibited from reviewing national preparatory acts that are not binding on the EU authority.

[198] See Case C-269/99 *Kühne* [2001] para 58 and Case C-562/12 *Liivimaas Lihaveis* [2014] para 75.

the necessary corollary being that a private party must gain standing before domestic courts. In the words of Dougan,

> the whole thrust of the Court's remedies jurisprudence in general and the judgment in *Borelli* in particular appeared to support the position that, where the Member State fails to comply with the obligation to provide access to judicial process, the Court will intervene in the national legal system and order that jurisdiction to entertain the Community claim be accepted, even if this means creating competence where there was none before.[199]

An exception must arguably be made for situations where the Member State has failed to identify an appropriate court with jurisdiction to rule on the sort of claim at issue. The Union operates according to a principle of institutional autonomy, implying that it is for the legal system of each Member State to determine which court or tribunal has jurisdiction to hear disputes involving individual rights derived from Union law.[200] There is some support in the Court's jurisprudence for the position that the duty to ensure effective judicial protection applies to national courts only as regards actions falling within their jurisdiction.[201] In *Connect Austria*, the Court held that a national court or tribunal that would be competent to hear a case 'if it was not prevented from doing so by a provision of national law which explicitly excluded its competence', has the obligation to disapply that provision.[202] Moreover, in *E.ON Földgaz*, the Court found that the right to effective judicial protection in Article 47 of the Charter precluded national legislation 'concerning the exercise of rights of action before the court or tribunal *having jurisdiction* to review the lawfulness of acts of a regulatory authority' that did not allow the claimant standing.[203] In case of a 'gap in jurisdiction', it can be argued that 'the individual's only recourse lies in an action for reparation against the Member State under *Francovich*'.[204]

It is therefore submitted that a national court or tribunal *that has jurisdiction* to rule on a particular category of claims, is bound to exercise that jurisdiction upon the request of a private party whose Union rights are adversely affected by an infringement. The principle of effective judicial protection dictates that standing must be granted, regardless of the standing doctrine normally applicable in the relevant Member State.

[199] M Dougan, 'The *Francovich* Right to Reparation: Reshaping the Contours of Community Remedial Competence' (2000) 6 *European Public Law* 103, 121. Prechal has also suggested that the Court's 'remedies jurisprudence' may amount to a 'direct empowerment by Community law … of the national courts to extend their existing powers or to assume, on the basis of Community law alone, new powers which do not exist under national law': see Prechal, *Directives in EC Law* (n 21) 171–72.

[200] See, inter alia, Case 179/84 *Bozzetti* [1985] para 17 and Joined Cases C-10 to C-22/97 *IN.CO.GE* [1998] para 14.

[201] See Dougan, *National Remedies Before the Court of Justice* (n 3) 9–12.

[202] Case C-462/99 *Connect Austria* [2003] para 41 and Joined Cases C-585/18, C-624/18 and C-625/18, *A.K* [2019]. Conversely, see Case C-54/96 *Dorsch Consult* [1997] and Case C-111/97 *EvoBus Austria* [1998], where the Member State had failed to designate a court with jurisdiction to deal with the relevant category of claims. On this distinction, see further Dougan, *National Remedies Before the Court of Justice* (n 3) 9–12.

[203] Case C-510/13 *E.ON Földgaz* [2015] para 51 (emphasis added). See also Joined Cases C-924/19 PPU og C-925/19 PPU *FMS* [2020] para 146.

[204] M Dougan, 'The Vicissitudes of Life at the Coalface: Remedies and Procedures for Enforcing Union Law before the National Courts' in P Craig and G de Búrca (eds), *The Evolution of EU law* (Oxford University Press 2011) 407, 432, with reference to Joined Cases C-6/90 and C-9/90 *Francovich* [1991].

VII. The Legality and Legitimacy of a Court-made Doctrine of Standing

Having concluded that a Union law doctrine of standing can be inferred from the principle of effective judicial protection, under Article 47 of the Charter, it is not hard to imagine critical voices raising concerns. Such criticism could extend both to the *legality* and the *legitimacy* of such a doctrine. By adopting a positivist conception of law (separating the question of the validity of law from that of its moral force),[205] it is possible to keep apart the issues of legal validity and legitimacy.

In order to determine what constitutes valid law in the Union context, we need to identify the 'ultimate rule of recognition' or 'basic norm' of Union law, by which the validity of any rule can be evaluated.[206] The primary law of the Union is perceived as the 'higher law' of the Union, hence inferior norms are valid when they are within the Treaties.[207] The division of competences between the Union and the Member States is regulated by Article 5 TEU, laying down the principles of conferral, subsidiarity and proportionality.[208] These principles have, however, not proved 'capable of curbing the Court's jurisprudence'.[209]

When it comes to the Court's competence to craft standing rules, one also needs to pay regard to the division of competences between the Union institutions. This is a matter of the *horizontal*, rather than *vertical*, separation of powers within the Union. The argument would be that if standing rules are to be established at all, they should be created by legislation. This very argument was raised against state liability by Germany, but rejected by the Court in *Brasserie du Pêcheur*.[210] The Court held that the principle of state liability was inherent in the system of the Treaty, and given the lack of express regulation it was for the Court,

> in pursuance of the task conferred on it by [now Article 19(1)] of the Treaty of ensuring that in the interpretation and application of the Treaty the law is observed, to rule on such a question in accordance with generally accepted methods of interpretation, in particular by reference to the fundamental principles of the Community legal system and, where necessary, general principles common to the legal systems of the Member States.[211]

[205] For a positivist account, see, for instance, HLA Hart, *The Concept of Law*, 2nd edn (Clarendon Press 1997). Hart has held that 'the certification of something as legally valid is not conclusive of the question of obedience, and … its demands must in the end be submitted to a moral scrutiny' (ibid 210).

[206] See, respectively, ibid 100–23 and H Kelsen, *Pure Theory of Law* (University of California Press 1967) 193–221.

[207] MP Maduro, *We, the Court: The European Court of Justice and the European Economic Constitution: A Critical Reading of Article 30 of the EC Treaty* (Hart Publishing 1998) 30. Yet, as he points out, a different perspective may be taken at the national level (ibid 30–31).

[208] Although the limits stemming from the principle of conferral are primarily of relevance for the Union legislature, it is also considered that the ECJ needs to respect these limits. See Beijer, *The Limits of Fundamental Rights Protections by the EU* (n 8) 183.

[209] The expression is borrowed from T Konstadinides, *Division of Powers in European Union Law: The Delimitation of Internal Competence between the EU and the Member States* (Kluwer Law International 2009) 134.

[210] Joined Cases C-46/93 and C-48/93 *Brasserie du Pêcheur* [1996] para 27. See further A Biondi and M Farley, *The Right to Damages in European Law* (Wolters Kluwer 2009) 21–23.

[211] Joined Cases C-46/93 and C-48/93 *Brasserie du Pêcheur* [1996] para 27.

The Court identified various sources for liability: the principle of full effectiveness of Union law and the effective protection of Union rights; the duty of loyal cooperation now enshrined in Article 4(3) TEU; and Article 340(2) TFEU, regulating the non-contractual liability of the Union itself.

Although the Court has not lent an ear to arguments of illegality, the *legitimacy* of the Court's rulings is still open to assessment. A shift in the decision-making authority from the national level to the European clearly raises legitimacy concerns. The concept of legitimacy evades precise definition, yet the term tends to be used in both a descriptive and a normative sense.[212] Whereas descriptive legitimacy refers to the fact that the subjects of the norm *believe* it to be legitimate, normative legitimacy is concerned with whether the norm *satisfies specified conditions* for possessing legitimacy. Here, the term is used in the latter sense, and the primary yardstick is whether the Court stays within the proper scope of the judicial function and is not unduly intruding into the domain of domestic courts.[213]

The Court may interpret Union law only within the limits of the powers conferred upon it.[214] But although the role of the Court is to *interpret and apply* the law rather than legislate from the bench, the Court is not 'denied all interpretative manoeuvring space [having to] behave as the imaginary – legalistic – mouth of the law'.[215] Given the indeterminacy of Union law, this fiction could hardly be upheld. It must still be kept in mind that where the Court appears to overstep the line between the resolution of concrete cases and the laying down quasi-legislative measures, it lays itself open to accusations of judicial activism.[216]

The Court has on occasion been criticised for pushing the envelope of its legal mandate.[217] The criticism against *Francovich* is captured by Weatherill:

> The argument, in short, is that the Court is dangerously promiscuous in its reliance on 'effectiveness'. Reasoning on the basis of what is 'inherent' in the Treaty doubtless offers creative scope for extending the penetration of EU law into national legal orders. But it also strains Article 5 TEU and, the other side of that coin, it erodes varied choices made in the name of national autonomy while concentrating a high level of law-making power on the Court of Justice.[218]

[212] D Bodansky, 'Legitimacy in International Law and International Relations' in JL Dunoff and MA Pollack (eds), *Interdisciplinary Perspectives on International Law and International Relations* (Cambridge University Press 2012) 321, 327.

[213] Compare Lenaerts, 'The Court's Outer and Inner Selves' (n 11) 13–14. Conversely, Bobek adopts a more descriptive approach, arguing that in a shared legal order such as the EU, the acceptance by national courts should function as the main yardstick of legitimacy; see M Bobek, 'Of Feasibility and Silent Elephants: The Legitimacy of the Court of Justice through the Eyes of National Courts' in M Adams et al (eds), *Judging Europe's Judges: The Legitimacy of the Case Law of the European Court of Justice* (Hart Publishing 2013) 197.

[214] See Case C-265/13 *Torralbo Marcos* [2014] para 27 and Case C-205/15 *Toma* [2016] para 22.

[215] M Adams et al, 'Introduction: Judging Europe's Judges' in Adams et al (eds), *Judging Europe's Judges* (n 213) 1, 2.

[216] Wilman, *Private Enforcement of EU Law Before National Courts* (n 29) 13 with reference to S Garben, 'Sky-High Controversy and High-Flying Claims? The Sturgeon Case Law in Light of Judicial Activism, Euroscepticism and Eurolegalism' (2013) 50 *CML Rev* 15.

[217] See for instance R Widdershoven, 'The Principle of Loyal Cooperation: Lawmaking by the European Court of Justice and the Dutch Courts' in FAM Stroink and ECHJ Linden (eds), *Judicial Lawmaking and Administrative Law* (Intersentia 2005) 3, 21–22.

[218] S Weatherill, *Law and Values in the European Union* (Oxford University Press 2016) 191. Other legal scholars have also criticised the incursion of the Court's *Francovich* jurisprudence into domestic remedial structures; see, eg, C Harlow, 'A Common European Law of Remedies?' in C Kilpatrick, T Novitz and P Skidmore (eds), *The Future of Remedies in Europe* (Hart Publishing 2000) 69.

It cannot be denied that the Court through its case law has gone a long way in sidelining domestic procedural autonomy. The high watermark of incursion into domestic enforcement regimes was set by *Francovich*. The establishment of a Union doctrine of standing for the protection of rights is modest in comparison, given the leeway granted to the Member States when it comes to determining the appropriate type of action and the procedural rules applicable.[219] It is submitted that the Court's dictating of standing conditions is indeed legitimate. With the introduction of Article 47 of the Charter (and Article 19 TEU) with the Treaty of Lisbon, the Court has obtained a more visible and legitimate legal basis upon which to develop its case law on effective judicial protection.[220] Standing rules are not of such a technical nature as to require the involvement of the legislature. But most importantly, the disapplication of domestic provisions pursuant to the principle of effectiveness is not sufficient and should therefore 'be complemented by a more direct positive obligation through the recognition of EU-wide procedural standards'.[221] As I see it, this is not so much a matter of undue incursion into domestic remedial structures but of 'ensuring respect for the European rule of law'.[222] I subscribe to the view voiced in legal scholarship that the establishment of positive standards for national procedures 'highlights a maturation of the EU legal order from a fundamental rights perspective'.[223]

Domestic rules on standing are embedded in the constitutional traditions of the Member States.[224] Pursuant to Article 4(2) TEU, the Union must respect the national identities of the Member States, inherent in, inter alia, the constitutional structures. Requiring that Union rights should be effectively enforced, however, can hardly be seen as an undue interference in the Member States' constitutional traditions. There are good reasons for ratcheting up the level at which the decision on standing is made. As held by Milutinović, standing forms an 'indispensable part of a legally enforceable right [and construing] the issue as a matter of national law is not satisfactory, as any national solution would affect not only the exercise, but also the content of the rights derived directly from the Treaty'.[225]

Hence, insofar as there are Union rights at stake, the issue of standing cannot be left to the Member State to decide; rather it must be determined at the Union level. Yet the princple of sincere cooperation enshrined in Article 4(3) TEU also calls for some deference on the part of the Court.[226] If the Court were to go far in requiring the Member States to provide standing to individuals whose individual rights are not impaired – in

[219] See further ch 7, section V.

[220] S Drake, 'More Effective Private Enforcement of EU Law Post-Lisbon: Aligning Regulatory Goals and Constitutional Values' in S Drake and M Smith (eds), *New Directions in the Effective Enforcement of EU Law and Policy* (Edward Elgar 2016) 12, 35.

[221] van Cleynenbreugel, 'Judge-Made Standards of National Procedure' (n 15) 94.

[222] Compare the argument made in support of state liability in Biondi and Farley, *The Right to Damages in European Law* (n 210) 29.

[223] van Cleynenbreugel, 'Judge-Made Standards of National Procedure' (n 15) 99.

[224] E Rehbinder, 'Locus Standi, Community Law and the Case for Harmonization' in H Somsen (ed), *Protecting the European Environment: Enforcing EC Environmental Law* (Blackstone Press 1996) 151, 162.

[225] V Milutinović, *The 'Right to Damages' under EU Competition Law: From Courage v Crehan to the White Paper and Beyond* (Kluwer Law International 2010) 230. He writes this with reference to Arts 101 and 102 TFEU, but the argument has relevance to all rights derived from Union law.

[226] See further van Cleynenbreugel, 'Judge-Made Standards of National Procedure' (n 15) 97.

the name of *effectiveness* – it would risk upsetting the balance enshrined in the Treaties, and possibly run counter to the principle of subsidiarity. After all, there are various ways of rendering Union law effective in the Member States.[227]

The Court's role in elaborating standing conditions is particularly apt following the changes made with the Lisbon Treaty.[228] The enactment of Article 19 TEU and Article 47 of the Charter provides evidence of Member States' willingness to 'affirm the grip which EU law has on the autonomy in the matter of procedure and remedies'.[229] Such a harmonisation of standing rules to ensure the protection of rights can be seen, along with developments such as direct effect, supremacy and state liability, as an aspect of the *constitutionalisation* of the European Union.[230]

[227] See further ch 13, sections IV and V on the interplay between various enforcement routes.

[228] One test of the descriptive legitimacy of the Court's case law is the effect on successive amendments to the Treaties; see A Arnull, 'The Rule of Law in the European Union' in A Arnull and D Wincott (eds), *Accountability and legitimacy in the European Union* (Oxford University Press 2002) 241, 243.

[229] Weatherill, *Law and Values in the European Union* (n 218) 192.

[230] Similarly Micklitz, 'The ECJ Between the Individual Citizen and the Member States' (n 188) 351. The crux of the constitutionalisation thesis is that the Union has transformed from an organisation governed by principles of public international law towards an entity characterised by constitutional values and principles. This process renders the relationship between the Union and its Member States 'indistinguishable from analogous legal relationships in constitutional federal states', see JHH Weiler, 'The Transformation of Europe' (1990) 100 *Yale Law Journal* 2403, 2413. On the constitutionalisation of Union law, see further JHH Weiler, 'The Reformation of European Constitutionalism' (1997) 35 *Journal of Common Market Studies* 97.

6

What Standing is Not About: Distinguishing Direct Effect, Invocability and Standing

I. Introduction

This chapter is devoted to addressing what standing is *not* about, essentially to demarcate for separate treatment the issue of standing. It sets out to show that the right to initiate proceedings before domestic courts must be kept distinct from *direct effect* (section II) and the right to invoke Union law provisions in the course of ongoing proceedings – *the 'invocation right'* (section III). These matters are often conflated in legal scholarship, and the following is an attempt to clarify the confusion.

II. Direct Effect

A. Why Direct Effect and Standing Should Not be Conflated

The relationship between direct effect and standing can be confusing, and this is partly because of the Court's linking of direct effect and the creation of rights. In *Van Gend en Loos*, the Court found that Treaty provisions may have direct effect, and thereby create rights the national courts have a duty to protect.[1] In *Firma Molkerei*, the Court stated, upon finding the conditions for direct effect fulfilled, that 'every time a rule of Community law confers rights on individuals, those rights [...] may be safeguarded by proceedings brought before the competent national courts.'[2] Also in legal scholarship, there has been a tendency to infer standing directly from the direct effect of Union law. By way of illustration, Ross has asserted that 'direct effect is a basic entitlement creating standing to sue for individuals seeking to enforce their Community law rights.'[3]

Direct effect, along with supremacy, is one of the 'central pillars of the legal order' the Court has developed with a view to securing the uniform and effective application

[1] Case 26/62 *Van Gend en Loos* [1963].
[2] Case 28/67 *Firma Mokerei* [1968].
[3] M Ross, 'Beyond Francovich' (1993) 56 *MLR* 55, 72. Along similar lines, S Kadelbach, 'European Administrative Law and the Law of a Europeanized Administration' in C Joerges and R Dehousse (eds), *Good Governance in Europe's Integrated Market* (Oxford University Press 2002) 167, 199.

of Union law in the Member States.[4] However, directly effective provisions do not necessarily confer rights, let alone standing to enforce the relevant provisions before domestic courts. As Dougan has pointed out, '[t]he issue of whether a given provision of Union law has direct effect is conceptually entirely distinct from the question of who should be recognised as enjoying standing to enforce that provision before the domestic courts'.[5]

In the following, I review the doctrine of direct effect, and explain how it relates to invocability and standing. It will be argued that direct effect is not a *sufficient* condition for relying on Union law before domestic courts, since the direct effect of a provision tells us little about 'who should be entitled to take advantage of that direct effect in practice'.[6] Moreover, it will be argued, direct effect is not a *necessary* condition either, since it does not have a 'monopoly over the question of the … application of EU norms'.[7]

B. Unpacking Direct Effect

In the following, I take a closer look at the doctrine of direct effect, and substantiate the claim that direct effect concerns the *quality or status* of the norm. The thrust of the argument is that direct effect is concerned with the justiciability of the norm in question. This is why concluding that a provision satisfies the criteria for direct effect does not tell us who may benefit from that effect in practice.

In the seminal ruling in *Van Gend en Loos*, the Court held that the provisions in the Treaty are not merely obligations of result addressed to the states but that citizens may rely on EU law directly before national courts. This means that EU law is also the law of the land, susceptible to judicial application in the Member States. While the judgment was restricted to whether Treaty provisions could produce direct effect, the Court has subsequently extended the doctrine to encompass provisions contained in regulations, directives, decisions, international agreements, Charter provisions and even general Union law principles.[8]

Direct effect can apply both horizontally and vertically, yet the direct effect of *directives* cannot be pleaded against individuals.[9] That being said, the Court has mitigated the effect of this lack of 'horizontal direct effect' of directives by various constructions. First, the concept of vertical direct effect has been expanded by widening the definition of the state.[10] Second, the Court has adopted a fairly narrow interpretation of what constitutes a 'direct obligation' on an individual.[11] Third, domestic courts are obliged to

[4] M Dougan, *National Remedies Before the Court of Justice: Issues of Harmonisation and Differentiation* (Hart Publishing 2004) 95.

[5] Dougan, 'Who Exactly Benefits from the Treaties? The Murky Interaction Between Union and National Competence over the Capacity to Enforce EU Law' (2009) 12 Cambridge Yearbook of European Legal Studies 73, 80. Similarly P Wennerås, *The Enforcement of EC Environmental Law* (Oxford University Press 2007) 75.

[6] Dougan, 'Who Exactly Benefits from the Treaties? (n 5) 80.

[7] D Leczykiewicz, 'The Constitutional Dimension of Private Law Liability Rules in the EU' in D Leczykiewicz and S Weatherill (eds), *The Involvement of EU Law in Private Law Relationships* (Hart Publishing 2013) 209.

[8] See further, M Bobek, 'The Effects of EU Law in National Legal Systems' in C Barnard and S Peers (eds) European Union Law, 3rd edn (Oxford University Press 2020) 154, 161–164.

[9] See Case C-91/92 *Faccini Dori* [1995] para 20; and Case C-282/10 *Dominguez* [2012] para 42.

[10] See Case C-188/89 *Foster* [1990] para 18.

[11] See, eg, Case C-201/02 *Wells* [2004] para 57, where the Court stated that 'mere adverse repercussions on the rights of third parties … do not justify preventing an individual from invoking the provisions of a directive against the Member State concerned'.

interpret national law in conformity with a directive to the extent possible (harmonious interpretation).[12] Fourth, general principles of Union law and Charter rights can be invoked in horizontal proceedings, with a view to having incompatible national provisions set aside.[13]

In *Van Gend en Loos*, the ECJ established the requirements that a provision must be clear, unconditional, containing no reservation on the part of the Member State, and not dependent on any implementing measure.[14] In subsequent years, these initial conditions have been loosened, so the current test seems to be that the provision at issue must be 'unconditional and sufficiently precise'.[15] As Prechal points out, the purpose of the conditions for direct effect is judicial application.[16] Hence, what these criteria boil down to is that the provision needs to be justiciable, meaning that it must be capable of being applied by a court. To cite Advocate General Van Gerven in *Banks*:

> The clarity, precision, unconditional nature, completeness or perfection of the rule and its lack of dependence on discretionary implementation measures are in that respect merely aspects of one and the same characteristic feature which that rule must exhibit, namely it must be capable of being applied by a court to a specific case.[17]

Union law can be invoked 'for purposes of "exclusion" or "substitution" of a [domestic] legal rule'.[18] In the first situation, Union law is used as a stand of review (and if there is incompatibility the national act must be set aside), whereas in the second situation the invoked norm is to apply instead.[19] The distinction between these two forms of invocability is illustrated by the Court's ruling in *Becker*, where the Court held that

> wherever the provisions of a Directive appear, as far as their subject matter is concerned, to be unconditional and sufficiently precise, those provisions may, in the absence of implementing measures adopted within the prescribed period, be relied upon as against any national

[12] See Case C-106/89 *Marleasing* [1990] para 8.

[13] The Court has recognised the existence of a general principle of Union law eliminating discrimination on grounds of age, as expressed by Directive 2000/78/EC (Equal Treatment in Employment and Occupation), and held that conflicting national law had to be set aside in the context of horizontal disputes between two private parties; see Case C-144/04 *Mangold* [2006] and Case C-555/07 *Kücükdeveci* [2010]. These rulings were confirmed in Case C-441/14 *Dansk Industri* [2016]. The right to an annual period of paid leave, under Art 31(2) of the Charter, as expressed by Directive 2003/88, can also be relied on in proceedings between private parties; see Case C-684/16 *Max Planck* [2018] para 74.

[14] Case 26/62 *Van Gend en Loos* [1963].

[15] A Union provision is *unconditional* if it is not subject, in its implementation or effects, to the taking of any measure either by the institutions of the Union or by the Member States, and a provision is *sufficiently precise* where the obligation it imposes is set out in unequivocal terms; see Case C-236/92 *Comitato* [1994] paras 9–10.

[16] S Prechal, 'Direct Effect Reconsidered, Redefined and Rejected' in JM Prinssen and A Schrauwen (eds), *Direct Effect: Rethinking a Classic of EC Legal Doctrine* (Europa Law Publishing 2002) 17, 22.

[17] AG Van Gerven in Case C-128/92 *Banks* [1993] para 27. In the words of Edward, 'Is this particular norm one that a judge can apply in this particular situation, or has it not yet reached the province of the judiciary?': see D Edward, 'Direct Effect – Myth, Mess or Mystery?' in Prinssen and Schrauwen (eds), *Direct Effect: Rethinking a Classic of EC Legal Doctrine* (n 16) 3, 3. Direct effect is thus concerned with the separation of powers; see further S Prechal, 'Does Direct Effect Still Matter' (2000) 37 *CML Rev* 1047, 1065.

[18] AG Legér in Case C-287/98 *Linster* [2000] para 57. This reflects the French distinction between 'invocabilité de substitution' and 'invocabilité d'exclusion'.

[19] S Prechal, *Directives in EC Law* (Oxford University Press 2005) 104–05. The Union law provision can be applied where a national provision does not exist, or where it has been excluded in the process of national law application since it violated the Union norm; see N Poltorak, *European Union Rights in National Courts* (Wolters Kluwer 2015) 122.

> provision which is incompatible with the Directive or in so far as the provision define rights which individuals are able to assert against the state.[20]

Where a union norm grants discretion, the claimant cannot require national authorities to fulfil the obligation in a certain manner.[21] The existence of discretionary power does not, however, rule out the possibility of *judicial control*.[22] After all, judicial review is a means of controlling the exercise of discretionary public power.[23]

Some scholars have argued that provisions invoked in the context of legality review do not have to be directly effective.[24] Such a view cannot be upheld, as the Court has explicitly stated that 'a national court is not required, solely on the basis of EU law, to disapply a provision of its national law which is contrary to a provision of EU law if the latter provision does not have direct effect'.[25] Other scholars have argued that there is a distinction between *subjective* and *objective* direct effect, or between a *broad* and a *narrow* definition.[26] As I see it, such distinctions are of limited value. Direct effect is about identifying which norms are susceptible to direct judicial application. The criteria are the same, regardless of whether the Union law provision is relied on for purposes of 'exclusion' or 'substitution'.[27] Nevertheless, the application of these criteria varies depending on the specific situation.[28] Where the claimant seeks to obtain a positive application of an EU law provision, he will need more guidance from the provision, as compared to where he is merely seeking review of the legality of national measures, but this is catered for in the conditions that the rules must be 'sufficiently precise' for the purposes of proceedings.[29]

There has been a long-running debate on whether or not the conferral of rights is a precondition for direct effect, but this debate seems to have come to a rest.[30] As Prechal points out, the question whether a provision has direct effect relates to '*the quality ascribed to it*, namely whether it can be invoked by those concerned within the national legal system', whereas the question whether a provision creates individual rights 'is *a matter of its content*'.[31] Van Dam has used a similar formulation, pointing out

[20] Case 8/81 *Becker* [1982] para 25.

[21] See Case C-216/02 *Zuchtverband für Ponys* [2004], addressed in ch 3, section IV.B.

[22] See, eg, Case C-72/95 *Kraaijeveld* [1996], where a directive was invoked as a standard for assessing the compatibility of national law with EU law.

[23] M Dougan, 'Judicial Review of Member State Action under the General Principles and the Charter: Defining the Scope of Union Law' (2015) 52 *CML Rev* 1201, 1212.

[24] See, eg, K Lenaerts and T Corthaut, 'Of Birds and Hedges: The Role of Primacy in Invoking Norms of EU Law' (2006) 31 *EL Rev* 287 (emphasising instead primacy). Direct effect is thus defined narrowly as the capacity of a Union law provision to create individual rights that can be enforced before national courts. For a thorough account of the relationship between direct effect and supremacy, see M Dougan, 'When Worlds Collide! Competing Visions of the Relationship between Direct Effect and Supremacy' (2007) 44 *CML Rev* 931.

[25] Case C-573/17, *Poplawski* [2019] para 68. This clarification was much needed in light of the Court's ruling in Case C-384/17 *Dooel Uvoz-Izvoz Skopje Link Logistic N&N* [2018], indicating the opposite.

[26] See further W Van Gerven, 'Of Rights, Remedies and Procedures' (2000) 37 *CML Rev* 501, 506; and Prechal, *Directives in EC Law* (n 19) 234–37.

[27] To the same effect, see Prechal, *Directives in EC Law* (n 19) 241–43.

[28] Poltorak, *European Union Rights in National Courts* (n 19) 126.

[29] Wennerås, *The Enforcement of EC Environmental Law* (n 5) 29.

[30] For an overview of this debate, see, inter alia, C Hilson, 'The Visibility of Environmental Rights in the EU Legal Order: Eurolegalism in Action?' (2018) 25 *Journal of European Public Policy* 1589, 1600.

[31] S Prechal, 'Member State Liability and Direct Effect: What's the Difference After All?' (2006) 17 *European Business Law Review* 299, 305 (emphasis in original).

that direct effect 'relates to the *status* of the rule, whereas the question of whether a rule confers rights on individuals relates to the *content* of the rule'.[32] Consequently, locating rights is not of importance for the purposes of determining the direct effect of a Union law provision.

Since direct effect concerns the quality or status of the norm, this means that the question of whether or not a norm has direct effect must be distinguished from the question of who, in the case at hand, can enforce that rule.[33] The issue of direct effect relates to whether Union law is apt for autonomous enforcement *by anyone at all*, whereas the question of capacity to enforce concerns exactly *who* can enforce Union law.[34] The Court has been laconic as to the entitlement to rely on directly effective norms. A commonly used formula is that 'those concerned' should be able to invoke the norm, but the Court has not provided much guidance as to what exactly it means to be a 'concerned' individual.[35] The personal scope of the invocation right will be addressed in more detail in section III.C.

C. Alternative Means of Rendering Union Law Susceptible to Judicial Application

Direct effect is not the only route available to those seeking to invoke Union law provisions before domestic courts. In the words of Robin-Olivier:

> [T]he effects of EU law in national courts have diversified and grown more complex to such an extent that *Van Gend en Loos*... no longer gives an accurate idea of the ways through which EU law penetrates member states through its enforcement in national courts.[36]

The principles of direct effect and the principles of effectiveness and effective judicial protection are often mentioned together, which could suggest that the last two principles only come into play as regards directly effective provisions.[37] It is submitted that this is not the case but that the Union law principles pertaining to standing also apply where a person brings an action under national law with Union origins.[38] Direct effect is 'just one *technique* by which a right ... can be brought to the individual'; Union law

[32] C van Dam, *European Tort Law*, 2nd edn (Oxford University Press 2013) 288 (emphasis in original).

[33] J Engström, 'The Europeanisation of Remedies and Procedures Through Judge-Made Law: Can a Trojan Horse Achieve Effectiveness? Experiences of the Swedish Judiciary' (PhD thesis, European University Institute 2009) 25.

[34] Dougan, 'Who Exactly Benefits from the Treaties?' (n 5) 90.

[35] See, eg, Case 41/74 *Van Duyn* [1974] para 12.

[36] S Robin-Olivier, 'The Evolution of Direct Effect in the EU: Stocktaking, Problems, Projections' (2014) 12 *International Journal of Constitutional Law* 165, 166.

[37] Ruffert, for instance, calls the doctrine of direct effect 'the first limb of the Community law approach to rights and remedies'; see M Ruffert, 'Rights and Remedies in European Community Law: A Comparative View' (1997) 34 *CML Rev* 307, 310.

[38] To the same effect, see Prechal, *Directives in EC Law* (n 19) 150. A different solution, she points out, 'would lead to an anomaly, namely, as long as the person was invoking the directive he would have standing, while as soon as he relied on national law (with Community origins) his *locus standi* would potentially be curtailed'.

can also become operative in other ways.[39] First, a directive may specify the right holder and the essential content of the right, while allowing the Member States discretion in defining the body liable to meet the claim, which may hamper the direct effect of these provisions.[40] However, where the state has exercised its discretion and defined the body that should be the debtor of these rights, the directive can be relied upon in the event of defective implementation.[41] Second, if a directive is correctly implemented in the Member State, a private party may rely on national law before the court.[42] The relevant legal provision stems from EU law, but it is given effect through the application of national law. Third, where correct implementation is lacking, the authorities of the Member States are still obliged to interpret national provisions in conformity with EU law if the former lend themselves to such interpretation. Obligations contained in a directive can therefore be placed on individuals, having been transformed into obligations of national law through judicial interpretation.[43] This form of indirect effect 'allows individuals to secure their EU rights indirectly by virtue of national law … independently of direct effect'.[44]

I will argue that, for the principles of equivalence, effectiveness and effective judicial protection to come into play, the only requirements are that the Union law provision is cognisable within the domestic legal order – that it is law of the land – and that it is justiciable, and hence can be pleaded as a source of applicable law before the domestic courts.[45] That is the case as regards directly effective Treaty provisions, provisions in regulations and provisions in directives that are implemented domestically or satisfy the conditions for direct effect. I subscribe to the view held by Engström that the crucial circumstance triggering the right to an effective judicial remedy is '*the existence of a right, legal position or interest that can be derived from the Community law regime in some way*, either through direct effect, indirect effect or through the implementation of a directive'.[46]

[39] S Beljin, 'Rights in EU Law' in S Prechal and B van Roermund (eds), *The Coherence of EU Law. The Search for Unity in Divergent Concepts* (Oxford University Press 2008) 97, 112.

[40] Joined Cases C-6/90 and C-9/90 *Francovich* [1991] paras 25 and 26; and Case C-334/92 *Wagner Miret* [1993] para 17.

[41] See Case C-441/99 *Gharehveran* [2001] para 44 (further addressed in ch 4, section III.D).

[42] Upon implementation EU law is rendered national law, while remaining EU law in terms of content; see Beljin, 'Rights in EU Law' (n 39) 111. The Member States must ensure that the rights under the national implementing measures can be asserted by judicial process by the individuals concerned; see Prechal, *Directives in EC Law* (n 19) 143.

[43] D Curtin, 'Directives; The Effectiveness of Judicial Protection of Individual Rights' (1990) 27 *CML Rev* 709, 724. For an illustration of how a private party, through the doctrine of consistent interpretation, can rely on an EU right contained in a directive against another private party, see Joined Cases C-397/01 to C-403/01 *Pfeiffer* [2004].

[44] S Drake, 'More Effective Private Enforcement of EU Law Post-Lisbon: Aligning Regulatory Goals and Constitutional Values' in S Drake and M Smith (eds), *New Directions in the Effective Enforcement of EU Law and Policy* (Edward Elgar 2016) 12, 22.

[45] Similarly Engström, 'The Europeanisation of Remedies and Procedures Through Judge-Made Law' (n 33) 89–92. See also Poltorak, *European Union Rights in National Courts* (n 19) 59, who holds that if the application of substantive provisions of a directive is possible via national law, the claims resulting from these provisions must be effectively protected.

[46] Engström, 'The Europeanisation of Remedies and Procedures Through Judge-Made Law' (n 33) 91 (emphasis in original).

III. The Right to Invoke Union Law Provisions When Already before the Court

A. Why the Invocation Right Should Not be Conflated with the Right to Standing

In the following, I address the 'invocation right', meaning the right to invoke Union law provisions in the course of ongoing proceedings. There has been a tendency to conflate this right with the right to initiate proceedings. The Court itself has also on a few occasions cast its rulings in the language of standing, although the ruling in question concerned whether the claimant could rely on a Union law provision to assist his case.[47] In legal literature, case law relating to the invocation right is often discussed as a matter of standing, with the result that the category of persons granted *locus standi* is perceived broadly.[48]

The ruling relied on most frequently in support of a wide category of enforcers is *Verholen*, where the Court was asked whether a husband could rely on the non-discrimination provision of Directive 79/7/EEC (Equal Treatment in Social Security) in order to set aside national discriminatory provisions that applied to his wife. The Court answered in the affirmative, and held that the right to rely on the Directive could not be confined to persons coming within the personal scope of the Directive, as others may have a 'direct interest' in the enforcement.[49] Building on this case, it is a commonly held misconception that the Member States must grant standing to those with a 'direct interest' in compliance with the obligations contained in Union law.[50] While the ruling was cast in the language of standing, it did in fact concern the right to invoke Union law arguments once before the court, given that the claimant already had standing as a matter of domestic law.[51]

There is a need to distinguish the category of persons entitled to initiate proceedings for the enforcement of Union law (standing) and those who have the right to rely on Union law provisions once before the court (admissibility of pleas).[52] In order to initiate

[47] See Joined Cases C-87/90, C-88/90 and C-89/90 *Verolen* [1991] para 24 and Case C-174/02 *Streekgewest* [2005] para 18. Verholen has also been cited in subsequent cases concerning *locus standi*, see, inter alia, Case C-13/01 *Safalero* [2003] para 50.

[48] See, eg, T Tridimas, *The General Principles of EU Law*, 2nd edn (Oxford University Press 2006) 453–55; and M Ruffert, 'Rights and Remedies in European Community Law: A Comparative View' (1997) 34 *CML Rev* 307, 331–32.

[49] Joined Cases C-87/90, C-88/90 and C-89/90 *Verolen* [1991] para 23.

[50] See, eg, JH Jans, 'Legal Protection in European Environmental Law: An Overview' in H Somsen (ed), *Protecting the European Environment: Enforcing EC Environmental Law* (Blackstone Press 1996) 49, 78; Wennerås, *The Enforcement of EC Environmental Law* (n 5) 110 and Koen Lenaerts, Kathleen Gutman and Ignace Maselis, *EU Procedural Law* (Oxford University Press 2014) 119.

[51] Similarly Engström, 'The Europeanisation of Remedies and Procedures Through Judge-Made Law' (n 33) 144; and Poltorak, *European Union Rights in National Courts* (n 19) 240.

[52] To the same effect, see T Eilmansberger, 'The Relationship between Rights and Remedies in EC Law: In Search of the Missing Link' (2004) 41 *CML Rev* 1199, 1205–06; G Jurgens, 'Introduction of a Relativity-Related Requirement in Dutch Administrative Law' (2007) 4 *Journal for European Environmental & Planning Law* 260, 268; and Poltorak, *European Union Rights in National Courts* (n 19) 128 ff. As Barents explains, in proceedings characterised by a strict system of pleas, 'the factual and legal grounds raised in the application initiating the proceedings delimit the subject-matter of the dispute'; see R Barents, 'EU Procedural Law and Effective Legal Protection' (2014) 51 *CML Rev* 1437, 1450.

proceedings, the claimant needs to have *locus standi*. If the Union law issue is raised in the course of an ongoing proceeding, the question is rather whether the claimant – or alternatively the defendant – is entitled to *invoke* or rely on the relevant Union law provision. As Engström points out, although both issues concern the persons who can enforce a norm in court, they are not concerned with the exact same thing:

> *Locus standi*, understood narrowly, is … a strictly procedural question of *who has the right to be a party to a trial concerning a certain matter*. When someone has standing or *locus standi*, that person 'holds the key to the courtroom', and has a right to bring a claim or challenge an action in front of a court. *Locus standi* does not tell us what remedies there are, neither what legal rules, circumstances or interests a claimant successfully can rely on to be successful with the claim.[53]

As Engström observes, the Court seems to have developed two different standards: on the one hand, a wider circle that must have the right to rely on Union law once having entered the courtroom, and, on the other, a narrower circle that must have a right to an available remedy and standing.[54] These lines of case law should not be conflated, because it would lead to an undue incursion into domestic standing doctrines.

The invocation right is closely linked to the principles of direct effect, supremacy, effectiveness and, not least, loyalty. By relying on Union law provisions in the course of an ongoing proceeding, the private party ensures the application of Union law in the Member States, and thus contributes to rendering these provisions effective in practice.[55] Accordingly, the Court has been generous in granting invocation rights, and since the invocation right arises when proceedings are already commenced, standing is not an issue. In the words of Eilmansberger:

> As long as a subjective legal position is restricted to an entitlement to rely upon the rule in a judicial proceeding, there can be no objection to a generous or indeed entirely unrestricted conferral of such a right. Only if an individual right is to be provided with the means of enforcement by way of offensive remedies and appropriate causes of action, does the classic concern regarding the true subjective rights arise, namely the scary vision of an *actio popularis*.[56]

The category of persons granted standing as a matter of Union law is narrow compared to those being entitled to invoke Union law provisions once before the court.[57] As seen

[53] Engström, 'The Europeanisation of Remedies and Procedures Through Judge-Made Law' (n 33) 128 (emphasis in original). She draws on PH Lindblom, 'In dubio pro natura! Några civilprocessuella frågor inom miljöratten' (2000) 5 *Juridisk Tidsskrift* 805.

[54] Engström, 'The Europeanisation of Remedies and Procedures Through Judge-Made Law' (n 33) 129.

[55] As Thorson points out, 'the "right to rely" is difficult to distinguish from the national court's obligation to take European Union law into account when performing judicial review,' as it 'aims to ensure that domestic courts do not hand down rulings which are contrary to Union law'; see B Thorson, *Individual Rights in EU Law* (Springer 2016) 126.

[56] Eilmansberger, 'The Relationship between Rights and Remedies in EC Law' (n 52) 1205–06. As he says, the invocation right 'has a somewhat modest content. It serves to make sure that the courts do what, in many cases, they are supposed to do anyway, namely apply the law relevant to the case.'

[57] The distinction between standing and invocability also finds its parallel in proceedings before the Union courts. Pursuant to Art 277 TFEU, the inapplicability of a measure of general application forming the basis of a contested decision can be pleaded incidentally in the course of an ongoing proceeding. The provision may not, however, be invoked in the absence of an independent right of action; see Case T-154/94 *CSF and CSME v Commission* [1996] para 16.

in chapter 3, section IV and chapter 5, section IV), the right to bring an action before national courts is primarily reserved to those exhibiting a Union right, and Member States are generally not obliged to extend standing beyond right holders.

B. Unpacking the Invocation Right

The invocation right can be defined as 'the procedural right to invoke a Union law in order to review a national norm (or an action by a national authority) from the point of view of its compliance with Union law'.[58] The invocation right is granted with a view to ensuring that Union law is rendered effective in the Member States, rather than to protect the legal position of the individual. Hence, the invocation right is not a 'right' properly so called, and it does not trigger the principle of effective judicial protection.[59]

Union law can be used as a standard for assessing the legality of executive decisions or legislative norms. An executive decision can violate Union law regardless of whether it is the *legislative basis* or the *decision itself* that is contrary to Union law requirements.[60] In the first case, the claimant (or occasionally the defendant) seeks to exclude the application of national law; in the second, he seeks to subject the administration directly to Union law requirements.[61] The Union law compatibility of legislative provisions can be challenged not only in the context of challenging an individual administrative decision; a private party may also plead violation of a Union law provision defensively when criminal proceedings are brought against him, or raise the compatibility of national norms with Union law collaterally in litigation with another private party. Although the procedural setting is different, the subject of review is the same, namely, the review of a national public act.[62]

The scope of the invocation right is decisive for the restrictions Member States can place on the pleas in law that may be raised in support of an action. The admissibility of pleas differs between the Member States and, moreover, is often dependent on the (administrative, criminal or civil) nature of the proceedings.[63] In most Member States there are no restrictions as to the rules a claimant can rely on once he has established *locus standi*. He may rely on all rules of law before the courts, regardless of whether these

[58] Poltorak, *European Union Rights in National Courts* (n 19) 129.

[59] D Leczykiewicz, 'Private Party Liability in EU Law: In Search of the General Regime' (2009) 12 *Cambridge Yearbook of European Legal Studies* 257, 278. Dougan seems to be of a different opinion, holding that the principle of effective judicial protection comes into play if Union law envisages the creation of a right in favour of the claimant, 'regardless of whether this is categorised as a subjective personal right or merely a right of standing to enforce in the general interest'; see Dougan, 'Who Exactly Benefits from the Treaties?' (n 5) 100. Along the same lines, Wennerås, who asserts that the Court has adopted 'an autonomous and broad interpretation of rights that does not distinguish between objective and subjective rights'; see Wennerås, *The Enforcement of EC Environmental Law* (n 5) 310.

[60] On this distinction and how it may play out in a national context, see JH Jans, 'Legal Protection in European Environmental Law: An Overview' (n 50) 88–91.

[61] This distinction is taken up in section III.D.

[62] M De Mol, 'The Novel Approach of the CJEU on the Horizontal Direct Effect of the EU Principle of Non-Discrimination: (Unbridled) Expansionism of EU Law?' (2011) 18 *Maastricht Journal of European and Comparative Law* 109, 125.

[63] S Prechal, 'Protection of Rights: How Far?' in Prechal and van Roermund (eds), *The Coherence of EU Law* (n 39) 155, 175.

rules are specifically enacted to protect his rights or interests. Hence, 'once through the bottle-neck of standing criteria', persons granted standing may voice also public interest considerations.[64] Such a liberal approach to the pleas that can be brought forward is, however, not found everywhere. For example, in the Netherlands, the administrative court may not annul a decision based on the violation of a norm that clearly does not serve the interest of the claimant.[65] The interesting question from the perspective of EU law is the extent to which the Member States may impose such limitations pertaining to invocability of Union norms.

C. The Extent of the Invocation Right

In the legal literature support can be found for the position that the invocation right accrues to those with a 'Union law interest'[66] or 'effective interest' in the application of the norm.[67] According to Downes and Hilson, 'a person with an interest will be able to rely on the provisions … if upholding this interest supports *effet utile*'.[68] Póltorak argues that 'a given entity should have the interest for invoking a Union provision if the invocation serves the effective achievement of the aims of the provision in question'.[69] Dougan is on to something similar:

> It seems that the Court will usually be persuaded to transform a mere factual involvement in any given situation, into a concrete legal capacity to enforce the applicable Union law, based on an analysis of the claimant's direct interest in the subject matter of the relevant provision, and of his or her 'added value' in securing the effective enforcement of Union law.[70]

While I do not object to these views, these requirements do not, I believe, present severe obstacles to the enforcement of Union law. The 'added value' or 'effectiveness' criterion is easily fulfilled, since by invoking Union law, one renders the Union law provisions operative in practice. As to the interest requirement, the Court seems to require that individuals can rely on Union law where this would assist their case. The interest requirement seems to be construed liberally, since 'the ECJ will readily find this condition fulfilled for the sake of ensuring the effectiveness' of Union law.[71] The requirement is primarily a means of highlighting that the courts of the Member States need not address *abstract questions of Union law*. In other words, the courts are not required to address arguments of Union law that have no bearing on the concrete case.[72]

[64] J Ebbesson, *Access to Justice in Environmental Matters in the EU* (Kluwer Law International 2002) 26 (in the environmental law context).

[65] See further R Ortlep and R Widdershoven, 'Judicial Protection' in JH Jans, S Prechal and RJGM Widdershoven (eds), *Europeanisation of Public Law*, 2nd edn (Europa Law Publishing 2015) 375.

[66] Poltorak, *European Union Rights in National Courts* (n 19) 251.

[67] C Hilson and T Downes, 'Making Sense of Rights: Community Rights in EC Law' (1999) 24 *El Rev* 121, 133 with reference to AG Fennelly in Case C-226/97 *Lemmens* [1998].

[68] ibid 133.

[69] Poltorak, *European Union Rights in National Courts* (n 19) 251.

[70] Dougan, 'Who Exactly Benefits from the Treaties?' (n 5) 91.

[71] Wennerås, *The Enforcement of EC Environmental Law* (n 5) 25.

[72] Similarly, the Court has held that 'the justification for a request for a preliminary ruling is not that it enables advisory opinions on general or hypothetical questions to be delivered, but rather that it is necessary for the effective resolution of a dispute'; see Case C-3/16 *Aquino* [2017] para 45. See also Case C-73/16 *Puškár* [2017] para 123.

Union law provisions can be relied on for a variety of purposes, and the question whether the provision grants rights is not necessarily relevant.[73] In the following, I examine three different contexts in which Union law can be invoked: first, as a standard for reviewing the legality of Member States' action in administrative proceedings; second, as a means to review legislative provisions in the context of a horizontal proceeding; and, third, as a defence in criminal proceedings.

When a private party seeks to rely on Union law to *challenge administrative decisions*, the Court does not seem to look into the protective scope of the provisions invoked, to see if the claimant's interests are covered. In *Smith and Nephew*, for example, the Court found that the holder of an original marketing authorisation could rely on the provisions of Article 5 of Directive 65/65/EEC (Medicinal Products), in proceedings before a national court in order to challenge the validity of an authorisation issued by the competent national authority to one of its competitors for a proprietary medicinal product bearing the same name.[74] The provision invoked was not intended to protect competitors but rather to make sure the product was neither harmful nor lacked therapeutic efficacy. There are also other cases where the Court, rather than addressing which interest the claimants had in the application of the norm, primarily examines whether the Union law norms are susceptible to judicial application.[75] The Court tends to reiterate the statement from *Van Duyn* that 'the useful effect [of a directive] would be weakened if individuals were prevented from relying on it before their national courts and if the latter were prevented from taking it into consideration as an element of Community law'.[76]

In *proceedings between private parties*, the compatibility of a legislative provision with Union law can be dealt with as a preliminary issue. Although not directly binding on the private party, Union law may still alter the legal framework of the dispute, and hence have a bearing on the outcome of the proceedings. The Court has allowed Union law to be invoked this way, without requiring that the norm invoked protects the individual concerned. In *CIA Security* the Court was asked whether a party in a civil dispute could invoke the government's failure to notify a draft technical regulation to the Commission as required under Directive 83/189/EEC (former Notification Directive).[77] CIA Security sought to defend itself against a claim that the undertaking sold alarm systems that did not fulfil the requirements laid down by Belgian legislation. They argued that the Belgian rules were invalid, as they had not been notified to the Commission in accordance with the Directive. The Court found that the failure to notify constituted a substantial procedural defect, rendering the technical regulations concerned inapplicable, with the effect that they were unenforceable against individuals.

[73] S Prechal and L Hancher, 'Individual Environmental Rights: Conceptual Pollution in EU Environmental Law?' 2002 *The Yearbook of European Environmental Law* 89, 94; and Prechal, *Directives in EC Law* (n 19) 99–100.

[74] Case C-201/94 *Smith and Nephew* [1996].

[75] See, eg, Case C-127/02 *Waddenzee* [2004] paras 64–69, where two environmental organisations were entitled to rely on Art 6(3) of Directive 92/43/EC (Habitats).

[76] See Case 41/74 *Van Duyn* [1974], reiterated, inter alia, in Case 51/76 *Verbond van Nederlandse Ondernemingen* [1977] para 23; Case C-287/98 *Linster* [2000] para 32; and Case C-127/02 *Waddenzee* [2004] para 66.

[77] Case C-194/94 *CIA Security* [1996].

The Court did not look into the protective scope of the provision invoked to determine whether CIA Security could rely on the Directive.

The Court adopted the same approach in *Unilever*,[78] this time in proceedings involving a contract between two private parties.[79] Central Foods refused to pay for olive oil supplied by Unilever since the oil was not labelled in accordance with Italian law. Unilever instituted proceedings and argued that the national labelling law was not binding, since it had been adopted in breach of the standstill provision provided for in the Notification Directive. The Court found that the failure to postpone the adoption of the rules in accordance with the Directive constituted a procedural defect, so as to render the technical regulations inapplicable. Although the Court stated explicitly that the provisions invoked did not create rights, it still found that the Directive could be relied upon by the claimant with a view to having national law disapplied.[80]

While it may be difficult to reconcile these cases with the line of case law rejecting horizontal direct effect, that is not the aspect meriting consideration here.[81] Rather, these rulings illustrate how provisions that are not meant to confer rights on individuals may still be relevant in the resolution of disputes between private parties, since in both cases 'it was the status and validity of public law regulatory standards which determined the private law obligations between the parties, either non-contractual (*CIA Security*) or contractual (*Unilever*)'.[82]

By allowing CIA Security and Unilever to rely on the Directive, the outcome of the legal proceedings was altered. Yet, as Nebbia has pointed out, the Court's main concern seems to have been the individuals' contribution to ensuring the effective application of the Directive, and 'the fact that certain individuals are able to derive benefits from this situation is defined as a mere "windfall benefit"'.[83]

In the *context of criminal proceedings*, a private party may seek to exclude the application of the national rule prohibiting his conduct. The inapplicability of a national provision incompatible with Union law would mean that the conduct was legal, and the individual would avoid punishment.[84] *Stoeckel* concerned an executive of a company who was criminally charged with employing women to work night shifts, contrary to the French labour code.[85] He pleaded in his defence that the French law was contrary

[78] Case C-443/98 *Unilever* [2000].

[79] Weatherill criticises the ruling, pointing to the contractual aspects of the dispute; see S Weatherill, 'Breach of Directives and Breach of Contract' (2001) 26 *EL Rev* 177, 180–81.

[80] See Case C-443/98 *Unilever* [2000] para 51, where the Court held that the Directive does 'not in any way define the substantive scope of the legal rule on the basis of which the national court must decide the case before it. It creates neither rights or obligations for individuals.' This was reiterated in Case C-98/14 *Berlington Hungary* [2015] para 108.

[81] Some scholars have sought to explain such rulings by distinguishing between direct and incidental horizontal effect, see, inter alia, A Arnull, 'Editorial: The Incidental Effect of Directives' (1999) 24 *EL Rev* 1. The Court seems to reject such incidental horizontal effect, see Case C-282/10 *Dominguez* [2012] para 42 and Case C-573/17, *Poplawski* [2019] para 64.

[82] Prechal, *Directives in EC Law* (n 19) 117.

[83] P Nebbia, 'Damages Actions for the Infringement of EC Competition Law: Compensation or Deterrence?' (2008) 33 *El Rev* 23, 30.

[84] D Leczykiewicz, 'Effectiveness of EU Law Before National Courts: Direct Effect, Consistent Interpretation and Member State Liability' in A Arnull and D Chalmers (eds), *Oxford Handbook of European Union Law* (Oxford University Press 2015) 212, 217.

[85] Case C-345/89 *Stoeckel* [1991].

to Directive 76/207/EEC (Equal Treatment), as the prohibition only applied to women. The Directive concerns the right of workers, and Stoeckel as an employer did not fall within the personal scope of the Directive. Even so, the Court found that Stoeckel could invoke the Directive as a defence in the criminal proceedings lodged against him.

All these cases illustrate how the scope of the invocation right cannot be determined with reference to individual rights. This does not mean, however, that the invocation right is granted indiscriminately. The Court has often stated that directly effective norms of EU law can be invoked by 'those concerned'[86] or 'interested'.[87] The requirement of an interest implies that the claimant is not entitled to make abstract arguments of Union law infringements that go beyond his personal interest in the case.[88] Yet the Court does not often review the interest requirement, but rather presumes that a relevant interest exists.[89] The interest of Mr Stoeckel was, for instance, rather obvious, as the application of Union law would mean that he would avoid punishment.

The interest requirement finds its clearest expression in *Verholen*. The Court was asked whether an individual could rely on the non-discrimination provision of Directive 79/7/EEC (Equal Treatment in Social Security) in proceedings before the national courts in order to set aside national discriminatory provisions that applied to his spouse. As a consequence of the alleged discrimination, the claimant had his pension reduced. The Court answered in the affirmative, holding that

> the right to rely on the provision of Directive 79/7 is not confined to individuals coming within the scope *rationae personae* of the directive, in so far as the possibility cannot be ruled out that other persons may have a *direct interest* in ensuring that the principle of non-discrimination is respected as regards persons who are not protected.[90]

The Court went on to state that in the present case, an individual who bears the effects of a discriminatory national provision may be allowed to rely on the Directive only if his wife, who is the victim of the discrimination, herself comes within the scope of the Directive. This seems intended to clarify that Member States are not required to entertain abstract arguments of Union law infringement, and the private party must demonstrate that he will benefit from invoking Union law arguments. If the claimant's wife was not covered by the Directive, he would not have had a sufficient interest in challenging the Union law compatibility of the national legislation, as the breach would not have been to his detriment.

The requirement of an interest also finds support in the Court's ruling in *Streekgewest*.[91] The claimant, a local body responsible for collecting domestic waste

[86] See, eg, Case 41/74 *Van Duyn* [1974] para 12.

[87] Case C-213/03 *Syndicat* [2004] para 47.

[88] The interest must not necessarily be identical to that protected by the Union law provision invoked; see further Engström, 'The Europeanisation of Remedies and Procedures Through Judge-Made Law' (n 33) 138–39.

[89] Wennerås, *The Enforcement of EC Environmental Law* (n 5) 25.

[90] Joined Cases C-87/90, C-88/90 and C-89/90 *Verolen* [1991] para 23 (emphasis added).

[91] Case C-174/02 *Streekgewest* [2005]. This case has been analysed in legal scholarship from the perspective of standing, see, eg, K Lenaerts, K Gutman and I Maselis, *EU Procedural Law* (Oxford University Press 2014) 119–20. The Court did not, however, have to rule on the issue of standing, since the private party already had access to court as a matter of domestic law. To the same effect, see AM Keessen, *European Administrative Decisions: How the EU Regulates Products on the Internal Market* (Europa Law Publishing 2009) 191; and Engström, 'The Europeanisation of Remedies and Procedures Through Judge-Made Law' (n 33) 144.

in the Netherlands, brought an action against the Dutch Ministry of Finance to seek the reimbursement of levies on waste paid pursuant to a law introducing a tax for the protection of the environment. The tax revenue was reserved for funding state aid. The claimant alleged a breach of the standstill obligation contained in (now) Article 108(3) TFEU, and the Court was asked whether the provision could be relied upon by a litigant who is not affected by the distortion of cross-border competition arising from an aid measure. The Court answered in the affirmative and stated that

> [a]n individual may have an interest in relying before the national court on the direct effect of the prohibition on implementation referred to in the last sentence of Article [108(3)] of the Treaty not only in order to erase the negative effects of the distortion of competition created by the grant of unlawful aid, but also in order to obtain a refund of a tax levied in breach of that provision. In the latter case, the question whether an individual has been affected by the distortion of competition arising from the aid measure is irrelevant to the assessment of his interest in bringing proceedings. The only fact to be taken into consideration is that the individual is subject to a tax which is an integral part of a measure implemented in breach of the prohibition referred to in that provision.[92]

The Court's ruling is hardly remarkable, given its findings in *Van Calster*, where the Court held that a method of financing aid by means of a tax forms an integral part of the aid measure.[93] The consequences of a failure by the national authorities to comply with standstill obligation must also apply to that aspect of the aid. Consequently, the national authorities are required in principle to repay charges levied in breach of Union law. As this is the case, the claimant's interests in relying on the Article 108(3) TFEU was evident.[94]

It is submitted that the interest requirement implies that a private party cannot challenge a domestic decision or norm for compliance with Union law without regard to his specific situation.[95] That there is no right to require abstract judicial review of legislative provisions is evident from the Court's ruling in *Sodemare*.[96] A private undertaking operating nursing homes contested the rejection of its request to be contracted for the provision of social security services of a healthcare nature by the Lombardy region in Italy. The Court found that the undertaking could not rely on the Treaty provision concerning freedom to provide services (now Article 56 TFEU) in order to challenge the rules at issue, since the provision did not cover its situation: the claimant was established in Italy and the residents reside in these homes permanently or for an indefinite period.[97] The ruling illustrates that the role of the national court is primarily to examine

[92] Case C-174/02 *Streekgewest* [2005] para 19. See also Case 175/02 *Pape* [2005] para 14.

[93] Joined Cases C-261/01 and C-262/01 *Van Calster* [2003].

[94] It can be inferred from Case C-174/02 *Streekgewest* [2005] that denying interested parties the right to rely on directly effective Union law provisions by a requirement that they fall within the protective scope of the provision – that they are right holders – does not seem possible. To the same effect see S Prechal et al, *'Europeanisation' of the Law: Consequences for the Dutch Judiciary* (The Hague, Raad voor de Rechtspraak 2005), 19. See, however, Prechal, 'Protection of Rights: How Far?' (n 63) 177, who takes the Court's statement to mean that 'the protective scope of [Art 108(3) TFEU] covers more persons than competitors only'. Thorson has held that 'the ruling may arguably interpreted as accepting a relatively wide range of right holders'; see Thorson, *Individual Rights in EU Law* (n 55) 260.

[95] Such a requirement has been expressed in the context of annulment proceedings under Art 263(4), see Case 85/82 *Schloh v Council* [1983] para 14.

[96] Case C-70/95 *Sodemare* [1997].

[97] ibid para 40.

the way the law applies to the claimant, and not to review the domestic law in the abstract. Consequently, where a national court considers the Union law compatibility of a statute, it may restrict its decision to the case at hand, and avoid dealing with the question of whether the statute or provision is contrary to Union law in other circumstances. Union law only requires the setting aside of a legislative provision to the extent that it is contrary to Union law *as applied to the claimant*.

Given the broad scope of the invocation right, one may ask what justification the Court may have for this incursion into the domestic procedural landscape. The answer is to be found in the Court's efforts on behalf of the effectiveness of the supremacy principle. In *Simmenthal*, an Italian rule determining that only the Constitutional Court was competent to set aside norms conflicting with Union law, was found unacceptable, since it would in practice undermine the supremacy of EU law.[98] The Court's reasoning in *Simmenthal* also explains why the invocation right is granted as generously as it is. 'Every national court', the Court held,

> must, in a case within its jurisdiction, apply Community law in its entirety and protect rights which the latter confers on individuals and must accordingly set aside any provision of national law which may conflict with it, whether prior or subsequent to the Community rule. Accordingly any provision of a national legal system and any legislative, administrative or judicial practice which might impair the effectiveness of Community law by withholding from the national court having jurisdiction to apply such law the power to do everything necessary at the moment of its application to set aside national legislative provisions which might prevent Community rules from having full force and effect are incompatible with those requirements which are the very essence of Community law.[99]

This ruling clearly illustrates how the Court looks unfavourably upon domestic rules restricting the supremacy of Union law. In the words of Delicostopous, 'substantive supremacy depends, existentially, on procedure and therefore substantive law spills over procedural law. In doing so, substantive EC supremacy leads to further procedural primacy.'[100]

The supremacy of Union law would surely be jeopardised if private parties were hindered from invoking provisions of Union law in the course of an ongoing proceeding, which means that legislative provisions constituting such a hindrance must be set aside.

D. The Consequences of Successfully Invoking a Breach of Union Law

The case law addressed in the preceding sections indicates that the claimant is, as a matter of EU law, entitled to plead the violation of Union law norms provided he has an *interest* in raising such a plea. When it comes to the consequences attached to a finding

[98] Case 106/77 *Simmenthal* [1978].
[99] ibid paras 21–22. This has been repeated in subsequent rulings; see, inter alia, Case C-187/00 *Kutz-Bauer* [2003] para 73 and Case C-556/17, *Torubarov* [2019] para 73.
[100] JS Delicostopous, 'Towards European Procedural Primacy in National Legal Systems' (2003) 9 *European Law Journal* 599, 609.

of non-compliance, there is a need to distinguish between individual administrative decisions and normative acts.

The right to rely on Union law to review a national *administrative decision* does not necessarily entail the right to have the decision annulled.[101] The possibility of upholding the decision is particularly relevant in the case of procedural infringements. The Court held in *Kamino* that Union law does not categorically require the annulment of an administrative decision in the case of infringements of procedural provisions.[102] The case concerned an administrative decision adopted without the right of defence being complied with. As to the consequences resulting from this procedural defect, the Court first noted that in the absence of Union regulation, those consequences are governed by national law, provided that the principles of equivalence and effectiveness are met. The Court nevertheless went on to state that the obligation of the national court to ensure EU law is fully effective does not mean a decision adopted without complying with the rights of defence must be annulled. An infringement of this principle must result in the annulment of the decision in question only if the outcome of the procedure could have been different had it not been for that infringement.[103]

The Court has also seems to have granted the domestic court considerable leeway in determining what measures were required to remedy the failure to conduct an environmental impact assessment in *Wells*.[104] The claimant challenged the renewal of a permit to conduct mining activities in a field close to her home. The permit was granted without a prior environmental impact assessment, as allegedly required by the Directive 85/337/EEC (former EIA Directive).[105] The Court held that if the project should have been subject to an assessment of its environmental effects pursuant to the Directive, the competent authorities would, under the principle of cooperation in good faith laid down in (now) Article 4(3) TEU, have to

> take all general or particular measures for remedying the failure to carry out such an assessment. In that regard, it is for the national court to determine whether it is possible under domestic law for a consent already granted to be revoked or suspended in order to subject the project in question to an assessment of its environmental effects, in accordance with the requirements of [the Directive], or alternatively, if the individual so agrees, whether it is possible for the latter to claim compensation for the harm suffered.[106]

The Court, then, seems to allow for the possibility that the planning permission granted without the required environmental impact assessment would neither be suspended nor revoked, but instead the claimant would obtain compensation for the harm suffered.[107] This possibility has not been mentioned in the Court's later case law, however. In *Inter Environnement Wallonie and Terre wallonne*, the Court held that a national court is

[101] To the same effect, see Leczykiewicz, 'Effectiveness of EU Law Before National Courts' (n 84) 239–40.
[102] Joined Cases C-129/13 and C-130/13 *Kamino* [2014].
[103] ibid paras 75–80. However, the Court has found that making the burden of proof of causality fall on the claimant is capable of making the exercise of the rights conferred on the person 'excessively difficult': see Case C-72/12 *Altrip* [2013] para 52; and Case C-137/14 *Commission v Germany* [2015] para 59.
[104] Case C-201/02 *Wells* [2004].
[105] Now Directive 2011/92.
[106] Case C-201/02 *Wells* [2004] paras 68–69.
[107] Leczykiewicz, 'Effectiveness of EU Law Before National Courts' (n 84) 239.

obliged to take 'all the general or particular measures provided for by its national law in order to remedy the failure to carry out such an assessment, including the possible suspension or annulment' of the contested measure.[108] This was reiterated in *Comune di Corridonia*.[109] The Court added that the Member State concerned is 'likewise required to make good any harm caused' by the breach, but this seems to come *in addition to* the general obligation to nullify the unlawful consequences of the breach.[110] The Court has moreover required Member States to give the infringement due consideration and weight.[111]

Where Union law serves as a parameter for assessing *normative acts*, the incompatible provisions must normally be disapplied. The obligation to set aside norms conflicting with Union law was laid down by the Court in *Simmenthal*, and stems from the principle of supremacy.[112] As the Court held in *Minister for Justice and Equality*, it follows from the principle of primacy that

> bodies called upon, within the exercise of their respective powers, to apply EU law are obliged to adopt all the measures necessary to ensure that EU law is fully effective, disapplying if need be any national provisions or national case-law that are contrary to EU law. This means that those bodies, in order to ensure that EU law is fully effective, must neither request nor await the prior setting aside of such a provision or such case-law by legislative or other constitutional means.[113]

In the words of Dougan, 'the principle of primacy is virtually inseparable, if not altogether indistinguishable, from its remedy of disapplication'.[114] The Court has stressed, however, that a distinction must be drawn between 'the power to disapply, in a specific case, a provision of national law that is contrary to EU law and the power to strike down such a provision, which has the broader effect that that provision is no longer valid for any purpose'.[115] The obligation to set aside legislative provisions contrary to Union law does not mean the infringing provisions are to be rendered inapplicable for all purposes, and hence become in effect null and void.[116] The further consequences of the disapplication of incompatible domestic provisions, such as the validity of contracts entered into in reliance on the legal regime in the Member State, must be determined according to domestic law.[117]

[108] Case C-41/11 *Inter Environnement Wallonie and Terre wallonne* [2012] para 63.

[109] Joined Cases C-196/16 and C-197/16 *Comune di Corridonia* [2017] para 35. See also Case C-261/18 *Commission v Ireland* [2019] para 75.

[110] ibid 36.

[111] The Court has opened up for the possibility that a national court may maintain during a short period certain effects of a national measure incompatible with EU law, subject to the satisfaction of strict conditions; see Case C-41/11 *Inter Environnement Wallonie and Terre wallonne* [2012] paras 46–58. See, however, Case C-463/11 *L v M* [2013], where the Court did not accept a domestic rule whereby a failure to conduct an environmental impact assessment was irrelevant to the legal validity of that plan. The Court has also opened up accepting, under strict conditions, national rules regularising a decision *a posteriori*, despite a failure to carry out an environmental impact assessment of a project as required under Directive; see Joined Cases C-196/16 and C-197/16 *Comune di Corridonia* [2017] paras 37–41.

[112] Case 106/77 *Simmenthal* [1978] paras 21–22.

[113] Case C-378/17, *Minister for Justice and Equality* [2018] para 50.

[114] M Dougan, 'Primacy and the Remedy of Disapplication' (2019) 56 *CML Rev* 1459, 1466.

[115] Case C-378/17, *Minister for Justice and Equality* [2018] para 50.

[116] Joined Cases C-10/97 to C-22/97 *IN.CO.GE* [1998] para 21.

[117] Case C-34/67 *Lück* [1968] and Case C-159/00 *Sapod Audic* [2002].

When addressing the obligation to set aside legislative provisions incompatible with Union law an important caveat is in place: a *procedural* infringement does not necessarily result in the norm's being inapplicable. The consequence of the failure to comply with the provisions of the Directive 83/189/EEC (former Notification Directive) came up in *Lemmens*, where a driver charged with driving a vehicle under the influence of alcohol sought to rely on the fact that national administrative rules regulating the use of breath analysers had not been notified to the Commission as required under the Directive. The Court held that a failure to notify makes such regulations inapplicable only insofar as it creates obstacles to the free movement of goods.[118] Advocate General Fennelly elaborated, and held that

> [t]he inapplicability of national provisions which are on their face incompatible with Community provisions is not universal in its effect, but depends on the result the Directive seeks to achieve. The conflicting national provisions are, therefore, only inapplicable in so far as this is required for the purposes of '[facilitating] the free movement of goods by preventing the creation of new barriers to trade', as the objective of the Directive is described.[119]

In the absence of any express regulation, the effects of procedural infringements must be assessed in light of the aim and purpose of the obligation and the directive in general.[120]

[118] Case C-226/97 *Lemmens* [1998]. The case was thereby distinguished from Case C-194/94 *CIA Security* [1996], see section III.C. It should be noted that the Court's ruling in *Lemmens* is interpreted in various ways in legal scholarship. The Court can either be seen as limiting the circle of persons entitled to rely on the Directive or the material scope of the Directive; see further Thorson, *Individual Rights in EU Law* (n 55) 257. As I see it, the question answered by the Court was not whether the defendant could invoke the notification provision, but rather the consequences that stem from the lack of notification. To the same effect, Eilmansberger, 'The Relationship between Rights and Remedies in EC Law' (n 52) 1244, fn 188; and Prechal, 'Protection of Rights: How Far?' (n 63) 171, fn 76.

[119] AG Fennelly in Case C-226/97 *Lemmens* [1998] para 26.

[120] Wennerås, *The Enforcement of EC Environmental Law* (n 5) 126.

7

The Relationship between Standing and (Substantive) Remedies

I. Introduction

In a book on standing, one may wonder why the issue of remedies is addressed. Standing, the argument would go, is a matter of *procedure*, whereas remedies concern *substance*. Yet separating procedure from substance is not always easy, and the Court has not been too concerned about this (rather blurry) divide either.[1] On occasion the Court has prescribed the availability of particular Union law remedies in domestic courts, and has also implicitly required a legal avenue for the vindication of these remedies. In the process the Court has largely brushed out the distinction between the procedural and substantive aspects of a claim. Since the conditions for standing depends on the remedy sought, there is a need to devote space to the issue of remedies. Understanding Union law requirements as to remedies is a prerequisite for outlining the Union approach to standing.

In the following, I examine how the Court has approached the issue of remedies (sections II and III) and look more closely at the relationship between standing and remedies (sections IV and V).

II. Remedial Autonomy and its Limitations

Pursuant to the principle of national remedial autonomy, the Member States have considerable leeway in arranging the remedies their national courts can apply, both in general and in actual cases. The remedy a judge can award depends on the form of action taken by the claimant, and it is generally up to the claimant to decide from the options available in the domestic legal system:

> [I]ndividuals are often provided with parallel, and sometimes cumulative, possibilities of adjudication [and what] cause of action an individual chooses to bring and what particular

[1] Similarly Havu, who points out that '[t]he issues of remedies and procedure are intertwined'; see K Havu, 'EU Law in Member State Courts: "Adequate Judicial Protection" and Effective Application – Ambiguities and Nonsequiturs in Guidance by the Court of Justice' (2016) 8 *Contemporary Readings in Law & Social Justice* 158, 159.

> relief he seeks depends on a variety of factors, the most important of course being the desired result of the litigation.[2]

It is generally for the national court, not the ECJ, to legally classify the actions brought before the national court.[3]

Although there are certain differences across the Member States when it comes to the type of remedies courts have at their disposal, the overall framework tends to coincide. In proceedings against the state there is the possibility of declaratory relief or annulment of an administrative act. Most courts also possess the power to award damages, and some also injunctive orders.[4] In proceedings against private parties, there is – in addition to declaratory relief, injunctions and damages – also the possibility of awarding contractual remedies.

Declarations merely pronounce particular practices or conditions to be illegal, and declaratory relief is normally used in an anticipatory manner, to obtain a judgment when harm is imminently threatened.[5] An *injunction* is a remedy that can take the form of either a mandatory or a prohibitory injunction. Whereas a prohibitory injunction aims to prevent the continuance or an infringement of a right, a mandatory injunction aims to redress a past infringement of a right by compelling the doing of an act that will realise that right.[6] These forms of injunctions therefore entail respectively *negative* and *positive* obligations.[7] It should be noted that the courts of the Member States are not obliged to grant injunctions going beyond the original Union right, such that a right mirroring a prohibition cannot via enforcement be turned into a positive obligation, for example.[8] *Damages* is a monetary remedy, aimed at compensating economic harm that has already occurred. It is a substitute remedy, because it is incapable of restoring or replacing the rights that have been violated. *Contractual remedies* are remedies that aim at invalidating or otherwise making ineffective contractual arrangements entered into in violation of EU law.[9]

Remedies can be classified according to various criteria. First, a distinction can be drawn between *primary* and *secondary* remedies. Whereas a primary remedy aims at

[2] J Engström, 'The Europeanisation of Remedies and Procedures Through Judge-Made Law: Can a Trojan Horse Achieve Effectiveness? Experiences of the Swedish Judiciary' (PhD thesis, European University Institute 2009) 250.

[3] Joined Cases C-397/98 and C-410/98 *Hoechst* [2001] para 81; Case C-446/04 *Test Claimants in the FII Group Litigatin* [2006] para 201; and Case C-94/10 *Danfoss* [2011] para 32.

[4] C Harlow, 'A Common European Law of Remedies?' in C Kilpatrick, T Novitz and P Skidmore (eds), *The Future of Remedies in Europe* (Hart Publishing 2000) 69, 75.

[5] D Shelton, *Remedies in International Human Rights Law*, 3rd edn (Oxford University Press 2015) 287.

[6] I Lianos, 'Competition Law Remedies in Europe' in D Geradin and I Lianos (eds), *Handbook on European Competition Law: Enforcement and Procedure* (Edward Elgar 2013) 362, 388.

[7] F Wilman, *Private Enforcement of EU Law Before National Courts: The EU Legislative Framework* (Edward Elgar 2015) 289. He holds that injunctions are a 'tailor-made' remedy, since the nature, effect and formulation of injunctive measures depend on the concrete situation; see F Wilman, 'The End of the Absence? The Growing Body of EU Legislation on Private Enforcement and the Main Remedies It Provides For' (2016) 53 *CML Rev* 887, 913.

[8] B Thorson, *Individual Rights in EU Law* (Springer 2016) 89–90 and 144. To illustrate his point he makes reference to Art 102 TFEU, prohibiting the abuse of a dominant position. A refusal to deal may constitute an infringement of the said provision, but this does not mean that domestic courts are obliged to grant a mandatory injunction prescribing a positive obligation to enter into a contract.

[9] Wilman, *Private Enforcement of EU Law Before National Courts* (n 7) 20.

safeguarding and enforcing a primary right, a secondary remedy constitutes a new claim emerging as a reaction to the infringement of the primary right.[10] Secondary remedies, such as an award of damages, are of a compensatory nature and arise as a consequence of Union law infringements, insofar as Member States are required to annul the unlawful consequences of a breach of Union law.[11] *Second*, remedies can be classified according to their purpose. Generally speaking, remedies may fulfil different functions, such as terminating ongoing infringements (or restoring compliance); compensating victims; deterring or preventing future infringements, or restoring the *status quo ante*.[12]

The remedial autonomy of the Member States is not unrestricted. The discretion afforded to the Member States is curtailed where the Union legislature has taken action. As we saw in chapter 3, section II, there is secondary legislation regulating the domestic enforcement of substantive EU law provisions in specific areas.[13] In the absence of specific regulation, Member States are generally not required to provide for any particular remedy, provided the private party has the opportunity to enforce his Union law rights and obtain appropriate redress.[14] Reference can be made to the ECJ's ruling in *Von Colson*, where the Court addressed the adequacy of domestic remedies that served to implement obligations under Directive 76/207/EEC (Equal Treatment). The case concerned a female claimant who had suffered discrimination based on gender when applying for a vacant position, and who had been compensated with mere reliance costs. The Court held that although the full implementation of the Directive did not require any specific form of remedy, the remedy chosen must be 'such as to guarantee *real and effective judicial protection* [and] it must also have real *deterrent effect* on the employer'. It went on to state that where a Member State chooses to award compensation, 'that compensation must in any event be *adequate* in relation to the damage sustained'.[15] Compensation should therefore amount to more than purely nominal compensation, such as the reimbursement of only expenses incurred in connection with the application.[16]

What constitutes an 'effective' and 'adequate' remedy may vary depending on the circumstances. Factors to be taken into account are not only the nature of the infringement,

[10] T Eilmansberger, 'The Relationship between Rights and Remedies in EC Law: In Search of the Missing Link' (2004) 41 *CML Rev* 1199, 1199, fn 2.

[11] Case 6/60 *Humblet* [1960]; and Joined Cases C-6/90 and C-9/90 *Francovich* [1991] para 36.

[12] E Hjelmeng, 'Competition Law Remedies: Striving for Coherence or Finding New Ways?' (2013) 50 *CML Rev* 1007, 1007–08.

[13] While some of these directives and regulations stipulate in fairly general terms that the Member States shall provide adequate, effective and deterrent remedies, others are more elaborate as to the type of remedy to be provided. By way of illustration, Art 3 of Directive 1999/44/EC (Sale of Consumer Goods) gives the consumer the right to reparation or replacement of non-conforming goods.

[14] This is also the case in relation to Art 13 ECHR; see, inter alia, *Öneryildiz v Turkey* App no 48939/99 (ECtHR, 2004) para 146, where the Court made clear that 'the protection afforded by Article 13 does not go so far as to require any particular form of remedy'.

[15] Case 14/83 *Von Colson* [1984] para 23 (emphasis added). See also Case C-271/91 *Marshall II* [1993] para 26, where the Court held that a state opting for financial compensation must 'enable the loss and damage actually sustained – to be made good in full'; and Joined Cases C-46/93 and C-48/93 *Brasserie du Pêcheur* [1996] para 82, where the Court held that reparation for loss or damage must be 'commensurate with the loss or damage sustained'.

[16] Case 14/83 *Von Colson* [1984] para 28. Although the Court derived these requirements from Art 6 of the Directive, this provision is seen as an expression of the general principle of judicial protection; see, inter alia, Case C-185/97 *Coote* [1998] para 21.

but also the timing of the proceedings and the nature of the relationships between the claimant and the defendant. Past infringements should, for example, be redressed by retrospective remedies (such as compensatory-based damages or restorative injunctions), whereas future infringements should be met by prospective remedies (such as preventive injunctions and declaratory relief).[17] In the case of an ongoing infringement, interim relief may also be appropriate with a view to securing the effectiveness of the final judgment. Moreover, contractual remedies may be relevant where there is a contractual dimension to the parties' legal relationship.[18] Whether the claimant is claiming the infringement of a Union right or is rather (exceptionally) enforcing the law in the public interest also has a bearing on the remedy that needs to be provided. The enforcers of the latter category are first and foremost entitled to claim remedies serving preventive ends, in the sense of bringing an end to the violation or compelling performance of an obligation under Union law (such as injunctions and declarations of nullity).[19]

A remedy is effective to the extent that it achieves its aims, which are primarily about terminating infringements and compensating the individuals concerned.[20] Although the Court also stresses the deterrent effect of a remedy, one should be cautious about stretching this element too far. The Member States are, for example, not obliged to provide for punitive damages in the case of Union law infringements, although this would clearly serve as a deterrent factor.[21] It must be kept in mind that the obligation to provide effective and deterrent sanctions is not necessarily exhausted by the provision of a private remedy.[22] If the remedy is not sufficiently deterrent, it can be supplemented by a public sanction, for instance a fine.

As a deviation from the relatively lenient requirements of 'adequacy' and 'effectiveness', the Court has on occasion elaborated more on the types of remedies that need to be provided in the case of an infringement. Particularly within the area of state aids, we find examples of a more assertive approach by the Court. National courts are entrusted with policing compliance, with the obligation to give prior notification of state aid to the Commission pursuant to Article 108(3) TFEU.[23] Remedies available before domestic

[17] A Wechsler and B Tripković, 'Conclusions: Enforcement in Europe as a Market of Justice' in H-W Micklitz and A Wechsler (eds), *The Transformation of Enforcement* (Hart Publishing 2016) 377, 402–03.

[18] Wilman, *Private Enforcement of EU Law Before National Courts* (n 7) 307.

[19] Similarly S Prechal and L Hancher, 'Individual Environmental Rights: Conceptual Pollution in EU Environmental Law?' 2002 *The Yearbook of European Environmental Law* 89, 108; and E Hjelmeng, 'Private Enforcement of Article 9 Commitment Decisions – "Objective" vs "Subjective" Direct Effect' in M Andenæs and K Lilleholt (eds), *Remedies and Substantive Law – European Dimensions of Economic and Private Law. University of Oslo Faculty of Law Research Paper No 2011-18*, 35.

[20] Similarly Hjelmeng, 'Competition Law Remedies' (n 12) 1010. The Court has explicitly stated that the purpose of Member State liability is 'not deterrence or punishment, but compensation for the damage suffered by individuals as a result of breaches of Community law by Member States'; see Case C-470/03 *A.G.M-COS.MET* [2007] para 88.

[21] See Case C-407/14 *Camacho* [2015]. Where punitive damages are available for similar domestic actions, the principle of equivalence, may, however, require that such damages be provided, see Joined Cases C-295/04 to C-298/04 *Manfredi* [2006] para 93. For a further account, see E Büyüksagis et al, 'Punitive Damages in Europe and Plea for the Recognition of Legal Pluralism' (2016) 27 *European Business Law Review* 137.

[22] M Dougan, 'Who Exactly Benefits from the Treaties? The Murky Interaction Between Union and National Competence over the Capacity to Enforce EU Law' (2009) 12 *Cambridge Yearbook of European Legal Studies* 73, 107.

[23] Art 108(3) TFEU provides that the Member States shall not put its proposed measures into effect 'until this [notification] procedure has resulted in a final decision'. National courts do 'no more than preserve, until the final decision of the Commission, the rights of individuals faced with a possible breach by State authorities of the prohibition laid down by [Art 108(3)] of the Treaty'; see Case C-354/90 *FNCE* [1991] para 14.

courts in the event of an infringement include preventing the payment of unlawful aid; recovery of unlawful aid; recovery of illegal interest; damages; and interim measures against unlawful aid.[24] Still, the type of remedy granted largely depends on what is provided for under national law.[25]

The Court has also recognised the existence of certain autonomous 'Union law remedies', and set out for itself the constitutive conditions governing entitlement to these specific remedies. It has left to domestic law only the specific conditions for their exercise, and procedural rules, subject to the requirements of equivalence and effectiveness.[26] To the extent that entitlement to a particular remedy is anchored in the Union legal order, we are dealing with a Union law right. It is a secondary, remedial right arising as a consequence of a Union law violation. Póltorak writes (with reference to compensation and restitution) that

> [t]hese are substantive rights derived from the EU law system. At the same time they are remedies, both because of their source, which is the principle of effectiveness, and because of their aims – protection of individual rights derived from the EU system aiming at restoration of the infringed rights. They are thus of a double character – they have the characteristics of a right and of a remedy.[27]

The Union law remedies are, in other words, *secondary rights* arising as a result of an infringement of a primary right. The remedies that should be properly classified as such will be elaborated on in the following.

III. The Right to Specific Union Law Remedies

The case law of the Court is still evolving, and there is no agreement in the legal scholarship as to what constitutes a Union law remedy. Still, it is submitted that at least the right to reimbursement of unlawfully levied charges, the right to have unlawful state aids recovered and the right to damages against the state constitute Union law remedies. Arguably, the right to damages for competition law infringements, now codified in Directive 2014/104/EU (Competition Damages), also qualifies as such.[28]

The most well-known and addressed Union law remedy is the right to damages from the Member States for violations of their Union law obligations. This remedy will be discussed at some length in chapter 10, and is therefore left out in the following.

The right of an individual to a refund of taxes and charges levied by a Member State in breach of the rules of EU law was addressed by the Court in *San Giorgio*.[29] The claimant sought to reclaim taxes that were unlawfully levied, but pursuant to Italian law, he had to

[24] Commission notice on the enforcement of State aid law by national courts of 9 April 2009, C 85/01 paras 26 et seq. The possibility of a direct action against the beneficiary of the aid is not required unless this follows from the principle of equivalence; see M Heidenhain, *European State Aid Law* (Beck 2010) 775.

[25] See, inter alia, Case C-354/90 *FNCE* [1991] para 12; and Case C-39/94 *SFEI* [1996] para 40.

[26] AP Komninos, 'Private Enforcement in the EU with Emphasis on Damages Actions' in Geradin and Lianos (eds), *Handbook on European Competition Law* (n 6) 288, 236.

[27] N Poltorak, *European Union Rights in National Courts* (Wolters Kluwer 2015) 14.

[28] See Art 3. This remedy is addressed further in ch 3, section IV.C.

[29] Case 199/82 *San Giorgio* [1983]. The right to recovery was, however, recognised already in Case 177/78 *Pigs and Bacon Commission v Mc Carren* [1979] para 25.

prove that the amount unlawfully levied was not passed on to his customers. The Court held that the entitlement to the repayment of charges levied contrary to Union law was a 'consequence of, and adjunct to' the rights conferred on individuals by the Union provisions prohibiting such charges.[30] The rationale underlying this principle is that a Member State must not profit and an individual who has been required to pay the unlawful charge must not suffer loss as a result of the imposition of the charge.[31] The right to repayment follows directly from the substantive Union law provision infringed.[32]

Where state aid has been granted in violation of the standstill provision in Article 108(3) TFEU, the national court must in principle order the full recovery of the unlawful aid from the beneficiary. The Court held in *SFEI* that 'a national court requested to order the repayment of aid must grant that application if it finds that the aid was not notified to the Commission, unless by reason of exceptional circumstances repayment is inappropriate'.[33] The Court has described recovery as 'the logical consequence of a finding that aid is unlawful'.[34] The main objective pursued in recovering unlawfully paid state aid is to eliminate the distortion of competition caused by the competitive advantage afforded by such aid.[35]

It was also long believed that the Court had established a right to interim relief in the form of an injunction, but, as will be seen, this does not seem to be the case. The obligation to provide interim protection was first stated by the Court in *Factortame*, where the Court held that the procedural rule prohibiting the suspension of the operation of an Act of Parliament – due to the principle of parliamentary sovereignty – had to be set aside.[36] The conditions under which interim protection had to be awarded were spelled out by the Court in *Zuckerfabrik* and *Atlanta*, where the validity of Union law secondary legislation was at issue. The Court found that while a preliminary ruling on the validity of Union law is pending, a domestic court may grant interim relief if it has serious doubts about the validity of the measure; interim relief is deemed necessary to avoid serious and irreparable harm; and the court takes due account of the Union interest.[37] The doubt as to whether these conditions were also applicable where the compatibility of national measures with Union law was the subject of the dispute was eventually clarified in *Unibet*.[38] The Court distinguished the case from *Zuckerfabrik* and *Atlanta*, since the application for interim relief did not

> seek to suspend the effects of a national provision adopted in accordance with a Community regulation where the legality of that regulation is contested, but rather the effects of national legislation where the compatibility of that legislation with Community law is contested.[39]

[30] Case 199/82 *San Giorgio* [1983] para 12. See also Case C-398/09 *Lady & Kid* [2011] para 17; and Case C-69/14 *Târşia* [2015] para 24.

[31] AG Fennelly in Joined Cases C-397/98 and 410/98 *Hoechst* [2000] para 45.

[32] The Member States are under an obligation to repay amounts of tax levied in breach of EU law with interest; see Case C-591/10 *Littlewoods Retail* [2012] para 26.

[33] Case C-39/94 *SFEI* [1996] para 71.

[34] Case C-275/10 *Residex* [2011] para 33.

[35] ibid para 34.

[36] Case C-213/89 *Factortame* [1990] para 23.

[37] See Joined Cases C-143/88 and C-92/89 *Zuckerfabrik* [1991] para 33; and Case C-465/93 *Atlanta* [1995] para 32.

[38] Case C-432/05 *Unibet* [2007].

[39] ibid para 79.

The Court held that as a matter of principle, interim relief should be available until the compatibility with Union law of an act is determined, if this is necessary to ensure the effectiveness of the final judgment.[40] The need for interim relief is at times indispensable in order for the remedy eventually awarded to serve its purpose. For instance, in the context of competition law, time is of the essence. It is hardly possible to imagine that a claim for a prohibitory injunction will be of value absent interim relief pending the final outcome of the case.[41] Yet the granting of interim relief is governed by the criteria laid down by the national law applicable before that court, subject to the requirements of equivalence and effectiveness.[42] Insofar as this is not a proper Union law remedy, it will not be addressed separately in the following.

The concept of Union law remedies cannot be addressed without mentioning some critical voices.[43] As Williams has explained, the ECJ's 'remedies' jurisprudence is understood in two different ways. Either the ECJ is regarded as requiring the existence of a cause of action *of some kind*, or, alternatively, the Court is seen as requiring a *particular* cause of action.[44] It has been suggested that private parties are perhaps not entitled to a specific remedy; rather they are entitled to *access to court* and *effective redress*. Hence, if Member States can provide an alternative, equally effective remedy, they are free to do so, and '[t]he need to make a certain remedial right available will … only come into play when there is a deficiency in the national system'.[45] There is some support for this position in the Court's jurisprudence. In *Marks & Spencer*, the Court held that wrongfully levied tax must in principle be reimbursed to the trader unless there are other ways of remedying that infringement under national law.[46] Moreover, in *Recheio*, the Court accepted that a national court on its own motion transferred an action for reimbursement by a taxpayer into an action for annulment of the decision imposing the unlawful tax.[47] The extent to which the Member States are at liberty to provide a different type of remedy will be further addressed in chapter 10, section IV in relation to state liability.

[40] ibid para 75. See also Case C-213/89 *Factortame* [1990] para 21, where the Court spoke of the necessity of interim relief 'in order to ensure the full effectiveness of the judgment to be given on the existence of the rights claimed under Community law'.

[41] E Hjelmeng, *Privat Håndhevelse av EØS-Avtalens Konkurranseregler* (Fagbokforlaget 2003) 165.

[42] Case C-432/05 *Unibet* [2007] paras 81–82. Member States are, moreover, entitled to restrict interim relief to those who bring proceedings on the merits; see Case C-416/10 *Križan* [2013] para 107. In Case C-432/05 *Unibet* [2007] para 72, the Court included the caveat that 'where it is uncertain … whether an action to safeguard respect for an individual's rights under Community law is admissible, the principle of effective judicial protection requires the national court to be able, none the less, at that stage, to grant the interim relief necessary to ensure that those rights are respected'.

[43] In particular Engström, 'The Europeanisation of Remedies and Procedures Through Judge-Made Law' (n 2) 250–63.

[44] R Williams, 'Case C-47/07, Masdar (UK) Ltd v Commission, Judgment of the Grand Chamber of 16 December 2008, and Case C-446/04, Test Claimants in the FII Group Litigation v Commissioners of Inland Revenue, Judgment of the Grand Chamber of 12 December 2006 [2006]; ECR I-11753' (2010) 47 *CML Rev* 555, 569–70.

[45] Engström, 'The Europeanisation of Remedies and Procedures Through Judge-Made Law' (n 2) 260.

[46] Case C-309/06 *Marks & Spencer* [2008] para 62.

[47] Case C-30/02 *Recheio* [2004] paras 16–17.

IV. Distinguishing Standing to Pursue Union Law Remedies and the Right to Obtain Such Remedies

Where Union law entitles a private party to a particular remedy, the content of this remedy, both as regards the material and personal scope, is basically determined pursuant to Union law. This remedial right must be upheld and enforced in the Member States. This means that where the Court has required the Member State to provide a particular remedy and has established the constitutive conditions, the notion of standing loses some of its importance. By recognising an individual's right to a particular remedy, the Court has at the same time obliged the Member State to ensure that this remedy can be pursued in court.[48] As Póltorak puts it,

> where the Court has ordered the implementation of offensive remedies – such as restitution compensation or injunction claims – these remedies require initiating separate court proceedings, hence it can be argued that these remedies also include the right to initiate proceedings.[49]

The question of standing is determined by who has the right to that particular remedy; in other words, the entitlement to the remedy and the right to pursue that remedy in court largely converge. For instance, when the Court stated in *Courage* that 'any individual' who has suffered loss because of a breach may claim compensation, it laid down a rule on standing.[50] The Court has also made clear that access to court must be provided for those pursuing *Francovich* damages. In *Köbler*, where the Court stated the principle of liability also for courts adjudicating in the last instance, it held that 'it is for the Member States to enable those affected to rely on that principle [of state liability] by affording them an appropriate right of action'.[51] This means that the Member States cannot restrict access to court through restrictive standing requirements. But since the entitlement to that remedy is limited to certain persons, the right to initiate proceedings is similarly curtailed.

A difficulty arises from the fact that these secondary – or remedial – rights are incomplete. Although the basic conditions for obtaining compensation and restitution have been defined by the Court, national law may still influence their content. For instance, the right to reimbursement of unlawfully levied charges and recovery of unlawful state aid means that the courts of Member States 'in principle' must order reimbursement or recovery. Reimbursement may, for instance, be denied where the charges have been passed on,[52] and recovery may be excluded based on considerations of legitimate expectations.[53] In relation to state liability in damages, the Court has held

[48] Similarly Eilmansberger, 'The Relationship between Rights and Remedies in EC Law' (n 10) 1239–40.

[49] Poltorak, *European Union Rights in National Courts* (n 27) 64. Similarly W Van Gerven, 'Of Rights, Remedies and Procedures' (2000) 37 *CML Rev* 501, 512.

[50] V Milutinović, *The 'Right to Damages' under EU Competition Law: From Courage v Crehan to the White Paper and Beyond* (Kluwer Law International 2010) 221.

[51] Case C-224/01 *Köbler* [2003] para 45.

[52] See Case 199/82 *San Giorgio* [1983]; and Joined Cases C-192/95 to C-218/95 *Comateb* [1997] para 21.

[53] See, inter alia, Case C-5/89 *BUG-Alutechninik* [1990] paras 14–16.

that in order to determine the loss or damage for which reparation should be granted, the national court may examine 'whether the injured person showed reasonable diligence in order to avoid the loss or damage or limit its extent'.[54] Similarly, as regards liability for competition law infringements, the Court has, for instance, left it to the domestic legal order to determine the detailed conditions for establishing causality, as long as the principles of equivalence and effectiveness are complied with.[55] Given these examples, the remedies can be classified as *hybrids*, based partly on Union law, partly on domestic law. The exact division of competences is rather obscure, a matter to be further explored in chapter 10. For present purposes, it is sufficient to mention that although the conditions for obtaining such a remedy are met prima facie, a claim will not necessarily succeed on the merits.

Still, it seems that the Member States cannot restrict *standing* through categorical rules on causality or other legitimate defences. This seems to be the implication of the Court's ruling in *Kone*.[56] Although the ruling does not explicitly address standing conditions, it has a direct bearing on access to judicial process.[57] The reference for a preliminary ruling arose in the context of a follow-on damages claim against an elevator cartel in Austria. The claimant brought proceedings against a cartel member, claiming damages for the loss suffered as a result of its supplier's (which was not a member to the cartel) setting higher prices than would have been achievable in the absence of the cartel (so-called 'umbrella pricing'). According to Austrian law, compensation could not be claimed against the cartel members, as the loss was caused by a supplier who was not a party to the cartel. The 'adequate causal link' required under Austrian law was not present and, moreover, the loss allegedly suffered due to umbrella pricing was not considered within the protective scope of the competition rules. The ECJ found the total exclusion of umbrella claims unacceptable. Recalling its holding in *Manfredi*, the Court first stated that it is for the domestic legal systems of each Member State to lay down the detailed rules on causation, provided that the principles of equivalence and effectiveness are complied with.[58] National law cannot, however, categorically and regardless of the particular circumstances of the case determine that a direct causal link does not exist when there is no contractual link with the cartel, as this would put the effectiveness of EU competition rules at risk.[59]

The ruling is rather short. The Court states that national law cannot categorically, a priori, exclude umbrella claims. However, the Court still leaves in place the requirement of a causal link, which means that damages need not be awarded in any particular case.[60]

[54] Case C-524/04 *Test Claimants in the Thin Cap Group Litigation* [2007] para 124.

[55] Case C-557/12 *Kone* [2014]; and Case C-435/18 *Otis II* [2019].

[56] Case C-557/12 *Kone* [2014].

[57] On the Court's distinct approach to standing in the field of competition law, see ch 3 section IV. C .

[58] This in contrast to AG Kokott, who defined causation as a concept of EU law; see her Opinion in Case C-55/12 *Kone* [2014] para 34.

[59] ibid para 33.

[60] The Court did not develop a uniform doctrine of causality, hence '[n]ational legal tradition will probably play an important role in the application of the conditions defined by the Court in *Kone*'; see A Svetlicinii and M Botta, '"Umbrella Pricing" in Private Enforcement of EU Competition Law and US Antitrust Law: Another Transatlantic Divergence?' (2016) 41 *EL Rev* 399, 406. In recital 11 to Directive 2014/104/EU (Competition

The Court therefore seems to have replaced a categorical rule on causality with a case-by-case approach.[61] This means that standing cannot be excluded through abstract rules on causation.[62] Individuals who have an arguable claim that they have suffered harm from a competition law infringement should be granted access to court, where the issue of causality can be assessed on the merits.[63] Although standing cannot be restricted *a priori* referring to the doctrine of remoteness, this does not necessarily mean that the notion of remoteness has no role to play in the domestic legal system. Remoteness cannot, however, be determined in the abstract, but must be assessed on a case-by-case basis.

The ECJ followed the same approach in *Otis II*, where the Court held that compensation may also be claimed from members of a cartel by persons who are not active as suppliers or customers on the relevant market affected by a cartel.[64] Although the Court left in place the requirement of a causal link, and refrained from defining that notion, it made clear that standing cannot be denied with reference to to the 'objective of protection' of Article 101 TFEU. The ruling makes clear that national law must not 'entirely bar claims by alleged harm-sufferers that are not active on the exact market affected by a cartel but are harmed more indirectly'.[65]

This conclusion would also apply to other defences available under domestic law, such as contributory negligence or unjust enrichment. Whether these defences are of use in a concrete case depends on the *facts of the case*, which means that Member States are not entitled to rely on general doctrines limiting the ability of the private party to obtain the remedy. In *Courage*, the Court held that whereas an absolute bar on the right of a party to a restrictive agreement on claiming damages is incompatible with Union law, this right can be excluded where the claimant bears 'significant responsibility for the distortion of competition'.[66] Similarly, in *Comateb* – upon acknowledging considerations of unjust enrichment – the Court held that 'traders may not be prevented from *applying to the courts* having jurisdiction … for reparation of loss caused by the levying of charges not due, irrespective of whether those charges have been passed on'.[67] Hence the Court is not opposed to a rule of national law preventing damages in the case of contributory negligence or unjust enrichment,

Damages), it is stated that causality is not dealt with in the Directive, hence indicating that this is a matter that in principle is left to national law.

[61] A Sanchez-Graells, 'When the CJEU opens the Umbrella, Lawyers and Economists get ready for a Warm Shower of Damages Claims' at www.howtocrackanut.com/blog/2014/06/when-cjeu-opens-umbrella-lawyers-and.html.

[62] On the requirement of causation, see ch 10, section III.D.

[63] On the requirement of an arguable claim, see ch 4, section IV.

[64] Case C-435/18 *Otis II* [2019].

[65] K Havu, 'Private Enforcement of Competition Law: Notes Regarding the Roles of EU and National Law on the Basis of Recent Preliminary Rulings' (2020) 2 *Europarättslig tidskrift* 193, 200.

[66] Case C-453/99 *Courage* [2001] para 31.

[67] Joined Cases C-192/95 to C-218/95 *Comateb* [1997] para 34 (emphasis added).

provided that it is not an absolute defence but can be established as a matter of fact. In the words of Engström,

> no absolute bars to the exercise of this remedial right are accepted. It must be possible to have access to court and have a judicial instance evaluate the reasonableness of depriving the individual of a right to damages in the circumstances of the case at hand.[68]

The above indicates that EU law is 'more concerned with the possibility of an action, than with the eventual relief [and it] is valuable to the Union project if national courts hear cases and take a stand on whether or not Union law has been respected'.[69] A private party who has an arguable claim that his Union rights have been violated must be able to address the court and request redress, but whether the action is successful eventually depends on the merits of his case.

V. Alternative Forms of Legal Recourse

Having discussed Union law remedies at length, there is a need to recall the starting point of national *remedial autonomy*. Where Union law does not require any specific type of remedy, it is left to the Member States to decide on the remedies to be provided, as long as they are effective and adequate. Due to the discretion granted to the Member States in this regard, it is not feasible to tie EU law standing requirements to the remedies provided. As will be seen, the Court has linked standing requirements to the *type of action*, rather than to the substantive remedy sought. Judicial review proceedings may serve as an illustration. The Court has on several occasions ruled on the possibility for third parties to challenge administrative acts in court.[70] A successful challenge may result in a variety of remedies, such as annulment (*ex tunc* or *ex nunc*), injunctive relief or damages, but the Court has not paid particular regard to this issue. Rather, the Court considers access to court of paramount importance, regardless of the type of (adequate) redress afforded to a successful claimant. As pointed out by Engström,

> the right to judicial review is more a right to a *cause of action* than for example, the right to compensation or the right to restitution [since the] protection of the legal position lies rather in the judiciary's control and in erasing the negative effects of an unlawful measure than granting a new right like compensation or restitution.[71]

The principle of effective judicial protection does not necessarily require the provision of a certain type of legal recourse; what matters is that the claimant's rights are effectively protected. The Court of Justice considers the system of legal protection as a whole to determine whether the requirement of effective judicial protection has been met. The duty to provide effective judicial protection is largely an obligation of result, and there

[68] Engström, 'The Europeanisation of Remedies and Procedures Through Judge-Made Law' (n 2) 230.

[69] Thorson, *Individual Rights in EU Law* (n 8) 147. He writes this in the context of interim measures, but the statement is of broader relevance.

[70] See, inter alia, Case C-104/13 *Olainfarm* [2014]; and Case C-510/13 *E.ON Földgaz* [2015].

[71] Engström, 'The Europeanisation of Remedies and Procedures Through Judge-Made Law' (n 2) 156–57.

are various ways to achieve this end. Opinions are divided as to whether this remedial discretion also applies in relation to what I have called 'Union law remedies', particularly *Francovich* liability. Whether the Court has introduced an autonomous Union law remedy or whether the Member States can fend off such a claim with reference to an alternative legal avenue will be addressed separately in chapter 10, section IV, and therefore left out in the following.

As will be seen, the Court has adopted a pragmatic approach, where the focus is on the individual claimant's situation, rather than on the legal system as such. This 'hands off' approach shows the Court's reluctance to interfere with domestic procedural and remedial structures. In the context of administrative review, the leeway given to the Member States was made clear by the Court already in *Safalero*.[72] The claimant in the main proceeding, a producer of scale aeroplane models, imported radio controls from another Member State. Italian administrative authorities seized the goods sold to a retailer, as the equipment did not bear a stamp required under Italian law. Safalero sought to challenge the seizure, alleging that the Italian rules were contrary to Union law as they hindered the free movement of goods. Under Italian law, only the addressee of the decision could challenge it, and consequently Safalero was not granted standing. The Court nevertheless held that Italian law afforded sufficient judicial protection through another legal avenue: as Safalero was fined for selling goods non-compliant with the aforementioned labelling requirements, he could have the compatibility of the Italian rules with Union law assessed in the course of challenging the fine.

The Court adopted a similar approach in *Unibet*, where it was asked whether a free-standing action for judicial review of legislation had to be made available to challenge the Swedish law on lotteries.[73] The claimants in the main proceedings had purchased advertising space in various Swedish newspapers in order to promote their gaming services. The Swedish Government took legal action against the newspapers for infringing the law on lotteries, which prohibited the marketing of lotteries that had not been granted a licence. No administrative action or criminal proceedings were brought against the betting companies, but the companies initiated judicial proceedings requesting a declaration that they were entitled to promote their activities, arguing that the Swedish legislation infringed their freedom to provide services. They also applied for interim relief and damages for loss suffered. The request for declaratory relief was held inadmissible, on the basis that it constituted an abstract review of legality foreign to the Swedish legal system, and the Court was asked whether the exclusion of this legal avenue was compatible with Union law.

The Court took the view that the principle of effective judicial protection was complied with. It held that the principle of effective judicial protection does not require the existence of a free-standing action, provided the compatibility of national legislative provisions with Union law can be examined as a preliminary issue in the context of an alternative legal avenue. The betting companies had two alternative judicial routes to contest incidentally the applicability of the law on lotteries. First, they could initiate an

[72] Case C-13/01 *Safalero* [2003].
[73] Case C-432/05 *Unibet* [2007].

action for damages based directly on EU law. The Court emphasised that the national court had to ensure that Swedish law was examined for Union law compliance, regardless of whether the claim for damages was unsuccessful, due to a lack of damage or causal link.[74] Second, they could apply for an exception to the prohibition on the promotion of their services in Sweden, and challenge before the court any decision rejecting that application. In the context of the court proceedings, it could argue that the Swedish statute was incompatible with Union law, and seek to have the law disapplied. The Court stressed, however, that the effectiveness requirement would not be fulfilled if the claimants could only test the legality of a national rule *by first breaking it*.[75]

The above cases reveal the Court to have an open mind with regard to national variations in the procedural framework. The Court has still not been clear as to what constitutes an adequate alternative legal recourse, but it must be required that both the formal and substantive aspects of judicial protection are fulfilled, which means that the claimant must be provided *both* with effective access to court *and* effective redress.[76] Whether another remedy is sufficient to afford adequate judicial protection must be assessed in each individual case; a mere reference to the general availability of alternative remedies will not suffice.[77] The existence of a favourable remedy in domestic legislation is not sufficient to ensure judicial protection where the procedural conditions for obtaining the remedy fail to meet the requirements of equivalence or effectiveness, either by being less favourable than those applicable to similar domestic actions, or by making the exercise of Union rights impossible or excessively difficult.[78]

The adequacy of the alternative legal route at the disposal of the claimant was not assessed in *Safalero*.[79] The Court seems to have accepted a situation that required the interested party to infringe the law in order to be granted effective judicial protection.[80] Keeping in mind the Court's statement in *Unibet*, that the effectiveness requirement would not be fulfilled if the claimant could only test the legality of a national rule by first breaking it, it may be questioned whether Safalero was afforded effective judicial protection at all. At the same time, there is one difference that merits consideration. In contrast to the situation in *Unibet*, the proceedings for imposing the fine had already been instigated, as the law had already been infringed. Since that was the case, the pending proceedings could be used for the protection of the claimants' rights.[81] This rather dubious distinction serves to illustrate the Court's pragmatic and context-specific approach to the question of effective judicial protection.

[74] Arnull raises the critique that '[r]equiring the national court to address the compatibility question come what it may is inconsistent with the principle of procedural economy'; see A Arnull, 'Annotation of Unibet' (2007) 44 *CML Rev* 1763, 1775.

[75] Case C-432/05 *Unibet* [2007] para 64. This was confirmed by the Court in Case C-583/11 P *Inuit* [2013] para 104.

[76] On these two aspects of the principle of effective judicial protection, see ch 3, section III.C.

[77] Similarly, Engström, 'The Europeanisation of Remedies and Procedures Through Judge-Made Law' (n 2) 263, fn 625.

[78] See Case C-326/96 *Levez* [1998] (equivalence); and Case Case C-63/08 *Pontin* [2009] (effectiveness).

[79] T Tridimas, *The General Principles of EU Law*, 2nd edn (Oxford University Press 2006) 453.

[80] Poltorak, *European Union Rights in National Courts* (n 27) 155.

[81] ibid 159.

Although a single remedy does not satisfy the requirements of the principle of effective judicial protection, the aggregate of remedies provided under domestic law may do so.[82] The Court has, however, found that requiring a claimant to bring two parallel proceedings could be contrary to the principle of effective judicial protection. In *Impact*, the Court was asked whether a specialised court was obliged to apply a directive directly, despite this being entrusted to the general courts under domestic law. The Court answered that this was indeed the case if the bringing of a separate claim based directly on the directive before the ordinary court 'would involve procedural disadvantages liable to render excessively difficult the exercise of the rights conferred on [the claimant] by Community law'.[83]

The Court has been careful not to prescribe in detail the kinds of measures that need to be taken to fulfil the obligation to provide effective judicial protection. Rather, the Court leaves the Member States sufficient room for making choices as to the legal avenues provided. That said, the Court indicated in *Unibet* that if the national legal system provides no legal avenue that enables a private party to ensure that his Union rights are respected, the Member State concerned must provide for a self-standing action to have the court review the compatibility of a national provision with Union law.[84] As General Sharpston put it, 'in certain circumstances Community law may require a new remedy where that is the only way to ensure that a Community right can be protected'.[85]

[82] See, inter alia, Joined Cases C-192/95 to C-218/95 *Comateb* [1997] (the aggregation of reimbursement and damages). This coincides with the jurisprudence from the ECtHR under Art 13 ECHR, see, inter alia, *Edwards v the United Kingdom* App no 46477/99 (ECtHR, 2002) para 101.

[83] Case C-268/06 *Impact* [2008] para 55.

[84] S Prechal and R Widdershoven, 'Redefining the Relationship between "Rewe-Effectiveness" and Effective Judicial Protection' (2011) 4 *Review of European Administrative Law* 31, 41–42; and Poltorak, *European Union Rights in National Courts* (n 27) 95–96.

[85] AG Sharpston in Case C-432/05 *Unibet* [2006] para 35.

8

Standing to Seek Judicial Review of Administrative Decisions

I. Introduction

In chapter 5, section IV, it was argued that the principle of effective judicial protection requires Member States to provide a claimant with standing where three conditions are met: the claimant is the holder of a Union right; this right is adversely affected; and the claimant has a (vested and present) interest in the proceedings. In the following, I illustrate how these criteria are to be applied where a claimant seeks judicial review of an administrative decision.[1] To provide a conceptual background to the issue of standing in administrative proceedings, I review in brief typical standing doctrines found in Member States in section II. Delineating the category of enforcers poses particular problems when diffuse interests are at stake, and in sections III and IV I therefore take a closer look at two particular sectors, namely, environmental law and telecommunications. The purpose is to shed light on the thorny issue of diffuse rights, and on how aspects of factual concern serve to distinguish those with the requisite interest to sue.

The vast body of the Court's case law pertaining to standing has been handed down in the context of proceedings for judicial review of administrative decisions.[2] This is due to the fact that a large number of the rules stemming from Union law presuppose the existence of administrative organs that can implement the rights and duties and intervene in the case of non-compliance.[3] Both the *addressee* of an unfavourable decision and *third parties* adversely affected by a decision may want to seize the court, with a view to having an administrative decision reviewed.

[1] This chapter is a more detailed version of HK Ellingsen, 'Judicial Review of Administrative Decisions in Domestic Courts – Union Law requirements on the *locus standi* of individuals' in L Cadiet, B Hess and M Requejo Isidro (eds), *Approaches to Procedural Law: The Pluralism of Methods* (Nomos 2017) 509.

[2] Administrative decisions is here defined as 'legal acts … which are passed in the exercise of public authority and which may affect the rights and legitimate interests of citizens and legal persons', see further Z Szente, 'Conceptualising the Principle of Effective Legal Protection in Administrative Law' in Z Szente and K Lachmayer (eds), *The Principle of Effective Legal Protection in Administrative Law*: A European Perspective (Routledge 2016) 5, 11 (with the exclusion of normative acts). Union law may affect not only the category of standees, but also the types of acts open to challenge – see Case C-97/91 *Borelli* [1992]; Case C-269/99 *Kühne* [2001]; and Case C-562/12 *Liivimaas Lihaveis* [2014]. On the possibility of challenging a failure to act, see AM Keessen, *European Administrative Decisions: How the EU Regulates Products on the Internal Market* (Europa Law Publishing 2009) 179.

[3] N Fenger, *EU-rettens påvirkning af dansk forvaltningsret* (DJØF 2013) 9.

An addressee who is denied a benefit to which he is entitled under Union law, must be entitled to challenge the refusal in court.[4] Moreover, an addressee of a decision imposing a sanction must be granted standing pursuant to the principle of effective judicial protection where the decision infringes his Union rights.[5] That notwithstanding, since addressees are mostly granted standing as a matter of domestic law, it is primarily with respect to *third parties* that Union law will have a role to play. Hence, the focus in the following will be on trilateral relationships, involving not only the public authority and the addressee, but also a third party.[6]

II. Standing Doctrines in the Member States

The range of persons entitled to challenge an administrative decision varies considerably between the Member States.[7] A rough distinction can be drawn between *rights-based* and *interest-based* approaches to standing. In states belonging to the first category – such as Germany – standing in administrative proceedings is generally limited to persons asserting the impairment of a subjective public right.[8] This test implies a 'three-step scrutiny' of the provision in question: there must be a generally binding statutory provision; the provision must aim at the protection of individual interests; and the persons concerned must be given the power to enforce their legally protected interests.[9] Even in legal systems where standing is not conditioned on the existence of rights, access to court often depends on the claimant's having an interest in seeking judicial review. The interest required varies greatly; it may, for instance, be qualified as a 'sufficient interest', which is the case in France, or a 'legal interest', such as in Denmark.[10] These broad formulas do not, however, shed much light on the content of these doctrines, and there are great variations as regards both the type of interests that are cognisable for standing purposes and the magnitude of the adverse effects on the claimant. The strictness of domestic standing doctrines tends to be influenced by what is seen to be the function of the court in the context of judicial review.[11]

The court's function can either be tuned to the protection of individual rights or interests, or it can rather be a means of keeping public authorities within their powers.

[4] Case 222/86 *Heylens* [1987] para 14.

[5] See Case C-682/15 *Berlioz* [2017] para 51, where the Court held that 'protection against arbitrary or disproportionate intervention by public authorities in the sphere of the private activities of any natural or legal person constitutes a general principle of EU law'. See also A de Moor-van Vugt, 'Administrative Sanctions in EU Law' (2012) 5 *Review of European Administrative Law* 5, 34. Of particular importance in this context is the right to legality and proportionality of penalties laid down in Art 48 of the Charter of Fundamental Rights.

[6] By means of illustration, an individual may want to contest a permit granted to another individual that does not live up to the demands of EU law; see, eg, Case C-201/02 *Wells* [2004], addressed further in ch 6, section III.D.

[7] The criteria for standing may also vary depending on the sector of administrative law or the remedy sought; see further M Eliantonio et al, *Standing Up for Your Right(s) in Europe – A Comparative Study on Legal Standing (Locus Standi) before the EU and Member States' Courts* (Intersentia 2013) 71–72.

[8] In environmental cases, Germany operates with a more liberal standard; see J Ebbesson, *Access to Justice in Environmental Matters in the EU* (Kluwer Law International 2002) 28.

[9] S Prechal, *Directives in EC Law* (Oxford University Press 2005) 103.

[10] For an overview of various doctrines, see Eliantonio et al, *Standing Up for Your Right(s) in Europe* (n 7) 149 ff.

[11] S Prechal and L Hancher, 'Individual Environmental Rights: Conceptual Pollution in EU Environmental Law?' 2002 *The Yearbook of European Environmental Law* 89, 106.

These functions can be referred to as *recours subjectif* and *recours objectif* respectively.[12] Neither of these two models exists in pure form in the Member States; rather they can be regarded as 'the opposing ends of a sliding scale on which all existing standing regimes can be placed [and most jurisdictions] are somewhere in between'.[13] The two functions of legal control tend to result in different rules on standing. Where the courts have a wider responsibility for controlling the legality of governmental action and ensuring public accountability, this militates against restricting access to the judicial procedure, since it could prevent a matter from being brought before a court, and render public action immune from challenge.[14]

Domestic standing doctrines cannot necessarily be applied when the proceedings engage with issues of EU law. As I argued in chapter 5, section IV, if the three criteria constituting the Union doctrine of standing are fulfilled, a claimant must be granted standing. In the following sections I take a closer look at this Union law doctrine by examining two distinct sectors, namely, environmental law and telecoms. The aim is to illustrate how the Union doctrine of standing may add to the the standing doctrines in place in the Member States.

III. Illustration I: Standing in the Area of Environmental Law

A. Introduction

Environmental protection is one of the fundamental objectives of the European Union.[15] Article 37 of the Charter states that the Union must ensure a 'high level of environmental protection'. This provision is nevertheless 'a weakened version of European environmental protection: it offers no substantive, or procedural environmental rights, making it of limited use for individual applicants'.[16] We should not be surprised, however, also to see a 'greening' of the Charter, in the sense that the right to a healthy environment is read into other Charter provisions.[17] As of now, though, environmental rights are only

[12] As pointed out by Barents, in the latter context, judicial protection is 'more the result and less the aim' of the proceedings; see R Barents, 'EU Procedural Law and Effective Legal Protection' (2014) 51 *CML Rev* 1437, 1446.

[13] T Zwart, 'Comparing Standing Regimes from a Separation of Powers Perspective' (2002) 53 *Northern Ireland Legal Quarterly* 391, 404. Similarly S Beljin, 'Rights in EU Law' in S Prechal and B van Roermund (eds), *The Coherence of EU Law. The Search for Unity in Divergent Concepts* (Oxford University Press 2008) 91, 97–98.

[14] See further R Gordon and R Moffatt, *EU Law in Judicial Review*, 2nd edn (Oxford University Press 2014) 87–88.

[15] See, inter alia, Art 3(3) TEU and Art 191(2) TFEU. See also Case 240/83 *ADBHU* [1985] para 13.

[16] See S Bogojevic, 'EU human rights law and environmental protection: the beginning of a beautiful friendship?' in S Douglas-Scott and N Hatzis (eds.) *Research Handbook on EU Law and Human Rights* (Elgar 2017) 451, 467. She points out that the Court couples Art 37 with other Charter rights, primarily with protection of health and the right to effective judicial protection (ibid 461).

[17] The term 'greening' is borrowed from A Boyle, 'Human Rights and the Environment. Where Next?' in B Boer (ed), *Environmental Law Dimensions of Human Rights* (Oxford University Press 2015) 201, 203, with reference to the tendency of the ECtHR to read environmental protection into other articles of the Convention (see, *inter alia, Kyrtatos v Greece* App no 41666/98 (ECtHR, 2003) para 52). For an account of how the case

found in provisions of secondary legislation. In the following, I examine the extent to which private parties are entitled to initiate legal proceedings where such environmental norms are breached. In section III.A, I address the issue of environmental Union rights, and thereafter, in section III.B, I look into what it means for a claimant to be affected in his rights.

B. Individual Rights Deriving from Environmental Provisions

There is a vast amount of secondary legislation – mostly directives – in the environmental sphere, imposing obligations of both a procedural and a substantive nature. The extent to which these provisions grant individual rights is, however, subject to disagreement. That the Union legal order grants individuals *procedural* environmental rights is undisputed. The obligation to carry out an environmental impact assessment under Directive 2011/92/EU (Consolidated Environmental Impact Assessment Directive), for instance, confers on the individuals concerned a corresponding right to have environmental effects assessed.[18] The range of procedural environmental rights expanded with the accession of the EU to the Aarhus Convention, which establishes various rights of the public with regard to the environment.[19]

The issue of substantive rights – meaning rights intended to protect a given level of environmental quality – has been more controversial.[20] Substantive environmental obligations are not explicitly framed as rights, as is the case for procedural environmental obligations.[21] There is also a rather common perception that EU environmental law is different from other areas of Union law.[22] Two features of environmental law measures have been seen as preventing them from granting enforceable rights to individuals: first, that these measures do not protect the interests of individuals; second, that the concepts used in environmental legislation are too vague and open-ended to confer rights. These features will now be addressed in turn, and it will be argued that EU environmental law is not that different from other areas of Union law.

law of the ECtHR with respect to environmental protection is likely to 'reinforce EU … environmental law in providing new remedies for the victims of pollution', see N de Sadeleer, *EU Environmental Law and the Internal Market* (Oxford University Press 2014) 112–25.

[18] Case C-420/11 *Leth* [2013].

[19] Convention on Access to Information, Public Participation in Decision-Making and Access to Justice in Environmental Matters, signed on 25 June 1998. Two directives were adopted to implement the Convention: Directive 2003/4/EC (Access to Environmental Information) and Directive 2003/35/EC (Public Participation and Access to Justice).

[20] Gill-Pedro states that 'it is clear from the case-law that individuals are not granted, under EU law, a substantive right to a healthy environment', rather they are granted standing to challenge the state's failure to comply with substantive environmental obligations; see E Gill-Pedro, 'EU Environmental Rights as Human Rights: Some Methodological Difficulties Facing European Courts' in S Bogojevic and R Rayfuse (eds), *Environmental Rights in Europe and Beyond* (Hart Publishing, 2018) 201, 215.

[21] See C Hilson, 'The Visibility of Environmental Rights in the EU Legal Order: Eurolegalism in Action?' (2018) 25 *Journal of European Public Policy* 1589, 1606. He holds that procedural rights 'offer a somewhat less powerful Eurolegalism: Procedural rights are important … however, they lack the salience and force of their substantive cousins'.

[22] See, inter alia, Prechal and Hancher, 'Individual Environmental Rights: Conceptual Pollution in EU Environmental Law?' (n 11) 109. The disagreement pertaining to substantive environmental rights is addressed in Prechal, *Directives in EC Law* (n 9) 109.

As to the first feature, we may recall from chapter 4, section III that provisions merely protecting public interests do not grant rights to individuals. There is, however, no watershed between individual and public interests. The Court has, in the context of its case law on the correct implementation of directives, held that directives that aim, inter alia, at the protection of human health may grant rights to individuals. The right to clean air was made explicit in *Commission v Germany*, concerning the proper implementation of one of the first air quality directives, laying down limit values for air pollution. The Court held that since the limit values were imposed specifically to protect human health, the Directive intended to grant rights, and the Member States had to make sure that 'the person concerned can ascertain the full extent of their rights, and where appropriate, rely on them before national courts'.[23] Provisions protecting other forms of individual interests, such as the interest in the legitimate use of water, can also be seen as granting rights[24].

Rights enshrined in directives aiming at the protection of individual interests such as human health trigger the right to effective judicial protection.[25] Directives setting environmental limit values or quality objectives – which 'form the core of much of the [Union] environmental law'[26] – must therefore be seen as granting individual rights.[27] This means, for instance, that provisions in Directive 2008/50/EC (Air Quality), Directive 2006/118/EC (Groundwater) and Directive 2009/148/EC (Asbestos) grant rights.[28]

The Court's anthropocentric approach to environmental rights implies that directives that do not aim at protecting individuals – but rather the environment *as such* – do not give rise to individual rights.[29] For instance, Directives 2009/147/EC (Birds) and 92/43/EC (Habitats) – which have been called 'the backbone of Europe's nature conservation law'[30] – protect species and habitats, regardless of their value for individuals. As de Sadeleer has pointed out, since

> environmental protection is much more than impairment of health, an exclusive anthropocentric approach will not suffice to address major environmental problems such as biodiversity losses, ozone layer depletion, and climate change.[31]

[23] Case C-59/89 *Commission v Germany* [1991] para 18. Similar formulations are found in Case C-361/88 *Commission v Germany* [1991] para 15.

[24] Case C-197/18 *Wasserleitungsverband Nördliches Burgenland* [2019].

[25] To the same effect, see E Rehbinder, 'Locus Standi, Community Law and the Case for Harmonization' in H Somsen (ed), *Protecting the European Environment. Enforcing EC Environmental Law* (Blackstone Press 1996) 151, 158.

[26] H Somsen, 'The Private Enforcement of Member State Compliance with EC Environmental Law: An Unfulfilled Promise?' (2000) 1 *Yearbook of European Environmental Law* 311, 336.

[27] As pointed out by Van Dam, 'immission levels (eg the maximum pollution of air or water) will generally protect the individual, whereas emission levels (eg the maximum output of substances from a certain source) will generally not'; see C van Dam, *European Tort Law*, 2nd edn (Oxford University Press 2013) 289, fn 49.

[28] Similarly ibid 289; and Ebbesson, *Access to Justice in Environmental Matters in the EU* (n 8) 62.

[29] The anthropocentric approach to environmental protection focuses on environmental protection for the sake of human beings, as opposed to the ecocentric approach, which advocates the protection of nature for its own sake, regardless of human interests; see LH Lieb, *Human Rights and the Environment: Philosophical, Theoretical and Legal Perspectives* (Martinius Nijhoff Publishers 2011) 3.

[30] S van Holten and M van Rijswick, 'The Governance Approach in European Union Environmental Directives and Its Consequences for Flexibility, Effectiveness and Legitimacy' in M Peeters and R Uylenburg (eds), *EU Environmental Legislation: Legal Perspectives on Regulatory Strategies* (Edward Elgar 2014) 13, 24.

[31] de Sadeleer, *EU Environmental Law and the Internal Market* (n 17) 105.

This shortcoming has, as will be seen in chapter 13, section III, been acknowledged by the ECJ, which has opened up to associational standing to protect the environment as such.

The second potential barrier to private enforcement, mentioned above, has to do with the ability to ascertain the *content and scope* of the right. For the courts to be able to infer that the Member State has failed to comply with an obligation laid down in a directive, the minimum content of the obligation must be ascertainable. Hence, the ability to rely on legal provisions in the courts largely depends on the amount of discretion afforded by these provisions.[32] In the words of Prechal and Hancher,

> the ascertainability of the scope of the right is a criterion which helps to decide whether a provision confers rights as such. The content of the alleged right must be sufficiently concrete or delineated. Hence, provisions involving discretion may not give rise to rights.[33]

There has been a tendency – evident in the field of environmental law – to resort to new modes of governance implying more informal and flexible measures, rather than set rules. An aspect of this is an increased use of framework directives.[34] Yet since a certain amount of discretion does not prevent the finding that a provision grants rights, provisions in framework directives should not be dismissed at the outset; rather a concrete assessment must be made. In *Commission v Luxembourg*, the Court found that the water quality objectives contained in Directive 2000/60/EC (Water Framework Directive) constituted precise obligations that were to be implemented in the Member States.[35] Moreover, in *Weser*, the Court held that the obligation to prevent deterioration of the status of all bodies of surface water and groundwater in the Water Framework Directive was applicable to individual projects, and that a Member State is required to refuse authorisation for project that would run contrary to the requirements of the Directive.[36] In these cases, the Court was not called upon to take a stance on whether the provisions contained in the Directive grant rights. Advocate General Sharpston did broach the issue in her Opinion in *Commission v Luxembourg*, however. She noted that although the issue did not need to be decided, the provisions regulating standards for water quality arguably do grant rights to individuals.[37] Support for this stance can be found in

[32] van Holten and van Rijswick, 'The Governance Approach in European Union Environmental Directives and Its Consequences for Flexibility, Effectiveness and Legitimacy' (n 30) 16.

[33] Prechal and Hancher, 'Individual Environmental Rights: Conceptual Pollution in EU Environmental Law?' (n 11) 102.

[34] Included also are soft law, coregulation, self-regulation, voluntary agreements and the open method of coordination; see RD Kelemen, *Eurolegalism: The Transformation of Law and Regulation in the European Union* (Harvard University Press 2011) 29. For a discussion on the use of framework directives in the environmental sphere, see M Bogaart, 'The Emergence of the Framework Directive in EU Environmental Policy: An Exploration of Its Function and Characteristics' in Peeters and Uylenburg (eds), *EU Environmental Legislation: Legal Perspectives on Regulatory Strategies* (n 30) 48.

[35] Case C-32/05 *Commission v Luxembourg* [2006] paras 74–75.

[36] Case C-461/13 *Weser* [2015] para 50.

[37] AG Sharpston in Case C-32/05 *Commission v Luxembourg* [2006] paras 75 and 86. Interestingly, in Case C-664/15 *Protect* [2017] paras 44 and 45, the Court speaks of the 'rights' that environmental NGOs derive from the Water Framework Directive, and stresses the importance of ensuring effective judicial protection of these rights.

Land Nordrhein-Westfalen, where the Court held that individuals could pursue such infringements by judicial process.[38]

Based on the foregoing, it can be concluded that EU environmental law is not so very different from other areas of Union law after all, and that arguably individuals can derive not only procedural, but also substantive rights from the Union legal order.

C. Adverse Effect on the Claimant

Acknowledging that environmental provisions may grant rights is one thing; determining the range of persons that must be entitled to rely on these rights to initiate proceedings is quite another. In order to be granted standing, it is submitted, a claimant must demonstrate that an infringement has an *adverse effect* on his rights.

There are clear indications in the Court's jurisprudence that the right to seize the court is reserved to affected individuals. In *Commission v Germany*, the Court stated that whenever exceeding the limit values in Directive 82/884/EEC (former Air Quality Directive) could endanger human health, the 'persons concerned' must be in a position to rely on mandatory rules in order to assert their rights.[39] Similarly, the Court held in *Commission v the United Kingdom* – concerning Directive 80/778/EEC (former Drinking Water Directive) – that Member States must lay down provisions necessary to ensure that the 'persons entitled to exercise those rights' enjoy judicial protection.[40] These formulations indicate that access to justice depends on considerations of actual effects.[41] In the words of Ebbesson:

> One may infer from this [reference to 'persons concerned'] that no *actio popularis* is intended, whereby anyone would be able to initiate judicial proceedings, regardless of whether he or she is affected by the excess of the air quality limits. ... Persons may invoke the right to human health in a particular case, basically because they are likely to be affected by the violation in question; that is what makes them 'concerned'.[42]

The criterion of being 'concerned' is rather too vague and open-ended to serve as guidance for determining the category of people with the requisite interest to sue. The Court

[38] Case C-535/18, *Land Nordrhein-Westfalen* [2020] para 132.

[39] Case C-59/89 *Commission v Germany* [1991] para 19.

[40] Case C-340/96 *Commission v the United Kingdom* [1997] para 37.

[41] Harlow has argued the opposite, however, namely that the Court's acknowledgement of such environmental rights 'amounts to creating an *actio popularis* in national courts', and calls this 'an unwarranted extension of EC law'; see C Harlow, 'Access to Justice as a Human Right: The European Convention and the European Union' in P Alston (ed), *The EU and Human Rights* (Oxford University Press 1999) 187, 199. Jans argues along the same lines, stating that 'rights can be bestowed on individuals by quality standards that have a very general protective aim [and it] would indeed seem that the Court desires a public interest civil action to be available in the event of a breach of directly effective environmental quality standards by the Member States'; see JH Jans, 'Legal Protection in European Environmental Law: An Overview' in H Somsen (ed), *Protecting the European Environment* (n 25) 81.

[42] Ebbesson, *Access to Justice in Environmental Matters in the EU* (n 8) 61. See Case C-535/18, *Land Nordrhein-Westfalen* [2020], where the Court distinguished between the obligations of non-deterioration of groundwater bodies and surface water as set out in Directive 2000/60.

addressed the issue of standing in *Janecek*, where it used the narrower term 'directly concerned', which seems to imply that not necessarily anyone whose environmental rights are somehow affected should be entitled to seize the court.[43] The criteria of 'direct concern' was also used in *Wasserleitungsverband Nördliches Burgenland*.[44]

The *Janecek* case concerned a claimant who was seeking an injunction ordering the public administration to act in accordance with rules laid down in Directive 96/62/EC (former Air Quality Directive). The Directive set objectives for harmful pollutants, requiring Member States to monitor and assess air quality to ensure that it met those objectives, and to prepare and implement air quality plans containing measures to achieve those objectives. Measures taken at an air quality measuring station near the central ring road showed that the limit value fixed for emissions was greatly exceeded. Mr Janecek brought an action for an order requiring the Freistad Bayern to draw up an air quality action plan in his district in accordance with Article 7(3) of the Directive. Pursuant to German law, the claimant could not rely on an entitlement to have an action plan drawn up. The ECJ held that the Directive places Member States under a clear obligation to draw up action plans where there is a risk of exceeding the limit values or alert thresholds. The Court stated in general terms that

> whenever the failure to observe the measures required by the directive which relate to air quality and drinking water, and which are designed to protect public health, could endanger human health, the persons concerned must be in a position to rely on the mandatory rules included in those directives.[45]

Moving on to the concrete case, the Court held that the natural or legal persons

> *directly concerned* by a risk that the limit values or alert thresholds may be exceeded must be in a position to require the competent authorities to draw up an action plan where such a risk exists, if necessary by bringing an action before the competent courts.[46]

Although the Court limited the right to bring proceedings to those 'directly concerned', it was laconic as to the further content of this requirement.[47] The Court was keen to stress, however, that the claimant lived in close geographical proximity to the measuring station, which could mean that the Court emphasised that he was particularly affected by the infringement. From the Court's ruling we can infer that the principle of effective judicial protection at least requires that claimants in that claimant's position should be granted standing.[48]

The ECJ went into further detail on the aspect of factual concern in *Wasserleitungsverband Nördliches Burgenland*.[49] The Court was asked whether the claimants

[43] Case C-237/07 *Janecek* [2008]. The requirement of 'direct concern' was repeated by the Court in Case C-404/13 *ClientEarth* [2014] para 56, concerning the duty on Member States to establish air quality plans under Directive 2008/50/EC (Air Quality).

[44] Case C-197/18 *Wasserleitungsverband Nördliches Burgenland* [2019].

[45] Case C-237/07 *Janecek* [2008] para 38.

[46] ibid para 39 (emphasis added). See also Case C-723/17 *Craeynest* [2019] para 56.

[47] On the remaining uncertanties, see JH Jans, 'Harmonization of National Procedural Law Via the Back Door? Preliminary Comments on the ECJ's Judgment in Janecek in a Comparative Context' in M Bulterman et al (eds), *Views of European Law from the Mountain, Liber Amicorum Piet Jan Slot* (Wolters Kluwer 2009) 267, 274–75.

[48] Similarly ibid 274.

[49] Case C-197/18 *Wasserleitungsverband Nördliches Burgenland* [2019].

in the main proceedings – an individual owning a domestic well, a public law body providing household water and a municipality operating a municipal well – should be granted *locus standi* with a view to seeking an amendment of an inadequate Nitrate Action Programme. Directive 91/676/EEC (Nitrates) requires all Member States to prepare such programmes to reduce and avoid water pollution caused by nitrates from agricultural sources. The Court stated that 'at least the natural or legal persons directly concerned by an infringement' of provisions of a directive must be in a position to require the competent authorities to observe such obligations, 'if necessary by pursuing their claims by judicial process'.[50] The Court proceeded to give additional clarification as to when the condition of 'direct concern' would be fulfilled:

> In order to determine whether natural and legal persons such as the applicants in the main proceedings are directly concerned by an infringement of the obligations provided for in Directive 91/676, it is necessary to examine the purpose and the relevant provisions of that directive, the proper application of which is asserted before the referring court.[51]

The Court stated that the purpose of the Nitrates Directive was to combat water pollution by nitrates from agricultural sources, and that nitrate levels in groundwater that exceed or could exceed the prescribed level must be considered to be such as to interfere with the legitimate use of water. Consequently, the Court held,

> a natural or legal person having the option of drawing and using groundwater is directly concerned by that threshould being exceeded or the risk of it being exceeded, which is capable of limiting that person's option by interfering with the legitimate use of that water.[52]

How to delineate the class of persons 'directly concerned' by an infringement of EU environmental law depends on the type of measure in question. For example, the range of persons concerned in the case of a breach of measures for groundwater protection may be more narrowly construed than in a case on air quality standards.[53] In relation to certain environmental directives such as the Directive 2008/50/EC (Air Quality), the number of adversely affected individuals may be great. Nevertheless, the fact that the class of persons adversely affected is broad does not reduce an individual's need for judicial protection.[54] Consequently, in such cases, the principle of effective judicial protection may require states to guarantee standing to a wide range of persons.[55]

In order to benefit from the right to effective judicial protection, the effects on the claimant must presumably meet a certain threshold. A requirement that everyone affected – regardless of how remotely – should be able to initiate proceedings would have a serious impact on domestic standing rules in some Member States. Although

[50] ibid para 32.
[51] ibid para 35.
[52] ibid para 40. Similarly, Case C-535/18, *Land Nordrhein-Westfalen* [2020], as regards Directive 2000/60 (Water Framework Directive).
[53] Ebbesson, *Access to Justice in Environmental Matters in the EU* (n 8) 61–62.
[54] N Fenger, *Forvaltning og Fællesskab: Om EU-Rettens Betydning for den Almindelige Forvaltningsret: Konfrontation og Frugtbar Sameksistens* (DJØF 2004) 694.
[55] R Ortlep and R Widdershoven, 'Judicial Protection' in JH Jans, S Prechal and RJGM Widdershoven (eds), *Europeanisation of Public Law*, 2nd edn (Europa Law Publishing 2015) 378.

it may be difficult to ascertain the exact number or identity of the persons affected by the challenged measure, the situation of the claimant can indicate that he is sufficiently affected to be granted standing. The Court stated in *Wasserleitungsverband Nördliches Burgenland* that it was no requirement for establishing *locus standi* that values over the threshold involve danger to the health of the claimants. The decisive point in the case at hand was that exceeding the threshold was such as to prevent the applicants from being able to make normal use of the water from their wells, or at the very least, to force them to incur costs for its decontamination.

The claimant in *Janecek* did not demonstrate that his health was impaired by the violation in question, and this cannot be a requirement under Union law, as the purpose of these directives is precisely to *prevent* detrimental effects to human health. A relevant criterion for establishing 'direct concern' – which the Court arguably hinted at in *Janecek* – may be geographical proximity. Advocate General Cosmas suggested adopting such an approach in his Opinion in *Greenpeace*, concerning standing pursuant to Article 263(4) TFEU for the enforcement of environmental law. 'An intervention in the environment', he pointed out,

> is located in a specific geographical area, and the extent of its impact is lessened the further away one is from the area of intervention. Accordingly, persons close to the construction works suffer its consequences in a different, more intense manner than persons farther away, the latter being at a greater radius from the epicenter of the intervention in the environment.[56]

He also suggested that the gravity of the impact a measure has or may have on a person may bring about a situation such as to ground standing.[57] Advocate General Cosmas was not able to convince the Court to afford environmental claimants standing under Article 263(4) TFEU by referring to the actual effects on the claimants,[58] yet this may be a viable line of argumentation in the domestic context. As we saw in chapter 5, section III, belonging to a 'closed class' cannot be a requirement to be afforded standing in domestic courts. Rather than relying on the *Plaumann* formula, one needs to distinguish those particularly affected from those whose interest is more tenuous and remote. As pointed out by one scholar,

> air pollution in a city matters much more to the inhabitants of that city than to people living thousands kilometers away [and] environmental damage resulting from the installation of a hydroelectric power plant concerns the inhabitants of the region much more than it would concern people who do not reside there.[59]

The threshold to demonstrating an adverse impact is unlikely to be very high, due to the need to enlist individuals as private enforcers of EU law. Still, a negligible impact on the individual is not necessarily enough to grant a right of access to court.[60]

[56] AG Cosmas in Case C-321/95 P *Greenpeace* [1997] para 104.
[57] ibid para 106.
[58] Case C-321/95 P *Greenpeace* [1998] paras 27–34.
[59] E Vitorelli, 'Collective Due Process of Law: Reconciling Representation and Participation' in Cadiet, Hess and Isidro (eds), *Approaches to Procedural Law* (n 1) 345, 359–60.
[60] As to the possible *de minimis* exception, see ch 5, section IV.C.

IV. Illustration II: Standing in the Telecommunications Sector

A. Introduction

In the following, I address the range of private parties that can challenge decisions from national regulatory authorities (NRAs) operating within the telecommunications sector. This sector belongs (along with others such as electricity and postal services) to the regulated network industries, which used to be dominated by state-controlled monopolies. Extensive liberalisation has taken place, but former monopolists – so-called incumbents – continue to hold strong market power. This is partly because they own infrastructure that it would be economically ineffective to duplicate.[61] Because of such 'natural monopolies', *ex post* control by competition law is not sufficient to render these industries competitive.[62] *Ex ante* regulatory powers are perceived as necessary, and NRAs are entrusted with supervising and regulating matters such as access rights and tariffs.[63]

The regulation of telecommunications markets comprises different stages: first, the NRA has to define the market; second, it has to conduct a market analysis, which includes identifying undertakings having significant power on the relevant market; third, upon identifying undertakings with significant power on the relevant market, it needs to impose regulatory obligations in order to achieve the objectives of telecommunications regulation, which includes guaranteeing adequate services and fostering competition.[64] The EU regulatory framework identifies the conditions under which intervention may take place, and sets out the measures that may be adopted.[65] The purpose of intervention is, in the short run, to create 'an ecosystem in which incumbent operators are subject to effective competitive constraints [hence] [s]ector specific regulation can be said to be truly successful where it is no longer necessary'.[66]

The Court has expressed itself on the standing rights of third parties against the decisions of NRAs in the field of telecommunication law in three subsequent rulings: *Tele2*, *Arcor* and *T-Mobile Austria*.[67] These cases concerned the interpretation of Article 4(1) of Directive 2002/21/EC (Telecom Framework Directive) and its precursor, Article 5a(3) of Directive 90/387/EEC, which stated that users and undertakings 'affected' by a decision of a regulatory authority have the right to appeal a decision. Although these rulings concerned the interpretation of specific provisions of

[61] A Ottow, 'Europeanization of the Supervision of Competitive Markets' (2012) 18 *European Public Law* 191, 192.

[62] In the words of Posner, '[c]ompetition is … not a viable regulatory mechanism under conditions of natural monopoly … direct controls are necessary to ensure satisfactory performance'; see RA Posner, 'Natural Monopoly and Its Regulation' (1968) 21 *Stanford Law Review* 548, 548.

[63] Ottow, 'Europeanization of the Supervision of Competitive Markets' (n 61) 191–92.

[64] H Weyer, 'Case C-426/05, Tele2 Telecommunication GmbH v Telekom-Control-Kommission, Judgment of the Court (Second Chamber of 21 February 2008, [2008], ECR-I-685" (2009) 46 *CML Rev* 1737, 1737.

[65] PI Colomo, 'EU Competition Law in the Regulated Network Industries' *LSE Law, Society and Economy Working Papers 08/2016*, 8.

[66] ibid 2.

[67] Case C-426/05 *Tele 2* [2008]; Case C-55/06 *Arcor* [2008]; and Case C-282/13 *T-Mobile Austria* [2015].

secondary law, it is submitted that the rulings of the former Court have wider significance, as the Court held that the standing provision in the Framework Directive was a concrete manifestation of the principle of effective judicial protection.[68] The interpretation will therefore have a bearing on similar rules found in other acts of EU law relating to the regulated network industries.[69] Moreover, the rulings may shed light on the Union standard of *locus standi* more generally.[70] That the said provisions merely reflect the general principle of effective judicial protection finds support in the fact that the Court's approach in these cases was echoed in *E.ON Földgaz*, although this time with a basis in Article 47 of the Charter.[71]

In the following, I take a closer look at the range of persons that need to be granted standing where an NRA operating within the telecommincations sector has breached its Union law obligations. In section IV.B, I address the issue of rights in the aforementioned sector, before asking, in section IV.C, what it means for a claimant to be affected in his rights.

B. Individual Rights in the Telecommunications Sector

The EU regulatory framework in the telecommunications sector may grant rights to individuals both directly and indirectly. As to the first of these, an obligation binding on the NRA may be owed to a private party (which has been referred to as 'individual rights under public law'[72]). As to the second, the regulatory obligations placed on an undertaking with significant power on the relevant market may also serve to protect individuals and hence provide them with rights. These two categories of rights will be addressed in turn.

Most commonly, judicial proceedings will serve to protect individual rights of the first type, that is, rights *held against the public authority*. The EU regulatory framework in the telecommunications sector may protect users of network facilities.[73] The Court's ruling in *E.ON Földgaz* is well suited to illustrate how the Court approaches the issue of rights of users of network facilities. Although the case concerned the transmission of electricity, the reasoning also has relevance in relation to other network facilities with bottleneck features (such as the 'local loop' in the telecommunications sector). The Court was asked about the *locus standi* of a company to challenge a decision of an NRA amending the criteria for deciding on applications for long-term reserve capacity in the gas pipeline. E.ON had lodged four requests for long-term reserve capacity allocation at the entry-point of the gas system interconnector between Hungary and Austria.

[68] In Case C-426/05 *Tele2* [2008] para 32, the Court held that the principle of effective judicial protection was the 'origin of' the standing provision in the Directive; and in Case C-55/06 *Arcor* [2008] para 174, it held that it was an 'expression of' that principle.

[69] To this effect, see AG Szpunar in Case C-282/13 *T-Mobile Austria* [2014] para 3. He referred specifically to Art 22(3) of Directive 97/67/EC (Postal Services); Art 37(17) of Directive 2009/72/EC, now Article 60(8) of Directive (EU) 2019/944 (Electricity); and also Art 41(17) of Directive 2009/73/EC (Natural Gas).

[70] Similarly N Poltorak, *European Union Rights in National Courts* (Wolters Kluwer 2015) 245.

[71] Case C-510/13 *E.ON Földgaz* [2015].

[72] AG Szpunar in Case C-282/13 *T-Mobile Austria* [2014] para 72.

[73] In Case C-55/06 *Arcor* [2008], the Court held that Art 3(3) of Regulation (EC) No 2887/2000 (on unbundled access to the local loop), requiring that rates are set according to cost-orientation, granted rights to network users.

Due to the limited capacity available, the Hungarian gas system operator requested the regulatory authority to specify how to handle the requests, and the regulatory authority instructed the network operator to draft new rules on capacity allocation, thereby withdrawing its earlier decision in the matter. The Court held that Article 5 of Regulation (EC) No 1775/2005 on conditions for access to the natural gas transmission networks, read in conjunction with the Annex to that Regulation, set out the principles that the transmission operator must respect in order to ensure that the access of market participants to the transmission network takes place on non-discriminatory and transparent conditions. The regulatory authorities are required to ensure observance of these principles when exercising their powers, and operators such as E.ON have a corresponding right to have decisions adopted in accordance with the criteria of transparency and non-discrimination.

The Court has held that competitors too may derive rights from a provision binding an NRA if the decision adopted pursuant to that provision aims to safeguard competition.[74] In *T-Mobile Austria*, the Court held that the procedure for the transfer of rights to use radio frequencies pursuant, in particular, to Article 5(6) of Directive 2002/20/EC (Authorization Directive), aims at safeguarding competition, and therefore also protects competitors.[75] Hence, the general market interest and the interest of the individual competitor largely overlap since, in the words of Advocate General Szpunar,

> [t]he position of competing undertakings is taken into account by provisions of EU law under which the regulatory authority is required to take measures to prevent changes in the market position of competing undertakings which are so significant as to be capable of leading to the distortion or restriction of competition.[76]

Not only obligations binding on the NRA may give rise to individual rights; such rights can also be the mirror image of regulatory obligations placed on an undertaking with significant market power. This is the *second* category of rights presented above. The Court's ruling in *Tele2* serves to illustrate how to locate rights in the latter context. The Court was asked whether an undertaking providing electronic communications and network services had the right to challenge an administrative decision taken in the context of a market analysis procedure concerning its competitor. We may recall from the previous section that such an analysis is conducted to determine whether a market is effectively competitive, or whether the imposition of regulatory obligations on an undertaking is required to foster effective competition.[77] Under Austrian law, the right to challenge such a decision was limited to parties to the administrative proceedings, which in the context of this procedure included only undertakings in respect of which specific obligations were imposed, amended or withdrawn by the regulatory authority. The Court stated that it was necessary to determine whether such a competitor may derive rights from Union law, and whether their rights may be affected by an NRA decision that is not addressed to them.[78]

[74] Case C-282/13 *T-Mobile Austria* [2015] para 41.
[75] ibid paras 41–46.
[76] AG Szpunar in Case C-282/13 *T-Mobile Austria* [2014] para 81.
[77] See section IV.A.
[78] Case C-426/05 *Tele2* [2008] para 33. If that is the case, the Court held, they should be entitled to a right of appeal in order to make that decision amenable to judicial review.

The Court found that certain obligations imposed on an undertaking with significant power on the relevant market – such as the obligation of non-discrimination between competitors and the obligation to give competitors access to specific network facilities – constituted protective measures adopted in the interests of users and competitors, and therefore capable of conferring rights on the latter.[79]

As the above illustrates, the Court has adopted a liberal approach to individual rights in the telecoms sector, evidence of which can be found *both* in the fact that provisions aimed at safeguarding competition may give rise to rights, and in the fact that rights may be the corollary of regulatory obligations placed on an undertaking with significant market power. Given the broad scope of rights in the telecoms sector, there is a need to determine who can draw on these rights by initiating legal proceedings. In what follows, I therefore address what it means for these rights to be *affected*.

C. Adverse Effect on the Claimant

The Court has used the formulation that standing must be granted to those 'affected' or 'adversely affected' in their rights by the challenged measure.[80] What effect the decision must have on the right holders is not clear, and the Court has not given much guidance. Although there is no watershed between these categories, it can be inferred from the Court's case law that a claimant's rights can be affected in at least two different ways: either the decision can have an impact on his *contractual position* with the addressee of the decision, or – in the absence of a contractual relationship with the addressee – his *competitive position* can be affected through the market mechanisms.

In the majority of the cases addressed in the preceding section, the claimants were adversely affected due to the fact that they had concluded or intended to conclude a contract with the addressee of the administrative decision. In *Tele2*, where the Court was asked about the right to challenge a decision taken in the context of a market analysis procedure, the Court found that the claimant's rights would be affected by a decision amending or withdrawing the regulatory obligations of its competitor. The Court was brief on the issue of impact, and merely stated that users or undertakings competing with an undertaking with significant market power 'must be considered to be potential beneficiaries of the rights corresponding to the specific regulatory obligations imposed by a national regulatory authority', and consequently may be regarded as being 'affected within the meaning of [the Directive] by decisions of that authority which amend or withdraw those obligations'.[81]

The claimant's right of access to the network facilities of its competitor were conferred on it by Union law, since the NRA had required the dominant undertaking to grant access rights on specific terms. This contractual aspect was not mentioned by the Court. Advocate General Maduro gave a more detailed assessment of the claimant's situation. He stressed that Tele2 was a competitor of the undertaking having significant market power, but was also a contractual partner of that undertaking whose legal

[79] ibid para 34.
[80] See, inter alia, ibid para 48.
[81] ibid para 36.

position would be adversely affected by a decision adopted in the course of market analysis proceedings.[82] Consequently, a decision to withdraw obligations imposed on an undertaking with significant market power 'will affect the rights under Community law of competing operators which, like Tele2, are contractual partners of that undertaking'.[83]

The Advocate General added, however, that competitors who are not in a contractual relationship with an undertaking having significant market power should also have a right of appeal under Article 4 of the Directive, where they are beneficiaries of rules designed to promote competition and are adversely affected by a decision such as that in the proceedings.[84] This seems to be a reference to the second category of effects addressed above, namely, the possibility of being affected in one's competitive position through the market mechanisms. This will be taken up below.

That an administrative decision can have an impact on the contractual position of another private party is also evident from the Court's ruling in *Arcor*, concerning the authorisation by German authorities of access rates to the local loop of Deutsche Telecom. The Court was asked whether Arcor, as beneficiary of access, must have the right of appeal to contest the rates on the ground that they had not been set on the basis of cost orientation as required under Union law (Regulation EC No 2887/2000 on unbundled access to the local loop). Under German law, only the participants in the proceedings – here the undertaking submitting rates for approval – could challenge the decision. The Court found that Arcor, having concluded a contract with the notified operator concerning access to the local loops, was a party affected within the meaning of the Framework Directive, because a decision concerning access to the local loop necessarily affects its rights as a party to such a contract.[85]

The Court does not seem to require that a contractual link with the addressee is already established in order to be granted standing. In *Arcor*, the Court stated explicitly that the rights of a beneficiary can also be potentially affected by such a decision in the absence of a contractual link with the network operator.[86] The Court stated that a beneficiary acquires the status of 'party affected' when his rights are 'potentially affected by such a decision by reason of its content and the activity exercised or *envisaged* by that party'.[87] This cannot, however, be taken to mean that any hypothetical future activity is sufficient to demonstrate a sufficient interest in seeking judicial review.[88]

The absence of a contractual link did not prevent the Court from requiring standing for the claimant in *E.ON Földgaz*. We may recall from the previous section that the case concerned a decision modifying the rules on capacity allocation in the gas pipeline. The claimant had not concluded a contract with the network manager, but the Court found this irrelevant, since the status of network user within the meaning of the Regulation covers all potential customers of the network manager.[89] Without any

[82] AG Maduro in Case C-426/05 *Tele2* [2007] para 15.
[83] ibid para 31.
[84] ibid paras 34–37.
[85] Case C-55/06 *Arcor* [2008] para 177.
[86] ibid.
[87] ibid para 176 (emphasis added).
[88] The Court has in its case law on the free movement rights refused to acknowledge purely hypothetical events: see Case 180/83 *Moser* [1984] para 18 and Case C-299/95 *Kremzow* [1997] para 16.
[89] Case C-510/13 *E.ON Földgaz* [2015] para 45.

further discussion, the Court stated that an operator such as E.ON 'must be regarded as potentially having its rights infringed by a decision of the regulatory authority'.[90] Advocate General Cruz Villalón was more explicit as to the issue of impact. He held that 'where the [claimant's] interest is sufficiently clear and is reflected in economic consequences, the combination of a right conferred by EU law and the economic loss suffered requires the Member States to guarantee access to justice'.[91] He held that in addition to having a right granted by the Regulation, E.ON had a clear financial interest at stake, and these two factors combined to lead him to conclude that 'when viewed in the light of the right to effective legal protection, the decision denying that E.ON lacked *locus standi* [*sic*] owing to the want of a 'legal interest' is difficult to reconcile with that right'.[92]

The Court did not address what particular interest the claimant had in initiating proceedings. Nevertheless, E.ON's financial interest was rather obvious, and stemmed from the fact that the undertaking had lodged four requests for long-term capacity allocation with the network manager. Although the Court stressed that all potential customers of the network manager have the status of network users, a potential customer would have to demonstrate an intention to enter into a contract with the manager.

To sum up: it can be concluded that one way of demonstrating an adverse impact is to refer to a (prospective) contractual relation with the addressee. If the prospects of or the terms of such a contract may be negatively affected by the decision of the NRA, this may be sufficient to ground standing. In the following I look at the second way by which a claimant can obtain standing, namely, by demonstrating an adverse impact on his market position.

In *T-Mobile Austria*, the Court made clear that a claimant can gain standing if he incurs loss due to a distortion of the competitive process. The Court was asked whether a telephone network operator such as T-Mobile Austria was 'affected' for the purposes of the former Framework Directive by a decision transferring the right to use radio frequencies. The decision was adopted in the context of a procedure for the authorisation of the modification of the ownership structure of competing undertakings. The Court held that standing should be granted to 'other undertakings providing electronic communications networks or services and which may be competitors of that addressee, in so far as the decision in question is likely to have an impact on their position on the market'.[93]

The Court held that the procedure for the transfer of rights to use radio frequencies aims at safeguarding competition, and that T-Mobile Austria was a direct competitor on the electronic communications services market with the parties to the transaction. Consequently, the Court held that

> T-Mobile Austria must … be regarded as being 'affected' by a decision of an NRA, such as that at issue in the main proceedings, since the transfer of rights to use radio frequencies … modifies the respective shares of radio frequencies granted to those undertakings and, consequently, has an impact on T-Mobile Austria's position on that market.[94]

[90] ibid para 48.
[91] AG Cruz Villalón in Case C-510/13 *E.ON Földgaz* [2014] para 50.
[92] ibid para 55.
[93] Case C-282/13 *T-Mobile Austria* [2015] para 37.
[94] Case C-282/13 *T-Mobile Austria* [2015] para 47.

The Court did not address the extent of the impact on the claimant's market position. Presumably it must be required that the effect on its market position reaches a certain threshold. The situation in the market needs to be assessed, taking into account, inter alia, the number of actors operating in the market. Advocate General Szpunar held that a competitor is affected where the decision relates to activities or transactions that have a 'significant impact' on the claimant's market position.[95] He drew a parallel to the case law governing *locus standi* in actions pursuant to Article 263(4) in the context of state aid and control of concentrations.[96] As argued in chapter 5, section III.C, however, the standing doctrine before the Union courts provides a misleading comparator when determining the right of private parties to gain standing before domestic courts. It needs to be taken into account that a claimant seeking to gain access to domestic courts is not only representing his own economic interest; he is at the same time representing the broader market interest. For this reason, the threshold for demonstrating the necessary interest to sue should not be equated to that under the *Plaumann* test.

[95] AG Szpunar in Case C-282/13 *T-Mobile Austria* [2014] para 82.
[96] ibid paras 83–85.

9

Standing to Seek Judicial Review of Legislative Acts

I. Introduction

The aim of this chapter is to address the right to seek judicial review of legislative acts.[1] Member States must answer for infringements of Union law regardless of which organ of the state is responsible for the infringement,[2] and this means that they are also held to account when they act in the capacity of a legislature.[3] Legislative breaches can be divided into two subcategories: first, the Member State may have failed in its obligations to transpose Union law (correctly) into national law; and second, the legislature may (outside of the implementation context) enact or have enacted rules that conflict with Union law.[4]

Legislative acts often require decisions by the administration or the courts to be executed. It is primarily through such decisions that the rights of individuals are affected, and the need for judicial protection arises.[5] Yet a legislative scheme or provision may be contrary to Union law *in and of itself*, regardless of implementing measures. A licensing regime may, for example, constitute an illegal restriction on the freedom of establishment or the freedom to provide services (see Articles 49 TFEU and 56 TFEU respectively),[6] or a state aid measure in the form of a legislative regime (such as a tax exception) may be illegal if the Member State has failed to comply with the standstill obligation contained in Article 108(3) TFEU.[7] Where a legislative provision affects a private party in the absence of implementing measures, this gives rise to the question whether a private party must be able to challenge the measure directly?

[1] By 'legislative acts', I mean binding laws of a general nature adopted by either parliament or the executive pursuant to the authorisation of parliament. For an examination of the notion of legislative act in various European legal systems and in the EU legal system, see AH Türk, *The Concept of Legislation in European Community Law: A Comparative Perspective* (Kluwer Law International 2006).

[2] Joined Cases C-46/93 and C-48/93 *Brasserie du Pêcheur* [1996] para 32.

[3] See, eg, Joined Cases C-128/09 to C-131/09, C-134/09 and C-135/09 *Boxus* [2011].

[4] JH Jans and AP Duijkersloot, 'State Liability' in JH Jans, S Prechal and RJGM Widdershoven (eds), *Europeanisation of Public Law*, 2nd edn (Europa Law Publishing 2015) 435, 466.

[5] J Engström, 'The Europeanisation of Remedies and Procedures Through Judge-Made Law: Can a Trojan Horse Achieve Effectiveness? Experiences of the Swedish Judiciary' (PhD thesis, European University Institute 2009) 169.

[6] See, inter alia, Case C-302/97 *Konle* [1999].

[7] See Case C-368/04 *Transalpine Ölleitung* [2006] concerning a rebate on energy taxes.

In the following analysis I examine the extent to which Member States are required to provide for a *free-standing* action for judicial review of legislative acts that are alleged to be in violation of Union rights (sections II and III). I will argue that this is not the case, provided that the legislative measure can be challenged incidentally in the course of an alternative legal proceeding, for instance a damages action. Yet in exceptional circumstances, where alternative legal avenues are wanting, Member States are required as a matter of EU law to allow for such a free-standing action.[8] Where a claimant wants to challenge domestic legislation allegedly infringing his Union rights, although the law has not (yet) been applied to him, the absence of a particular factual context makes it challenging to decide whether he can demonstrate the requisite interest to sue. It will be argued that standing must be granted primarily to a right holder who either has to modify his conduct to comply with the relevant legislation, or risk being sanctioned.

II. Review of Legislative Acts in the Member States

To provide a conceptual background to the issue of judicial review of legislative acts, there is a need to explore briefly how legislative acts are examined for compatibility with superior norms in the Member States. To this end, a distinction must be drawn between acts adopted by parliament and delegated legislation. Control of the legality of delegated legislation is not very controversial. Administrative lawmaking requires parliamentary authorisation, and this authorisation 'binds the executive to the will of parliament and often contains restrictions for its use, which are enforced by courts'.[9] Judicial review of primary legislation is more controversial, since is 'carries the weight of democratic parliamentary will'.[10] Although most Member States provide for the possibility of constitutional review of such legislative acts, such review is not available in states adhering to a system of parliamentary supremacy.[11]

In Member States that adhere to a system of constitutional review, there are divergences on key issues of institutional design. First, in some states constitutional review can be exercised by all courts in the system, whereas in others such review is conducted by a centralised institution, such as a constitutional court outside the judicial hierarchy ('diffuse' and 'centralised' models respectively). Second, there are differences in how the

[8] The principle of effective judicial protection is presumably not directly effective in the sense that a court is required, as a matter of EU law, to entertain a case that is beyond its jurisdiction, see ch 5, section VI.C.

[9] Türk, *The Concept of Legislation in European Community Law* (n 1) 9. For a brief overview, see M Eliantonio et al, *Standing Up for Your Right(s) in Europe – A Comparative Study on Legal Standing (Locus Standi) before the EU and Member States' Courts* (Intersentia 2013) 63–64.

[10] M Dougan, 'Who Exactly Benefits from the Treaties? The Murky Interaction Between Union and National Competence over the Capacity to Enforce EU Law' (2009) 12 *Cambridge Yearbook of European Legal Studies* 73, 77.

[11] Dworkin draws a distinction between majoritarian and constitutional democracies; see R Dworkin, *Freedom's Law: The Moral Reading of the American Constitution* (Oxford University Press 1996) esp 17–18. States belonging to the former category adhere to the idea of parliamentary supremacy, whereas states belonging to the latter regard judicial review of legislation as essential to a democratic state. In real life, however, this is not a rigid dichotomy, and it must be stressed that some states that in principle allow for judicial review (such as Sweden and Denmark) save it for exceptional circumstances.

issue of constitutionality is raised: concrete review is related to a case already before the court, whereas abstract review is unconnected to a specific case. Thus, while concrete review often occurs incidentally in the course of (civil, administrative or criminal) proceedings because the result of the case depends on the constitutionality of a statute, abstract review typically occurs when a legislative provision is deemed intrinsically inconsistent with the constitution.[12] There are also states that allow for constitutional complaints, where individuals can challenge a statutory norm if it interferes with their constitutional rights in and of itself, without any further judicial decision or individual administrative act.[13] In the context of concrete review, the court may limit itself to deciding whether the statute is unconstitutional as applied, and the decision only has effect *inter partes*, whereas if a statute is challenged in the abstract, the court must address the constitutional issue in its entirety, and the decision has effect *erga omnes*.

In Member States that allow for statutes to be challenged in the abstract, the standing rules vary. Kay categorises standing rules according to their broad purpose. While what he calls 'injury standing' has the main purpose of securing a remedy for an injury suffered as a result of a violation of constitutional rules, 'inquiry standing' is primarily meant to clarify the meaning of constitutional rules so as to facilitate their observance.[14] Most jurisdictions adhere to the former category, and have adopted relatively stringent standing criteria, requiring that the claimant show that the act in question has an actual impact on his actions; but there are jurisdictions belonging to the latter camp that allow for a more open standing.[15]

Domestic systems of constitutional review are not directly applicable where the infringement pertains to Union law. But although Union law is not normally perceived as superior law in the Member States, it is often granted a special status in the legal systems due to the principle of supremacy. Supremacy 'in practice … often amounts to giving directives and Community law in general a higher ranking in the hierarchy of norms which are valid within a national legal system'.[16] The Court held in *Simmenthal* that the national courts are under a duty to set aside any legislative measure conflicting with Union law, and that any national provision withholding that power is incompatible with Union law.[17] The ruling did not, however, address the question whether it is sufficient that the Union law issue can be raised incidentally in a concrete case, or whether it must be subject of an independent action. This question is to be addressed in the following.

[12] For a further account of these distinctions, see VF Comella, 'The European Model of Constitutional Review of Legislation: Toward Decentralization?' (2004) 2 *International Journal of Constitutional Law* 461. For a more detailed account of the various models of constitutional review found in Europe, see M De Visser, *Constitutional Review in Europe: A Comparative Analysis* (Hart Publishing 2014).

[13] For a general overview over constitutional complaints in Europe, see G Dannemann, 'Constitutional Complaints: The European Perspective' (1994) 43 *International Comparative Law Quarterly* 142.

[14] RS Kay, 'Standing to Raise Constitutional Issues: A Comparative Analysis' in RS Kay (ed), *Standing to Raise Constitutional Issues: Comparative Perspectives* (Bruylant 2005) 1, 2.

[15] See further ibid.

[16] S Prechal, *Directives in EC Law* (Oxford University Press 2005) 95. Similarly de Búrca, who points out that 'the legislative rights which are created at Community level generally acquire a form of constitutional status at the national level where they take priority over national law'; see G de Búrca, 'The Language of Rights and European Integration' in J Shaw and G More (eds), *New Legal Dynamics of European Union* (Oxford University Press 1995) 30.

[17] Case 106/77 *Simmenthal* [1978] paras 21–22.

III. Situations Where Incidental Review is Sufficient from the Perspective of Union Law

Whether the Member States need to provide for a self-standing action for judicial review of legislative acts came up before the Court in *Unibet*, addressed in chapter 7, section V.[18] We may recall that the Court held that the Member States are required to provide for a self-standing action in exceptional circumstances where alternative means of legal recourse are lacking. The judgment suggested that the Member States can rely on their domestic enforcement rules only to the extent that they provide sufficient protection for individual Union rights.[19] The overall enforcement regime in place in the Member State must be examined in order to determine whether individual Union rights are given adequate legal protection.

Member States do not have to provide for a self-standing action for judicial review where the affected individual can challenge the legislation through an alternative legal avenue. Whether such legal recourse is available depends both on the specifics of the domestic legal system and on the specific facts of the case. Where the claimant satisfies the criteria for liability in damages laid down in the '*Francovich* jurisprudence' (see chapter 10), he may initiate an action for damages. As the Court made clear in *Unibet*, to comply with the principle of effective judicial protection, the national court must ensure that domestic legislation is examined for Union law compliance, regardless of whether the claim for damages is unsuccessful, due to a lack of damage or causal link.[20] A claimant may also seek an individual decision that can be subject to challenge, and plead the Union law violation in the course of the proceedings. Whether this latter option is available to the claimant depends on how the legislative measure is crafted. For instance, in the case of a licensing scheme, the claimant may be well served by applying for a licence, thereby provoking an individual decision that in turn can be subject to judicial review.[21] This will allow the domestic court to examine whether the legislative scheme is in compliance with Union law.

What it means for an alternative recourse to be available is not entirely clear. A central question is whether the claimant is required to avail himself of a legal avenue that is clearly futile, if that will enable him to have the Union law compatibility of the legislative measure assessed. One way of reading the Court's ruling in *Unibet* is that the mere possibility of raising the compatibility issue is sufficient to satisfy the effectiveness requirement, regardless of the actual chances of receiving damages.[22] The ruling can also be taken to account for the position that where the legislative provision allows for exceptions, the possibility of requiring an exception in order to challenge the refusal can be conceived of as fulfilling the requirement of an effective remedy, even though it is clear from the outset that such an exception will not be granted.

[18] Case C-432/05 *Unibet* [2007].

[19] G Anagnostaras, 'The Quest for an Effective Remedy and the Measure of Judicial Protection Afforded to Putative Community Law Rights' (2007) 32 *EL Rev* 728, 728.

[20] Case C-432/05 *Unibet* [2007] para 59.

[21] This possibility would not be open to a private party whose market position is adversely affected by an unlawful grant of state aid to its competitor; see Case C-368/04 *Transalpine Ölleitung* [2006] para 49.

[22] Anagnostaras, 'The Quest for an Effective Remedy' (n 19) 738.

Such a reading sits, however, oddly, with the Court's ruling in *Hoechst*.[23] The case arose in the context of an action for compensation in damages. The claimant in the main proceedings had been denied a tax advantage pursuant to national legislation that was allegedly contrary to Union law. The action was held inadmissible, with the argument that the claimant had failed to act diligently to avoid the loss and damage. It could have filed an application for tax exception and challenged the unfavourable decision before the court. The Court found, however, that the exercise of rights conferred by Union law would be rendered impossible or excessively difficult if claims for restitution or compensation were rejected or reduced solely because the persons concerned had not applied for a tax advantage that national law clearly denied them.[24]

Although the Court's ruling in *Hoechst* could indicate that an individual does not have to resort to a legal avenue that has no prospect of success, the matter here is not fully comparable with that addressed by the Court in *Unibet*. What constitutes an effective remedy must be seen in relation to what the claimant seeks to achieve with his action. The main interest of an individual affected by a statute incompatible with Union law is normally to have the court declare that he can go about his business without being restricted by the statute. The crux of the matter should therefore be whether a preliminary finding of incompatibility will enable the claimant to do so.

The Court did not address this issue in *Unibet*, but Advocate General Sharpston elaborated. She referred to the explanation by the Swedish Government that a decision by a national court to the effect that the prohibition on promotion of gaming services ran counter to Union law would be examined closely by the Government and most likely lead to a change in the law. Advocate General Sharpston found the remedial structure in Sweden adequate from the perspective of effective judicial protection, but stressed that she proceeded

> on the twin premises that, if the national court decides the preliminary issue as to the compatibility with Community law of the prohibition on promotion in Unibet's favour, it will grant Unibet some form of substantive relief and that that relief will be effective [but] if the damages route does not in fact afford protection that, in practical terms, allows Unibet to enforce its rights under Community law once they are recognized by the national court, a new remedy must necessarily be created if Sweden is to respect its obligations under Community law.[25]

That the effectiveness of the damages actions depends on the granting of some kind of substantive relief to the claimant cannot, however, be inferred from the laconic judgment of the Court.[26] A preliminary finding of incompatibility will not necessarily result in the legislature's stepping in and changing the law.[27] And even if such a change were to take place, 'there would inevitably be a delay and it might not have retrospective effect'.[28]

[23] Joined Cases C-397/98 and C-410/98 *Hoechst* [2001].
[24] ibid para 106. This finding has its parallel in the case law of the ECtHR, which has held that in order to be considered 'effective', a remedy must offer reasonable prospects of success; see, inter alia, *Akdivar and others v Turkey* App no 21893/93 (ECtHR, 1996) para 66.
[25] AG Sharpston in Case C-432/05 *Unibet* [2006] para 56.
[26] Anagnostaras, 'The Quest for an Effective Remedy' (n 19) 738.
[27] AM Keessen, *European Administrative Decisions: How the EU Regulates Products on the Internal Market* (Europa Law Publishing 2009) 193; and A Arnull, 'Annotation of Unibet' (2007) 44 *CML Rev* 1763, 1175.
[28] Arnull, 'Annotation of Unibet' (n 27) 1775.

Where a private party does not benefit from a change in the law, it can be questioned whether an incidental review of the legislative measure has afforded him effective judicial protection. It is arguable that the Court's ruling in *Unibet* should be understood to mean that the mere finding that a legislative provision is incompatible with Union law gives the claimant the legal certainty needed to go on with his business.

IV. A Free-standing Action as an Avenue of Last Resort

While in some cases it may be possible to obtain judicial review of a legislative measure through an alternative legal avenue, this may not always be the case. The key aim of this section is to identify lacunae in the system of legal protection offered at the domestic level, in order to outline the exceptional situation in which a free-standing action for judicial review of legislative measures is required under Union law.

There are several examples of private parties' breaking the law in order to manoeuvre themselves into a position where they could have the court rule on the compatibility of the legislative measure in question. By way of illustration, in *Klas Rosengren and Others*, the appellants in the main proceedings had imported wine from Spain with a view to challenging Swedish law prohibiting the direct import of alcoholic beverages by private parties.[29] When criminal proceedings were brought against them, they pleaded in their defence that the prohibition was contrary to (now) Article 34 TFEU (free movement of goods) or Article 37 TFEU (discrimination on the grounds of nationality in the operation of state monopolies). We saw in chapter 6, section III.C that a private party has the right to plead in his defence that the application of domestic law would run contrary to Union law. Yet, as the Court made clear in *Unibet*, the ability of a private party to raise Union law arguments defensively in the context of proceedings brought against him would not be sufficient, and effective judicial protection would not be ensured, if the claimant could only test the legality of a national rule by first breaking it.[30] That statement cannot, however, be taken to mean that Member States should allow individuals to seize the court and have legislation reviewed, regardless of their concrete interest. Considering that legislation is of general application, and often directed at the public at large, it would in practice mean that Member States would have to provide for open standing.

The Court's ruling in *Unibet* offers little guidance in determining the range of persons that should be entitled to challenge legislative provisions. This can be explained by the fact that the ruling did not really concern the issue of *locus standi* but rather restrictions as to the availability of a specific form of procedure. As pointed out by Póltorak, 'Restrictions on *locus standi* are those which refer to the entity bringing the action while restrictions of availability of procedures are those which refer to the scope – the subject of a given procedure.'[31] But since the ruling entails that access to court must be provided

[29] Case C-170/04 *Klas Rosengren and Others* [2007]. For a comparable fact pattern, see Case C-142/05 *Mickelson and Roos* [2009].

[30] Case C-432/05 *Unibet* [2007] para 64.

[31] N Poltorak, *European Union Rights in National Courts* (Wolters Kluwer 2015) 159.

to have the court assess the compatibility of a national provision with Union law, the Court is implicitly saying that standing must be granted.

When considering the extent to which a person can be considered affected in his rights by virtue of the mere existence of a legislative measure, the jurisprudence of the ECtHR may also give guidance in this context. Importantly, though, it is the case law under Article 34 that is of relevance, since the State Parties are not required to provide for abstract judicial review of statutes pursuant to Article 13 ECHR.[32] We may recall from chapter 5, section IV.C that only 'victims' of a convention infringement are granted standing before the Strasbourg Court. It is only in wholly exceptional circumstances that the risk of a future violation may confer the status of 'victim' on an individual applicant.[33] In *Tanase v Moldova*, the Court held that

> [i]n order to claim to be a victim of a violation, a person must be directly affected by the impugned measure: the Convention does not envisage the bringing of an *actio popularis* for the interpretation of rights it contains or permit individuals to complain about the provision of national law simply because they consider, without having been directly affected by it, that it may contravene the Convention.[34]

Despite that, 'it is open', the Court held,

> to a person to contend that a Law violates his rights, in the absence of an individual measure of implementation, if he is required either to modify his conduct or risk being prosecuted or if he is a member of a class of people who risk being directly affected by the legislation.[35]

As to the first category of 'potential victims', there are several cases where the ECtHR has afforded standing to an applicant who faced a situation where he had to alter his conduct or risk being prosecuted. In *Dudgeon v the United Kingdom*, a male homosexual was granted standing to challenge a law prohibiting and sanctioning homosexual conduct between male adults. Although the provision had not been enforced for years, the ECtHR still found that the applicant had to be considered a 'victim' of an infringement of Article 8 ECHR (private life), as he had to live in fear that he might be prosecuted under the said Act.[36] Moreover, in *SAS v France*, a Muslim woman was entitled to challenge the French ban on wearing a full-face veil. The Court held that women in her situation are

> confronted with a dilemma comparable *mutatis mutandis* to that which the Court identified in the *Dudgeon* and *Norris* judgments …: either they can comply with the ban and thus refrain from dressing in accordance with their approach to religion; or they refuse to comply and face prosecution.[37]

[32] *James and Others v the United Kingdom* App no 8793/79 (ECtHR, 1986) para 85. On the relationship between Arts 13 and 34, see ch 5, section IV.C.

[33] *Asselbourg and 78 others v Luxembourg* App no 29121/95 (ECtHR, 1999), where the Court held that to be considered a potential victim, an applicant must produce 'reasonable and convincing evidence of the probability of the occurrence of a violation concerning him or her personally, mere suspicions or conjectures are not enough in that respect'.

[34] *Tănase v Moldova* App no 7/08 (ECtHR, 2010) para 104.

[35] ibid.

[36] *Dudgeon v the United Kingdom* App no 7525/76 (ECtHR, 1981). See also *Norris v Ireland* App no 10581/83 (ECtHR, 1988).

[37] *SAS v France* App no 43835/11 (ECtHR, 2014) para 57.

Conversely, the fact that the applicants did not face the threat of sanctions has been used as an argument to deny standing. In *Oardiri v Switzerland* and *Ligue des Muslumans de Suisse and others v Switzerland* (the Minarets Cases),[38] the applicants sought to challenge a constitutional amendment prohibiting the building of minarets, pleading the violation of their rights under Article 9 ECHR (freedom of religion) and 14 ECHR (non-discrimination). The applicants were denied standing, and the ECtHR stressed, inter alia, that the prohibition was not subject to sanctions, and that the applicants were therefore not prevented from exercising their freedom of religion.

The other class of 'potential victims' set out by the ECtHR in *Tanase v Moldova* were those belonging to a 'class of people who risk being directly affected' by the legislation. The ruling in *Burden and Burden v the United Kingdom* serves to illustrate how this latter category is to be delineated. The ECtHR allowed two sisters standing to challenge inheritance tax legislation that was allegedly discriminatory and thus a violation of Article 14 ECHR, seen in relation to their right to peaceful enjoyment of their possessions under Article 1 of the First Protocol. The Court found that since it was highly probable that one of them in the near future would have to pay inheritance tax upon the death of the other, they were directly affected by the law in question.

After this brief *tour d' horizon* in the case law of the ECtHR, it needs to be examined whether this strand of case law can also give indications as to who should be granted standing pursuant to the principle of effective judicial protection under EU law. We have seen that standing accrues to those whose Union rights are adversely affected (chapter 5, section IV.C). A private party cannot, based on the principle of effective judicial protection, claim a right to initiate judicial review proceedings based on abstract arguments that legislation conflicts with Union law. A requirement that the claimant is sufficiently affected ensures that the litigation is concrete, and alleviates the courts from having to deal with hypothetical and abstract legal questions.[39]

There are valid reasons for arguing that the principle of effective judicial protection grants standing to right holders required either to modify their conduct or otherwise risk being sanctioned. A private party subject to legislation incompatible with Union law also faces a dilemma: either he has to forgo an activity that may turn out to be completely legitimate, or he may ignore the statute and risk being exposed to sanctions.[40] The Court's statement in *Unibet*, to the effect that an individual should not be placed in a position in which he can only test the compatibility of a law by breaking it, arguably means that those who face this dilemma should be granted standing. A statute contrary to Union law places limitations on an individual's freedom to act, and making anticipatory relief available would also further the effectiveness of Union law by eliminating this 'chilling effect'. Whether the claimant faces such a dilemma must be determined in view of the facts of the case; the probability of the legislative measure's being executed to the

[38] *Ouardiri v Switzerland* App no 65840/09 (ECtHR, 2011); and *Ligue des musulmans de Suisse and Others v Switzerland* App no 66274/09 (ECtHR, 2011).

[39] This is what Bickel has called the 'passive virtues' of judicial decision-making, see AM Bickel, *The Least Dangerous Branch: The Supreme Court at the Bar of Politics*, 2nd edn (Yale University Press 1986) ch 4. He argued that the law on standing would ensure that the court deals with specific disputes, rather than abstract questions of (constitutional) law.

[40] This dilemma is also pointed out by SM Thio, *Locus Standi and Judicial Review* (Singapore University Press 1971) 57–58.

detriment of the claimant must be assessed. Yet, as Kay has pointed out, special considerations arise in the context of judicial review of legislation. This type of judicial review

> obliges a court considering such a claim to estimate the likelihood and imminence of such a law being brought to bear on the claimant to his or her disadvantage. Such a speculative injury is bound to yield imprecise and, therefore, to some extent, inconsistent results.[41]

Whereas demonstrating the threat of sanctions is one way of demonstrating adverse effects on a claimant's Union rights, it is not necessarily the only way. In *Unibet* the Court did not say that only those who face the threat of sanctions should be entitled to an effective remedy, and it is quite illustrating that the betting company did not face prosecution – proceedings were only initiated against the Swedish media. The ruling can therefore arguably be seen as an example of the second category set up by the ECtHR, consisting of '*[members] of a class of people who risk being directly affected* by the legislation'. In *Unibet*, the claimants had purchased advertising space in the Swedish media, but were hindered from purchasing additional advertising space due to the legislative prohibition and the injunctions obtained by Swedish administrative authorities. The undertakings were therefore adversely affected by the legislative prohibition. Whether the Court would have reached the same conclusion in the absence of such a contract is more doubtful. For a claimant to demonstrate that he has a special interest in the subject matter of the action, he must demonstrate that his factual situation falls within the scope of the relevant Treaty provision. The Court's ruling in *Alpine Investments* indicates that the possibility of a cross-border element may be sufficient for invoking Article 56 TFEU.[42] On the other hand, the Court has held that the purely hypothetical prospect of exercising the right of freedom of movement is not sufficient to establish a connection with Union law.[43] Consequently, an individual does not come within the scope of the Treaty if the effects of national rules are 'purely hypothetical'.[44] In such circumstances, it may in theory be that the legislative provision is contrary to Union law but the claimant is not in a position to have the Court intervene.[45]

To conclude, Member States may need to provide for a self-standing action for judicial review of legislation in exceptional cases, where an affected individual lacks an alternative legal avenue. This prompts the question of what remedy national courts must afford? Where a legislative measure is challenged incidentally in the course of civil, administrative or criminal proceedings, the court can limit itself to assessing the actual application of the norm to the case at hand. In other words, the claimant (or occasionally

[41] Kay, 'Standing to Raise Constitutional Issues: A Comparative Analysis' (n 14) 5.

[42] The Court's ruling in Case C-384/93 *Alpine Investments* [1995] para 19, where the Court held that '[t]he freedom to provide services would become illusory if national rules were at liberty to restrict offers of services [and the] prior existence of an identifiable recipient cannot therefore be a condition for application of the provisions on the freedom to provide services'.

[43] Case C-299/95 *Kremzow* [1997] para 16.

[44] Case 180/83 *Moser* [1984] para 18. However, the Court has not provided clear parameters that allow us to determine where to draw the line between uncertain and purely hypothetical events; see further N Nic Shuibhne, *The Coherence of EU Free Movement Law: Constitutional Responsibility and the Court of Justice* (Oxford University Press 2013) 173–77.

[45] See Case C-70/95 *Sodemare* [1997], addressed in ch 6, section III.C. The Court held that the claimant was not in a position to challenge a legislative provision for conformity with Union law, since the case was confined in all respects within a single Member State.

the defendant) asserts that the statute is contrary to Union law *as applied* in the course of such concrete review. Since it is a concrete case that triggers the review, the court may, if it deems it appropriate, omit the question whether the statute is valid and applicable in other circumstances. This is different when the statute is challenged directly, prior to its execution. It is submitted that the principle of effective judicial protection cannot entail an obligation for the courts to review the legislative provision in the abstract and render it void or inapplicable with *erga omnes* effect. The Court emphasised in *Unibet* the importance of individuals' obtaining an *examination* of the question of Union law compatibility.[46] This means Member States are required under Union law to make available a legal avenue so that a court can take a stance on whether a legislative measure is in conformity with Union law. It seems to follow implicitly from the Court's ruling *Unibet* that it is sufficient for the courts to make a declaration of incompatibility.[47]

[46] Case C-432/05 *Unibet* [2007] paras 49 and 56.

[47] The solution adopted in the United Kingdom under the Human Rights Act 1998 could serve as an example of how such a regime might be structured. The court has no power to invalidate legislation, but pursuant to s 4 of the Act, the court may make a formal declaration of incompatibility. A finding of incompatibility with the Convention empowers the relevant government minister to amend the legislation by a 'fast track' procedure laid down in s 10.

10

Standing to Seek Compensation from the State

I. Introduction

The aim of this chapter is to outline the criteria for having a right of action for compensation against the state. The right to compensation pursuant to *Francovich* can be seen as a 'Union law remedy', and as we may recall from chapter 7, section IV, in the context of such remedies, issues of substance and procedure tend to merge. The Court has not only laid down the entitlement to compensation, but also required that this remedy can be pursued in court.[1] As Van Gerven has held, when the Court has enumerated the conditions for liability to arise, it entails 'the inevitable conclusion that the plaintiff is entitled to *ask for reparation* for the harm sustained in a court of law'.[2]

The *Francovich* case law can therefore be seen as prescribing a *right of action* before a national court for damages incurred as a result of the infringement. The constitutive conditions spelled out in the Court's jurisprudence regulate not only who has a right to redress, but also who has a right of access to court. Put differently, the conditions not only regulate the right to *obtain* compensation, but also the right to *pursue* a claim for compensation. Conversely, if these criteria are not met, domestic courts are not, as a matter of EU law, obliged to allow the suit, and the claim can be dismissed at the admissibility stage. Yet it should be stressed that standing is based on a prima facie assessment of the claim brought forward, and domestic courts need to entertain a suit if the claimant has an arguable claim on the merits.[3]

There is a vast body of jurisprudence from the Court pertaining to state liability, and this jurisprudence has been the subject of a vast number of scholarly publications; it is not my intention to provide an original contribution to this scholarship.[4] Nevertheless, a book on standing would be incomplete without accounting for the possibility of

[1] Similarly T Eilmansberger, 'The Relationship between Rights and Remedies in EC Law: In Search of the Missing Link' (2004) 41 *CML Rev* 1199, 1239–40; and N Poltorak, *European Union Rights in National Courts* (Wolters Kluwer 2015) 64.

[2] W Van Gerven, 'Of Rights, Remedies and Procedures' (2000) 37 *CML Rev* 501, 512 (emphasis added).

[3] In order to have a right of action in damages, the claimant must demonstrate that he is *arguably* entitled to relief pursuant to the *Francovich* criteria, but the threshold for arguability is not high; see ch 7, section IV.

[4] See, inter alia, A Biondi and M Farley, *The Right to Damages in European Law* (Wolters Kluwer 2009); P Aalto, *Public Liability in EU Law: Brasserie, Bergaderm and Beyond* (Hart Publishing 2011); B Roosebeke, *State Liability for Breaches of European Law* (Springer Fachmedien 2007).

initiating an action for damages against the state. In the following, I seek to outline the *constitutive conditions* that must be fulfilled for an individual to have the right to claim compensation in domestic courts.[5] Where these cumulative conditions are met, prima facie, the claimant has, under EU law, a right to judicial process.

In section II, I give a brief overview of the state liability doctrine, before moving on, in section III to outline the criteria for having a right of action in damages against a state. In section IV, I ask whether we are dealing with an autonomous remedy, or rather a remedy of last resort.

II. The Contours of the State Liability Doctrine

In most European legal systems, state liability 'has been built on the framework of tort law, which addresses the same set of problems everywhere: the foundation of liability, causation, justification or excuses, and remoteness of damage'.[6] Despite this common framework, there are differences as regards both the availability and the extent of liability. Some Member States operate with restrictions to liability, such as immunities relating to administration of justice or to the legislative process.[7] Other States set high hurdles for such a liability to occur.[8] However, when it comes to Union law infringements, domestic limitations may have to yield. The Court has required Member States to make available damages actions, regardless of whether this remedy already exists under domestic law, and has also set out the constitutive conditions pursuant to which this remedy can be claimed and obtained.[9]

The seminal case on state liability was *Francovich*. The case concerned the failure of the Italian state to implement Directive 80/987/EEC (Employer Insolvency). Pursuant to the Directive, the Member States were to set up a guarantee fund for the benefit of workers whose wage claims would otherwise not be covered. The claimants claimed to have suffered loss as a consequence of the state's failure to do so, and sued for compensation. The Court found that the state can incur liability in the case of non-implementation of a directive, provided three conditions are met: the result prescribed by the directive must entail the grant of rights to individuals; it must be possible to identify the content of those rights from the directive; and there must be a causal link between the Member

[5] As to the *extent* of compensation, the Member States are granted considerable discretion; see Case C-118/08 *Transportes Urbanos* [2010] para 31. The Court has nevertheless required such compensation to be 'commensurate with the loss or damage sustained' (see Joined Cases C-46/93 and C-48/93 *Brasserie du Pêcheur* [1996] para 82 and Case C-373/95 *Maso* [1997] para 36) and 'adequate' (see Joined Cases C-94/95 and C-95/95 *Bonifaci* [1997] para 53 and Case C-373/95 *Maso* [1997] para 41). The Court has, inter alia, declined to accept statutory ceilings, see Case C-271/91 *Marshall II* [1993] para 30.

[6] D Shelton, *Remedies in International Human Rights Law*, 3rd edn (Oxford University Press 2015) 91.

[7] Aalto, *Public Liability in EU Law* (n 4) 61.

[8] J Engström, 'The Europeanisation of Remedies and Procedures Through Judge-Made Law: Can a Trojan Horse Achieve Effectiveness? Experiences of the Swedish Judiciary' (PhD thesis, European University Institute 2009) 208. For a comparative account of state liability in Europe, see K Oliphant (ed), *The Liability of Public Authorities in Comparative Perspective* (Intersentia 2016).

[9] For a presentation of how this Union remedy has been received in the Member States, see R Condon and B van Leeuwen, 'Bottom Up or Rock Bottom Harmonization? Francovich State Liability in National Courts' (2016) 35 *Yearbook of European Law* 229.

State's failure and the loss suffered by the individual. The principle of Member State liability was found to be 'inherent in the system of the Treaty'.[10]

In *Francovich*, the Court only addressed liability for the situation in which Member States fail to implement a directive. However, in *Brasserie du Pêcheur* and *Factortame*,[11] the Court made clear that Member State liability was not confined to lack of implementation of directives, but also extended to other types of infringements. The claimant in the first case, a French brewery, sought damages for the losses it had incurred due to the German purity regulation ('*Reinheitsgebot*'), imposing content and labelling requirements that hindered the export of beer to Germany; whereas the claimants in the second case, Spanish fishermen, sought to cover the loss they had suffered as a result of the Merchant Shipping Act's excluding foreign vessels from fishing in the territorial waters of the United Kingdom. The Court held that the conditions under which Member State liability would arise depended on the nature of the infringement; and where the states were afforded a wide discretion, three conditions needed to be fulfilled: the rule of law infringed must be intended to confer rights on individuals; the breach must be sufficiently serious; and there must be a direct causal link between the breach and the damage sustained.[12]

The discrepancy between the conditions laid down in *Francovich* and *Brasserie du Pêcheur* were reconciled in *Dillenkofer*. The Court held that the conditions for liability are the same, regardless of the breach committed. The condition that there should be a sufficiently serious breach, although not expressly mentioned, was nevertheless implicit in the Court's *Francovich* ruling.[13] Although the conditions for liability are the same regardless of the type of breach, the conditions are vague enough to cater to the differences inherent in the functions served by the various state organs, and the characteristics of the Union law provision infringed.

The Court already made clear in *Brasserie* that the principle of state liability applies whichever public authority is responsible for the breach.[14] The Member State is responsible for breaches committed not only by central government institutions, but also by local and regional authorities.[15] Liability can arise from acts of the executive and legislative and even the judicial branches of government.[16] Moreover, the Court has found not

[10] Joined Cases C-6/90 and C-9/90 *Francovich* [1991] para 35.

[11] Joined Cases C-46/93 and C-48/93 *Brasserie du Pêcheur* [1996].

[12] ibid para 51.

[13] Joined Cases C-178/94, C-179/94, C-188/94, C-189/94 and C-190/9 *Dillenkofer* [1996] para 23.

[14] Joined Cases C-46/93 and C-48/93 *Brasserie du Pêcheur* [1996] para 32. This was reiterated, inter alia, in Case C-224/01 *Köbler* [2003] para 31 and Case C-429/09 *Fuss* [2010] para 46.

[15] Case C-302/97 *Konle* [1999]. Whether the state can be held liable pursuant to *Francovich* must be kept distinct from the question of which organ is responsible for making reparation pursuant to domestic law in the Member State concerned; see *Konle*, para 62.

[16] See, inter alia, Case C-5/94 *Hedley Lomas* [1996] (administrative decision); Case C-392/93 *British Telecom* [1996] (legislative act); and Case C-224/01 *Köbler* [2003] (judicial decision). Scholars are divided as to whether the *Foster* jurisprudence applies, implying that the state is to be held liable for the conduct of organisations or bodies 'subject to the authority or control of the State or had special powers beyond those which result from the normal rules applicable to relations between individuals'; see Case C-188/89 *Foster* [1990] para 18. Póltorak and Fredriksen assume this is the case: see Poltorak, *European Union Rights in National Courts* (n 1) 325; and HH Fredriksen, *Offentligrettslig erstatningsansvar ved brudd på EØS-avtalen* (Fagbokforlaget 2013) 131; whereas Dougan finds good reasons 'for not treating *Foster* as a relevant authority in the context of *Francovich* [since to] hold Member States responsible for breaches committed by an "emanation of the state" would in fact amount to an unfair allocation of financial responsibility in respect of breaches of Community law'

only that breaches of public law duties will incur liability, but also that Member States can be held liable when breaching obligations of a private law character.[17]

III. The Criteria for Having a Right of Action in Damages

A. Infringement of a Rule Intended to Confer Rights on Individuals

The first condition for having a right of action in damages is that the infringed rule must be intended to confer rights on individuals. The Court has used a variety of formulations, such as a rule of law 'for the protection of the individual'[18] or a rule of law 'intended to protect individuals'.[19] Yet the Court held in *Sison* that these expressions are 'mere variations on a single legal concept, which is expressed … by the formula "intended to confer rights on individuals"'.[20]

That the *infringed* rule must entail the grant of rights is somewhat imprecise. As pointed out in legal scholarship, the provision breached does not have to be correlative to the right of the claimant.[21] For instance, in *Francovich*, the Member State's breach was the failure to implement a Directive, whereas the substantive right at issue was the right to financial protection in the case of the insolvency of the employer. Similarly, in *Köbler*, the Member State breached the duty to make a reference for a preliminary ruling (now Article 267 TFEU), whereas the right conferred on the claimant stemmed from, inter alia, (now) Article 45 TFEU. This means that 'the Member States' breach of a procedural obligation may be seen as a violation of the primary substantive rights, and hence an indirect correlation between the breach and the violated right can be established'.[22] Yet it is mostly the case that the provision infringed is the same as the provision granting rights.

The concept of Union law rights was elaborated on in chapter 4, section III. It was argued that the protective scope of the provision (and the ascertainability of the right) needs to be taken into account. The protective scope of the provision is also what underlies the condition to be addressed in the following, namely, legally relevant harm.

See M Dougan, *National Remedies Before the Court of Justice: Issues of Harmonisation and Differentiation* (Hart Publishing 2004) 254–55.

[17] Case C-429/09 *Fuss* [2010] (where Stadt Halle acted as an employer) and Case C-242/95 *GT-Link* [1997] (a public undertaking abused its dominant position contrary to (now) Art 102 TFEU). Dougan argues, however, that the *Francovich* action is grounded in public law; see M Dougan, 'Addressing Issues of Protective Scope within the Francovich Right to Reparation' (2017) 13 *European Constitutional Law Review* 124, 159–62.

[18] Case C-282/90 *Vreugdenhil v Commission* [1992] para 19; and Case C-390/95 P *Antillean Rice Mills and Others v Commission* [1999] para 58.

[19] Case T-4/01 *Renco v Council* [2003] para 60.

[20] Case T-341/07 *Sison* [2011] para 33.

[21] D Leczykiewicz, 'The Constitutional Dimension of Private Law Liability Rules in the EU' in D Leczykiewicz and S Weatherill (eds), *The Involvement of EU Law in Private Law Relationships* (Hart Publishing 2013) 199, 217–18; and Dougan, 'Addressing Issues of Protective Scope within the Francovich Right to Reparation' (n 17) 126–31.

[22] Leczykiewicz, 'The Constitutional Dimension of Private Law Liability Rules in the EU' (n 21) 218. See Joined Cases C-6/90 and C-9/90 *Francovich* [1991] and Case C-224/01 *Köbler* [2003].

B. Legally Relevant Harm

For a claimant to have a right of action in damages, he must also, it is submitted, have suffered *legally relevant harm*. The occurrence of harm is not a criterion the Court has listed for state liability to occur, yet it is clear that compensation is not to be awarded in the absence of harm.[23] The requirement of harm is implicit in the condition of causation, in that the Court requires a causal link between the infringement and the harm suffered.[24] This gives rise to the question what constitutes legally relevant harm. The issue of legally relevant harm is closely related to the issue of rights, yet these notions should be kept apart: whereas the issue of rights concerns whether the claimant is protected by the provision invoked, the issue of legally relevant harm concerns the *extent* of the protection. In other words, a claimant holds a right if he belongs to the group of persons protected by the infringed provision; but he has suffered a legally relevant harm only if the provision infringed protects against the type of harm suffered.

The criterion of legally relevant harm has seldom been addressed by the Court, and is also under-theorised in legal scholarship.[25] Whether this criterion is to be determined according to Union law or domestic law can be questioned. The Court has repeatedly held that the *extent* of compensation is to be determined pursuant to the domestic law of the Member States, subject to fulfilment of the principles of equivalence and effectiveness, which could be taken to mean that this discretion also extends to determining the type of harm to be compensated. In fact, the Court has used formulations that could indicate that this is indeed the case. In *Brasserie du Pêcheur*, for example, it held that 'it is for the domestic legal system of each Member State to set the criteria for determing the extent of reparation', provided that the principles of equivalence and effectiveness are complied with.[26] Although this could indicate that it is generally left to the Member State to determine what type of harm is to be compensated, it will be argued that this is not in fact the case. I subscribe to the view held by Fredriksen that 'harm' must be an *autonomous Union law concept*, and that it is merely the principles pertaining to the meting out of the compensation that are left to the remedial autonomy of the Member States.[27] In other words, a distinction must be drawn between what constitutes relevant harm and the amount of compensation awarded.

When it comes to determining what constitutes legally relevant harm, it must be taken into account that infringement of Union law by the Member States tends to result in pure economic loss.[28] Not all forms of economic loss are recoverable under Union law; rather it seems to follow from the Court's case law that the state is only liable for harm of the type the infringed provision was meant to prevent. A first indication of such a stance is to be found in *Rechberger*, where the claimants sought compensation from

[23] Poltorak, *European Union Rights in National Courts* (n 1) 332.

[24] ibid.

[25] See, however, Dougan, 'Addressing Issues of Protective Scope within the Francovich Right to Reparation' (n 17).

[26] See Joined Cases C-46/93 and C-48/93 *Brasserie du Pêcheur* [1996] para 90. See also Case C-470/03 *A.G.M.-COS.MET* [2007] para 94.

[27] Fredriksen, *Offentligrettslig erstatningsansvar ved brudd på EØS-avtalen* (n 16) 155.

[28] For an overview of how different national systems have approached the need for 'floodgates' to limit the scope of liability for pure economic loss, see B Thorson, *Individual Rights in EU Law* (Springer 2016) 162–63.

Austria, since they had not obtained a refund for a pre-paid holiday trip following the bankruptcy of the travel organiser. They argued that their loss was caused by Austria's failure to properly implement Article 7 of Directive 90/314/EEC (Package Travel). The Court stressed the protective purpose of the norm, in stipulating that the provision 'is designed to safeguard all the consumer rights mentioned in that provision and thus to protect consumers against all the risks defined therein and resulting from the insolvency of the travel organisers'.[29] What the Court seems to be saying is that the loss suffered is of a kind the Union law provision is meant to protect against, and consequently that the harm is legally relevant.

The Court went into even more detail on the issue of relevant harm in its ruling in *Leth*.[30] We may recall from chapter 5, section IV.E that the case concerned a claim for compensation due to an alleged failure to comply with the Directive 85/337/EEC (former EIA Directive). The claimant in the main proceedings was the owner of a house situated close to an airport, and consent to an extension of the airport was granted without a prior environmental impact assessment's having been conducted. Ms Leth brought proceedings, claiming damages to compensate for the devaluation of her property and a declaration as to future losses.[31]

That Member States were required to make good harm caused by the failure to carry out an environmental impact assessment had been established by the Court in *Wells*.[32] Yet the Court did not conclude directly that Leth had a right to compensation for all her economic loss where such an assessment was lacking. The infringed provisions should be examined to see whether the loss suffered fell within the scope of protection afforded by the Union law.[33] The Court concluded that the economic damage was covered by the objective of the Directive, insofar as the damage was the direct consequence of the environmental effects of a public or private project. Such economic damage had to be distinguished from damage that did not have its direct source in the environmental effects and which, therefore, was not covered by the objective of protection pursued by that Directive.[34]

From the Court's ruling in *Leth* it can be concluded that the type of economic damage for which compensation can be claimed must be determined by interpreting the Union law provision infringed. What constitutes legally relevant harm must be determined with reference to Union law, rather than domestic law. The further content of this criterion still needs to be clarified. A question raised in legal scholarship is, for example, whether

> any given EU law right can or should be divided into the pursuit of primary and secondary objectives – such that only the interests legally protected by the primary objectives of the relevant provisions are apt to provide the basis for a right to reparation; while those interests legally protected only on a purely secondary basis would fall outside the legitimate protective scope of the EU system of non-contractual state liability.[35]

[29] Case C-140/97 *Rechberger* [1999] para 61.
[30] Case C-420/11 *Leth* [2013].
[31] The Court held that Directive 85/337 (EIA Directive) confers on individuals a right to have environmental effects assessed, see para 32.
[32] Case C-201/02 *Wells* [2004] para 66.
[33] Case C-420/11 *Leth* [2013] para 33.
[34] ibid 36.
[35] Dougan, 'Addressing Issues of Protective Scope within the Francovich Right to Reparation' (n 17) 142–43.

That the harm suffered is considered legally relevant does not necessarily mean that the claimant is entitled to claim and obtain compensation. In *Leth*, the Court was careful to distinguish the question of legally relevant harm from that of *causation*. After addressing the type of harm considered legally relevant, it went on to address the requirement of a direct causal link. Although the Court stressed that the existence of that direct causal link is a matter for the national courts to ascertain, in accordance with the guidelines laid down by the Court, it went quite far in suggesting that the requirement was not fulfilled in the present case.[36]

C. Sufficiently Serious Breach

The third criterion for having a right of action in damages, is that the state has committed a 'sufficiently serious' breach. In *Brasserie du Pêcheur*, the Court provided the criteria national courts must take into account in order to assess whether the condition has been met: the clarity and precision of the rule breached; the measure of discretion left to national authorities; whether the infringement and damage caused was intentional or involuntary; whether any error of law was excusable or inexcusable; whether the position taken by a Union institution may have contributed towards the omission; and the adoption or retention of a national measure or practices contrary to Union law.[37] These criteria have been reiterated by the Court in its subsequent case law.[38]

In its earlier case law on the liability of the Union organs – which is 'the opposite [side] of the same coin of public liability under the Treaty'[39] – the Court distinguished between legislative and administrative acts, and required a sufficiently serious breach only in relation to the former.[40] This differentiation between legislative and administrative acts was, however, left aside in *Bergaderm*, and replaced by a distinction based on the degree of discretion. 'The decisive test,' the Court held,

> for finding that a breach of Community law is sufficiently serious is whether the Member State or the Community institution concerned *manifestly and gravely disregarded the limits of its discretion* … Where the Member State or the institution in question has only considerably reduced, or even no, discretion, the mere infringement of Community law may be sufficient to establish the existence of a sufficiently serious breach.[41]

Hence, the Court has crafted a 'two-tiered system of liability', pursuant to which a form of strict liability applies where the infringed provision does not allow for discretion, while the claimants must prove more with respect to Union provisions granting the Member States broad discretionary authority.[42] Bearing in mind, however, that discretion tends

[36] Case C-420/11 *Leth* [2013] para 46.

[37] Joined Cases C-46/93 and C-48/93 *Brasserie du Pêcheur* [1996] para 56.

[38] See Case C-224/01 *Köbler* [2003] paras 54–55; and Case C-446/04 *Test Claimants in the FII Group Litigation* [2006] para 213.

[39] G Anagnostaras, 'State Liability and Alternative Courses of Action: How Independent Can an Autonomous Remedy Be?' (2001) 21 *Yearbook of European Law* 355, 372.

[40] See Case 5/71 *Schöppenstedt* [1971] (legislative action) and Case 145/83 *Adams* [1985] (administrative action) respectively.

[41] Case C-352/98 P *Bergaderm* [2000] paras 43–44 (emphasis added).

[42] A Ward, *Judicial Review and the Rights of Private Parties in EC Law* (Oxford University Press 2000) 224.

to be a matter of *degree*, one should be cautious about drawing sharp distinctions between the two categories.[43] Moreover, as the Court made clear in *Haim*, although a mere infringement may be sufficient to constitute a sufficiently serious breach where discretion is lacking, this is not necessarily the case, and all factors characterising a situation must be taken into account.[44]

Given the central role played by discretion, it is regrettable that the Court has not been more forthcoming on what is meant by the term. It is clear that the existence and scope of discretion must be determined with reference to *Union law* rather than domestic law.[45] Moreover, the discretion enjoyed by the state is broadly dependent on the degree of clarity and precision of the rule infringed.[46] Clearly, if the state acts in a legislative capacity and finds itself in an area where there is no Union harmonisation, it will have considerable discretion, since is only restricted by the Treaty provisions. But where a Member State is called upon to implement Union legislation, it may also have discretion in that regard. The liability of a Member State by reason of incorrect transposition is 'conditional on a finding of manifest and serious disregard by that State for the limits set on its discretion'.[47] This requirement is dictated by the concern that the legislative function should not be hindered by the prospect of damages actions.[48]

There are in particular two types of infringements the Court has perceived as being sufficiently serious in and of themselves, due to lack of discretion. First, if a Member State fails to transpose a directive or transposes it belatedly, it incurs liability for the harm suffered as a consequence thereof.[49] Second, a breach of Union law must be considered as sufficiently serious if it has persisted 'despite a judgment finding the infringement in question to be established, or a preliminary ruling or settled case-law of the Court on the matter from which it is clear that the conduct in question constituted an infringement'.[50] Provided the Member State is afforded discretion, it needs to be determined whether the limits of this discretion are 'manifestly and gravely disregarded'. The national court must take account of all the relevant factors characterising the situations before it, as listed in *Brasserie*. The clarity and precision of the rule breached is often the crucial element in this inquiry.[51]

[43] Similarly Van Gerven, who speaks about a 'sliding scale' of discretion; see W Van Gerven, 'Bridging the Unbridgeable: Community and National Tort Laws after Francovich and Brasserie' (1996) 45 *International and Comparative Law Quarterly* 507, 518.

[44] Case C-424/97 *Haim* [2000] paras 41–42.

[45] ibid para 40.

[46] Case C-278/05 *Robins* [2007] para 73.

[47] ibid para 75.

[48] AG Léger in Case C-118/00 *Larsy* [2001] para 61. In the context of non-contractual liability of the Union, this aspect has been highlighted by the Court in Joined Cases 83 and 94/76, 4, 15 and 40/77 *Bayerische HNL* [1978] para 5.

[49] This was perceived to be the case in *Francovich* and *Dillenkofer*, concerning respectively the failure to transpose and the belated transposal of Directive 90/314/EEC (Package Travel); see Joined Cases C-6/90 and C-9/90 *Francovich* [1991] and Joined Cases C-178/94, C-179/94, C-188/94, C-189/94 and C-190/94 *Dillenkofer* [1996].

[50] Joined Cases C-46/93 and C-48/93 *Brasserie du Pêcheur* [1996] para 57. This was found to be the case, inter alia, in Case C-118/00 *Larsy* [2001] (see paras 43–45) and Case C-429/09 *Fuss* [2010] (see para 58).

[51] See, inter alia, Case C-392/93 *British Telecom* [1996] paras 43–44 and Joined Cases C-283/94, C-291/94 and C-292/94 *Denkavit* [1996] paras 51–53, where the Court held that the provisions lacked precision and clarity and that guidance from the Court was lacking, hence rendering the error excusable. See, conversely, Case C-150/99 *Stockholm Lindöpark* [2001] para 40, where the Court stressed 'the clear wording' of the relevant directive.

The claimant must surmount the hurdle of showing, prima facie, a 'sufficiently serious' breach in order to have a right of action in damages, and this applies regardless of the organ responsible for the breach. Yet it has been further qualified when it comes to breaches committed by the judiciary, given the specific nature of the judicial function and the need for legal certainty. In *Köbler*, the Court restricted liability to exceptional circumstances where the court has 'manifestly infringed the applicable law'.[52] Liability can only incur for courts adjudicating at last instance.[53] Whether the liability for breaches committed by the judiciary is largely a matter of window-dressing will depend on the further content given to the requirement of 'manifest infringements'. The opinions in legal scholarship vary, from the position that the requirement 'cannot be regarded as an insurmountable obstacle'[54] to the position that '[t]he increase in the effective judicial protection following from the Köbler ruling is *de facto* limited'.[55]

D. Causation

The last requirement for having a right of action in damages – a 'direct causal link' between the unlawful act and the damage[56] – is perhaps the most difficult criterion to pin down. This is both because the Court has not gone into much detail on this requirement, and, not least, because the few rulings that do address the issue seem somewhat contradictory.

To start with, there is a need to clarify the notion of causation. In general (and somewhat circular) terms, causation means there has to be a causal link between the breach and the injury sustained. However, drawing a distinction between matters of fact and law –between *factual* and *legal* causation – is important in the causal inquiry.[57] As regards the first, it concerns whether the defendant factually caused the claimant's loss, which is an empirical matter. Member States employ various tests to assess factual causation (but-for tests, necessary cause and so on). Legal causation, on the other hand, concerns the scope of liability. The question is whether the defendant should be responsible for the loss occurred, and this is a matter of policy. Member States employ concepts such as foreseeability and adequate cause, and legal causation covers doctrines such as intervening causes and remoteness of damage.[58]

[52] Case C-224/01 *Köbler* [2003] para 53. This was confirmed in Case C-173/03 *Traghetti del Mediterraneo* [2006] para 32 and Case C-168/15 *Tomášová* [2016] para 24.

[53] The decisive matter is not whether the judicial organ is the highest court in the Member State, but rather whether it is 'the last judicial body before which individuals may assert the rights conferred on them by EU law'; see Case C-3/16 *Aquino* [2017] para 34.

[54] B Beutler, 'State Liability for Breaches of Community Law by National Courts: Is the Requirement of a Manifest Infringement of the Applicable Law an Insurmountable Obstacle?' (2009) 46 *CML Rev* 773, 775.

[55] Engström, 'The Europeanisation of Remedies and Procedures Through Judge-Made Law' (n 8) 222. Similarly Tridimas, who holds that '*Köbler* only applies *in extremis*'; see T Tridimas, 'Bifurcated Justice: The Dual Character of Judicial Protection in EU Law' in A Rosas, E Levits and Y Bot (eds), *The Court of Justice and the Construction of Europe: Analyses and Perspectives on Sixty Years of Case-law* (TMC Asser Press 2013) 367, 377.

[56] See, inter alia, Joined Cases C-46/93 and C-48/93 *Brasserie du Pêcheur* [1996] para 51 and Case C-118/08 *Transportes Urbanos* [2010] para 30.

[57] See further I Lianos, 'Causal Uncertainty and Damages Claims for the Infringement of Competition Law in Europe' (2015) 34 *Yearbook of European Law* 170, 177–85.

[58] ibid 179–82.

Limitations to liability in the Member States can be framed either as a matter of normative causation, or as a matter of legally relevant harm.[59] Yet the concepts of normative causation and legally relevant damage are closely connected, and sometimes hard to tell apart. The Court's ruling in *Leth* (addressed in chapter 5, section IV.E), supports the view that the Court has adopted an approach where the protective scope of the norm has to be assessed with a view to determining the type of harm considered legally relevant, and has singled out the issue of causation for separate treatment.

Whether causation is an autonomous Union concept, or is rather to be determined according to national law (within the bounds of the requirements flowing from the principles of equivalence and effectiveness) is disputed in legal scholarship.[60] The Court mostly leaves it to the domestic court to determine whether the requirement for a causal link has been met in the concrete case, yet this does not necessarily mean that the rules governing causation are left to national law.[61] In *Leth*, the Court held that 'It is, in principle for the national courts to apply the criteria, *directly on the basis of European Union law*, for establishing the liability of the Member States for damage caused to individuals.'[62] Yet in the absence of clear authority to the effect that there is a Union concept of causality, I am hesitant to draw that conclusion.

The Court has on occasion considered that it had the necessary information to determine the issue of causation itself, which could indicate that causality is to be determined pursuant to Union law. The clearest example of the Court's expressing its stance on the matter of causation is *Brinkmann*.[63] A German undertaking exporting tobacco to Denmark had been subject to charges that were contrary to Directive 79/32/EEC (Tobacco VAT), since their products were wrongly classified as cigarettes rather than smoking tobacco. The Court found that Denmark had failed to transpose the Directive into Danish law in a timely manner, which in and of itself constituted a sufficiently serious breach. Nevertheless, the Danish authorities had given immediate effect to the relevant provisions of the Directive, which meant that the requirement of a direct causal

[59] By way of illustration, whereas Germany largely limits liability through the application of the *Schutzzweck* doctrine (determining the protective scope of the infringed provision), France restricts liability through rules on normative causation (by requiring that the causal connection is 'direct'); see further C van Dam, *European Tort Law*, 2nd edn (Oxford University Press 2013) 285–87.

[60] That the requirement of a 'direct causal link' is based on Union law is suggested by, inter alia, T Tridimas, 'Liability for Breach of Community Law: Growing Up and Mellowing Down?' (2001) 38 *CML Rev* 301, 310, and W Van Gerven, 'The Emergence of a Common European Law in the Area of Tort Law: The EU Contribution' in D Fairgrieve, M Andenas and J Bell (eds), *Tort Liability of Public Authorities in Comparative Perspective* (The British Institute of International and Comparative Law 2002) 125, 133. There are also scholars who argue that causation is left to national law, subject to the requirements of equivalence and effectiveness: see, inter alia, Aalto, *Public Liability in EU Law: Brasserie, Bergaderm and Beyond* (n 4) 11; van Dam, *European Tort Law* (n 59) 323; and Engström, 'The Europeanisation of Remedies and Procedures Through Judge-Made Law' (n 8) 223–24.

[61] Tridimas, 'Liability for Breach of Community Law (n 61) 310. Similarly IC Durant, 'Causation' in H Koziol and R Schulze (eds), *Tort Law of the European Community* (Springer Vienna 2008) 47, 73. The Court has stated on several occasions that it is in principle for the national court to ascertain whether the loss and damage claimed flow sufficiently directly from the breach of EU law by the Member State, see, inter alia, Joined Cases C-46/93 and C-48/93 *Brasserie du Pêcheur* [1996] para 65 and Case C-524/04 *Test Claimants in the Thin Cap Group Litigation* [2007] para 122.

[62] Case C-420/11 *Leth* [2013] para 43 (emphasis added).

[63] Case C-319/96 *Brinkmann* [1998].

link between the belated transposition and the claimant's loss was not fulfilled.[64] The fact that the Court took it upon itself to determine the question of causation could indicate that it perceived the applicable concept as deriving from Union law rather than domestic law.

Although the Court has showed itself willing to address matters pertaining to causation, there is scarce support for the position that the causal link requirement has been harmonised at the Union level.[65] On the contrary, the case law of the Court lends support to the position that causation is not an autonomous Union concept but left to national law (within the bounds of the requirements flowing from the principles of equivalence and effectiveness).[66] The Court took such a stance in *Danfoss*. The case concerned a claim for compensation from a third party suffering from the 'passing-on' of unlawfully levied charges. The Court held that the domestic rule at issue – under which a direct causal link could only be established between the levying of unlawful charges and damage suffered by the taxable person – should not be interpreted 'in such a way as to make it virtually impossible or excessively difficult to obtain compensation for the damage suffered'.[67] This passage seems to rest upon the assumption that rules on causation are essentially left to domestic law.

When it comes to the liability of private parties for competition law infringements, the Court acknowledged that causality is, as a starting point, governed by domestic law. In *Manfredi*, the Court held that 'the detailed rules governing the exercise of [the right to compensation] including those on the application of the concept of "causal relationship"' were for the domestic legal system of each Member State to prescribe, subject to the requirement to observe the principles of equivalence and effectiveness.[68] In her Opinions in *Kone* and *Otis II*, Advocate General Kokott argued strongly in favour of an autonomous Union concept of causality.[69] There is, however, nothing in the Court's rulings to indicate that causality is to be regarded as a constitutive condition determined by EU law.[70] The Court found that national provisions that *a priori* limit the circle of persons entitled to claim compensation for harm caused by an anticompetitive behaviour, must be deemed incompatible with Article 101 TFEU.[71] These rulings can thus be seen as 'clarifying the outer limits imposed by European primary law', by prohibiting

[64] The Danish authorities had wrongly interpreted the Directive, but this infringement was not sufficiently serious to give rise to state liability; see Case C-319/96 *Brinkmann* [1998] para 31.

[65] Similarly Dougan, who holds that it does not seem accurate to claim that the causation requirement has been 'subjected to full judicial harmonization effectively pre-empting existing domestic rules in favour of a centralised Community standard' (Dougan, *National Remedies Before the Court of Justice* (n 16) 247), and Jans, who holds that '[o]ne cannot say that there is a fully developed European doctrine on causality' (see JH Jans, 'State Liability: In Search of a Dividing Line between National and European Law' in D Obradovic and N Lavranos (eds), *Interface between EU Law and National Law* (Europa Law Publishing 2007) 281, 290).

[66] Similarly Aalto, *Public Liability in EU Law: Brasserie, Bergaderm and Beyond* (n 4) 11; van Dam, *European Tort Law* (n 59) 323; Engström, 'The Europeanisation of Remedies and Procedures Through Judge-Made Law' (n 8) 223–24 and Dougan, 'Addressing Issues of Protective Scope within the Francovich Right to Reparation' (n 17) 131–32.

[67] Case C-94/10 *Danfoss* [2011] para 36.

[68] Joined Cases C-295/04 to C-298/04 *Manfredi* [2006] para 64.

[69] AG Kokott in Case C-557/12 *Kone* [2014] and Case C-435/18 *Otis II* [2019].

[70] See Case C-557/12 *Kone* [2014] and Case C-435/18 *Otis II* [2019].

[71] See ch 7, section IV.

the automatic exclusion of certain types of claims, but not as an examination of what constitutes a relevant causal link.[72] I agree with Havu, who holds that

> individuals who have suffered harm caused by competition infringements must be able to claim compensation, but it is, in the absence of EU law, for Member State laws to set out detailed rules governing the condition of causal link and its application.[73]

Given that the Court has never defined causality as a matter of EU law, Member States are not excluded from denying, on a case-by-case basis, compensation for harm suffered based on domestic doctrines such as remoteness, proximate causation or directness of injury.[74]

It is submitted that the same approach must be adopted in the context of state liability. Phrased differently, the requirement of a direct causal link is presumably to be determined pursuant to domestic law, which must be assessed for compliance with the requirements of equivalence and effectiveness. This clearly illustrates that what we are talking about here is a 'hybrid' remedy, based partly on Union law, partly on domestic law. This hybrid quality, it is submitted, spills over into the question of standing, in the sense that the standing conditions are also partly based on domestic law. If it is clear from the outset that, pursuant to domestic rules on causality, there is no causal link between the infringement and the harm suffered, a claimant does not have a right of action in damages against the state.[75]

IV. Autonomous Union Law Remedy or Remedy of Last Resort?

A. Introduction

Having gone through the constitutive conditions for having a right of action in damages against a state, I ask whether this legal avenue must be made available to a claimant at his choice. Generally speaking, the principle of effective judicial protection does not dictate a particular type of legal recourse but leaves Member States ample latitude, provided the claimant's rights are effectively protected.[76] In the following, I examine whether the *Francovich* doctrine constitutes an exception to this rule, calling for an autonomous action for which a Member State must provide, regardless of whether alternative legal avenues are available under national law. The Court has repeatedly stressed that the right to reparation is 'founded directly on Community law'[77] or 'flows directly from

[72] B Freund, 'Compensation for Remote Economic Losses Caused by Infringements of Art 101 TFEU – *Otis and Others v Land Oberösterreich and Others* (C-435/18)' (2020) 1 *GRUR International* 496, 500.

[73] K Havu, 'Private Enforcement of Competition Law: Notes Regarding the Roles of EU and National Law on the Basis of Recent Preliminary Rulings' (2020) 2 *Europarättslig tidskrift* 193, 200.

[74] To this effect, see PC de Sousa, 'EU and National Approaches to Passing on and Causation in Competition Damages Cases: A Doctrine in Search of Balance' (2018) 55 *CML Rev* 1751, 1771.

[75] This would be different if domestic rules on causality fail to comply with the principles of equivalence and effectiveness; see Case C-557/12 *Kone* [2014], addressed in ch 7, section IV.

[76] See ch 7, section II.

[77] Case C-66/95 *Sutton* [1997] para 33; and Case C-127/95 *Norbrook* [1998] para 111.

Community law'.[78] As the Court held in *Leth*, the conditions for state liability 'found a right in individuals to obtain redress on the basis of European Union law directly'.[79] But does this necessarily mean that Member States are prevented from offering alternative remedies in lieu of damages?

We may recall that the Court in *Safalero* held that a domestic court may refuse to grant standing, without infringing the principle of effective judicial protection, if the claimant is afforded sufficient judicial protection through another legal avenue.[80] The question to be answered is therefore whether a domestic court may hold a claim for damages to be inadmissible, with reference to the availability of alternative remedies. For the purpose of this inquiry, there is a need to distinguish two scenarios. First, I explore the extent to which a state may require the exhaustion of alternative remedies as a means for the private party to mitigate his losses; second, I examine the leeway also granted to Member States outside the scope of the mitigation principle, as a manifestation of the remedial autonomy of Member States.[81] As will be seen, the Court has allowed for some flexibility, yet one should be cautious in sidelining the state liability doctrine, since monetary compensation will often be the only means of providing judicial protection of Union rights.

B. Exhaustion of Other (Primary) Remedies as Fulfilment of the Mitigation Duty

The Court has repeatedly held that national courts may enquire whether the injured person showed reasonable diligence in order to avoid the loss or damage or limit its extent, and whether, 'in particular, he availed himself in time of all the legal measures available to him'.[82] Keeping in mind that damages is a *secondary remedy*, emerging as a reaction to rights infringement, the Court has accepted that a Member State may first require the claimant to avail himself of possible *primary remedies* to safeguard and enforce the primary right. It is clearly preferable to restore substantive legality, since this allows the violated norm to 'produce its desired effect with regard to the actual addressees of the rights and obligations it contains'.[83] Whereas an award of damages will serve the financial interest of the claimant, the restoration of substantive legality will also ensure the broader public interest pursued by the norm in question.[84]

[78] Case C-300/04 *Eman* [2006] para 70; and Case C-524/04 *Test Claimants in the Thin Cap Group Litigation* [2007] para 123.

[79] Case C-420/11 *Leth* [2013] para 42. This means that national courts cannot make liability subject to additional criteria; see, inter alia, Case C-429/09 *Fuss* [2010] para 66. The Court already held in Joined Cases C-46/93 and C-48/93 *Brasserie du Pêcheur* [1996] that reparation cannot be made subject to proof of fault beyond the condition of 'sufficiently serious breach', as this would 'be tantamount to calling in question the right to reparation founded on the Community legal order', see para 79.

[80] Case C-13/01 *Safalero* [2003], addresed in ch 7 section V.

[81] This division mirrors that of Anagnostaras, 'State Liability and Alternative Courses of Action' (n 39).

[82] Joined Cases C-46/93 and C-48/93 *Brasserie du Pêcheur* [1996] para 84. See Case C-524/04 *Test Claimants in the Thin Cap Group Litigation* [2007] para 124; and Case C 445/06 *Danske Slagterier* [2009] para 60.

[83] Anagnostaras, 'State Liability and Alternative Courses of Action' (n 39) 366.

[84] The Court has nevertheless on occasion refrained from requiring the Member State to provide for primary remedies, directing the claimant instead to seek reparation under *Francovich*; see, for instance, Case C-90/96 *Petrie* [1997] para 30.

Individuals are expected to conduct themselves prudently with a view to protecting their rights. The rationale behind a liability action is to compensate a victim for a violation he could neither prevent nor be blamed for, and this does not cover situations in which the claimant could have avoided or mitigated the loss by availing himself of appropriate legal remedies.[85] In legal scholarship there is wide support for the position that Member States are entitled to make the admissibility of such a claim dependent on the previous exhaustion of domestic remedies.[86]

The possibility of requiring the exhaustion of primary remedies was implied in *Stockholm Lindöpark*. Lindöpark was a development company running a golf course exclusively for the use of businesses. Under Swedish law, its activities were exempted from VAT, and the company was therefore prevented from deducting input VAT incurred on goods and services used for the purposes of this activity. The Court found that the Swedish law violated provisions of Directive 77/388/EEC (Sixth VAT Directive), and that the provisions in the Directive were sufficiently clear and precise to be considered directly effective. Lindöpark thus had the possibility of pursuing retroactively the debts it claimed was owed by the Swedish state, invoking the Directive. Consequently, the Court held that 'At first sight … an action for damages founded on the Court's case-law relating to the liability of Member States for breaches of Community law does not seem necessary.'[87]

This ruling seems to indicate that the right to damages is residual to other primary remedies afforded in the Member State concerned.[88] The Court has stressed, however, that it would be contrary to the principle of effectiveness to oblige injured parties to have recourse to all the legal remedies available to them, if that would give rise to 'excessive difficulties or could not reasonably be required of them'.[89] At least the Court's ruling in *Hoechst* indicates that claimants cannot be required to resort to an alternative legal avenue if it is clear from the outset that recourse to this avenue will not bring about any positive results. The Court held that it would render the exercise of Union rights 'impossible or excessively difficult' if a claimant were required to apply for grant of a Union right that national law clearly denied him, with a view to challenging the refusal in court.[90]

A similar statement was made in *Thin Cap Group Litigation*, regarding the compatibility of the United Kingdom's 'thin capitalisation' rules with (now) Article 49 TFEU (freedom of establishment). Pursuant to these rules, the ability of a resident company to deduct, for tax purposes, interest paid on loans granted by a non-resident parent company was restricted, such a restriction not applying if the loans were granted by a parent company resident in the state. As regards a claim for compensation or

[85] Anagnostaras, 'State Liability and Alternative Courses of Action' (n 39) 366.

[86] See, inter alia, Aalto, *Public Liability in EU Law: Brasserie, Bergaderm and Beyond* (n 4) 9; Engström, 'The Europeanisation of Remedies and Procedures Through Judge-Made Law' (n 8) 251–57; and S Prechal, 'Member State Liability and Direct Effect: What's the Difference After All?' (2006) 17 *European Business Law Review* 299, 301.

[87] Case C-150/99 *Stockholm Lindöpark* [2001] para 35. Similarly Joined Cases C-444/09 and C-456/09 *Gavieiro* para 87.

[88] Engström, 'The Europeanisation of Remedies and Procedures Through Judge-Made Law' (n 8) 255.

[89] Case C 445/06 *Danske Slagterier* [2009] para 62.

[90] Joined Cases C-397/98 and C-410/98 *Hoechst* [2001] para 106; see further ch 9, section III.

reimbursement, the Court found that the requirement of effectiveness would not be fulfilled if a company had to apply to the tax authorities for a certain classification of the interest paid, when such a classification was clearly not in compliance with domestic law.[91]

Given that the rules of mitigation of loss must be applied within the bounds of the principles of effectiveness and effective judicial protection, it must be determined whether it is *reasonable* to require the individual to have mitigated its loss though exercising another remedy.[92] If that is not the case, standing cannot be denied with reference to the availability of an alternative avenue. What is 'reasonably required' of the claimant must be determined based on the circumstances of the case.[93]

C. Exhaustion of Other Remedies as a Manifestation of Remedial Autonomy

Having seen that a state may hold a claim for compensation inadmissible if a claimant has failed to mitigate his losses by availing himself of available remedies, I now turn to explore the extent to which a state, as a manifestation of its remedial autonomy, may hold inadmissible an action for damages with reference to the availabililty of alternative remedies.

Although the claimant has not violated the mitigation duty by failing to pursue alternative courses of action, Member States are still afforded some leeway when it comes to determining the form of reparation. This was first made evident in the Court's rulings in *Bonifaci*[94] and *Maso*.[95] Following the Court's ruling in *Francovich*, Italy adopted a legislative decree implementing Directive 80/987/EEC (Employer Insolvency) and decided on the body to be responsible for making the payments under the guarantee scheme. The claimants had suffered loss as a result of the belated implementation of the Directive, and brought proceedings for damages against the state. The Court found that such an action was not required as a matter of Union law if the full retroactive application of the belatedly transposed Directive constituted adequate reparation. Such retroactive application would be sufficient unless the beneficiaries established

> the existence of complementary loss sustained on account of the fact that they were unable to benefit at the appropriate time from the financial advantages guaranteed by the Directive with the result that such loss must also be made good.[96]

Legal scholars have taken these rulings as to account for the position that the *Francovich* case law does not necessarily entail a right to monetary damages, and that Member

[91] Case C-524/04 *Test Claimants in the Thin Cap Group Litigation* [2007] para 126.

[92] Engström, 'The Europeanisation of Remedies and Procedures Through Judge-Made Law' (n 8) 255–56.

[93] See, eg, Case C-429/09 *Fuss* [2010] paras 80–86, where the Court found that a public sector employee, as the weaker party in the employment relationship, could not reasonably be required to make a prior application to his employer requesting the employer to comply with the requirements of maximum weekly working time provided for in Directive 2003/88/EC (Working Time).

[94] Joined Cases C-94/95 and C-95/95 *Bonifaci* [1997].

[95] Case C-373/95 *Maso* [1997].

[96] Joined Cases C-94/95 and C-95/95 *Bonifaci* [1997] para 53; and Case C-373/95 *Maso* [1997] para 41. This was reiterated in Case C-261/95 *Palmisani* [1997] para 35.

States do not have to provide for a damages claim when the claimant can receive effective judicial protection by other means.[97] Dougan, for example, finds it

> arguable that *Francovich* does not create a right specifically to damages against the Member State for its breach of Community law, but has instead introduced a general right to reparation in whatever form the Member States find it most convenient to provide.[98]

He suggests that this line of case law may be a reflection of the general principle that 'every breach of Community right must carry with it an effective level of redress', but that the precise form of such relief is as a starting point left to the Member State to decide.[99] Seen from this angle, *Francovich* can be seen as merely spelling out the *constitutive conditions* for this obligation to arise. Such a conclusion cannot, however, be drawn based on the rulings in *Maso* and *Bonifaci* alone. A key issue in explaining these cases may be the fact that the claimants' original rights under the Directive were of a financial character, and thus similar in nature to the right to compensatory damages.[100] Given that similarity, it would be undue formalism to require the availability of a damages action. After all, money is money.[101] In *Tomášová*, when the Court was asked whether an action for unjust enrichment had priority over reparation for damage, it responded that 'the relationship between a claim for that reparation and other remedies which could be available [is] determined by the national law of each Member State, in conformity with the principles of equivalence and effectiveness'.[102]

If the primary right is not of a financial character, this raises the question whether the Member State can meet a claim for monetary damages by offering reparation *in kind*. Prechal is clearly right to hold that whenever a claimant prefers such reparation, and it is practically possible, Union law does not stand in the way.[103] But the interesting question from the perspective of effective judicial protection is rather whether the state can fend off a claim for monetary compensation with reference to the possibility of obtaining reparation in kind. The Court's ruling in *Fuss* lends support to the view that the reparation does not necessarily have to be monetary in nature. The case concerned a violation of Directives 93/104/EC and 2003/88/EC (Working Time), and the Court found that additional time off could be provided in lieu of financial compensation. '[I]t cannot be concluded,' the Court added, 'that EU law favours one or other of those forms of reparation.'[104]

Despite the Court's sweeping statement, one should be cautious in reading this as a retreat to domestic remedial autonomy. Generally speaking, an action for damages must

[97] Engström, 'The Europeanisation of Remedies and Procedures Through Judge-Made Law' (n 8) 251–57; and Anagnostaras, 'State Liability and Alternative Courses of Action' (n 39) 378–81.

[98] Dougan, *National Remedies Before the Court of Justice* (n 16) 257.

[99] ibid 258. See further M Dougan, 'The Francovich Right to Reparation: Reshaping the Contours of Community Remedial Competence' (2000) 6 *European Public Law* 103.

[100] See Dougan, *National Remedies Before the Court of Justice* (n 16) 257–58.

[101] It is not necessarily possible to confer on individuals retroactively the actual right they were supposed to enjoy under Union law, and the passing of time may have reduced the value of the benefit belatedly conferred, hence possibly calling for a *Francovich* action; see Anagnostaras, 'State Liability and Alternative Courses of Action' (n 39) 361.

[102] Case C-168/15 *Tomášová* [2016] para 41.

[103] S Prechal, *Directives in EC Law* (Oxford University Press 2005) 296.

[104] Case C-429/09 *Fuss* [2010] para 96.

not necessarily be made available where alternative remedies exist to protect individual rights and ensure the application of EU law.[105] The latitude left to the domestic legal orders will vary depending on the type of infringement committed. In order to satisfy the requirement of effective judicial protection, the remedy needs to be adequate.[106] Where the claimant has suffered economic harm as a result of the infringement, it may prove difficult for the Member State to make up for these losses through means other than awarding compensation.[107] This means that for practical purposes, the *Francovich* doctrine still holds sway. Consequently, the opportunities available to a Member State to refuse to grant standing with reference to the possibility of pursuing other remedies are limited.

[105] To the same effect, Z Varga, 'National Remedies in the Case of Violation of EU Law by Member State Courts' (2017) 54 *CML Rev* 51, 77.

[106] See ch 7, section II.

[107] Similarly Engström, 'The Europeanisation of Remedies and Procedures Through Judge-Made Law' (n 8) 257.

11

Standing in Proceedings against Private Parties

I. Introduction

The aim of this chapter is to address the special challenges facing an individual seeking to enforce Union law against another private party. Where the defendant is a private party, the claimant must overcome certain hurdles in order to gain access to court. First, the infringed provision must bind individuals; second, it must be possible to invoke the provision in the context of a horizontal proceeding. But although these criteria are met, it can be challenging to determine the role of private individuals in the enforcement of the relevant obligations, because EU law 'blurs the boundaries between public and private law, between public and private enforcement, between individual and collective enforcement and … between judicial and administrative enforcement'.[1]

In the following, I take a closer look at the Union law requirements pertaining to standing when the defendant is a private party. In sections V and VI, a distinction is drawn between actions for injunctions and actions for contractual remedies. But before examining these procedural tracks, I want to say something about the special features of EU law in private legal relationships (section II), and address a matter of importance regardless of the type of action initiated, namely, the possibility of invoking Union law in proceedings against private parties (section III and IV).

II. Union Law and Private Legal Relationships

Union law reaches deeply into private legal relationships. The EU's intervention in private relationships has been described as 'pointilistic',[2] a 'patchwork',[3] 'islands in the ocean' of domestic private law,[4] and as 'accidental tourists in the field or private law'.[5]

[1] H-W Micklitz, 'Enforcement and Compliance: Editorial Introduction' in R Brownsword et al (eds), *The Foundations of European Private Law* (Hart Publishing 2011) 415, 415.

[2] W-H Roth, 'Transposing "Pointillist" EC Guidelines into Systematic National Codes – Problems and Consequences' (2002) 10 *European Review of Private Law* 761.

[3] MW Hesselink, 'The General Principles of Civil Law: Their Nature, Roles and Legitimacy' in D Leczykiewicz and S Weatherill (eds), *The Involvement of EU Law in Private Law Relationships* (Hart Publishing 2013) 131, 165.

[4] R Michaels, 'Of Islands and the Ocean: The Two Rationalities of European Private Law' in Brownsword et al (eds), *The Foundations of European Private Law* (n 1) 139.

[5] H Collins, 'The Hybrid Quality of European Private Law' in Brownsword et al (eds), *The Foundations of European Private Law* (n 1) 453, 454.

The Union has also been criticised for interfering with the integrity of domestic private law.[6] Concerns about the interference of EU law in the realm of domestic private law stem largely from its instrumental nature, meaning that legislative measures serve the policy goals of the Union.[7] The 'instrumentalist rationality' stands in contrast to the 'juridical rationality' seen as originating in domestic private law.[8] European private law is '*regulatory* private law; it does not start from party autonomy or freedom of contract, but is designed for the achieving, fostering or managing of particular markets or particular policy objectives'.[9] Its essence is captured by Cherednychenko:

> Whereas national private laws have been primarily concerned with justice between market participants rather than the pursuance of public goals, the EU has viewed private law, in particular contract law, as an instrument for achieving the collective objectives of European integration. Alongside the central objective of establishing the European internal market, these objectives include, in particular, the protection of consumers, workers, small- and medium-sized enterprises, the industry, and the environment as well as non-discrimination policy.[10]

The EU has never been concerned with the traditional distinction between public law regulation and private law, and EU law is therefore of a 'hybrid quality'.[11] The dichotomy between domestic and EU private law should not, however, be overstated. Private relationships are increasingly also subject to regulation at the domestic level, driven by social, economic or political concerns. States intervene to correct market failures or to realise social goals such as protection of weaker parties, freedom of choice and access to opportunities. Hence, regulation is expanding in areas such as consumer protection, employment relations and anti-discrimination, blurring the distinction between public and private law. One should not ignore, however, the heavy contribution of Union law to the 'process [of] making private law more "public"'.[12]

Union law may have a direct bearing on private legal relationships of both a contractual and a non-contractual nature. Some legislative measures focus on the individual transaction (a contract of purchase of goods or services by a consumer, or a contract of employment for a worker) and adjust the content of that individual contract.[13]

[6] See, inter alia. Roth, 'Transposing "Pointillist" EC Guidelines into Systematic National Codes' (n 2) 770.

[7] Instrumentalist rationality, according to Michaels, 'signifies that private law serves as a means to extra-legal ends, in particular those formulated in the EU Treaty and by the Court of Justice'; see Michaels, 'Of Islands and the Ocean' (n 4) 142.

[8] The term 'juridical rationality' is meant to 'capture a specific characteristic of this type of private law reasoning, namely that its expertise is a specifically law-based one, and the aim is to find answers to existing questions on the basis of the legal material itself – legal texts, legal precedents – rather than on the basis of some extra-legal goal'; ibid 142.

[9] H-W Micklitz, 'Administrative Enforcement of European Private Law' in Brownsword et al (eds), *The Foundations of European Private Law* (n 1) 563, 563.

[10] OO Cherednychenko, 'Public Supervision over Private Relationships: Towards European Supervision Private Law?' (2014) 22 *European Review of Private Law* 37, 38. Similarly, Collins has pointed out that the task of the Union legislature is 'one of problem solving, not justice between the market participants, and certainly not one of securing legal integrity or doctrinal coherence'; see Collins, 'The Hybrid Quality of European Private Law' (n 5) 453.

[11] Collins, 'The Hybrid Quality of European Private Law' (n 5) 453.

[12] P Mates and M Bartoň, 'Public versus Private Interests – Can the Boundaries Be Legally Defined?' 2011 *Czech Yearbook of International Law* 171, 185.

[13] H Collins, 'Social Dumping, Multi-Level Governance and Private Law in Employment Relationships' in Leczykiewicz and Weatherill (eds), *The Involvement of EU Law in Private Law Relationships* (n 3) 223, 227. See, eg, Directive 93/13/EEC (Unfair Terms) Art 6.

Other measures lay down rules of conduct, breach of which may constitute an infringement of the corresponding right of another private party. In contractual legal relationships, it is often the legal act – the contract – that needs to be assessed for compliance with Union law, whereas in non-contractual legal relationships, it is the factual conduct of the private party that needs to be addressed. That being said, the distinction between contractual and non-contractual legal relationships is not always easily drawn. It is not necessarily the concluding of a contract or its content that constitutes a Union law infringement. The infringement may, for instance, be committed at the pre-contractual stage.[14] Alternatively, Union law obligations can be read into the contract, which means that an infringement of these obligations can at the same time be seen as a breach of contract.[15] As will be seen, it is not readily apparent whether a Union law measure laying down rules of conduct gives rise to contractual remedies in the event of a breach.[16]

III. Various Ways to Invoke Union Law against Private Parties

Where a Union law obligation is placed on a private party, this may give rise to a corresponding right triggering the principle of effective judicial protection. We may recall the Court's holding in *Van Gend en Loos*, that EU rights arise not only when they are explicitly granted, but also 'by reason of obligations which the Treaty imposes in a clear and defined way upon individuals'.[17]

Identifying who is bound by an EU law obligation requires an interpretation of the relevant provision. Various Treaty provisions have been found to impose obligations on private parties. This is the case as regards Article 157 TFEU on equal pay for equal work regardless of gender,[18] the competition rules in Articles 101 and 102 TFEU, and also on occasion the free movement rights in the Treaty. The last provisions – because of their nature and substance, prohibiting obstacles to the internal market – tend to concern subjects traditionally handled by public bodies (such as import duties and licences).[19] Nevertheless, the Court in a series of cases has extended the application of the rules to restrictions imposed by private parties.[20] Private actions will, however, only rise to the

[14] For an overview of such pre-contractual duties, see T Wilhelmsson and C Twigg-Flesner, 'Pre-Contractual Information Duties in the Acquis Communautaire' (2006) 2 *European Review of Contract Law* 441.

[15] The possibility of reading such obligations into the contract varies between legal systems; see further EA Farnsworth, 'Comparative Contract Law' in M Reimann and R Zimmermann (eds), *The Oxford Handbook of Comparative Law* (Oxford University Press 2006) 899, 918–22.

[16] On this issue, see further section V.

[17] Case 26/62 *Van Gend en Loos* [1963].

[18] Case 43/75 *Defrenne v SABENA* [1976].

[19] M Claes, 'The European Union, Its Member States and Their Citizens' in Leczykiewicz and Weatherill (eds), *The Involvement of EU Law in Private Law Relationships* (n 3) 29, 37.

[20] Case 36/74 *Walrave and Koch* [1974]; Case C-415/93 *Bosman* [1995]; Case C-281/98 *Angonese* [2000]; Case C-309/99 *Wouters* [2002]; Case C-438/05 *Viking* [2007]; Case C-341/05 *Laval* [2007]; and Case C-171/11 *Fra.bo* [2012].

level of a restriction in exceptional circumstances. As Semmelmann holds, the case law appears to

> equate obstacles originating from the private sphere with public power on the basis of criteria such as the normative/regulatory/quasi-regulatory power and mere socio-economic power comparable to the one inherent in state action.[21]

The vast amount of secondary legislation regulating the relations between private parties *inter se* takes the form of directives. By way of illustration, in the area of consumer law there are directives on, inter alia, package travel, unfair terms and consumer rights;[22] whereas in the area of labour law there are directives on, inter alia, working time, transfers of undertakings and posted workers.[23] Although Member States are obliged to implement directives in their domestic legal order, the directive may well formulate rights and obligations for individuals.[24] As such, directives are *indirect* sources of rights and obligations.[25] There are also examples of regulations governing relations between private parties.[26] Since directives are directly applicable in the Member States, they are *direct* sources of rights and obligations.

The possibility of private enforcement of the obligations of individuals not only requires the provision in its substance to be addressed to individuals; it must also be possible to *rely on* the provision in the context of horizontal proceedings. This raises particular challenges in the case of directives due to the lack of horizontal direct effect.[27] It must, however, be kept in mind that there is a 'plurality of horizontal effect types'.[28] It is primarily though the correct implementation of Union law in the domestic legal orders that Union law provisions become binding on individuals. A claimant seeking to enforce obligations contained in a directive against a private defendant may also rely on the doctrine of harmonious interpretation to render Union law operational in the Member State.[29] The duty of consistent interpretation is rather far-reaching in horizontal cases too. The Court held in *Dansk Industri* that the requirement to interpret national law in conformity with EU law entails the obligation for national courts, where necessary, to change their established case law.[30] The possibility of harmonious

[21] C Semmelmann, 'The Public-Private Divide in European Union Law' in U Neergaard and R Nielsen (eds), *European Legal Method: in a multi-level EU legal order* (DJØF 2012) 183, 211. For an account of different 'levels of horizontality' in the case law on free movement, see N Nic Shuibhne, *The Coherence of EU Free Movement Law: Constitutional Responsibility and the Court of Justice* (Oxford University Press 2013) 100–13.

[22] Directive (EU) 2015/2302 (Package Travel); Directive 93/13/EEC (Unfair Contract Terms); Directive 2011/83/EU (Consumer Rights).

[23] See respectively Directive 2003/88/EC (Working Time); Directive 2001/23/EC (Transfer of Undertakings) and Directive 96/71/EC (Posting of Workers).

[24] S Prechal, *Directives in EC Law* (Oxford University Press 2005) 95–96.

[25] ibid.

[26] See, eg, Regulation (EC) No. 261/2004 (Denied Boarding Compensation).

[27] Case 152/84 *Marshall* [1986] para 48; Case C-106/89 *Marleasing* [1990] para 6; Case C-91/92 *Faccini Dori* [1994] para 20; and Case C-282/10 *Dominguez* [2012] para 37.

[28] PC de Sousa, 'Horizontal Expressions of Vertical Desires: Horizontal Effect and the Scope of the EU Fundamental Freedoms' (2013) 2 *Cambridge Journal of International and Comparative Law* 479, 480. On the various doctrines mitigating the effect of the 'prohibition of horizontal direct effect', see ch 6, section II.B.

[29] The Court has made clear that the duty of harmonious interpretation extends to all national provisions in an area covered by the directive, even though they are not enacted for its implementation; see Case C-106/89 *Marleasing* [1990] para 8.

[30] Case C-441/14 *Dansk Industri* [2016] para 33.

interpretation depends, however, on the rigidity of the national provisions at play, since the national courts are not required to interpret national law *contra legem*.[31]

IV. The Requirement of a Horizontal Right of Action

Provided that the Union law provision infringed is binding on the individual, and the provision can be relied on in a horizontal proceeding (either through direct applicability or direct effect, or by relying on national law with Union origins), it needs to be determined whether Member States must provide for a private right of action to affected individuals.

Certain directives and regulations intend to grant, or do grant, explicit rights to private parties, and also prescribe the type of remedies that must be afforded in the case of a violation. By way of illustration, Directive 93/13/EEC (Unfair Contract Terms) states that Member States must provide that unfair terms shall not be binding on the consumer;[32] Directive 85/374/EEC (Product Liability) entails a right to compensation in the case of defective products;[33] and Regulation (EC) No 261/2004 (Denied Boarding Compensation) grants private parties the right to compensation in the event of denied boarding, cancellations or delays.[34] Where such remedies are prescribed, the instrument clearly requires the availability of private enforcement actions. As far as the Unfair Terms Directive is concerned, this was made evident by the Court in *ERSTE Bank Hungary*. The Court found that a consumer must be entitled to bring a legal action in order to challenge an unfair contract term:

> [A]dequate and effective means to stop the use of unfair terms in consumer contracts must include provisions enabling the latter to be guaranteed effective judicial protection by making it possible for them to bring legal proceedings against the disputed contract including in the enforcement phase and under reasonable procedural conditions so that the exercise of their rights is not subject to conditions, in particular time-limits or costs which make it excessively difficult or impossible to exercise the rights guaranteed by [the Directive].[35]

Despite the *ad hoc* regulation of remedies in secondary legislation, instruments imposing obligations on private parties are mostly silent as to the legal avenues open to individuals in policing the norms laid down. Such instruments tend to leave it to the

[31] See Case C-268/06 *Impact* [2008] para 100; Case C-282/10 *Dominguez* [2012] para 25; Case C-176/12 *AMS* [2014] para 39; and Case C-441/14 *Dansk Industri* [2016] para 32.

[32] See Art 6(1). Pursuant to Art 3(1) of the Directive, a contractual term that has not been individually negotiated 'shall be regarded as unfair if, contrary to the requirement of good faith, it causes a significant imbalance in the parties' rights and obligations arising under the contract, to the detriment of the consumer'; see further Case C-421/14 *Banco Primus* [2017] paras 58–63.

[33] See Art 1. The injured person shall be required to prove the damage, the defect and the causal relationship between the defect and the damage (Art 4).

[34] See Art 1.

[35] Case C-32/14 *ERSTE Bank Hungary* [2015] para 59. This was reiterated in Case C-377/14 *Radlinger* [2016] para 46. The Court has repeatedly held that national courts must assess *ex officio* whether contractual terms are unfair and draw the necessary consequences thereof; see, inter alia, Joined Cases C-240/98 and C-244/98 *Océano Grupo* [2000] paras 26–29 and Case C-472/11 *Banif Plus Bank* [2013] paras 23–24. These obligations are, however, based on the premise that one of the parties to the contract initiates judicial proceedings; see Case C-32/14 *ERSTE Bank Hungary* [2015] para 63.

Member States to regulate the legal consequences of infringements. This raises the question whether these obligations have an impact on private law relationships, in the sense that a private party affected by a breach of these obligations can obtain redress in court. Member States often distinguish between private enforcement of private rights and public enforcement of public norms.[36] But since Union law does not operate according to a strict separation between public and private law, the possibility of private enforcement cannot be ruled out simply by referring to the public character of these norms.[37] In the absence of specific provisions regulating the civil law effects of infringements committed by private parties, the underlying aim and the general context of the provisions must be examined. Since the principle of effective judicial protection dictates that Member States must make available a legal avenue for private parties whose rights are impaired, there is a need to examine whether the relevant Union measure contains rights.

In the following, a distinction will be drawn between actions for injunctions and actions for contractual remedies. In the first type of proceedings, the claimant is seeking to bring an ongoing infringement to an end; in the second type he is seeking the amendment or (full or partial) invalidation of a contract entered into in violation of EU law.

V. Standing to Seek Injunctions

A. Introduction

Whether Union law gives rise to a private right of action for the enforcement of norms binding on individuals was addressed by the Court in *Muñoz*.[38] We may recall from chapter 3, section IV.B that the case concerned a suit brought by Muñoz against his competitor Frumar for its failure to comply with the labelling standards for table grapes enshrined in Regulations (EEC) No 1035/72 and (EC) No 2200/96. The Court found that the United Kingdom could not fend off a claim with reference to the public enforcement regime in place, but that Muñoz was entitled to initiate proceedings with a view to putting the infringement to an end. The ruling in *Muñoz* is rather laconic as to why a private suit had to be entertained. I argued that the ruling can be explained by the need to protect the rights of Muñoz as a competitor suffering the detrimental effects of a violation of the labelling requirements.

The following is an attempt to assess the broader implications of the ruling. First, I examine whether the ruling should be interpreted restrictively due to the nature of the Union law provision infringed. Second, I look at how such private actions lie in the wider enforcement landscape, keeping in mind that it is primarily left to the organs of the Member States to ensure that private parties comply with their Union law obligations.

[36] C Hodges, 'Objectives, Mechanisms and Policy Choices in Collective Enforcement and Redress' in J Steele and WH van Boom (eds), *Mass Justice: Challenges of Representation and Distribution* (Edward Elgar 2011) 104.

[37] Similarly Thorson, who argues that 'one cannot easily dismiss legislation as irrelevant only because it has "public law" characteristics'; see B Thorson, *Individual Rights in EU Law* (Springer 2016) 348.

[38] Case C-253/00 *Muñoz* [2002].

B. Extending the Rationale from *Muñoz* beyond the Enforcement of Regulations

In *Muñoz*, the Court addressed the private enforcement of provisions in a regulation, which unlike directives are directly applicable horizontally. This raises the question whether the findings in *Muñoz* are limited to provisions contained in regulations? Tridimas is of the opinion that '[t]he *Muñoz* principle … does not extend to directives', since directives may not themselves impose obligations on individuals.[39] In a similar vein, Tountolous argues that in view of the nature of directives as a legal instrument, the choice of the legal techniques for implementation is left to the discretion of the Member States, and that the Member State has complied with its Union law obligations when an effective control mechanism in public law has been established and effective, proportionate and dissuasive sanctions are adopted.[40]

The distinction between regulations and directives is spelled out in Article 288 TFEU. While regulations 'shall be binding in [their] entirety and directly applicable in all Member States', directives shall be binding 'as to the result to be achieved'. Regulations are subject to enforcement by national courts without the need for further implementing (legislative or executive) measures, whereas directives cannot impose obligations on private parties in the absence of domestic implementation. Despite these differences, it does seem somewhat contrived to tie the availability of a private right of action to the distinction between regulations and directives. A directive may be designed to result in the creation of rights and obligations for private parties, and *when these are transposed into national law*, Member States must ensure their effective enforcement.[41] To the extent that the content and scope of these obligations are laid down in concrete and precise terms, Member States are to some extent 'degraded to notaries, rubber-stamping what has been decided in Brussels'.[42] Directives are on occasion rather precise and constraining, not too dissimilar to regulations:

> Often little is left to the freedom to choose form and method. Member states can only comply by transcribing the text of the directive at issue into their national law, a tendency which has been reinforced by the ECJ, notably where the Court requires an accurate reproduction of the directive's terminology in national implementing legislation. Some member states have adopted the practice of transposing certain directives by mere reference in their national laws, illustrating the normative self-sufficiency of these directives.[43]

Given the blurry distinction between regulations and directives in terms of *content*, it is submitted that what matters is the degree of 'executive discretion' enjoyed by the Member State in the implementation of the relevant Union policy. This would mean, for example, that there may be a role for private enforcement in the event that a Union

[39] T Tridimas, *The General Principles of EU Law*, 2nd edn (Oxford University Press 2006) 546.
[40] V Tountopoulos, 'Market Abuse and Private Enforcement' (2014) 11 *European Company and Financial Law Review* 297, 303.
[41] Along the same lines F Wilman, *Private Enforcement of EU Law Before National Courts: The EU Legislative Framework* (Edward Elgar 2015) 478.
[42] N Reich, 'The Public/Private Divide in European Law' in H-W Micklitz and F Cafaggi (eds), *European Private Law after the Common Frame of Reference* (Edward Elgar 2010) 56, 68.
[43] S Prechal, 'Adieu à la Directive?' (2005) 1 *European Constitutional Law Review* 481, 484–85.

measure entails a prohibition regime. Conversely, if the measure envisions a licensing or authorisation regime, private enforcement is in principle ruled out, since such a regime *per definition* requires the involvement of a public authority. The amount of discretion afforded by the Union measure was also perceived as relevant by Advocate General Geelhoed in *Muñoz*. The obligations in question, he explained,

> lend themselves well to enforcement in civil proceedings [since] the content of those obligations is precisely determined and not subject to exceptions. Even if an authority of a Member State ... decides for whatever reason not to take action that does not give a producer of or dealer in fruit and vegetables the right to infringe the rule and thereby occasion loss to a third party.[44]

The broader implications of *Muñoz* have been questioned not only because of the type of instrument at issue in the case, but also because of the specifics of the provisions infringed. It has been suggested that the obligation stemming from *Muñoz* might be limited, since the Court deemed it relevant 'that it was the purpose of the regulations in question "to facilitate trade relations based on fair competition" [and if] a regulation does not state this to be one of its objectives, a civil remedy may not be available'.[45] The Court did not, however, explicitly state that the infringed rules were worthy of special treatment, and moreover the provisions in question are not easily distinguishable from other Union law provisions that seek to ensure fair trading and transparency in the market.[46] This may indicate that the 'logic of the *Muñoz* ruling might be applied more broadly'.[47]

C. Private Enforcement Regardless of Public Enforcement Mechanisms

The second aspect that merits consideration is how the private action required by the Court in *Muñoz* relates to the public enforcement regime in place in a Member State. Phrased differently, it can be asked whether the scope for private enforcement varies depending on the public enforcement regime in place. This covers two interrelated (sub-)questions: first, whether a private right of action is dependent on passivity on behalf of the public authorities responsible for enforcement; second, whether Member States may instead open up for claims against the competent public authorities, with a view to compelling them to take action against the infringing party.

As to the first, some scholars have suggested that the Court's reasoning in *Muñoz* may be influenced by the Court's not considering the public enforcement regime sufficiently effective in the case at hand.[48] But although Advocate General Geelhoed

[44] AG Geelhoed in Case C-253/00 *Muñoz* [2001] para 56.

[45] AJ de Moor-van Vugt and RJGM Widdershoven, 'Administrative Enforcement' in JH Jans, S Prechal and RJGM Widdershoven (eds), *Europeanisation of Public Law* (Europa Law Publishing 2015) 281.

[46] Wilman, *Private Enforcement of EU Law Before National Courts* (n 41) 59.

[47] ibid 60. One might also add that the Court's reasoning in *Muñoz* bears a clear resemblance to that followed in Case C-453/99 *Courage* [2001] concerning an action for damages (ibid 299). AG Jacobs argued in *AOB Bundesverband* that the *Courage* rationale applied equally to actions for injunctions; see AG Jacobs in Joined Cases C-264/01, C-306/01, C-354/01 and C-355/01 *AOB Bundesverband* [2003] para 105.

[48] J Engström, 'Effektivt rättsskydd i förvirring – Nationell prosess- och sanktionsrätt i ljuset av C-253/00 Muñoz' 2003 *Europarättslig tidsskrift* 167, 181; and Thorson, *Individual Rights in EU Law* (n 37) 141.

highlighted the fact that the designated enforcement authority declined to act,[49] there is nothing in the Court's ruling to indicate that the right to private redress depends on the availability and willingness of the public authority to take action.

As to the second, it has been suggested in legal scholarship that the need for introducing a right of action against a private infringer depends on the availability of remedies against the public authorities. Rehbinder's argument is that there is first and foremost a need for a horizontal right of action, 'where injunctory relief against the authorities is not available or the discretion the authorities normally enjoy in the field of enforcement is not reviewable'.[50] Fenger is of the opinion that the protection of individuals is best served by allowing an undertaking to sue a competent authority that fails to supervise and enforce the law against a competitor. Moreover, where the private party has suffered loss, the solution adopted in *Muñoz* is not, in his opinion, necessarily sufficient; rather, an action for failure to act combined with a claim for compensation against the state would be more appropriate.[51] These are valid arguments, and the Member States may well open up for such suits against the competent institutions. It has, however, been argued (chapter 2, section III) that a private party does not have a *right to enforcement*, meaning that a Member State is not obliged to entertain such suits. And neither does the availability of such suits relieve the state of its obligation to allow for private actions.

It could perhaps be argued that where the private party's interest is to bring the illegal conduct to an end – and thereby terminate the infringement – he could be equally well served through the route of public enforcement. It is nevertheless submitted that the duty of Member States to ensure effective protection of individuals' rights cannot be accomplished through a public enforcement regime. As the Court held already in *Humblet*, a substantive right 'has as its corollary that it provides the person whose interest it operates with the means of enforcing it himself by proceedings before the courts rather than by the intervention of a third party'.[52] I align myself with Dougan, who suggests that the ruling in *Muñoz* can be explained by the principle of parallelism (or symmetry), whereby an individual right requires an individual remedy:

> [T]he Member State was not entitled to reserve the power to pursue and punish infringements of Union law to the competent public authorities alone, where the relevant Union legislation actually created rights (however ill-defined) in favour of the claimant, since the principle of parallelism requires that those rights must be capable of vindication also by means of individual access to the courts.[53]

A 'public enforcement monopoly' is therefore not acceptable in relation to Union law provisions that grant rights to individuals.[54] So the possibility of submitting a complaint to a supervisory authority, or alternatively initiating proceedings against that authority

[49] AG Geelhoed in Case C-253/00 *Muñoz* [2001] para 2.

[50] E Rehbinder, 'Locus Standi, Community Law and the Case for Harmonization' in H Somsen (ed), *Protecting the European Environment. Enforcing EC Environmental Law* (Blackstone Press 1996) 151, 165.

[51] N Fenger, *Forvaltning og Fællesskab: Om EU-Rettens Betydning for den Almindelige Forvaltningsret: Konfrontation og Frugtbar Sameksistens* (DJØF 2004) 689.

[52] Case C-6/60 *Humblet* [1960].

[53] Michael Dougan, 'Who Exactly Benefits from the Treaties? The Murky Interaction Between Union and National Competence over the Capacity to Enforce EU Law' (2009) 12 *Cambridge Yearbook of European Legal Studies* 73, 106.

[54] Wilman, *Private Enforcement of EU Law Before National Courts* (n 41) 416.

with a view to provoking a public enforcement action, would be insufficient to ensure effective legal protection of the claimant's rights. Pursuant to the principle of effective judicial protection, a private party should not have to rely on the state to intervene to enforce his rights but should be able to *enforce them himself*.

Despite requiring a private legal avenue, the Court did not elaborate on the issue of standing in *Muñoz*. The Court was primarily concerned with the question of whether the Member State was at all required to allow for private enforcement of the norms in question, which is explained by the fact that the barrier hampering access to court was the lack of a legal avenue for individuals. Yet by holding that Muñoz should be able to initiate a private action against Frumar, the Court implicitly held that he should be granted standing.[55] Advocate General Geelhoed suggested that the rules on standing should reflect the conditions governing standing for private parties in annulment proceedings before the EU courts, namely, the requirement of 'direct and individual concern', now enshrined in Article 263(4) TFEU. The Court did not endorse this view, but was rather laconic as to how Muñoz was affected by the non-compliance with the labelling standards. Yet Muñoz was presumably one of the few actors operating on the relevant market, and it must be assumed that he was adversely affected by the conduct of his competitor.[56] It can be inferred from the ruling that a right holder in the position of Muñoz needs to be granted standing to ensure compliance with Union law. But as Engström asks, 'Would the Court have reached another conclusion had he been a consumer, or a small grower?'[57] The Court stressed that *competitors* of the infringer must be able to enforce the applicable rules by way of initiating a civil action, which seems to imply that standing does not extend to any private party.[58] Whether a competitor is sufficiently affected by non-compliance with regulatory norms needs to be determined by taking into account, inter alia, the number of actors operating on the relevant market and their market shares.[59]

Now to the extent that a Union law measure lays down detailed, justiciable norms for the protection of individuals, they should be enforceable, it has been argued, by way of an individual right of action. Placing the enforcement of EU law in the hands of individuals, rather than administrative organs, may produce certain negative effects. First, it may create the risk of over-deterrence.[60] To avoid over-deterrence, Member States could try to steer incentives through rules on court fees and available remedies.[61] Second, adversarial legal proceedings may be seen as inapt to deal with the broader policy issues inherent in Union law. Thus a private enforcement regime may produce fragmented

[55] Similarly J Engström, 'The Europeanisation of Remedies and Procedures Through Judge-Made Law: Can a Trojan Horse Achieve Effectiveness? Experiences of the Swedish Judiciary' (PhD thesis, European University Institute 2009) 145.

[56] Similarly Fenger, *Forvaltning og Fællesskab* (n 51) 709.

[57] Engström, 'The Europeanisation of Remedies and Procedures Through Judge-Made Law' (n 55) 195.

[58] Wilman, *Private Enforcement of EU Law Before National Courts* (n 41) 361.

[59] On the requirement of being 'affected', see ch 5, section IV.C.

[60] See J-U Franck, 'Rights, remedies and effective enforcement in air transportation: *Ruijssenaars*' (2017) 54 *CML Rev* 1867, 1883–84.

[61] For insights on how private enforcement regimes can be tailored to avoid what she calls 'remedial overkill', see JM Glover, 'The Structural Role of Private Enforcement Mechanisms in Public Law' (2011–2012) 53 *William & Mary Law Review* 1137, 1189–98.

and incoherent policy.[62] The need for expert knowledge can be accommodated by inviting competent public authorities to intervene and to expound the law, for example as *amicus curiae*.[63]

VI. Standing to Seek Contractual Remedies

A. Introduction

An injunction to stop unlawful conduct may well be of value, for example, to competitors or repeat players on the market. Other claimants will not necessarily stand to gain from such proceedings, and may thus have a hard time demonstrating a sufficient interest to sue. A claimant may rather be interested in obtaining contractual remedies, be they in the form of a right to free himself from the contract; an amendment of its terms; or the non-bindingness of certain provisions.

The provisions on market freedoms are of a deregulatory nature, aiming to facilitate voluntary exchange.[64] Yet the Union legal order does not constitute a laissez-faire system; contractual freedom is curtailed in various respects. The reason may be to protect a public interest such as the interest in a well-functioning market (which is the primary aim of Article 101 TFEU, prohibiting agreements disrupting free competition in the internal market); to protect the weaker party to the contract (such as employers or consumers); or sometimes both. Consumer law belongs to the 'core of European regulatory private law',[65] and in the following I will use the area as an illustration, though construed broadly to also cover investor protection.[66] The Court has held that the principle of effective judicial protection applies with respect to consumer rights.[67]

B. The Scope for Privately Enforcing 'Conduct of Business' Rules

The EU has adopted several measures with a view to protecting consumers and bolstering consumer confidence in the internal market. In the area of consumer protection, there are several measures where the emphasis is placed on the individual transaction, and which adjust the content of the individual contract. By way of illustration, Directive 93/13/EEC (Unfair Contract Terms) states that unfair terms shall not bind the consumer.[68] There are also various directives regulating pre-contractual conduct, such

[62] See S Burbank, S Farhang and H Kritzer, 'Private Enforcement' (2013) 17 *Lewis & Clark Law Review* 637, 667, who (writing in a US context) hold that when giving a large role to private litigation in implementation, 'resulting policy will tend to be confused, inconsistent and even straightforward contradictory'.

[63] This is the solution provided for in the Regulation (EC) No 1/2003 (Competition Enforcement), Art 15(3).

[64] Thorson, *Individual Rights in EU Law* (n 37) 129.

[65] Micklitz, 'Administrative Enforcement of European Private Law' (n 9) 581.

[66] For an overview of the area of employment law, see Collins, 'Social Dumping, Multi-Level Governance and Private Law in Employment Relationships' (n 13).

[67] See, eg, Case C-169/14 *Sánchez Morcillo* [2014], as regards Directive 93/13/EEC (Unfair Contract Terms).

[68] See Art 6(1).

as the provision of information to (potential) customers. Such rules can be found, inter alia, in Directive 2008/48/EC (Credit Agreements for Consumers).[69]

There are also, however, EU law instruments that lay down 'conduct of business' rules, and determining their relevance for domestic private law may raise challenges. Occasionally, the directive explicitly regulates the civil law consequences of a breach of its substantive provisions. With Directive 2019/2161 (Enforcement and Modernisation, known as the Omnibus Directive), consumers were provided with individual remedies where they have been harmed by unfair commercial practices (see Directive 2005/29/EC).[70] The private law implications of the Unfair Commercial Practices Directive had been debated for years.[71] Article 5(1) provided that unfair commercial practices 'shall be prohibited', yet there was no agreement as to whether an individual consumer who had concluded a contract under the impact of an unfair commercial practice was entitled to judicial protection.[72] Pursuant to Article 11 of the Directive, persons or organisations regarded under national law as having a legitimate interest in combating unfair commercial practices needed to be able to take legal action and/or to bring unfair commercial practices before an administrative authority.[73] Whether the Directive merely protected the *collective interest of consumers* (public interest) or the *interest of the individual consumer too* (private interest) was an open question.[74] Many scholars were of the opinion that the unfair commercial practices legislation should merely be perceived as a public law means to regulate the behaviour of market participants.[75] There were clear indications of the instrument's public interest orientation in the Directive and its preamble, and in *Bankia*, the Court clarified that a breach of the obligations in the Directive would therefore not, as a matter of EU law, lead to the full or partial annulment of the concluded agreement.[76]

With the Omnibus Directive, a clear framework for individual remedies was introduced. The Unfair Commercial Practices Directive now prescribes that '[c]onsumers harmed by unfair commercial practices, shall have access to proportionate and effective

[69] See Arts 4–6.

[70] See the Unfair Commercial Practices Directive, Art 11a.

[71] See D Poelzig, 'Private or Public Enforcement of the UCP Directive? Sanctions and Remedies to Prevent Unfair Commercial Practices' in W van Boom, A Garde and O Akseli (eds), *The European Unfair Commercial Practices Directive: Impact, Enforcement Strategies and National Legal Systems* (Ashgate 2014) 235.

[72] A commercial practice is considered unfair, inter alia, if it is deemed to be misleading; see Art 5(4)(a).

[73] See also Art 13, which required Member States to lay down penalties that were effective, proportionate and dissuasive.

[74] The ECJ was invited to address the issue in Case C-388/13 *Nemzeti* [2015] but left the question of rights open. AG Wahl emphasised, however, that the Directive merely protected the collective interests of consumers and did not apply to individual contractual relationships; see his Opinion in Case C-388/13 *Nemzeti* [2014] paras 30–32.

[75] To this effect, H-W Micklitz, 'A Common Approach to the Enforcement of Unfair Commercial Practices and Unfair Contract Terms' in van Boom, Garde and Akseli (eds), *The European Unfair Commercial Practices Directive* (n 71) 173, 191; and Thorson, *Individual Rights in EU Law* (n 37) 133–34, To the same effect, H Collins, 'The Unfair Commercial Practices Directive' (2005) 1 *European Review of Contract Law* 417, 425.

[76] See Case C-109/17 *Bankia* [2018] para 33, where the Court held that 'a contract used as an enforceable instrument cannot be declared invalid solely on the ground that it contains terms that are contrary to the general prohibition of unfair commercial practices laid down in Article 5(1) of that directive'. See also Case C-453/10 *Pereničová* [2012] paras 40–43, where the Court held that erroneous information in a contract could be considered 'misleading', but that this was only one element of several in the assessment of the unlawfulness of the contractual term under Directive 2004/39/EC (Unfair Contract Terms).

remedies, including compensation for damage suffered by the consumer and, where relevant, a price reduction or the termination of the contract'.[77]

There are still Union law instruments containing 'conduct of business' rules that do not regulate the civil law consequences of non-compliance with the norms laid down. To determine whether individual legal recourse is required to comply with the principle of effective judicial protection, we therefore need to look into the protective scope of the provisions in question, to see if they aim at (also) protecting individual market participants. Taking individual rights as a starting point, a distinction can arguably be drawn between directives when it comes to their relevance to private legal relationships, based on differences in protective scope. An individual right must be accompanied by an individual remedy, and consequently, the Member States cannot refuse to enforce such regulatory standards through private law remedies. In the following, we shall take a closer look at Directive 2014/65/EU (MiFID II), to shed light on its private law implications. As Collins points out, 'as soon as the individual consumer is given the chance to be a complainant in his own right – to have private right of redress – we enter the territory of private law'.[78]

MiFID II[79] contains a regulatory framework for investment services in financial instruments by banks and investment firms and for the operation of regulated markets. The Directive contains provisions to ensure investor protection. These 'conduct of business' obligations include a general duty of care, requiring the investment service provider to act honestly and fairly in the best interest of its clients, and also include more specific rules, such as information and disclosure obligations, and the duty to ensure the suitability and appropriateness of the service, instrument or product for the client.[80] With this Directive, typical pre-contractual and contractual duties of information are turned into regulatory standards subject to enforcement by supervisory authorities.[81] Put differently, many private law duties of care and loyalty have been '[transformed] into contract-related regulatory duties of financial institutions within a financial supervisory framework'.[82]

Member States must designate competent public authorities to monitor compliance, and enforce the rules in the event of an infringement.[83] Yet the Member States' obligations are not necessarily exhausted by the establishment of a public enforcement regime. There is no agreement in legal scholarship as to the private law implications of MiFID II. By way of illustration, Andenas and Della Negra argue that 'Member States

[77] Directive 2005/29/EC, Art 11a.

[78] Collins, 'The Hybrid Quality of European Private Law' (n 5) 455.

[79] Directive 2014/65/EU (MiFID II). The Directive is adopted in accordance with the four-level regulatory approach called the 'Lamfalussy process'. The MiFID II regime includes, in addition to the said Directive, Regulation (EU) No 600/2014 (MiFIR) and a number of implementing measures.

[80] MiFID II, Arts 24–25, and Commission Delegated Regulation (EU) 2017/565. These provisions revise and expand the obligations laid down in the predecessor directive, Directive 2004/39/EC (MiFID I), Art 19, and some of the literature used in the following pertains to the latter Directive. For a comparison between the 'conduct of business' rules in the two Directives, see D Busch, 'MiFID II: Stricter conduct of business rules for investment firms' (2017) 12 *Capital Markets Law Journal* 340.

[81] F Della Negra, 'The Private Enforcement of the MiFID Conduct of Business Rules. An Overview of the Italian and Spanish Experiences' (2014) 10 *European Review of Contract Law* 571, 575–76.

[82] Cherednychenko, 'Public Supervision over Private Relationships' (n 10) 39–40.

[83] MiFID II, Arts 67–70.

have a duty to provide investors with private law remedies for a firm's failure to respect the EU conduct of business rules unless the Member States prove that other legal remedies already ensure full compliance with the principle of effectiveness';[84] whereas Wallinga is of the opinion that 'judicial enforcement through private law means falls outside the harmonization scope of … MiFID II'.[85]

In order to determine whether the Directive is of a strictly 'public law' character, we need to look into the protective scope of the provisions laid down therein. MiFID II has a twofold aim, namely, investor protection and market integrity.[86] The instrument seems to protect the interests not only of investors as a collective, but also of the individual investor.[87] This interpretation finds support in MiFID II Article 75, whereby Member States shall ensure the setting up of efficient and effective complaints and redress procedures for the out-of-court settlement of consumer disputes. The protective orientation is rendered explicit in MiFID II Article 69(2), requiring Member States to 'ensure that mechanisms are in place to ensure that compensation may be paid or other remedial action be taken in accordance with national law for any financial loss or damage suffered as a result of an infringement of this Directive'.[88] That the Directive entails the grant of rights also finds support in legal scholarship.[89]

If one draws the conclusion that MiFID II grants rights to individuals that need to be enforceable by the individuals concerned, the issue of appropriate redress looms large. As observed by Della Negra, this finding 'opens up a "Pandora's box": what are the remedies (eg contract law, tort law, invalidity, liability) and procedures … that ensure an effective investor protection?'[90] In *Bankinter*, the Court was asked about the contractual consequences that flowed from MiFID I when an investment firm failed to comply with the assessment requirements laid down in Article 19(4) and (5) of the Directive.[91] The aforementioned provisions required the firm providing an investment service to a (potential) client to conduct, respectively, a suitability or appropriateness assessment ('know your customer'). As to the consequences of a failure to comply with these obligations, the Court held that it was for the internal order of each Member State

[84] M Andenas and F Della Negra, 'Between Contract Law and Financial Regulation: Towards the Europeanisation of General Contract Law' (2017) 28 *European Business Law Review* 499, 512.

[85] M Wallinga, 'Why MiFID & MiFID II Do (Not) Matter to Private Law: Liability to Compensate for Investment Losses for Breach of Conduct of Business Rules' (2019) 27 *European Review of Private Law* 515, 528.

[86] See MiFID II, recitals 68 and 70. These rationales are closely connected. Protection of consumers against abusive practices is both an end in itself and a means to ensure a prosperous financial market through the strengthening of investor confidence.

[87] Bush even argues that the 'conduct of business' rules (in MiFID I) should be treated as consumer protection provisions and that national courts should determine *ex officio* whether there has been an infringement, see D Busch, 'The Private Law Effect of MiFID: The Genil Case and Beyond' (2017) 13 *European Review of Contract Law* 70, 92.

[88] The fact that this obligation is included in a provision regulating 'supervisory powers' cannot detract from this conclusion.

[89] See, inter alia, N Reich, 'The Interrelation between Rights and Duties in EU Law: Reflections on the State of Liability Law in the Multilevel Governance System of the Union: Is There a Need for a More Coherent Approach in European Private Law?' (2010) 29 *Yearbook of European Law* 112, 150–52; and Della Negra, 'The Private Enforcement of the MiFID Conduct of Business Rules' (n 81) 576–77. Conversely, V Mak, 'The "Average Consumer" of EU Law in Domestic and European Litigation' in Leczykiewicz and Weatherill (eds), *The Involvement of EU Law in Private Law Relationships* (n 3) 333, 343–44.

[90] Della Negra, 'The Private Enforcement of the MiFID Conduct of Business Rules' (n 81) 579.

[91] Case C-604/11 *Bankinter* [2013].

to determine the contractual consequences where an investment firm fails to comply with the requirements laid down in Article 19(4) and (5), subject to the observance of the principles of equivalence and effectiveness.[92]

C. A Right to Judicial Proceedings in the Case of Rights Infringements

In the previous sections, we have seen that it is not readily apparent whether a Union law measure containing obligations for private parties is of relevance to individual contractual relationships. In such circumstances, it is 'via an analysis of the issue of rights that one may establish whether or not legislation should have a "private law" aspect – meaning that it is relevant for legal relations between individuals'.[93]

Finding that a Union measure is relevant to legal relations between individuals only takes us so far. The interest of an affected individual consists in obtaining a judicial termination of whether there has been an infringement of his rights and, if so, obtaining an appropriate remedy. In the following, I will substantiate the claim that although Union law does not always require Member States to afford any particular contractual remedies, they must nevertheless provide a legal avenue, through which an individual can have the court determine whether his Union rights have been infringed. Put differently, while Member States are granted considerable leeway when it comes to the *outcome of* court proceedings, they are not with regard to enabling *access to* court.

It does not follow from the right to judicial protection that all contracts or contractual terms that run counter to individual rights must be invalidated.[94] Rather, what matters is whether 'the rights appear in an area in which there are overriding policy reasons that require the rules granting rights to be mandatory and invariable'.[95] Such 'overriding policy reasons' have, for instance, led to specific provisions in Directive 89/665/EEC (Procurement Remedies Directive laying down the 'ineffectiveness' of contracts if the contract-awarding authority has committed certain grave infringements of the substantive provisions in the public procurement directives,[96] and Article 101(2) TFEU, stating that forbidden anti-competitive agreements are 'automatically void'. In the absence of specific regulation, Member States are not necessarily obliged to provide for contractual remedies in the event of an infringement of Union law. Member States are entitled to align the remedial response to the severity of the infringement, and also to protect the private defendant from excessive legal consequences.

In *Wall*, concerning a contract award procedure that ran contrary to Article 49 TFEU (right of establishment) and Article 56 TFEU (freedom to provide services), the Court held that there was no obligation under Union law to annul the contract; this question was to be determined on the basis of national law, within the bounds of the principles

[92] ibid para 57. This was reiterated in Case C-312/14 *Banif Plus Bank* [2015] para 79.
[93] Thorson, *Individual Rights in EU Law* (n 37) 348.
[94] ibid 134.
[95] ibid.
[96] See Art 2d.

of equivalence and effectiveness.[97] In *Sapod Audic*, concerning the contractual consequences of a Member State's breach of Directive 83/189/EEC (former Notification Directive), the Court held that this was 'a question governed by national law, in particular as regards the rules and principles of contract law which limit or adjust that sanction in order to render its severity proportionate to the particular defect found'.[98]

The Court seems to leave considerable leeway to Member States to determine how to remedy a breach. Hence, as Wilman points out,

> it should not be too readily assumed that the principles of (civil) law, such as *pacta sunt servanda*, the protection of the rights of third parties and legitimate expectations and the freedom of contract, will always and unconditionally be sacrificed at the altar of effectiveness of EU law and sincere cooperation.[99]

But although Union law does not entitle the private party to a particular outcome – such as the nullity of a contract – it is submitted that he must as a matter of Union law be entitled to *judicial process* when his rights are infringed. There are several rulings indicating that the Court places emphasis on the possibility of an action, toning down the importance of the relief eventually awarded. As made clear in chapter 7, section IV, one must distinguish standing to pursue a remedy from the right to obtain a remedy. The Court has repeatedly held that a private party must not be prevented from applying to the courts for a remedy where he alleges that his Union rights are infringed.[100] Hence, while it may well be that the claimant is not entitled to the remedy sought (such as the full or partial annulment of the contract), whether an alleged infringement is of such a character as to give rise to contractual remedies should be determined at the merits stage. In other words, the claimant must be entitled to judicial proceedings, thus enabling the court to assess the circumstances of the case and give the Union law infringement *due consideration*. Whether the claim is based directly on a violation of the regulatory duties contained in the Union law instrument, or based instead on national doctrines should not matter from the perspective of EU law. Private law doctrines such as misrepresentation, breach of a duty of care, undue influence or fiduciary duty can provide a basis for a claim. Such doctries are often formulated vaguely, thereby allowing for considerations of breach of various Union norms.[101]

Arguably, the court must take a stand on whether or not Union law has been infringed. Enforcement is 'not only essential for achieving compensation, deterrence and vindication: it also defines the boundaries of rights and duties'.[102] In *Unibet*, the Court found that in the context of an action for damages, the domestic court had to examine whether there was a violation of Union law, although the other conditions for liability were not fulfilled.[103] Similarly, it is submitted that the domestic court needs to

[97] Case C-91/08 *Wall* [2010] paras 63–65.
[98] Case C-159/00 *Sapod Audic* [2002] para 52. See also Case C-227/08 *Martín Martín* [2009] para 32.
[99] Wilman, *Private Enforcement of EU Law Before National Courts* (n 41) 320.
[100] See, eg, Joined Cases C-192/95 to C-218/95 *Comateb* [1997]; and Case C-55/12 *Kone* [2014], addressed further in ch 7, section IV.
[101] See further Mak, 'The "Average Consumer" of EU Law' (n 89) 343–46.
[102] A Wechsler and B Tripković, 'Conclusions: Enforcement in Europe as a Market of Justice' in H-W Micklitz and A Wechsler (eds), *The Transformation of Enforcement* (Hart Publishing 2016) 377, 398.
[103] Case C-432/05 *Unibet* [2007] para 59.

determine whether there has been an infringement of Union law, regardless of whether that infringement is considered grave enough to give rise to contractual remedies. The interest of the individual here overlaps considerations of *effet utile*. From the point of view of the effectiveness of Union law, it is desirable that national courts determine whether Union law has been respected.[104] Not only does this serve as a means to clarify the content of these obligations, it may also serve a deterrent function, particularly if coupled with publicity measures.[105]

What interest a private party will have in a finding of an infringement if the national court still declines to afford a contractual remedy must be determined in light of the facts of the concrete case. It may incentivise the defendant to amend his conduct such that it benefits the claimant in his future dealings with the entity. Alternatively, the finding of an infringement may be of value to the claimant by forming a basis for subsequently negotiating a settlement between the parties to the dispute.[106] The obligation on domestic courts to take a stand on Union law compliance also offers the claimant a form of procedural justice that may be of value regardless of the outcome of the case.[107] It can thus be argued that the principle of effective judicial protection also requires verification by the court as to whether applicable Union law norms have been complied with. For that to be possible, a claimant must be granted standing.

[104] Thorson, *Individual Rights in EU Law* (n 37) 147.

[105] On the 'naming and shaming' associated with disclosure of measures taken, see further de Moor-van Vugt and Widdershoven, 'Administrative Enforcement' (n 45) 278–79.

[106] Wilman, *Private Enforcement of EU Law Before National Courts* (n 41) 346–47.

[107] The theory of procedural justice proposes that individuals are more likely to accept and comply with adverse results if they perceive of the dispute resolution process as fair; see, for instance, TR Tyler, *Why People Obey the Law* (Yale University Press 1990). This means, inter alia, that those involved should be able to present their arguments, be listened to and have their views taken into account by a neutral and unbiased decision maker: see ibid 163–64.

12

Enforcing the Rights of Others

I. Introduction

In the context of judicial protection of rights, the *right holder* is, of course, the main actor. If a Union norm is considered to create an individual right, the right holder himself is entitled to seize the court and obtain redress in the case of a violation. However, one may ask if the principle of effective judicial protection dictates standing not only to the person whose rights are infringed, but also to certain third parties. Here, there is a need to distinguish between two constellations: on the one hand, the ability of third parties to initiate proceedings *on behalf of the right holder*; and, on the other, the ability to initiate proceedings *on his own behalf* where the claimant is affected by the breach of another person's rights. In the following, I will look into the latter, and examine whether a claimant may gain standing under EU law where he is directly affected by the violation of another person's rights.

There are various ways the principle of effective judicial protection can be brought into play, although the claimant is not the primary right holder under EU law. In the following, a distinction is drawn between various third parties: claimants whose rights are affected (section II); indirect victims (section III); sucessors of rights (section IV) and third parties suffering economic harm through the infringement of the rights of others (sections V and VI).

II. Claimants Whose Rights are (Also) Affected

A claimant may, of course, have to be granted standing to challenge a measure infringing the rights of another person if that decision *at the same time* impairs his own rights. In that case he is to be perceived as a direct victim of an infringement. This constellation may, for instance, be relevant in relation to so-called 'derived rights' of family members of Union citizens. To illustrate, Directive 2004/38/EC (Citizenship Directive) grants rights in the host state to close family members,[1] whereas rights against the home state can be based on Article 21(1) TFEU.[2] In addition, a derived right of residence to a

[1] See Arts 6, 7 and Art 2(2). On the interpretation of these provisions, see, inter alia, Case C-127/08 *Metock* [2008] and Case C-40/11 *Iida* [2012].

[2] Case C-456/12 *O and B* [2104] paras 49–50 and Case C-673/16 *Coman* [2018] paras 23–24. To invoke Art 21(1) TFEU against the home state, the Union citizen must have made use of his right to freedom of movement; see Case C-256/11 *Dereci and Others* [2011] paras 60–61. The Court has acknowledged, however, that

third-country family member of a Union citizen can be derived from Articles 45, 49 and 56 TFEU.[3] These rights are granted with a view to making effective the free movement rights of the Union citizen. As held by the Court in *Ymeraga*:

> Any rights conferred on thid-country nationals by the Treaty provisions on Union citizenship are not autonomous rights of those nationals but rights derived from the exercise of freedom of movement by a Union citizen. The purpose and justification of those derived rights are based on the fact that a refusal to allow them would be such as to interfere with the Union citizen's freedom of movement by discouraging him from exercising his rights of entry into and residence in the host Member State.[4]

Consequently, such derived rights exist, in principle, only where these are necessary to ensure that EU citizens can exercise their free movement and residence rights effectively.[5]

Article 31(1) of the Citizenship Directive states that 'persons concerned' shall have access to judicial procedures in order to appeal or seek review of any decision 'taken against them'.[6] This provision must be interpreted in light of the principle of effective judicial protection. Pursuant to the principle of effective judicial protection, a Member State needs to grant standing both to the third-country national to pursue his derived right of residence,[7] and to the Union citizen whose right to free movement may be impaired.[8]

III. Claimants Indirectly Affected by a Union Law Infringement

In highly exceptional circumstances it may be that an 'indirect victim' of a rights violation has to be granted standing. The case law of the ECtHR may provide guidance in this respect, given the correspondence between Article 47(1) of the Charter and Article 13 ECHR. It has been argued that the requirement of being a 'victim' under Article 13 ECHR has its parallel in the 'victim test' developed under Article 34 of the Convention.[9] What merits our attention for present purposes is the case law pertaining to *indirect victims*. The ECtHR has accepted applications from close relatives who are affected by the infringement of another person's Convention rights. The standing of indirect victims is primarily of relevance in the case of deaths or disappearances giving rise to issues under Article 2 of the Convention (right to life).[10] Provided that the alleged

exceptionally, Art 20 TFEU can be relied on also in the absence of such a cross-border element, see, inter alia, Case C-34/09 *Zambrano* [2011] and Case C-133/15 *Chavez-Vilchez and others* [2017].

[3] Case C-370/90 *Singh* [1992]; Case C-60/00 *Carpenter* [2002]; Case C-291/05 *Eind* [2007]; Case C-457/12 *S and G* [2014].

[4] Case C-87/12 *Ymeraga* [2013] para 35. This was reiterated in Case C-86/12 *Alokpa* [2013] para 22.

[5] See AG Sharpston in Case C-456/12 and Case C-457/12 *O and S* [2013] para 49.

[6] This right accrues to third-country nationals envisaged in Art 3(2); see Case C-89/17 *Banger* [2018] para 52.

[7] By implication Case C-459/99 *MRAX* [2002] paras 100–02.

[8] The Directive also contains certain rights that are not dependent on the Union citizen; see, eg, Art 13 on the departure of the Union citizen. Such rights can presumably only be enforced by the third-country nationals themselves.

[9] See ch 5, section IV.C.

[10] See, eg, *McCann v the United Kingdom* App no 18984/91 (ECtHR, 1995); and *Varnava and Others v Turkey* App nos 16064/90, 16065/90, 16066/90, 16068/90, 16069/90, 16070/90, 16071/90, 16072/90 and 16073/90 (ECtHR, 2009).

violation is linked to the death of the primary victim, complaints by close relatives can also be admitted.[11] The applicant must demonstrate a sufficiently close link with the immediate victim, and the Court has also placed emphasis on whether the applicant has a personal interest in pursuing a complaint before the Court.[12] This means that it is first and foremost spouses, parents and children who will satisfy these criteria.[13] In order for close relatives to be considered indirect victims there must be

> special factors which give the suffering of the applicant a dimension and character distinct from the emotional distress which may be considered as inevitably caused to relatives of a victim of a serious human rights violation.[14]

The transferring of the indirect victim test to the Union law context needs to be reserved for highly exceptional circumstances. Given the nature of *Union law rights*, an infringement rarely affects third parties to such a degree as to merit a comparison. Still, if a Member State, when acting within the scope of EU law, infringes the essential provisions of the Charter, such as Article 19, a situation comparable to that noted above may occur. Pursuant to Article 19 of the Charter, no one may be removed, expelled or extradited to a state where there is a serious risk of being subjected to the death penalty, torture or other inhuman or degrading treatment or punishment. Where a Union citizen has made use of his right to free movement within the Union, his situation may fall within the scope of Union law for the purposes of Article 51(1) of the Charter.

Consider, for instance, the situation addressed by the Court in *Petruhhin*.[15] The case concerned an Estonian citizen who was arrested in Latvia for crimes allegedly committed in Russia. Mr Petruhhin appealed the decision to extradite him to Russia, and the Latvian court asked, inter alia, whether the requested Member State must verify that the extradition would not prejudice the rights protected by the Charter. The Court held that insofar as the competent authority of the requested Member State was in possession of evidence of a real risk of inhuman treatment of individuals in the state concerned, it was bound to assess the existence of that risk when it decided on the extradition request.[16] Should the Member State violate Article 19 of the Charter, and the extradited Union citizen would disappear or die following the extradition, his close relatives must arguably be granted standing along the lines of the Strasbourg case law.

IV. Rights of Successors: Assignment of Claims and Third Party Contracts

Where there has been a *succession of rights*, the successor should arguably be able to invoke the right before the court and obtain protection pursuant to Article 47 of the

[11] *De Donder and De Clippel v Belgium* App no 8595/06 (ECtHR, 2011). On the standing of indirect victims as regards complaints pertaining to other provisions of the Convention, see DJ Harris et al, *Harris, O'Boyle & Warbrick: Law of the European Convention on Human Rights* (Oxford University Press 2014) 91–94.

[12] See *Koch v Germany* App no 497/09 (ECtHR, 2012) paras 43–44.

[13] See, however, *Yaşa v Turkey* App no 63/1997/847/1054 (ECtHR, 1998), where a nephew was granted standing before the ECtHR following the murder of his uncle.

[14] *Cakici v Turkey* App no 23657/94 (ECtHR, 1999) para 98.

[15] Case C-182/15 *Petruhhin* [2016].

[16] ibid Paras 58–59.

Charter. A specific form of succession is the assignment of claims to a third party. The issue of judicial protection following an assignment was touched upon, but not resolved, in *Sähköalojen ammattiliitto*.[17] The case concerned Polish posted workers, who alleged that their employer did not pay them the minimum remuneration due to them under collective agreements allegedly applicable pursuant to Directive 96/71/EC (Posting of Workers). The workers individually assigned their claims to a Finnish trade union, so that it could seek recovery. The assignment of claims arising from employment relationships was prohibited under Polish law, and the Finnish court therefore asked the Court whether this prevented the union from pursuing these claims through judicial proceedings. The Court answered in the negative, holding that pursuant to the principle of *lex fori*, the standing of the trade union was governed by Finnish procedural law. Under Finnish law, the claimant had standing to bring proceedings on behalf of the posted workers. Moreover, the assignment of pay claims to the trade union was in conformity with Finnish law.

One might ask whether the principle of effective judicial protection *dictates* that standing must be provided where a claim has been lawfully assigned. The Court did not have to answer this question in *Sähköalojen ammattiliitto*, since the claimant already had standing pursuant to national law. There are, however, expressions that point in this direction. The Court held that Directive 96/71, read in the light of Article 47 of the Charter, prevents a rule of the sending Member State barring a trade union from bringing an action in the host state, where the claim is lawfully assigned.[18] The reference to Article 47 of the Charter in this case indicates that also those (lawfully) assigned a right can benefit from the principle of effective judicial protection.[19] If this is correct, it will benefit whole industries relying on claim assignment as a mode of business. For instance, in relation to Regulation (EC) No 261/2004 (Denied Boarding Compensation), there are companies specialising in the recovery of the standardised payments following flight delays.[20] There are also companies relying on the assignment of cartel-related damages claims.

Closely related to succession are contracts benefiting third parties. In *Coloroll Pension Trustees*, the Court was asked whether the dependants of an employee could rely on the right to equal pay laid down in (now) Article 157 TFEU against the trustees of an occupational pension scheme. By definition, such a pension is not paid to the employee but rather to his or her survivor. The case did not concern standing, as the case was already before the court, yet the Court's reasoning has relevance for purposes of standing too. It held that

> since the right to payment of a survivor's pension arises at the time of the death of the employee affiliated to the scheme, the survivor is the only person who can assert it. If the survivor were to be denied this possibility, this would deprive [Article 157 TFEU] of all its effectiveness as far as survivors' pensions are concerned.[21]

[17] Case C-396/13 *Sähköalojen ammattiliitto* [2015].

[18] ibid para 26.

[19] The Court has held that the assignment of claims cannot, in itself, have an impact on the determination of the court having jurisdiction; see Case C-352/13 *CDC Hydrogen Peroxide* [2015] para 35. The Court has, however, held that the assignee cannot rely on the consumer forum rule in the Brussels I Regulation; see Case C-498/16 *Schrems II* [2018].

[20] For an illustration, see Case C-94/14 *Flight Refund Ltd* [2016].

[21] Case C-200/91 *Coloroll Pension Trustees* [1994] para 19.

This is clearly an area where effectiveness and effective judicial protection interact.[22] I agree with Thorson that if a survivor pension is at issue, 'the fact that the survivor is the one enjoying the right to the pension must also mean that the survivor should enjoy the protection flowing from the ban on gender discrimination in this matter'.[23]

V. Third Parties Suffering from the 'Passing-on' of Unlawfully Levied Taxes

Private parties who have been subject to an unlawfully levied tax have a right to reimbursement as a matter of Union law. This remedial right to reimbursement is a direct consequence of 'the rights conferred on individuals by provisions of EU law prohibiting such taxes'.[24] Where the charged subject has sought to mitigate the costs of such taxes by passing them on to a third party – most notably customers – the question arises whether the third party has a claim against the Member State. The Court addressed this issue in *Danfoss*.[25] The claimants sought reimbursement from the Danish state, due to an excise duty on oil that had been levied on oil companies and passed on to the claimants through increased purchase prices. They relied on the argument that they had had to bear the financial consequences of the unlawful duty. The Court had previously accepted an exception to the principle of reimbursement of unlawfully levied charges where the charges have been passed on to the purchasers, since this would constitute unjust enrichment of the persons concerned.[26] With reference to this exception, the Court held that

> [i]t appears from this that the right to the recovery of sums unduly paid helps to offset the consequences of the duty's incompatibility with EU law by neutralising the economic burden which that duty has unduly imposed on the operator who, in the final analysis, has actually borne it.[27]

The Court made reference to the principle of national procedural autonomy, and the requirement to observe the principles of equivalence and effectiveness, and found that it would be sufficient if reimbursement could be claimed from the taxable person. However, if that were to prove impossible or excessively difficult, the principle of effectiveness requires that the purchaser be able to bring his claim for reimbursement against the tax authorities directly.

[22] See ibid para 23, where the Court pointed out that 'the effectiveness of Article 119 would be considerably diminished *and* the legal protection required to ensure real equality would be seriously impaired' if the provision could not be relied upon in the case at hand (emphasis added).

[23] B Thorson, *Individual Rights in EU Law* (Springer 2016) 309.

[24] Case C-69/14 *Târsia* [2015] para 24; and Case C-205/15 *Toma* [2016] para 32. See further ch 7, section III on this 'Union remedy'.

[25] Case C-94/10 *Danfoss* [2011].

[26] See, inter alia, Case C-398/09 *Lady & Kid* [2011] paras 18–20. A presumption that the charges have been passed on is, however, incompatible with Union law; see Case 199/82 *San Giorgio* [1983] para 14 and Joined Cases C-441/98 and C-442/98 *Kapniki Michailidis* [2000] para 42.

[27] Case C-94/10 *Danfoss* [2011] para 23.

The Court did not address the issue whether the claimants were the holders of any (primary) Union rights. This is remarkable, given that the Court has seen the right to reimbursement as a consequence of, and an adjunct to, the rights conferred on individuals by the European Union provisions prohibiting such charges.[28] The reasoning of the Court in *Danfoss* rather seems to suggest that reimbursement can be sought even in the absence of a rights infringement. Hence the Court is in effect disentangling the remedy from the right.

The Court's ruling in *Danfoss* is difficult to reconcile with its jurisprudence pertaining to reimbursement. One way of seeing it, is that the end consumer obtains the position of right holder once the 'passing-on' has taken place.[29] This is seemingly the position of Advocate General Kokott, who held that

> [t]he final consumer to whom an indirect charge levied contrary to European Union law … has been passed on, is … also to be regarded as an individual on whom rights have been conferred by the European Union provisions prohibiting such charges. He too must be able to obtain repayment of the charge passed on to him.[30]

Hence, by passing on the charge, it could also be argued that the tax payer is also passing on the Union right. Seen from this angle, this is a variation of the succession category addressed in section IV.[31]

The result in *Danfoss* is not unreasonable. After all, it was the claimants who finally had to bear the overcharge, and it was their property rights that were thereby affected. Moreover, where a charge has been passed on, it is only the third party who has any incentives to sue.[32] I agree with Thorson, who holds that

> the ruling seems to reveal some of the Court's thinking. A key point is clearly that the whole idea of speaking of rights in this area in the first place is based on a policy consideration: that the levying of illegal charges is a matter which should be rectified. When the notion of rights conceptually undermines protection efforts rather than helping to achieve that goal, the Court abandons the rights approach and considers instead whether national solutions are sufficiently effective.[33]

It would have been preferable if the Court in *Danfoss* had stressed effectiveness aspects, and placed emphasis on the deterrent effect served by such reimbursement claims. On the other hand, basing a claim for remedies solely on considerations of effectiveness would sit uneasily with the Court's jurisprudence, which generally makes access to court and effective redress dependent on a Union right's being infringed (chapter 3, section IV). Opening up for standing based solely on effectiveness considerations could

[28] Case 199/82 *San Giorgio* [1983] para 12. See also Case C-398/09 *Lady & Kid* [2011] para 17 and Case C-69/14 *Târşia* [2015] para 24.
[29] Thorson, *Individual Rights in EU Law* (n 23) 321.
[30] AG Kokott in Case C-94/10 *Danfoss* [2011] para 37.
[31] In legal scholarship, it has been suggested that there may be a parallel between the 'passing-on' of unlawfully levied charges and 'passing-on' in the context of competition law, see Thorson, *Individual Rights in EU Law* (n 23) 320. For a detailed account on the 'passing-on' problem, see M Strand, *The Passing-On Problem in Damages and Restitution under EU Law* (Edward Elgar 2017).
[32] Similarly Thorson, *Individual Rights in EU Law* (n 23) 321.
[33] ibid 324.

indeed be a slippery slope, slowly eroding the procedural autonomy of the Member States.

VI. Third Parties Suffering Economic Harm through the Infringement of the Rights of Others

The Court has not been explicit as to whether a private party can claim compensation from the State where he suffers economic harm through the infringement of another person's rights. In legal scholarship it has been suggested that such claims should, perhaps, not be limited to the circle of beneficiaries, but that others who might further the effectiveness of the law should be entitled to claim compensation.[34] As was seen in chapter 10, section III, a claim for compensation against the state cannot be based on considerations of effectiveness. Rather it will be asked whether the right to seek damages is limited to the right holder himself, or whether it also extends to secondary victims. This boils down to a question of whether the loss incurred by third parties is *legally relevant* in the context of state liability.

While Member States' tort laws diverge when it comes to acknowledging claims for compensation from third parties, a distinction can be made between, on the one hand, states that accept that the tortious act gives rise to a claim for whoever suffers loss as a consequence thereof, and, on the other, states that primarily acknowledge a claim for compensation from the primary victims, requiring a specific statutory provision in order to accept claims from secondary victims.[35]

In *Danfoss* (addressed in section V), the claimants had claimed not only reimbursement, but also compensation for the harm suffered. The Court held that domestic rules on causation, under which a causal link could be established only as between the unlawfuly levied charge and the damage suffered by the taxable person, may not be interpreted in such a way as to make it virtually impossible or excessively difficult to obtain compensation for the damage suffered.[36] The Court held that if it were to prove impossible or excessively difficult for the purchaser to obtain compensation from the taxable person, the purchaser should be able to bring his claim directly against the state. Hence, the Court seemed to presume that the purchaser was entitled to compensation in the first place.[37] It can be questioned whether this really was the case.

The relevant provision in *Danfoss* was Article 8(1) of Directive 92/81/EEC (Duties on Mineral Oils), containing an obligation not to levy the harmonised excise duty on fuel used for the purpose of air navigation other than private pleasure flying. While that was clearly a provision granting rights to individuals,[38] it has been argued that the

[34] J Engström, 'The Europeanisation of Remedies and Procedures Through Judge-Made Law: Can a Trojan Horse Achieve Effectiveness? Experiences of the Swedish Judiciary' (PhD thesis, European University Institute 2009) 216.

[35] SD Lindenbergh, 'The Protection of Secondary Victims: A Comparative Overview' in *Personal Injury Compensation in Europe Series: Fatal Accidents & Secondary Victims* (XPL Publishing 2005) 413, 414.

[36] Case C-94/10 *Danfoss* [2011] para 36.

[37] This seems to lie implicitly in the statement that the claimant should be able to obtain compensation for 'the damage suffered'; see ibid para 36.

[38] See Case C-346/97 *Braathens* [1999], addressed in ch 4, section III.D.

provision protects the *taxable person*, not those who in the end have to bear the costs of the charge. This prompts the question whether the ruling can be taken to account for the position that it is sufficient to demonstrate that the provision infringed confers rights, and that the claimant does not also have to demonstrate that he falls within the protective scope of the provision? Given the shortcomings in the Court's reasoning in *Danfoss*, this ruling can hardly be seen as conclusive in this regard.

The Court tends to use formulations suggesting that the right to compensation accrues to the right holder himself. The Court held already in *Brasserie* that the full effectiveness of EU law would be impaired if individuals were unable to obtain redress when 'their rights' were infringed by a breach of EU law.[39] This was made even more explicit in *Ullens de Schooten*, where the Court was asked whether a statutory provision allegedly incompatible with EU law, could give rise to compensation in a wholly internal situation. The Court stated that the non-contractual liability of a state for breaches of EU law can be engaged only if the infringed rule 'is intended to confer rights on those individuals [and it] must therefore be determined whether an individual in a situation such as that [the claimant in the main proceedings] derives rights from the relevant provisions of the … Treaty'.[40] Reference can also be made to the Court's ruling in *Francovich II*, where the Court somewhat ironically found that Mr Francovich himself was not entitled to reparation since he was not within the protective scope of the Employer Insolvency Directive.[41] So, despite paving the way for the principle of state liability, he was himself left empty-handed.

Since Member State liability is a manifestation of the principle of effective judicial protection of Union rights, it seems plausible that compensation is limited to harm suffered by the right holder himself. After all, Article 47 of the Charter grants judicial protection to those 'whose [Union] rights' are violated. In legal scholarship there is support for the position that

> it is necessary for the protection offered by the rule invoked to be effective in relation to the person who invokes it, and hence that person must be among those upon whom the rule concerned confers rights; conversely, a rule not protecting the person against the unlawfulness he invokes but protecting another person cannot be accepted as the source of the obligation to provide compensation.[42]

While generally speaking it must be assumed that only the loss incurred by the right holder is considered legally relevant, it cannot be excluded that third-party loss may be perceived relevant in exceptional circumstances, where there is a close link between the right holder and the third party. In *Gutknecht* and *FG Marine* – concerning liability for the *Union organs* – the General Court addressed claims for compensation by the previous owners of the company whose rights were allegedly infringed. The Court did not seem to pay particular regard to the fact that the shareholders' losses were derived

[39] Joined Cases C-46/93 and C-48/93 *Brasserie du Pêcheur* [1996] para 20.

[40] Case C-268/15 *Ullens de Schooten* [2016] para 46.

[41] Case C-479/93 *Franvovich II* [1995].

[42] K Lenaerts, K Gutman and I Maselis, *EU Procedural Law* (Oxford University Press 2014) 517. This is written in relation to the non-contractual liability of the Union institutions under Art 340(2) TFEU, but as the Court made clear in Joined Cases C-46/93 and C-48/93 *Brasserie du Pêcheur* [1996] para 42 and Case C-352/98 P *Bergaderm* [2000], the conditions are the same as those pertaining to Member State liability.

from the losses incurred by the companies.[43] In *Gutnecht*, the Court rejected the claim due to a lack of factual causality;[44] whereas in *FG Marine* the claim was rejected due to a breach in the chain of causation, since the claimants had failed to operate diligently to avoid loss.[45] Since the Court did not explicitly address the fact that the claimants were secondary victims, one should be careful in drawing conclusions from these rulings.[46] That the value of the company's shares falls as a consequence of an infringement of the company's rights is not necessarily sufficient for a shareholder to benefit from the principle of effective judicial protection. Yet it cannot be excluded that shareholders in exceptional circumstances might be able to have the 'corporate veil pierced in their favour'.[47] It seems plausible, as Milutinović has suggested, that this could be the case, for instance, 'where the management of the victim undertaking has failed to bring a claim or has brought the claim unsuccessfully'.[48]

If one accepts that certain third-party losses are considered relevant for the purposes of state liability, the exception should be construed narrowly. The claimant must at the very least demonstrate that he is closely affiliated to the primary victim of the infringement. The Court's ruling in *Danfoss* is difficult to fit into the Court's line of jurisprudence, and should be perceived as an outlier case. The Court should therefore consider deviating from the ruling – or at least explaining its stance properly – in order to make clear that claims for reimbursement and damages as a starting point depend on the infringement of a Union law right *belonging to the claimant.*

[43] HH Fredriksen, *Offentligrettslig erstatningsansvar ved brudd på EØS-avtalen* (Fagbokforlaget 2013) 476.

[44] Case T-561/08 *Gutknecht* [2011] paras 30–35.

[45] Case T-360/04 *FG Marine v Commission* paras 76–77.

[46] See Joined Cases C-663/17 P, C-665/17 P and C-669/17 P *Trasta Komercbanka* [2019], where the Court found that the shareholders of a company whose authorisation had been withdrawn did not satisfy the requirement of 'direct and individual concern' pursuant to Art 263(4) TFEU.

[47] The expression is borrowed from *Agrotexim and others v Greece* App no 14807/89 (ECtHR, 1995) para 62. The Court acknowledges shareholders as indirect victims 'only in exceptional circumstances, in particular where it is clearly established that it is impossible for the company to apply to the Convention institutions through the organs set up under its articles of incorporation or – in the event of liquidation – through its liquidators'; see ibid para 66.

[48] V Milutinović, *The 'Right to Damages' under EU Competition Law: From Courage v Crehan to the White Paper and Beyond* (Kluwer Law International 2010) 229.

13

Enforcement of Union Law in the Name of Effectiveness

I. Introduction

The focus in chapters 8 to 11 was on the individual claimant and protection of his individual rights. We saw how the principle of effective judicial protection requires Union law rights to be effectively protected in the Member States, which may entail extending national doctrines beyond their usual ambit, or even providing a right of action where one does not exist pursuant to domestic law. The aim of this chapter is to address EU intervention in domestic standing doctrines where rights are not at stake. I examine the extent to which private parties and NGOs, which are not affected in their Union rights, must be granted standing to enforce the duties and obligations placed on state organs and private parties in the name of effectiveness (*effet utile*). It will be argued that the Court of Justice is less demanding of Member States when it comes to enforcing Union obligations than enforcing Union rights.[1] The impact of Union law on domestic standing doctrines is therefore limited where individual rights are not at stake.

This chapter examines two closely interrelated questions: first, whether private enforcement is required at all; second, if it is, who should have standing to that end. When determining whether private enforcement is required to render Union law effective, regard must be had to the overall enforcement regime in the Member State concerned.[2] The extent to which private enforcement is called for depends on the alternative enforcement mechanisms in place in the relevant Member State. This requires us to take public enforcement mechanisms into account as well. Private and public enforcement must be analysed together in order to determine whether enforcement by public spirited individuals or organisations is a 'necessary part of the enforcement arsenal'.[3] It is through such an overall analysis of the enforcement system in place that potential lacunae can be detected. The need for private enforcement is pressing in areas where

[1] Similarly MJ Frese, *Sanctions in EU Competition Law: Principles and Practice* (Hart Publishing 2014) 96.

[2] As Wilman points out, it is the 'combination of [private and public] enforcement that determines the effectiveness of the measure in question'; see F Wilman, 'The End of the Absence? The Growing Body of EU Legislation on Private Enforcement and the Main Remedies It Provides For' (2016) 53 *CML Rev* 887, 930.

[3] The expression is borrowed from A Afilalo, 'Towards a "Common Law" of Europe: Effective Judicial Protection, National Procedural Autonomy, and Standing to Litigate Diffuse Interests in the European Union' (1999) 22 *Suffolk Transnational Law Review* 349, 403.

other means of enforcement are wanting. This means that the role of private enforcement may well vary depending on who is responsible for the infringement.

Since private enforcement 'has to be understood in a larger context – in relation to its public counterpart',[4] a distinction must be drawn between proceedings against a state (section IV) and proceedings against other private parties (section V). Where *the state* has failed to fulfil its obligations under EU law, the scope for private enforcement must be seen in relation to the public enforcement conducted at the centralised level (primarily) by the Commission. Conversely, in proceedings against private parties, the scope for private enforcement must be seen in relation to the public enforcement at the decentralised level, primarily carried out by designated public authorities. The question that needs to be asked is whether private enforcement is needed in order for the state to live up to the sanctioning requirements formulated by the Court in *Greek Maize*.[5]

II. Why a Rights-orientated Approach is Insufficient

The rights-orientated approach to standing is not necessarily sufficient from the perspective of Union law. First, not every Union law obligation translates into corresponding rights, as certain obligations may be imposed in order to pursue public values. Examples that spring to mind are nature conservation and the protection of endangered species.[6] Allowing for the vindication of the public interests involved may entail expanding standing beyond right holders, since 'the fish cannot go to court'.[7] Second, it may be the case that although Union law does create rights for individuals, these rights are unlikely to be enforced due to the low stakes involved. This is typically the case in the area of consumer protection, where the economic harm suffered by each individual tends to be insignificant.[8] The 'unchallenged existence of widespread minor illicit gains … incentivizes wrongful behaviour [and such] behaviour raises a *public* issue' that needs to be addressed.[9] Third, the infringed provision may be a protective norm, but in the particular case no private party is actually affected by the infringement. By way of illustration, the Court held in *Feryn* that a public statement made by a company director could constitute direct discrimination within the meaning of the Directive 2000/43/EC (Equal treatment irrespective of racial or ethnic origin), although there was no identifiable victim.[10] Where there is no individual victim to pursue the case, alternative means of reacting to the infringement may be required to protect the public interest involved.

[4] J Rathod and S Vaheesan, 'The Arc and Architecture of Private Enforcement Regimes in the United States and Europe: A View Across the Atlantic' (2016) 14 *University of New Hampshire Law Review* 303, 374.

[5] Case 68/88 *Greek Maize* [1989], addressed further in section V.B.

[6] See further ch 8, section III.B.

[7] AG Sharpston uttered these words at the hearing in Case C-115/09 *Bund für Umwelt und Naturschutz Deutschland (Trianel)* [2011]. Case C-441/17 *Commission v Poland* [2018], concerning logging in a Polish protected area, is illustrative in this regard.

[8] See further ch 5, section IV.G.

[9] C Hodges, 'Objectives, Mechanisms and Policy Choices in Collective Enforcement and Redress' in J Steele and WH van Boom (eds), *Mass Justice: Challenges of Representation and Distribution* (Edward Elgar 2011) 101, 107 (emphasis in original).

[10] Case C-54/07 *Feryn* [2008], further accounted for in section III.

In areas where the law does not create individual rights, 'a private enforcement system predicated on individuals litigating to protect their rights presents severe shortcomings'.[11] While only holders of individual rights may invoke the principle of effective judicial protection to obtain standing, this does not mean that others are barred from utilising Union law arguments to ensure access to court. Yet the argument must be that the claimant's contribution is indispensable in order to render Union law operative in the Member State. In other words, leaving aside the protection of individual rights and turning to the effectiveness of Union law per se entails a shift in perspective. The claimant is seen in a merely instrumental fashion, and the emphasis is on his contribution to the effective enforcement of Union law.

Member States are obliged to pursue infringements of Union law regardless of the benefits accrued by individuals. Effectiveness is not limited to protecting individual Union rights; the principle of effectiveness is in essence about 'ensuring the integrity and coherence of the Community legal order as a whole'.[12] To the extent that Member States rely on private parties to pursue infringements, it is appropriate to speak of the 'general interest function' of private enforcement.[13] From this angle, private parties are seen as 'law enforcers acting in the public interest, rather than as holders of subjective rights'.[14]

III. Starting Point: No Mandatory Public Interest Standing Without Specific Regulation

Member States have widely diverging approaches when it comes to determining public interest standing in judicial review proceedings. Whether such standing is allowed for in the legal orders largely depends on what is seen as the function of the legal process – rights protection or general legality review (see chapter 8, section II). In Member States emphasising the protection of individual rights, public interest standing is generally ruled out (except, perhaps, in carefully circumscribed circumstances). In states where judicial review proceedings are tuned towards subjecting governmental conduct to control, public interest standing tends to be looked upon more favourably.[15] Also when it comes to private enforcement of regulatory norms binding on private parties, there are many discrepancies to be found. There is limited analysis of the balance between public and private enforcement techniques in the different Member States.[16] Still, as explained in chapter 2, section IV, the Union mode of regulation – 'eurolegalism' – has

[11] M Smith and S Drake, 'Introduction' in S Drake and M Smith (eds), *New Directions in the Effective Enforcement of EU Law and Policy* (Edward Elgar 2016) 1, 10.

[12] M Accetto and S Zleptnig, 'The Principle of Effectiveness: Rethinking Its Role in Community Law' (2005) 11 *European Public Law* 375, 392.

[13] F Wilman, *Private Enforcement of EU Law Before National Courts: The EU Legislative Framework* (Edward Elgar 2015) 550.

[14] L Gyselen, 'Liability of Supranational, State and Private Actors: Comment from the Point of View of EU Competition Law' in J Wouters, J Stuyck and T Kruger (eds), *Principles of Proper Conduct for Supranational, State and Private Actors in the European Union: Towards a Ius Commune: Essays in Honour of Walter Van Gerven* (Intersentia 2001) 135, 144.

[15] See further M Eliantonio et al, *Standing Up for Your Right(s) in Europe – A Comparative Study on Legal Standing (Locus Standi) before the EU and Member States' Courts* (Intersentia 2013) 56.

[16] Hodges, 'Objectives, Mechanisms and Policy Choices in Collective Enforcement and Redress' (n 9) 104.

shifted European legal cultures in the direction of more private enforcement.[17] The extent to which private enforcement must be provided for *as a matter of EU law* will be addressed in the following.

The starting point is that public interest standing is not mandatory in the absence of specific legislative provisions to that effect. Whether the Member States were required to provide for associational standing was a question touched upon by the Court in *Feryn*.[18] The case concerned public statements made by a company director of Firma Feryn, to the effect that they did not recruit 'immigrants'. The Court was asked whether his statement constituted direct discrimination contrary to Article 2(2)(a) of Directive 2000/43/EC (Equal treatment irrespective of racial or ethnic origin), despite there being no identifiable individual claiming to be the victim of this discrimination. The Court answered in the affirmative, finding that the 'objective of fostering conditions for a socially inclusive labour market would be hard to achieve' if the scope of the Directive were limited to cases in which a victim brought legal proceedings.[19] The fact that Article 7 of the Directive only prescribed a legal avenue for persons who consider they have suffered discrimination, did not prevent the Court from finding that the Directive also protected the public interest of social inclusion:

> Article 7 of Directive 2000/43 does not preclude Member States from laying down, in their national legislation, the right for associations with a legitimate interest in ensuring compliance with that directive, or the body or bodies designated pursuant to Article 13 thereof, to bring legal or administrative proceedings to enforce the obligations resulting therefrom without acting in the name of a specific complainant or in the absence of an identifiable complainant. It is, however, solely for the national court to assess whether national legislation allows such a possibility.[20]

The Court's position seems to be that Member States are *entitled but not obliged* to provide for associational standing to pursue infringements where no victim is to be found. It has been asserted in legal scholarship that this creates a 'mismatch between the robust, teleological interpretation of the concept of direct discrimination, on the one hand, and the enforcement provisions, on the other'.[21] Another scholar has pointed to the

> fundamental contradiction that lies at the heart of EU equality law, namely the fact that, at a *substantive* level, discrimination directed against certain groups is prohibited, but at a *procedural* level, Member States are not required to provide enforcement mechanisms if an individual victim cannot be identified.[22]

As I see it, however, the Court's ruling is merely a reminder of the procedural autonomy enjoyed by Member States. Member States enjoy considerable discretion in crafting

[17] For an overview of the changes this 'eurolegalism' has brought about in various European jurisdictions, see RD Kelemen, *Eurolegalism: The Transformation of Law and Regulation in the European Union* (Harvard University Press 2011) 93–238.

[18] Case C-54/07 *Feryn* [2008].

[19] ibid para 24. The Court's ruling was confirmed in relation to Directive 2000/78/EC (Equal treatment in employment and occupation) in Case C-81/12 *Accept* [2013] para 36.

[20] Case C-54/07 *Feryn* [2008] para 27.

[21] M Ambrus, M Busstra and K Henrard, 'The Racial Equality Directive and Effective Protection against Discrimination: Mismatches between the Substantive Law and Its Application' (2010) 3 *Erasmus Law Review* 165, 168.

[22] SB Lahuerta, 'Enforcing EU Equality Law Through Collective Redress: Lagging Behind?' (2018) 55 *CML Rev* 783, 786.

their enforcement regime where individual rights are not at stake. Requiring Member States to provide public interest standing in the name of effectiveness would represent an incursion into the enforcement structures established at Member State level. It will be argued in the following that only exceptionally, where a Member State is in want of alternative means of effective enforcement, would the state have to enlist individuals as enforcers in the general interest.

The Union legislature has acknowledged the shortcomings of the rights-orientated approach to standing, and enacted secondary legislation that provides for standing for associations or organisations in particular fields. In the field of consumer protection, for example, there are directives that oblige Member States to provide consumer organisations with standing to pursue the broader interest of consumers.[23] The area of environmental law particularly stands out, due to the importance of the Aarhus Convention, which in Article 9 directly refers to requirements of access to justice. With respect to projects likely to have a significant effect on the environment, environmental organisations enjoy rights of participation in administrative procedures and a subsequent right to judicial review of any decision taken (see Article 6(1) and Article 9(2) of the Aarhus Convention respectively). Reference can be made to Directive 2011/92 (Consolidated EIA Directive), which requires that standing be afforded to members of the public concerned to seek judicial review of measures falling within the Directive.[24] Pursuant to the Directive, environmental organisations meeting any requirements under national law are to be regarded either as having sufficient interest, or as having a right that is capable of being impaired by such projects.[25] As the Court made clear in *Trianel*, environmental organisations must be entitled to bring proceedings for the protection of the *general public interest* rather than the rights of affected individuals.[26] National laws making access to court conditional on demonstrating that the challenged decision impaired an individual right cannot be applied to NGOs, which must also be able to rely on rules protecting only the public interest.

With respect to projects that are not likely to have a significant environmental impact, only Article 9(3) of the Aarhus Convention applies, prescribing that the public must have 'access to administrative or judicial procedures to challenge acts and omissions by private persons and public authorities which contravene provisions of its national law relating to the environment'. Article 9(3) of the Convention has not been implemented in Union law, and the provision does not satisfy the criteria of direct effect.[27] Yet domestic courts are required to interpret their procedural rules in accordance with the objectives of the provision to the extent possible, so as to enable environmental NGOs to challenge administrative decisions contrary to Union environmental law.[28]

[23] See, inter alia, Directive 93/13/EEC (Unfair Contract Terms), Art 7(2).

[24] See Art 11.

[25] See Art 11(3); Art 1(2).

[26] Case C-115/09 *Bund für Umwelt und Naturschutz Deutschland (Trianel)* [2011] para 46. The Court has held that although national law may lay down certain conditions in order to ensure that the organisation does in fact exist and is active, the Directive precluded a provision of national law that reserves the right to bring an appeal against a decision on projects falling within the scope of that Directive solely to environmental protection associations whose membership numbers at least 2,000; see Case C-263/08 *Djurgården-Lilla Värtans Miljöskyddsförening* [2009] paras 40–52.

[27] Case C-240/09 *Lezoochranárske zoskupenie* (Slovak Brown Bear) [2011].

[28] ibid para 51.

The Court speaks in the 'language of rights', and relies on the principle of effective judicial protection to broaden NGO standing in environmental matters.[29] *Protect*, which concerned the water quality objectives contained in Directive 2000/60/EC (the Water Framework Directive), must be considered a landmark ruling in this respect.[30] Austrian authorities had granted a permit to a facility producing snow for a ski resort, using water from a nearby river. An environmental NGO sought to challenge the decision on the ground that it contravened Article 4(1) of the Water Framework Directive, prohibiting deterioration of the status of all bodies of surface water, but was denied *locus standi*. With reference to Article 47 of the Charter, read in conjunction with Article 9(3) of the Aarhus Convention, the ECJ held that a duly constituted environmental organisation operating in accordance with the requirements of national law must be able to challenge a decision granting a permit for a project that may be contrary to the obligation set out in Article 4 of the Water Framework Directive.[31] The Court speaks of the exercise of the 'rights which environmental organisations derive' from Article 4 of the Directive, and stresses the importance of ensuring effective judicial protection of rights conferred by Union law.[32] Yet speaking of rights in this context seems artificial, and this use of vocabulary must be seen against the background of the special status enjoyed by the Aarhus Convention in the Union legal system.[33] In the words of Darpö, 'the Aarhus Convention and general principles of EU law cross-fertilise each other in the environmental area'.[34]

The aim of the following two sections is to outline the extent to which Member States are required to provide for private enforcement as a supplement to the public enforcement mechanisms already in place. In section IV, I concentrate on infringements committed by Member States, while infringements committed by private parties are examined in section V.

IV. Infringements Committed by Member States

A. The Insufficiency of Centralised Enforcement at the Union Level

When it comes to determining the enforcement regime that must be crafted at the domestic level with a view to holding *Member States* to account, there is first a need to

[29] The Court speaks about the 'rights' that environmental organisations derive from Union law; see Case C-243/15 *Lesoochranárske zoskupenie (Slovak Brown Bear)* II [2016] para 60. The relevant right was nevertheless of a procedural nature, namely, the right to participate in environmental decision-making. For a more detailed account, see M Eliantonio, 'The relationship between EU secondary rules and the principles of effectiveness and effective judicial protection in environmental matters: towards a new dawn for the "language of rights"?' (2019) 2 *Review of European Administrative Law* 95.

[30] Case C-664/15 *Protect* [2017].

[31] ibid para 58.

[32] ibid paras 44 and 45.

[33] Compare Case C-470/12 *Pohotovosť* [2014], where the Court held that a consumer protection association could not rely on Art 47 of the Charter to obtain leave to intervene in proceedings involving a consumer.

[34] J Darpö, 'Pulling the trigger: ENGO standing rights and the enforcement of environmental obligations in EU law' in S Bogojević and R Rayfuse (eds), *Environmental Rights in Europe and Beyond* (Hart Publishing 2018) 253, 267.

address the role of the Commission. This subsection seek to demonstrate that centralised enforcement at the Union level is insufficient to render Union law effective in the Member States.

It is the responsibility of the Commission, as the 'Guardian of the Treaties', to see to it that Member States comply with their Union law obligations. Pursuant to Article 17 TEU, the Commission shall 'promote the general interest of the Union and take appropriate initiatives to that end'. It shall, moreover, 'ensure the application of the Treaties, and of measures adopted by the institutions [and] oversee the application of Union law under the control of the Court of Justice of the European Union'. In the event that states fail to comply with their obligations, the Commission may initiate infringement proceedings under Article 258. A non-compliant state can be brought before the Court and ultimately be subject to penalties or lump sum payments in accordance with Article 260 TFEU.

Not only does the Commission look into systematic infringements arising from the legislative framework established in the Member States or from administrative practices, it also examines isolated incidents involving the incorrect application of Union law. In the case of general and persistent infringements, the Commission may 'bag several flies in one swat',[35] since the Court has accepted that the Commission may seek at the same time a finding that a provision of a directive has not been complied with *in a particular situation* and a finding that these provisions have not been complied with because of the adoption of a *general practice* contrary thereto.[36]

The Commission has various regulatory tools and techniques in its 'compliance promoting toolkit'.[37] Although infringement proceedings receive the most attention, such proceedings are not the only means of ensuring that Member States comply with their Union law obligations. All the same, infringement proceedings are the only mechanism based on deterrence; the other compliance mechanisms have a softer character, implying 'dialogue and mutual trust'.[38] Informal compliance mechanisms include so-called 'package meetings' between Commission officials and individual Member State officials to discuss matters of enforcement, or networks consisting of informal meetings with stakeholders with a view to assisting the Commission in addressing potential enforcement problems.[39] An alternative compliance mechanism that is worth particular mention is the EU pilot, an informal scheme that aims to resolve compliance problems without having recourse to the formal infringement proceedings. The scheme brings together the Commission, the Member State and the complainant, and aims to

[35] The expression is borrowed from LW Gormley, 'Infringement Proceedings' in A Jakab and D Kochenov (eds), *The Enforcement of EU Law and Values: Ensuring Member States' Compliance* (Oxford University Press 2017) 65, 73.

[36] Case C-494/01 *Commission v Ireland* [2005] para 27. On general and persistent infringements, see P Wennerås, 'A New Dawn for Commission Enforcement under Articles 226 and 228 EC: General and Persistent (GAP) Infringements, Lump Sums and Penalty Payments' (2006) 43 *CML Rev* 31.

[37] M Smith, 'The Visible, the Invisible and the Impenetrable: Innovations or Rebranding in Centralized Enforcement of EU Law?' in Drake and Smith (eds), *New Directions in the Effective Enforcement of EU Law and Policy* (n 11) 45, 47.

[38] DS Martinsen and M Hobolth, 'The Effectiveness of Transgovernmental Networks: Managing the Practical Application of European Integration in the Case of SOLVIT' in Drake and Smith (eds), *New Directions in the Effective Enforcement of EU Law and Policy* (n 11) 152, 157.

[39] See further Smith, 'The Visible, the Invisible and the Impenetrable' (n 37) 72.

provide informal solution to problems arising in the application of EU laws outside the ambit of internal market law.[40] The EU pilot works alongside the infringement proceedings and aims to induce Union law compliance; in practice, however, it functions 'as a portal or a first step to the infringement procedures'.[41]

The Commission has limited resources both in terms of manpower and money, and therefore lacks the capacity to police implementation and enforcement of the vast amount of Union law.[42] Neither is the Commission obliged to act on a complaint; it has full discretion whether to pursue a potential infringement committed by a Member State.[43] To this one may add that infringement proceedings are processes from which private parties are largely excluded: they do not have access to the process and cannot assert any rights in court; they cannot compel the Commission to take action, nor command access to documents the Commission may have acquired in the course of its investigation.[44]

Taking into account these structural features, public enforcement at the centralised level can hardly be perceived as sufficient to ensure the effectiveness of Union law at the domestic level. Gormley has compared infringement proceedings to a Swiss cheese: '[T]hey look attractive, have an initially diverting taste, but on closer examination, being full of holes, are not quite what one might first imagine.'[45] The limited enforcement capacity of the Commission is precisely what underlies the Court's 'dual vigilance' reasoning in *Van Gend en Loos*.[46] The system of decentralised enforcement is predicated on the notion that Member States are primarily to be held to account at the national level. The obligation to establish effective mechanisms to hold Member State to account is an aspect of the duty of loyal cooperation as enshrined in Article 4(3) TEU. This provision entails an obligation on Member States to 'take all the measures necessary to guarantee the application and effectiveness of [EU] law'.[47]

B. An Effective Regime for Holding Member States to Account at the National Level

Having concluded that Member States must themselves establish a system allowing private parties to hold public authorities to account, there is a need to address the content of this system. First of all, it should be stressed that a narrow focus on the possibility of enforcement through the ordinary judicial system may leave a blind spot,

[40] C Koops, 'EU Compliance Mechanisms: The Interaction Between the Infringement Procedures, IMS, SOLVIT and EU-Pilot' (2011) *Amsterdam Centre for European Law and Governance Working Paper Series 2011–08*, 20.

[41] ibid 23.

[42] RD Kelemen, 'The Impact of the Court of Justice on the European Law Enforcement Architecture' in H-W Micklitz and A Wechsler (eds), *The Transformation of Enforcement. European Economic Law in a Global Perspective* (Hart Publishing 2016) 163, 166.

[43] See, inter alia, Case 247/87 *Star Fruit v Commission* [1989] para 11.

[44] Smith, 'The Visible, the Invisible and the Impenetrable' (n 37) 57–58 (with further reference to Case 48/65 *Lütticke v Commission* [1966] and Case 247/87 *Star Fruit v Commission* [1989] as regards access to documents).

[45] Gormley, 'Infringement Proceedings' (n 35) 65.

[46] Case 26/62 *Van Gend en Loos* [1963].

[47] Case C-339/00 *Ireland v Commission* [2003] para 71.

since 'the constitutional tradition of the relevant Member State might treat enforcement more as a matter of good administration based around access to an institution like an ombudsman or mediator'.[48] There are various enforcement mechanisms outside the ambit of court proceedings that may be well suited to rendering Union law effective in the Member States. In addition to the above-mentioned ombudsman or mediator, reference can also be made to SOLVIT, an informal service provided by Member States' administrations to assist citizens and businesses running into problems resulting from a possible misapplication of internal market rules by the public administration in another Member State.[49] Although this mechanism is primarily of use to citizens or businesses affected in their Union rights, there are no formal standing requirements for lodging a complaint with SOLVIT. But although access is not restricted to holders of Union rights, the limited field of application – internal market rules – means the mechanism may fall short of affording protection to diffuse interests characterising areas such as environmental protection.

Where extra-judicial means of enforcement are lacking, this raises the question whether the Member States must allow for private enforcement before the courts. This is arguably not the case. There are various ways to organise the protection of general and diffuse interests in a given legal system, and litigation initiated by NGOs or public-spirited individuals is merely one of them.[50] A Member State could, for example, choose to set up an independent public watchdog with powers to initiate legal proceedings in the event of a Member State's failing to live up to its Union obligations.[51] If the focus is on the effectiveness of Union law, it should not matter who brings the action; what matters is simply that Union law is enforced. Whether the suit is initiated by a public-spirited citizen, an NGO or a public entity is unimportant from the viewpoint of effectiveness. Hence, the Court should show deference, provided that Union law can be enforced *at least by someone*.[52]

Although it may be of no importance from the point of view of Union law, standing rules may well matter to the Member State concerned. Member States should have a say in designating the entities that have a legitimate interest in the cessation and prohibition of infringements. Standing doctrines can take various forms theoretically. In the first, only certain organisations recognised by Member States would be entitled to sue. Alternatively, claimants can be acknowledged on an *ad hoc* basis, based either on

[48] M Dougan, 'Who Exactly Benefits from the Treaties? The Murky Interaction Between Union and National Competence over the Capacity to Enforce EU Law' (2009) 12 *Cambridge Yearbook of European Legal Studies* 73, 78.

[49] Commission Communication, 'Effective Problem Solving in the Internal Market ('SOLVIT') COM(2001) 702, 1.

[50] As Dougan has pointed out, Member States might 'prefer to entrust enforcement powers to a collective authority (whether public or private, such as an independent commission or a trade union) which is considered better placed to reach decisions about whether legal action would be justified in the general interest and taking into account a wider range of potentially competing considerations': Dougan, 'Who Exactly Benefits from the Treaties?' (n 48) 78.

[51] This option has been suggested for violations of environmental law provisions, see S Prechal and L Hancher, 'Individual Environmental Rights: Conceptual Pollution in EU Environmental Law?' 2002 *The Yearbook of European Environmental Law* 89, 112.

[52] Wennerås is on to something similar when he holds, 'it seems clear that national courts must in any event consider some plaintiffs to have a legal interest capable of being affected by infringements of rules protecting ecological interests'; see P Wennerås, *The Enforcement of EC Environmental Law* (Oxford University Press 2007) 113–14.

formal legislative criteria or on a concrete assessment of whether the claimant is a suitable enforcer. States should be able to lay down criteria to make sure the claimant is an adequate representative of the interests at stake, and this could, for example, take the form of membership numbers, organisational structure and funding.

The focus in the foregoing sections has been on how Member States should structure their enforcement regime in order to live up to the demands of EU law. A Member State's obligation to grant standing to a claimant in a concrete case must be seen against the backdrop of this general obligation to craft an effective enforcement regime. This means that in exceptional circumstances, a claimant may gain access to court by arguing that allowing him to sue is the only way of subjecting the challenged measure to judicial review.[53] The approach suggested by Afilao has some merit to it. He writes that if an association protecting diffuse interests initiates legal proceedings, and the national court brings the question of standing before the ECJ, the Court would announce that

> national courts must allow associational standing if there exist no effective alternative methods of enforcing particular diffuse interests protected by European law. The Court would then direct national courts to analyze, based on the specific facts of each case, the effectiveness of alternative remedies. The national courts would evaluate both the possibility that actions will be brought by plaintiffs with standing under national law and the effectiveness of non-judicial methods of enforcement. If the national court finds that the alternative remedies are not effective enough, the national court would be required by European law to give the association seeking relief standing. However, the ECJ would give the national courts a way out of granting standing to associations not adequately organized to represent the interests at stake or to be quality litigants.[54]

The Court, he holds, would supervise the 'experimentation by the national courts', and the role of the Court would essentially be to make sure 'the enterprise remains on track by correcting aberrant behaviour and ensuring that national courts do not let effectiveness fall below minimum standards'.[55]

I will refrain from predicting the Court's approach to such a preliminary reference, and merely point out that associational standing is, generally speaking, but one of many ways of ensuring enforcement. In assessing the adequacy of domestic enforcement regimes, there are good reasons for granting considerable leeway to Member States, in order to avoid 'upsetting the equilibrium of the domestic enforcement system'.[56]

V. Infringements Committed by Private Parties

A. Introduction

When it comes to infringements committed by private parties, individuals may also have an important role to play in monitoring, detecting and pursuing infringements.

[53] The alternative could be for the claimant to lodge a complaint with the Commission and hope for 'privately triggered public enforcement', yet due to the Commission's discretion in these matters, this may well turn out to be a dead end.

[54] Afilalo, 'Towards a "Common Law" of Europe' (n 3) 402.

[55] ibid 403.

[56] Dougan, 'Who Exactly Benefits from the Treaties?' (n 48) 78.

It is a common perception that public and private enforcement must be kept apart as they pursue different objectives. Whereas public enforcement is about applying EU law in the public interest and imposing sanctions on infringers to punish them and deter them from so acting in the future, private enforcement is a means to provide those affected by infringements with access to justice and redress for the harm suffered.[57] Hence, when considering the EU obligations relating to public and private enforcement respectively, 'the starting point is that these are to a great extent two largely *unrelated* matters [existing] for the most part independently from each other'.[58] This assumption will be questioned in the following, where I appraise the extent to which private enforcement can be seen as 'an enforcement instrument in the general interest'.[59]

Poor enforcement undermines the effectiveness of the Union rules in force. Private enforcement can serve as a supplement to public enforcement, since it could 'help to draw important resources into the overall "enforcement mix"'.[60] Private enforcement can promote deterrence and help ensure compliance, as it increases the risk of being detected and adds to the expected sanction.[61] The added value of private enforcement is greater where parties pursue infringements not already known, or, alternatively, not pursued by the Member States' competent authorities (*stand-alone actions*), as opposed to where a violation has already been established and the private party merely piggybacks on the findings of the government (*follow-on actions*). In the first situation, the private party also serves a detective function. When, on the other hand, the infringement is already detected and pursued by a governmental agency, the only supplemental function to perform is that of multiplying the costs of violations. The private party 'provides no independent research skills, no special litigation savvy, and no nonpoliticized incentives. She simply piles on and rounds up the tab.'[62]

The co-existence of public and private enforcement mechanisms could add to the effectiveness of Union law, since more potential enforcers are likely to result in increased rates of detection, deterrence and compliance. Put differently, 'the more enforcement tools there are in the 'toolbox', the higher is the probability of detecting and remedying [infringements]'.[63] This is indeed the rationale underlying the ECJ's case law on liability for competition law infringements, where the Court has stressed that the availability of actions for damages 'strengthens the working of the Community competition rules and discourages agreements and practices, which are frequently covert, which are liable to restrict and distort competition' and 'make[s] a significant contribution to the maintenance of effective competition in the Community'.[64] Outside the field of competition law, such an added value is not, I submit, sufficient to ground a Union duty to provide

[57] See Commission Communication, 'Towards a European Horizontal Framework for Collective Redress', COM (2013) 401, 10.

[58] Wilman, *Private Enforcement of EU Law Before National Courts* (n 13) 547.

[59] ibid 546.

[60] ibid 548.

[61] A Renda, 'Private Antitrust Damages Actions in the EU: Chronicle of an Attempted Golpe' in Micklitz and Wechsler (eds), *The Transformation of Enforcement* (n 42) 273, 275–76.

[62] See WB Rubenstein, 'On What a "Private Attorney General" Is – And Why It Matters' (2004) 57 *Vanderbilt Law Review* 2129, 2151 (writing in the context of the American enforcement system.)

[63] D Poelzig, 'Private or Public Enforcement of the UCP Directive? Sanctions and Remedies to Prevent Unfair Commercial Practices' in W van Boom, A Garde and O Akseli (eds), *The European Unfair Commercial Practices Directive. Impact, Enforcement Strategies and National Legal Systems* (Ashgate 2014) 235, 257.

[64] Case C-453/99 *Courage* [2001] paras 26–27.

standing to private parties; Member States are only required to provide for private enforcement to pursue infringements to the extent necessary to *fill a lacuna* created by the shortcomings of the enforcement system in place in the Member State.

B. The Legal Framework: Outlining EU Sanctioning Requirements

In order to determine whether the enforcement system in the Member State is deficient, there is first a need to determine the requirements that have to be met as a matter of EU law. This section will therefore take a closer look at the EU sanctioning requirements stemming from the principle of loyal cooperation under Article 4(3) TEU. Member States have a duty to ensure that private parties comply with their Union law obligations, and the Court has imposed certain requirements in order to ensure that Member States perform this task in a satisfactory manner.

Before addressing the requirements pertaining to *decentralised* enforcement, it bears mentioning that there are also elements of *centralised* enforcement with respect to offences committed by private parties. The Commission is empowered to enforce the competition rules contained in Articles 101 and 102 TFEU by imposing sanctions in the case of non-compliance. In the past decades, we have also witnessed an increased tendency to grant direct enforcement powers to EU level institutions and agencies. As Scholten puts it, '[e]nforcement of EU law has been moving to "Brussels"'.[65] This shift is an aspect of the broader 'agencification' in the EU.[66] The enforcement powers of EU institutions vary greatly, extending from the issuing of Opinions and recommendations to competent domestic authorities, to the direct imposition of sanctions.

An example of a rather extensive relocation of enforcement powers to the centralised level is found in the financial markets sector.[67] The European Central Bank (ECB) directly supervises credit institutions, and is empowered to withdraw authorisations or to impose administrative sanctions in response to violations.[68] In addition, three European Supervisory Authorities (ESAs) have been created: the European Banking Authority (EBA); the European Securities and Markets Authority (ESMA); and the European Insurance and Occupational Pensions Authority (EIOPA).[69] The enforcement machinery cannot be adequately mapped without taking into account this form of centralised enforcement. That being said, such centralised enforcement is the

[65] M Scholten, 'Mind the Trend! Enforcement of EU Law Has Been Moving to 'Brussels'' (2017) 24 *Journal of European Public Policy* 1.

[66] See M Chamon, *EU Agencies: Legal and Political Limits to the Transformation of the EU Administration* (Oxford University Press 2016). He defines 'EU agencies' as 'permanent bodies under EU public law, established by the institutions through secondary legislation and endowed with their own legal personality' (ibid 15); and 'agencification' as 'the process whereby the EU agencies take up an increasingly important role in the EU administration, both in a quantitative as well as in a qualitative sense' (ibid 45).

[67] For a detailed account, see A Ottow, 'The New European Supervisory Architecture of the Financial Markets' in M Everson, C Monda and E Vos (eds), *European Agencies in between Institutions and Member States* (Wolters Kluwer 2014) 123.

[68] See Regulation (EU) No 1024/2013 (European Central Bank supervision of credit institutions).

[69] See Regulation (EU) No 1093/2010 (EBA); Regulation (EU) No 1094/2010 (EIOPA) and Regulation (EU) No 1095/2010 (ESMA). These ESAs have various enforcement powers, see further A Ottow, 'Europeanization of the Supervision of Competitive Markets' (2012) 18 *European Public Law* 191, 214.

exception rather than the rule. Union law norms are primarily enforced by domestic government authorities, using administrative sanctions as the primary means of ensuring compliance.

As regards the further content of this duty to ensure compliance, the starting point is that Member States enjoy institutional and procedural autonomy. We may recall from chapter 3, section III.B that, pursuant to the principle of *institutional autonomy*, Member States are generally free to designate the public institutions responsible for performing tasks resulting from Union law. This is only a starting point, however, and Member States are on occasion obliged by secondary EU law to have in place a regulatory authority for the purpose of applying and enforcing EU law. Such an approach is to be found, for example, in legislation pertaining to the network industries, the financial markets sector and, not least, in the field of competition law.[70] The degree of detail provided for as a matter of EU law varies, yet considerable discretion tends to remain in the hands of the Member States when it comes to the precise structure, powers and functioning of the relevant authorities.[71]

The *procedural autonomy* of the Member States is also subject to exceptions. An unfettered procedural autonomy in this field could result in an enforcement deficit, where Member States have seized the opportunity to shirk their responsibilities. Yet, as Hodges has noted, there is a 'striking absence of enforcement policies' at the Union level.[72] The harmonisation of domestic enforcement throughout the EU can take place through informal instruments, such as networks' exchanging information on best practices.[73] Nevertheless, given the shortcomings of such informal persuasion, the EU legislator and the Court have developed sanctioning requirements to improve Member State enforcement.[74] The development of requirements for enforcement measures at domestic level can be described as '*enforcement norm-setting*'.[75] Such norm-setting can take place either through legislation, or through case law.

As to the first, the EU legislator increasingly imposes specific obligations with regard to monitoring and sanctioning. By illustration, Directive 2001/95/EC (Product Safety) not only lays down binding safety standards for consumer products, but also requires national authorities to monitor compliance with the product safety rules and to impose measures in the case of non-compliance, such as product recalls.[76] Many regulations and directives also indicate the ways in which an infringement of the rules should

[70] See, inter alia, Directive 97/67/EC (Postal Services), Art 22, Art 3 and Directive 2009/138/EC (Insurance and Reinsurance) chapter III and Regulation (EC) No 1/2003 (Competition Enforcement), Art 5.

[71] Wilman, *Private Enforcement of EU Law Before National Courts* (n 13) 48.

[72] C Hodges, 'Public and Private Enforcement: The Practical Implications for Policy Architecture' in R Brownsword et al (eds), *The Foundations of European Private Law* (Hart Publishing 2011) 437, 447. He holds that '[i]t is simply pointless to create a vast edifice of rules if they are going to be enforced differently, or to different extents, in different areas of the Community'.

[73] See further AJ de Moor-van Vugt and RJGM Widdershoven, 'Administrative Enforcement' in JH Jans, S Prechal and RJGM Widdershoven (eds), *Europeanisation of Public Law* (Europa Law Publishing 2015) 267. Ottow has called such networks 'the cement between the bricks of the national supervisory systems'; see Ottow, 'Europeanization of the Supervision of Competitive Markets' (n 69) 203.

[74] R Meeus, 'Fill in the Gaps: EU Sanctioning Requirements to Improve Member State Enforcement of EU Environmental Law' (2010) 7 *Journal for European Environmental & Planning Law* 135, 136.

[75] ibid.

[76] See ch IV of the Product Safety Directive.

be sanctioned, although these criteria often merely replicate the requirement already stemming from the case law of the Court. It was widely disputed whether the Union institutions could prescribe the imposition of criminal sanctions for the enforcement of Union norms,[77] but with the Lisbon Treaty this competence was made explicit.[78]

Specific enforcement provisions are the exception, rather than the rule. It is generally the case that no explicit rules have been provided for in secondary law to regulate the enforcement of the norms laid down therein. The Court has imposed certain requirements on decentralised enforcement, derived from the duty of loyal cooperation enshrined in Article 4(3) TEU, thereby curbing the sanctioning autonomy of the Member States.

In *Amsterdam Bulb*, the Court held that where an individual failed to observe Union law, the Member States were 'competent to adopt such sanctions as appear to them to be appropriate'.[79] The Court took a more assertive stance in *Greek Maize*, and fleshed out the principles that should govern Member States public enforcement. This is the seminal case on EU sanctioning requirements, and with respect to sanctions is 'what the *Dassonville* case and the *Cassis de Dijon* case are for the law on the free movement of goods'.[80] The case concerned two consignments of maize that were exported from Greece to Belgium and officially declared as Greek maize, while in fact they contained maize from Yugoslavia. The maize was thus released on the market without any agricultural levies being collected. The Greek authorities failed to take action against the authors of the fraud, so the Commission initiated infringement proceedings, claiming that Greece had failed to comply with the duty of loyal cooperation under (now) Article 4(3) TEU. The Court held:

> [W]here Community legislation does not specifically provide any penalty for an infringement or refers for that purpose to national laws, regulations and administrative provisions, [Article 4(3)] of the Treaty requires the Member States to take all measures necessary to guarantee the application and effectiveness of Community law. For that purpose, whilst the choice of penalties remains within their discretion, they must ensure in particular that infringements of Community law are penalized under conditions, both procedural and substantive, which are analogous to those applicable to infringements of national law of a similar nature and importance and which, in any event, make the penalty effective, proportionate and dissuasive. Moreover, the national authorities must proceed, with respect to infringements of Community law, with the same diligence as that which they bring to bear in implementing corresponding national laws.[81]

These observations have been repeated in several subsequent rulings.[82] The similarities with the case law pertaining to the protection of Union law rights spring to mind, and

[77] See further A Dawes and O Lynskey, 'The Ever-Longer Arm of EC law; The Extension of Community Competence into the Field of Criminal Law' (2008) 45 *CML Rev* 131.

[78] Pursuant to Art 83(2) TFEU, the EU is competent to introduce criminal sanctions 'to ensure the effective implementation of a Union policy in an area which has been subject to harmonisation measures'.

[79] Case 50/76 *Amsterdam Bulb* [1977] para 33.

[80] N Hækkerup, *Controls and Sanctions in the EU Law* (DJØF 2001) 172, with reference to Case 8/74 *Dassonville* [1974] and Case 120/78 *Cassis de Dijon* [1979].

[81] Case 68/88 *Greek Maize* [1989] paras 23–25.

[82] See, inter alia, Case C-326/88 *Hansen* [1990] para 17; Case C-7/90 *Vandevenne and others* [1991] para 11; Case C-186/98 *Nunes* [1999] paras 9–11; Joined Cases C-387/02, C-391/02 and C-403/02 *Berlusconi* [2005] para 65; and Case C-565/12 *LCL Le Crédit Lyonnais SA* [2014] para 44.

these two strands of case law can be seen to overlap. In a concrete case the Court may also have to address them both.[83] That being said, the case law on Member State sanctions and individual remedies should be kept apart both conceptually and doctrinally.[84] After all, in the present context, the focus is on the effectiveness of Union law per se (*effet utile*), rather than on the protection of any individual's legal position.

The conditions spelled out in *Greek Maize* 'apply to every aspect of the enforcement of Union law', covering the nature of the sanction, the conditions for its imposition, and also the character and level of the sanction imposed.[85] The general obligation of adequate enforcement also extends to ensuring that enforcement takes place in practice, and this covers the duty to introduce supervisory measures and inspection procedures.[86] The Commission has the opportunity under Article 258 TFEU to initiate infringement proceedings if a Member State fails to comply with its obligation to supervise and enforce private infringements of Union law.

The requirement of *equivalence* means that the sanctions laid down for infringements of EU law must be as severe as those imposed for similar infringements of domestic law, and also that the efforts of states to enforce the rules must correspond to similar infringements of domestic law. In other words, the principle applies both to the provision for sanctions and the application of such sanctions.[87] As Meeus has pointed out, the requirement of equivalence does not guarantee adequate enforcement of EU law in situations where a Member State does not enforce national legislation effectively.[88]

The principle of *proportionality* requires the severity of the sanction to correspond to the gravity of the breach.[89] The competent national authorities must take into account all the considerations specific to each case, including the behaviour of the party concerned and its good faith or its fraudulent intentions, in order to determine whether a penalty must be imposed at all, and, if it must, which one.[90] The principle contains not just a minimum, but also a maximum standard.[91] *Dissuasion* is concerned with guaranteeing future respect for a norm.[92] A sanction is dissuasive where it prevents an individual from infringing Union law, which means that one must take into account both the nature and the levels of the penalty and the likelihood of its being imposed.[93]

[83] See, eg, Case 14/83 *Von Colson* [1984], addressed in ch 7, section II, where the Court seems to regard compensation as a sanction too.

[84] M Dougan, 'From the Velvet Glove to the Iron Fist: Criminal Sanctions for the Enforcement of Union Law' in M Cremona (ed), *Compliance and the Enforcement of EU Law* (Oxford University Press 2012) 74, 86.

[85] ibid 83.

[86] AB Blomberg, 'European Influence on National Environmental Law Enforcement: Towards an Integrated Approach' (2008) 1(2) *Review of European Administrative Law* 39, 43.

[87] Hækkerup, *Controls and Sanctions in the EU Law* (n 80) 177.

[88] Meeus, 'Fill in the Gaps' (n 74) 141.

[89] See, eg, Case 21/85 *A. Maas & Co* [1986] para 15. The Court distinguished between, on the one hand, 'principal obligations whose observance is of fundamental importance to the proper functioning of a Community system' and, on the other, 'secondary obligations whose infringement should not be punished with the same rigour'.

[90] Case C-148/14 *Nordzucker* [2015] para 44.

[91] S Prechal, *Directives in EC Law* (Oxford University Press 2005) 91. For an illustration, see Joined Cases C-497/15 and C-498/15 *Euro-Team* [2017].

[92] C Harding, 'Member State Enforcement of European Community Measures: The Chimera of "Effective" Enforcement' (1997) 4 *Maastricht Journal of European and Comparative Law* 5, 11.

[93] AG Kokott in Joined Cases C-387/02, C-391/02 and C-403/02 *Berlusconi* [2004] para 89.

Presumably the required dissuasive effect covers both *general* and *specific* deterrence, referring to the discouraging effects on third parties and the perpetrator respectively.[94]

That a sanction should be *effective* means that it should be able to produce the desired effect.[95] The sanction must reinforce the value of the rule or principle infringed, and must *look backwards* in the sense that it must reflect the gravity of the infringement, while also *looking forward* in the sense of deterring future infringements.[96] The first aspect shows the overlap between effectiveness and proportionality, the latter shows how effectiveness and dissuasion also overlap. Not only the sanction as such, but also the conditions that must be fulfilled in order to impose the sanction, must meet the effectiveness requirement: such conditions must not be framed in such a way as to make it practically impossible or excessively difficult to impose the sanction.[97]

It is evident from the *Greek Maize* ruling that the Court (just as it does when it comes to private remedies) places significance of the *functional nature* of measures rather than their juridical form or label. Member States are granted considerable discretion as to the precise content of the sanction. In *Feryn*, concerning discriminatory statements of the director of a company, the Court suggested what would constitute an effective sanction in the case at hand:

> [T]hose sanctions may, where necessary, include a finding of discrimination by the court or the competent administrative authority in conjunction with an adequate level of publicity, the cost of which is to be borne by the defendant. They may also take the form of a prohibitory injunction, in accordance with the rules of national law, ordering the employer to cease the discriminatory practice, and, where appropriate, a fine. They may, moreover, take the form of the award of damages to the body bringing the proceedings.[98]

Considering the broad understanding given to the concept of sanctions, it should be seen as covering 'any aggravating measure formally imposed on a violator by a public authority (a judge or a public administration) in relation to the violation of a legal norm the violator concerned has committed'.[99] Such responses can be not only of a punitive, but also of a reparatory nature.[100] Whereas the first category comprises responses such as administrative fines, the latter covers responses such as withdrawal of an obtained advantage or an obligation to repay amounts wrongly received.[101] As we shall see, however, the award of private remedies may also be perceived as a sanction, and can thus constitute a means of fulfilling the obligations laid down in *Greek Maize*.

[94] To the same effect, Hækkerup, *Controls and Sanctions in the EU Law* (n 80) 174.

[95] KE Sørensen, 'Member States' Implementation of Penalties to Enforce EU Law: Balancing the Avoidance of Enforcement Deficits and the Protection of Individuals' (2015) 40 *EL Rev* 811, 816.

[96] Harding, 'Member State Enforcement of European Community Measures' (n 92) 9.

[97] AG Kokott in Joined Cases C-387/02, C-391/02 and C-403/02 *Berlusconi* [2004] para 88. By way of illustration, see Case C-177/88 *Dekker* [1990], where the Court found that a requirement of fault applicable in Dutch law rendered civil liability ineffective.

[98] Case C-54/07 *Feryn* [2008] para 39.

[99] Meeus, 'Fill in the Gaps' (n 74) 138.

[100] Similarly Prechal, *Directives in EC Law* (n 91) 87, fn 101, who uses the term in the sense of 'legal consequences laid down in a secondary norm for non-compliance with a primary norm of conduct'. The distinction between 'administrative sanctions' and 'administrative measures' is not clear-cut, and the terminology varies. As pointed out by de Moor-van Vugt, 'sanctions' is rarely used as an umbrella term for the response of Member States to infringements of Union law; 'penalty' or 'measure' tends to be preferred: see A de Moor-van Vugt, 'Administrative Sanctions in EU Law' (2012) 5 *Review of European Administrative Law* 5, 13.

[101] See further ibid 13–14 for an elaboration of the distinction.

C. The Interplay between Public and Private Enforcement

The *Greek Maize* jurisprudence primarily concerns the responsibilities of public authorities when enforcing Union law. Yet it can also be argued that this jurisprudence provides a basis for asking whether the entire enforcement system adopted by the Member States lives up to what is expected under the Treaties.[102] There is a close link between the provisions of redress for private parties and the discharge of the Member States' own enforcement responsibilities. The public and private enforcement mechanisms cannot be seen in isolation, since both contribute to ensuring the effectiveness of substantive Union law. In the words of Dougan,

> [t]he real question concerns the manner in which those two different perspectives on decentralized enforcement [public enforcement and private remedies] interact with each other and thereby mutually fulfil or even exhaust the Member States' overarching obligation under Article 4(3).[103]

This is the question that will be examined in the following. The Union draws on a 'full toolbox of enforcement techniques in order to promote high levels of compliance'.[104] Clearly, a Member State cannot be considered as having fulfilled its obligation to provide for effective enforcement simply by opening up for the possibility of private enforcement.[105] The interesting question is, however, the extent to which a Member State is required to allow for private suits due to deficiencies in its system of public enforcement.

Member States are afforded considerable discretion in crafting their enforcement regimes. Determining the proper mix of public and private enforcement is essentially left to the Member States. Hence, they may rely primarily on public enforcement, private enforcement or a balance of the two.[106] The balance between public and private enforcement is rooted in the national legal system, which could explain why the Court has taken a deferential stance. When determining whether to opt for public or private enforcement, factors to be taken into consideration include the existence of information and detection advantages, the type of sanction or remedy that is deemed appropriate and the differences in motives to sue.[107] What is considered the appropriate balance may well vary between different sectors due to the particularities of each field. This is not the place to elaborate on the merits and shortcomings of the respective enforcement mechanisms, or to assess the ideal mix of public or private enforcement; the important aspect is to note that the different modes of enforcement cannot be seen in isolation. When examining the need for private enforcement, account must be taken of the relevant public enforcement

[102] Dougan, 'Who Exactly Benefits from the Treaties?' (n 48) 84.

[103] ibid 107.

[104] H Collins, 'The Hybrid Quality of European Private Law' in Brownsword et al (eds), *The Foundations of European Private Law* (n 72) 453, 463.

[105] Case C-132/05 *Commission v Germany (Parmesan Cheese)* [2008] para 68. See also Case 72/85 *Commission v Netherlands* [1986] para 20.

[106] Prechal, *Directives in EC Law* (n 91) 88; and de Moor-van Vugt and Widdershoven, 'Administrative Enforcement' (n 73) 268.

[107] R van den Bergh, 'Private Enforcement of European Competition Law and the Persisting Collective Action Problem' (2013) 20 *Maastricht Journal of European and Comparative Law* 12, 15. He writes this in the context of competition law enforcement, but the observations hold true for enforcement of EU law in general.

mechanisms, since the need for private enforcement varies depending on how well established and effective the methods of public enforcement are in the respective area.

In the following, I address the issue of gaps in the enforcement mechanisms existing in the Member States, and ask what this implies in terms of standing. It will be argued that private enforcement may be called for in order to avoid an enforcement deficit, but that Member States still will have considerable leeway in determining who should be entitled to sue.

D. Locating Deficiencies in the Domestic Enforcement Regimes

What does it mean that a public enforcement regime is deficient? The need for private enforcement mechanisms to fill the gap is evident in situations where public enforcement mechanisms are lacking.[108] In fields where public enforcement plays a modest role, the legislature has on occasion stepped in and enacted instruments facilitating private enforcement. This is the case, inter alia, in the field of intellectual property.[109] In other policy fields – such as competition and financial services – public enforcement mechanisms are well-developed. But even though Member States have established authorities to monitor compliance with Union law rules and pursue infringements, there may be reasons why public enforcement does not work optimally. Of course, there are resource constraints, but there is also a risk of enforcement officials' shirking their responsibilities because of political influence, capture by the regulated industry or skewed incentives due to future career prospects.[110] Moreover, within the national systems, the legislative and executive powers generally serve the same purpose; in the EU system the interests of Member States and their executive powers may diverge from those of the EU, creating a principal–agent problem.[111] When implementing and enforcing Union law, 'Member States are likely to be torn between loyalty towards the [Union] and their own national interests'.[112] To that could also be added that Member States may have little to gain from enforcing EU law effectively, since 'the outcome of strict enforcement may be that companies and individuals in Member States that do comply diligently with Union law have a harder time surviving in bad economic weather'.[113]

A public enforcement regime must be perceived as deficient if the competent organ is not doing its job properly. It is clearly not sufficient for Member States to erect adequate sanctions systems; they also need to make sure that infringements are pursued in practice. All the same, it remains a difficult task determining the required extent of Member States' enforcement activity. What we need to know is 'how much compliance

[108] Wilman, *Private Enforcement of EU Law Before National Courts* (n 13) 551.

[109] Directive 2004/48/EC (IPR Enforcement Directive).

[110] These shortcomings tend to be highlighted in the American debate about private enforcement: see, eg, Hodges, 'Objectives, Mechanisms and Policy Choices in Collective Enforcement and Redress' (n 9) 105–06; and Rathod and Vaheesan, 'The Arc and Architecture of Private Enforcement Regimes in the United States and Europe' (n 4) 309–10.

[111] N Poltorak, *European Union Rights in National Courts* (Wolters Kluwer 2015) 39.

[112] M Accetto and S Zleptnig, 'The Principle of Effectiveness: Rethinking its Role in Community Law' (2005) 11 *European Public Law* 375, 382.

[113] de Moor-van Vugt and Widdershoven, 'Administrative Enforcement' (n 73) 263.

is enough?'[114] Harding has pointed out that the obligation of effective enforcement of Union law is both complex in its assessment and difficult in its realisation.[115] He therefore raises the important question whether the obligation of effective enforcement

> has anything more than a hortatory force, enabling European authorities such as the Court of Justice occasionally to remind Member States to do their best, without seriously intending to monitor or probe actual performance in enforcement, except in manifest cases of failure which cannot be ignored.[116]

It is submitted that although Member States cannot be required to ensure *full* compliance, they will nevertheless fail to meet Union law standards if their enforcement regimes suffer from such systemic weaknesses as addressed above, such as regulatory capture or undue political influence. Such weaknesses will necessarily affect the way cases are prioritised, and may well lead the competent organ to develop a practice of tolerating certain types of offences. Such a practice is clearly at odds with the obligation to impose effective, proportionate and deterrent sanctions.

Apart from the aforementioned deficiencies, Member States may also fail to comply with Union law obligations if they resort to compliance mechanisms that are deemed inadequate from the perspective of Union law. This raises the question whether Union law necessarily dictates *deterrence*-based as opposed to *compliance*-based enforcement strategies. Whereas the first strategy seeks to dissuade actual and potential infringers from breaking the law through fear of the consequences, the latter seeks to induce compliance through positive incentives, such as guidance.[117] Enforcement strategies can also be combined, which is the idea underlying Ayres and Braithwaite's *responsive regulation*. Their 'enforcement pyramid' entails a gradual escalation of measures applied to ensure compliance, from persuasive methods (such as advice and education) to a more punitive mode of enforcement (such as criminal prosecution).[118] An important question in this regard is whether Union law requires that the infringer must necessarily be sanctioned, or whether other means of ensuring compliance suffice from the perspective of Union law. Put differently, the question is whether the Member State can fend off a demand for judicial enforcement by an interested private party with reference to the availability of other, softer compliance mechanisms.

The requirement of dissuasiveness clearly indicates that the Union favours a 'deterrent-based' rather than a 'compliance-based' approach to enforcement.[119] This means that a Member State that finds out that the law has been violated will fail to comply with its enforcement obligations by seeking to induce compliance through soft mechanisms such as guidance and advice. It has been suggested in legal scholarship that

[114] Afilalo, 'Towards a "Common Law" of Europe' (n 3) 378.

[115] Harding, 'Member State Enforcement of European Community Measures' (n 92) 22.

[116] ibid.

[117] See further J van der Heijden, 'The Long, but Promising, Road from Deterrence to Networked Enforcement' in Drake and Smith (eds), *New Directions in the Effective Enforcement of EU Law and Policy* (n 11) 77, 81–83.

[118] I Ayres and John B, *Responsive Regulation: Transcending the Deregulation Debate* (Oxford University Press 1992), esp ch 2.

[119] Similarly A Ottow and K de Weers, 'Towards a European Enforcement Toolkit?' (2011) *The Europe Institute Utrecht Working Paper 01/11*, 56.

the requirements of equivalent, effective, proportionate and dissuasive sanctions, as laid down in both *Greek Maize* and secondary legislation, could merely indicate

> the top of the regulatory pyramid, by summing up what punitive enforcement measures a NRA must have at its disposal. Within this theory, NRAs are still free to use compliance-based measures, as long as the NRAs have a deterrent, punitive sanction as a last resort.[120]

This latter reading, however, sits rather uneasily with the EU's dominating mode of governance, the 'eurolegalism'. As we have seen in chapter 2, section IV, principal–agent problems cause lack of confidence in domestic authorities, which means that the Union organs have clear incentives to limit discretion in the hands of government officials and clearly spell out what their agents must do. Opening up for a more compliance-based style, whereby domestic authorities could work more cooperatively on issues that arise, would mean delegating wide discretion to domestic authorities in determining how to conduct their enforcement efforts. It would therefore seem that compliance mechanisms of a softer kind resonate less with the Court and the Union legislature. Nevertheless, a distinction must presumably be made between intentional or negligent infringements of a serious nature, and more excusable minor errors. In the latter case, the primary concern should be to restore *compliance* with Union law (rather than to punish the offender). Member States must presumably be entitled, as an element in an enforcement procedure, first to induce compliance through warnings, and impose a sanction where such softer measures do not produce the desired effect.[121]

E. The Need for Private Enforcement to Fill the Gaps in the Enforcement System

Having outlined what it means for the Member States to ensure an effective enforcement regime, the question is what this implies with respect to private enforcement. Where the public enforcement regime established at the domestic level suffers from serious deficits, the Member State concerned must adapt its system to ensure compliance with the Union standards. While this can be achieved by improving the system of public enforcement, it may be easier said than done. The state can alternatively open up for private enforcement initiatives to ensure Union law is rendered effective within its jurisdiction.[122] In that sense, then, the argument is not that Union law *dictates* private enforcement, but that this may be the most viable option to ensure effective enforcement in practice.[123]

To the extent that private enforcement is allowed for, a state can craft its standing rules in various ways. It is submitted that the Court is not in a position to formulate an autonomous approach to standing where individual rights are not at stake. The Court

[120] ibid 57.

[121] Similarly Meeus, 'Fill in the Gaps' (n 74) 156.

[122] The role of private enforcement in the case of public regulatory failure has also been addressed in JM Glover, 'The Structural Role of Private Enforcement Mechanisms in Public Law' (2011-2012) 53 *William & Mary Law Review* 1137, 1203–16.

[123] Similarly Poelzig, who holds that the principle of effectiveness demands private enforcement 'if this is the only way to ensure full effectiveness'; see Poelzig, 'Private or Public Enforcement of the UCP Directive?' (n 63) 247.

lacks a legal basis for formulating such a doctrine. The principle of loyal cooperation enshrined in Article 4(3) TEU clearly obliges the Member States to ensure that Union law is applied and enforced at the national level, yet there are various ways of complying with this obligation. Hence, to the extent that private enforcement is called for to avoid an enforcement deficit, Member States are granted considerable leeway in determining who should have standing. Rather than prescribing a particular standing regime to be applied in the Member States, the Court rejects domestic solutions that fall below the Union standard of effectiveness.

It is submitted that Member States may have to provide for private enforcement if the public enforcement regime has substantive shortcomings that cannot be remedied. A closely related question is whether a private legal avenue must be provided where the enforcement mechanisms as such are adequate, but where the competent domestic authority decides not to act *in a concrete case*. Put differently, the question is whether the Member State concerned must allow for a private action in order to avoid an enforcement deficit in the case at hand. In legal scholarship, the Court's ruling in *Muñoz* has been interpreted as requiring private suits in order to facilitate the effective enforcement of Union law in the individual case.[124] We may recall from chapter 3, section IV.B, that the Court in *Muñoz* found that it must be possible for a trader to enforce Union law obligations pertaining to quality standards for table grapes by means of civil proceedings instituted against a competitor. The Court highlighted how the possibility of bringing civil proceedings would strengthen the practical working of the Union rules in question and serve as a supplement to the public enforcement mechanisms by discouraging illegal practices.[125] It was submitted that Muñoz should be perceived as a right holder, and that the ruling thus can be explained with reference to the principle of effective judicial protection. While pursuing his own rights, he was at the same time contributing to the effective application of Union law in the true spirit of *Van Gend en Loos*.

Thorson, on the other hand, stressed the fact that that the public enforcement was deficient in the case at hand.[126] He holds that in *Muñoz*, the

> [e]nforcement of EU law was rendered excessively difficult, given that the existing enforcement mechanism (the public inspectorate) had not fulfilled its enforcement tasks and at the same time the court case had been dismissed. In practice then the application of Union law was near impossible.[127]

The argument seems to be that a private party (although not necessarily *any* private party) must be given a right to step into the shoes of domestic enforcement authorities where they fail to pursue an infringement. This holding is, however, predicated on the notion that the competent organ should have taken action. Whether competent organs are under a duty to enforce is, however, questionable.

Clearly, it is not sufficient to provide for sanctions on paper; they also have to be enforced by the competent authorities to ensure compliance with Union law.[128] Yet it does not seem to follow from the principle of loyal cooperation that the competent

[124] Case C-253/00 *Muñoz* [2002].
[125] ibid para 31.
[126] B Thorson, *Individual Rights in EU Law* (Springer 2016) 181.
[127] ibid 141.
[128] Blomberg, 'European Influence on National Environmental Law Enforcement' (n 86) 44.

organ must pursue *every possible offence*. The Court held in *Greek Maize* that Member States must not be less diligent in taking measures against infringements of Union law than against similar infringements of national law. Moreover, the Court made clear in *Spanish Strawberries* that the failure to pursue a violation of EU law could constitute a breach of the duty of loyal cooperation as enshrined in Article 4(3) TEU.[129] This does not mean, however, that each and every Union law infringement must be pursued and sanctioned.[130] Ensuring full compliance with Union law is neither possible nor desirable. In the words of Blomberg:

> EC law requires the fulfilment of all obligations deriving from it, which means in theory 100% compliance, thus compelling Member States to detect and enforce every breach. [Yet] it is common sense that such a result is an illusion and moreover, mandatory enforcement for various reasons is highly undesirable .... The question of effectiveness is therefore above all a matter of defining the desired, adequate level of enforcement.[131]

Effectiveness should be interpreted in light of what is feasible.[132] The principle of proportionality may also mean that sanctions should not be imposed for minor infringements.[133] Apart from this, I agree with Frese, who holds that the implications of the principle of effectiveness cannot be determined in the abstract, regardless of the area of law:

> Effective sanctioning in one area of EU law could mean that as many infringements as possible should be terminated and punished, whereas in other areas, case prioritisation may take place without jeopardising the effectiveness of EU law.[134]

The leeway granted to the Member States must be assessed for the relevant area of Union law. The Court has held, for instance, that the duty to combat fraud of Union funds also entails an obligation to initiate 'any proceedings under administrative, fiscal or civil law for the collection or recovery of duties or levies which have been fraudulently evaded or for damages'.[135] In other areas, such as competition law, there are reasons for allowing Member States some leeway in prioritising which infringements to pursue. Limited resources may not allow an authority to pursue every infringement, and the cost of pursuing a case may exceed the benefits of doing so.[136]

[129] Case C-265/95 *Commission v France (Spanish Strawberries)* [1997].

[130] To this effect, see Joined Cases C-145/15 and C-146/15 *Ruijssenaars* [2016].

[131] Blomberg, 'European Influence on National Environmental Law Enforcement (n 86) 44–45.

[132] Harding, 'Member State Enforcement of European Community Measures' (n 92) 22. As he points out (ibid 20), 'even those systems which employ a principle of "legality" (an obligation to prosecute when there are sufficient grounds for suspicion of an offence, as opposed to "opportunity", or discretion in that respect) in practice have to be selective and to prioritize'.

[133] Case C-148/14 *Nordzucker* [2015] para 44.

[134] MJ Frese, *Sanctions in EU Competition Law: Principles and Practice* (Hart Publishing 2014) 99.

[135] Case C-352/92 *Milchwerke Köln* [1994] para 23. The Court has also been demanding when it comes to the obligation to pursue and sanction breaches of the EU fisheries policy. Where Union legislation relating to the conservation and control of fishery resources has been breached, the competent authorities of the Member States are 'required to take penal or administrative action against the master of the vessel concerned or against any other peson responsible'; see Case C-140/00 *Commission v the United Kingdom* [2002] para 56.

[136] See further WPJ Wils, 'Discretion and Prioritisation in Public Antitrust Enforcement, in Particular EU Antitrust Enforcement' (2011) 34 *World Competition* 353. Member States are, however, clearly not entitled to tolerate cartels and other serious infringements. When asked whether national authorities might find an infringement of Art 101 TFEU without imposing a fine when the undertaking concerned had participated in a national leniency programme, the Court responded that 'the national competition authorities must proceed

Given that the domestic enforcement authorities have some (albeit limited) discretion in determining which cases to pursue, there are valid arguments against requiring the Member States to allow for private enforcement should the authority decline to take action. As Poelzig points out, if it is in the public interest not to enforce the law in a particular case, 'public authorities may exercise discretion not to enforce the law [but] a private person may still file a claim even though enforcement in the particular case would not be beneficial to the society'.[137] Where the enforcement authority makes use of its discretion and decides not to pursue and sanction a possible violation, the authority acts within the bounds of EU law. It would seem incoherent, from the perspective of Union law, if the Member State were still obliged to allow for private actions with a view to ensuring the effectiveness of Union law in its territory. It could, of course, be argued that private parties should be able to step in if the authority is passive in a situation outwith the ambit of its 'prosecutorial discretion'. In the absence of any legal authority, I would be hesitant to draw that conclusion. Further clarification from the Court is awaited.

VI. Concluding Remarks

We have seen that the Court of Justice is not as demanding of Member States when it comes to enforcing Union *obligations* as when enforcing Union *rights*. I agree with Engström, who sees the Court as somewhat 'reluctant to intrude into the national enforcement regimes and stretch its understanding of effectiveness beyond the protection of specific rights when it comes to requiring standing in front of national courts'.[138]

The criteria that can be derived from Article 4(3) TEU constitute a *negative test*. This implies that the Court will not dictate a particular means of enforcement, but once the Member State has made the choice, it may assess whether the enforcement mechanisms chosen – both in law and fact – satisfy the requirements of effectiveness and dissuasiveness. Because of the vagueness of these criteria, the enforcement requirements offer little guidance to the Member States, playing primarily a role in 'judging – retrospectively – whether a Member State has fulfilled its obligations' by taking adequate measures.[139]

It may nevertheless be the case that the overall enforcement regime suffers from structural flaws. If the public enforcement regime is perceived as inadequate, it is submitted that allowing for private enforcement may be the only way to restore the required level of effectiveness. In such circumstances, is still left to the Member States to structure their standing doctrines, provided that these allow for private suits to be pursued in practice.

Where private parties are entitled to pursue the public interest in the effective enforcement of Union rules, rather than their own private Union law right, it may well

by way of exception only not to impose a fine where an undertaking has infringed that provision intentionally or negligently'; see Case C-681/11 *Schenker & Co* [2013] para 46.

[137] Poelzig, 'Private or Public Enforcement of the UCP Directive?' (n 63) 254–55.

[138] J Engström, 'The Europeanisation of Remedies and Procedures Through Judge-Made Law: Can a Trojan Horse Achieve Effectiveness? Experiences of the Swedish Judiciary' (PhD thesis, European University Institute 2009) 142.

[139] Blomberg, 'European Influence on National Environmental Law Enforcement' (n 86) 46.

have an impact on the type of remedy that needs to be provided. Where the Member States are required to provide private enforcement with a view to ensuring the effectiveness of EU law, the claimant is not necessarily entitled to compensatory remedies such as monetary damages but may rather seek injunctions or declarations with a view to terminating infringements and restoring the status quo.[140] In certain fields, such as in relation to environmental protection, interim measures may also prove necessary if an action is to serve its purpose. But although monetary remedies are not required for the sake of protecting the claimant, it may be asked whether this might not change if the focus is shifted towards effectiveness per se. In order to enlist private parties to police Union law compliance, they need proper incentives, and the prospects of monetary awards are likely to have an impact on individuals' willingness to sue.[141] In addition, under the *Greek Maize* doctrine, Member States are required to ensure that the legal consequences are a sufficient deterrent, which may also serve to influence the remedies that must be provided to a claimant serving as an enforcer in the public interest. Providing a 'bounty' to private parties may encourage private actions and deter prospective infringers, yet '[f]rom a policy perspective, it would seem hard to justify enriching an individual whose capacity to bring legal proceedings derives from the effective protection of the public (rather than any strictly private) interest'.[142] Consequently it is submitted that a Member State, by providing for the possibility of pursuing injunctive or declaratory remedies, will live up to its obligations under EU law.

[140] Prechal and Hancher, 'Individual Environmental Rights' (n 51) 108. Similarly J Stuyck, 'Enforcement and Compliance: An EU Law Perspective' in Brownsword et al (eds), *The Foundations of European Private Law* (n 72) 514.

[141] On this matter, see further ch 14, section II.

[142] M Dougan, *National Remedies Before the Court of Justice: Issues of Harmonisation and Differentiation* (Hart Publishing 2004) 45.

14

Conclusions

I. Key Findings

In the introductory chapter, I identified the research question of this book: which standing rules must a Member State apply to live up to the demands of EU law? In this section, I present the key findings of the book, before moving on, in section II, to examine the extent to which the Court achieves what is has set out to do, namely, to ensure that rights are effectively protected and that Union law is rendered effective in the Member States.

In this book it has been argued that EU law primarily exerts its influence on national standing rules through the principle of effective judicial protection. Based on Article 47 of the Charter, an autonomous doctrine of standing can be formulated, meaning that when rights are at stake, it is not a matter of applying domestic standing doctrines within the confines of the principles of equivalence and effectiveness but rather of applying a doctrine whose content is determined at the Union level. Member States must grant standing when three criteria are met: the claimant is the holder of a Union right; this right is adversely affected by the (alleged) infringement; and the claimant demonstrates a vested and present interest in the proceedings. As of now, the Union doctrine of standing is only embryonic in form. It can be expected that the Court will be given the opportunity to elaborate on these criteria in future preliminary references.[1] When that occasion arises, the Court should take upon itself to spell out more fully the content of Member States' obligations by drawing its case law together and filling in the gaps.

It has been argued that the requirements placed on Member States are less strict when Union rights are not at stake. As an aspect of the duty of loyal cooperation, enshrined in Article 4(3) TEU, Member States are required to take all necessary measures to guarantee the application and effectiveness of EU law within their jurisdiction. The principle of *effet utile* cannot, however, form the basis of uniform standing rules. Rather than prescribing a particular means of enforcement, it serves to scrutinise *ex post* whether the selected enforcement mechanisms satisfy the effectiveness test, and strike down domestic solutions that unduly undermine the effectiveness of Union law.

[1] National courts can, in the formulation of their references for a preliminary ruling, 'steer the Court towards developing guiding standards, based upon the interpretation of ECHR provisions by the ECtHR'; see P van Cleynenbreugel, 'Judge-Made Standards of National Procedure in the Post-Lisbon Constitutional Framework' (2012) 37 *EL Rev* 90, 98.

To accommodate Union law requirements, national standing doctrines may have to yield. That domestic rules and doctrines pursuing legitimate public interests have to yield to Union law is, however, nothing new. On the contrary, it is the ordinary state of the law.[2] The influence of Union law on national standing doctrines can certainly lead to fragmentation at the domestic level, calling for separate treatment based on the origin – domestic or European – of the rule of substantive law at issue.[3] Yet concerns about Union law interventions in domestic standing regimes should not be overstated. First, the principle of effective judicial protection takes national legal systems as a source of inspiration, and absorbs national values, since the content of the principle is shaped by the 'constitutional traditions common to the Member States'.[4] This is a two-way process of fertilisation: influence goes from national law to EU law and from EU law back to national law.[5] Second, the incursions stemming from the princples of effective judicial protection and effectiveness are the bare minimum Member States must provide for to avoid Union law rights' becoming mere paper tigers.

II. Union Law Standing: No Panacea for Effectiveness and Effective Judicial Protection

Opening up for private enforcement does not guarantee that individuals will actually be vigilant to pursue their rights and police Union law compliance. Put differently, establishing a private right of action and formal rights of standing does not necessarily translate into an effective enforcement regime, where rights are effectively protected and the effectiveness of Union law is guaranteed. As Hodges has pointed out, 'a legal system that wishes to promote private enforcement of both private and public norms … would logically reduce barriers for private actors and incentivise them to take action'.[6] To ensure that private enforcement takes place in practice, there is a need to ensure that private parties have both the opportunities and the incentives to bring legal claims.[7]

A necessary precondition to bringing an action is, of course, to know that an infringement of one's rights has taken place. In the Union law context, this is not merely a matter of knowledge of relevant factual circumstances, but also of being able to ascertain whether the conduct in question constitutes an infringement of the relevant

[2] Weiler has called this the 'dark side of the moon' of direct effect; see JHH Weiler, 'Van Gend En Loos: The Individual as Subject and Object and the Dilemma of European Legitimacy' (2014) 12 *International Journal of Constitutional Law* 94, 103.

[3] Member States may 'resolve such problems … by permitting Union standards of judicial protection to "spill over" into wholly internal structures'; see M Dougan, 'The Vicissitudes of Life at the Coalface: Remedies and Procedures for Enforcing Union Law before the National Courts' in P Craig and G de Búrca (eds), *The Evolution of EU law* (Oxford University Press 2011) 407, 416.

[4] See, inter alia, Case C-222/84 *Johnston* [1986] para 18.

[5] A Ottow and K de Weers, 'Towards a European Enforcement Toolkit?' (2011) 1 *The Europe Institute Utrecht Working Paper 01/11*, 21.

[6] C Hodges, 'Objectives, Mechanisms and Policy Choices in Collective Enforcement and Redress' in J Steele and WH van Boom (eds), *Mass Justice: Challenges of Representation and Distribution* (Edward Elgar 2011) 101, 103.

[7] RD Kelemen, *Eurolegalism: The Transformation of Law and Regulation in the European Union* (Harvard University Press 2011) 56.

Union standard. Given the elusive concept of Union rights, it is, moreover, not always readily apparent for the claimant whether the infringed provision does grant him a right at all. But even if an individual is aware of the fact that his rights have been infringed, there may be barriers of various types that hamper his effective access to court. Such barriers can be of a practical or procedural nature.

Various practical considerations may play a role when a private party determines whether to initiate an action, such as the value of business relationships and emotional or psychological considerations, such as stress and frustration.[8] In addition, procedural rules may prevent a litigant from initiating proceedings. An individual's access to court will be illusory if the Member States have put restrictive rules on access to evidence and burden of proof in place, making it clear from the outset that the action is bound to fail.[9] Access to court can also be hampered if the Member State operates with short limitation periods. Excessive costs can also deter individuals from initiating proceedings. Domestic rules on evidence, limitation periods and costs are left to national law, assessed against the '*Rewe* criteria' of equivalence and effectiveness.[10]

The prospect of a positive net outcome will normally be a precondition of the choice to initiate proceedings. Where the cost of pursuing a claim is expected to exceed its value, the claim will mostly remain unenforced. Questions concerning cost of litigation are therefore closely connected to the question of available remedies:

> For any potential litigant weighing the potential costs and benefits of launching an action, the issues affecting litigation costs discussed above make up only half of the balance sheet and must be balanced against the damages, remedies, or other policy victories that courts may award them.[11]

In order to mobilise private parties in the enforcement of Union law, adequate incentives are required.[12] To incentivise suits, two options clearly spring to mind: first, the possibility of allowing for collective actions and thereby of lowering the share of the cost each claimant has to bear; second, the possibility of providing for punitive damages to increase the benefit of initiating actions. All the same, neither collective actions nor punitive damages are currently required as a matter of Union law.[13]

Given the high costs involved in litigation, legal proceedings are not for everyone.[14] As Weatherill puts it, 'Everyone may dine at the Ritz [but few] can afford to do so.'[15]

[8] F Wilman, *Private Enforcement of EU Law before National Courts: The EU Legislative Framework* (Edward Elgar 2015) 555.

[9] To reduce evidence barriers, the Union legislature has introduced specific rules on access to evidence and the burden of proof in specific fields: see, eg, Directive 2000/43/EC (Equal treatment irrespective of racial or ethnic origin), Art 8; and Directive 2014/104/EU (Competition Damages), Arts 5–7 and 9.

[10] Joined Cases C-442/98 *Kapniki Michailidis* [2000] (evidence); Joined Cases C-89/10 and C-96/10 *Q-Beef* [2011] and Case C-637/17 *Cogeco Communications* [2019] (limitation periods); and Case C-61/14 *Orizzonte* [2015] (legal costs).

[11] Kelemen, *Eurolegalism* (n 7) 71.

[12] S Burbank, S Farhang and H Kritzer, 'Private Enforcement' (2013) 17 *Lewis & Clark Law Review* 637, 675.

[13] See Case C-407/14 *Camacho* [2015] on punitive damages. EU-wide rules on collective redress may, however, be enacted in the near future, see ch 5, section IV.G.

[14] It follows from Art 47(3) of the Charter that legal aid shall be 'made available to those who lack sufficient resources insofar as such aid is necessary to ensure effective access to justice'. The Court found in Case C-279/09 *DEB* [2010] para 59 that it must not be 'impossible for legal persons to rely on that principle'.

[15] S Weatherill, *Law and Values in the European Union* (Oxford University Press 2016) 190. This is a reference to the utterance of 19th-century judge Sir James Matthew, who is known to have said that 'in England, justice is open to all, like the Ritz hotel'; see AG Jääskinen in Case C-61/14 *Orizzonte* [2015] para 1.

Large corporations may have little difficulty financing litigation, but this is different for individuals and organisations protecting diffuse interests.[16] The cost of litigation thus results in an imbalance in the types of infringements being pursued. As Micklitz has argued, the Union legal order is biased in favour of the enforcement of economic rights by businesses, at the expense of the social rights of individuals.[17]

The practical and legal barriers in individuals' access to court have resulted in the enactment of procedural devices, most notably the Regulation (EC) No 861/2007 establishing a European Small Claims Procedure. It has also resulted in an increase in alternative dispute resolution mechanisms, providing individuals with alternatives to formal court proceedings.[18] Such mechanisms offer a 'simple, fast and low-cost out-of-court solution to disputes'.[19] Yet since these mechanisms operate outside the ambit of ordinary court proceedings, they have clear shortcomings from an enforcement perspective. Generally speaking, alternative dispute resolution mechanisms do not create precedents, do not contribute to developing the law, and do not serve the purpose of general deterrence in the same manner as court judgments generally do.[20] Moreover, since only courts can refer questions to the ECJ, the use of such mechanisms excludes the involvement of the Court, thereby preventing the use of Article 267 TFEU to create a dialogue between domestic courts and the ECJ on the interpretation of Union law.

The procedural and practical barriers addressed may prevent individuals from pursuing their Union rights and policing Union law compliance. These features may imply that the American form of 'adversarial legalism' will not readily take root in the Member States.[21] Differences in legal culture can also prevent the 'Americanisation' of European law.[22] Wind argues, based on empirical research, that there are few signs of 'eurolegalism' in practice. The narrative that

> citizens and companies allegedly have discovered how to use national courts across the continent to claim their (EU) rights and thereby help enforce EU law [is] questionable as it is situated at a very abstract (almost moral) level holding limited empirical evidence when you dig a bit beneath the surface …. [L]ittle suggests that an increased number of national litigants, civil society mobilisation, preliminary rulings and competitive national courts are creating a European adversarial system which – on a broad scale – helps enhance the integration and harmonsation of European law.[23]

[16] Kelemen, *Eurolegalism* (n 7) 56.

[17] H-W Micklitz, 'The ECJ Between the Individual Citizen and the Member States – A Pleas for a Judge-Made European Law on Remedies' in H-W Micklitz and B de Witte (eds), *The European Court of Justice and the Autonomy of the Member States* (Intersentia 2012) 347, 377. He even calls for 'judicial activism to strengthen the position of private actors, individually and collectively, by applying and developing the acquis communautaire in the field of social judicial enforcement'; see H-W Micklitz, 'Administrative Enforcement of European Private Law' in R Brownsword et al (eds), *The Foundations of European Private Law* (Hart Publishing 2011) 563, 568.

[18] See, eg, Directive 2013/11/EU (Consumer ADR) and Regulation (EU) No 524/2013 (Consumer Online Dispute Resolution).

[19] Preamble to Directive 2013/11/EU (Consumer ADR) recital 5. Similarly, preamble to the Regulation (EU) No 524/2013 (Consumer Online Dispute Resolution) recital 8.

[20] Wilman, *Private Enforcement of EU Law before National Courts* (n 8) 380. Similarly, A Arnull, 'The Principle of Effective Judicial Protection in EU Law: An Unruly Horse?' (2011) 36 *EL Rev* 51, 68.

[21] Kelemen, however, is of the view that a transformation is taking place at the level of the Member States; one that is likely to encourage the spread of 'Eurolegalism': see in particular Kelemen, *Eurolegalism* (n 7) 57.

[22] See, eg, RA Kagan, 'The "Non-Americanisation" of European Law' (2008) 7 *European Political Science* 21; and R Kagan, 'Should Europe Worry about Adversarial Legalism?' [1997] *OJLS* 165.

[23] M Wind, 'Can Legal and Political Culture Explain the Success and Failure of European Law Compliance?' in H-W Micklitz and A Wechsler (eds), *The Transformation of Enforcement. European Economic Law in a Global Perspective* (Hart Publishing 2016) 69, 71.

While the adoption of features of the American system could bolster the development of a fully-fledged 'eurolegalism', such an adoption has not been seen as desirable. The Commission has warned on several occasions against generating a 'litigation culture' by opting for elements such as punitive damages, contingency fees, pre-trial discovery procedures, opt-out class actions and jury awards.[24] The irony is that it is exactly this combination of elements – this 'toxic cocktail' – that ensures the effectiveness of the American system of 'adversarial legalism'.[25]

At the present stage, the EU seems to convey the message that it desirable to ensure an effective private enforcement regime while at the same time avoiding excess litigation. Still, as Wilman has pointed out, there is an inherent tension between the ambition to see more private enforcement claims being brought and the desire to avoid a litigation culture: 'the EU might not be able to have its cake and eat it too'.[26]

This book has addressed one piece in the puzzle in the crafting of an effective regime for the enforcement of Union law at the domestic level. However, providing standing is no panacea for ensuring the effective protection of Union rights and the effectiveness of Union law in Member States. If the Union is serious about its determination to bolster private enforcement actions, the legislature and the Court need to work in tandem to make this happen. The Union legislature has enacted several legislative measures that facilitate private enforcement in particular fields, such as public procurement and competition law. Such a piecemeal approach provides for different enforcement regimes merely because they involve different areas of substantive law. Van den Bossche criticises this procedural and remedial 'particularism' and calls for a change:

> Fifty years after the *Van Gend en Loos* case, the EU legislature must act to guarantee access to justice, stop illegal practices and enable injured parties to obtain compensation in situations of harm caused by violations of rights granted under Union law, while ensuring appropriate safeguards to avoid abusive litigation, in all fields of EU law.[27]

While a more coherent approach may be deemed desirable, the Union organs cannot disregard the limits of their competence, as given specific expression in the principles of conferral and subsidiarity enshrined in Article 5 TEU. This also means that all changes cannot originate at the Union level. The Union organs will have to rely on the cooperation of their domestic peers in crafting an enforcement regime that adequately protects the rights of individuals and makes sure that Union law is rendered effective in practice.

[24] See recital 15 of the preamble to Commission Recommendation 2013/396/EU (Collective Redress) and *Green Paper on Consumer Collective Redress* COM(2008) 794, 12.

[25] The expression is borrowed from European Commission DG SANCO, MEMO/08/741, 2008, 4.

[26] Wilman, *Private Enforcement of EU Law before National Courts* (n 8) 489. Similarly Storskrubb and Ziller point to the 'inevitable tension between the development of access to justice and the growth of litigation, which sometimes creates unbearable pressures on the budgets devoted to justice'; see E Storskrubb and J Ziller, 'Access to Justice in European Comparative Law' in F Francioni (ed), *Access to Justice as a Human Right* (Oxford University Press 2007) 177, 203.

[27] A-M van den Bossche, 'Private Enforcement, Procedural Autonomy and Article 19(1) TEU: Two's Company, Three's a Crowd' (2014) 33 *Yearbook of European Law* 41, 73.

BIBLIOGRAPHY

Aalto, P, *Public Liability in EU Law: Brasserie, Bergaderm and Beyond* (Hart Publishing 2011)

Accetto, M and Zleptnig, S, 'The Principle of Effectiveness: Rethinking Its Role in Community Law' (2005) 11 *European Public Law* 375

Adams, M et al, 'Introduction: Judging Europe's Judges' in M Adams et al (eds), *Judging Europe's Judges: The Legitimacy of the Case Law of the European Court of Justice* (Hart Publishing 2013) 1

Afilalo, A, 'Towards a "Common Law" of Europe: Effective Judicial Protection, National Procedural Autonomy, and Standing to Litigate Diffuse Interests in the European Union' (1999) 22 *Suffolk Transnational Law Review* 349

Albors-Llorens, A, 'The Standing of Private Parties to Challenge Community Measures: Has the European Court Missed the Boat?' (2003) 62 *CLJ* 72

——, 'Judicial Protection before the Court of Justice of the European Union' in C Barnard and S Peers (eds), *European Union Law*, 2nd edn (Oxford University Press 2017)

Ambrus, M, Busstra, M and Henrard, K, 'The Racial Equality Directive and Effective Protection against Discrimination: Mismatches between the Substantive Law and Its Application' (2010) 3 *Erasmus Law Review* 165

Anagnostaras, G, 'State Liability and Alternative Courses of Action: How Independent Can an Autonomous Remedy Be?' (2001) 21 *Yearbook of European Law* 355

——, 'The Quest for an Effective Remedy and the Measure of Judicial Protection Afforded to Putative Community Law Rights' (2007) 32 *EL Rev* 728

Arnull, A, 'Editorial: The Incidental Effect of Directives' (1999) 24 *EL Rev* 1

——, 'The Rule of Law in the European Union' in A Arnull and D Wincott (eds), *Accountability and Legitimacy in the European Union* (Oxford University Press 2002) 241

——, 'Annotation of Unibet' (2007) 44 *CML Rev* 1763

——, 'The Principle of Effective Judicial Protection in EU Law: An Unruly Horse?' (2011) 36 *EL Rev* 51

——, 'Remedies before National Courts' in R Schütze and T Tridimas (eds), *Oxford Principles of European Union Law*, vol I: *The European Union Legal Order* (Oxford University Press 2018) 1011

Andenas, M and Della Negra, F, 'Between Contract Law and Financial Regulation: Towards the Europeanisation of General Contract Law' (2017) 28 *European Business Law Review* 499

Ayres, I and Braithwaite, J, *Responsive Regulation: Transcending the Deregulation Debate* (Oxford University Press 1992)

Barents, R, 'EU Procedural Law and Effective Legal Protection' (2014) 51 *CML Rev* 1437

Beijer, M, *The Limits of Fundamental Rights Protections by the EU: The Scope for the Development of Positive Obligations* (Intersentia 2017)

Beljin, S, 'Rights in EU Law' in S Prechal and B van Roermund (eds), *The Coherence of EU Law. The Search for Unity in Divergent Concepts* (Oxford University Press 2008) 91

Bengoetxea, J and Jääskinen, N, 'Rights and Diverse Effects in EU Law: A Hohfeldian Approach to the Doctrine of Direct Effect of Directives' in R Banakar (ed), *Rights in Context: Law and Justice in Late Modern Society* (Ashgate 2010) 277

Bergh, R van den, 'Private Enforcement of European Competition Law and the Persisting Collective Action Problem' (2013) 20 *Maastricht Journal of European and Comparative Law* 12

Betlem, G, 'Torts, A European Ius Commune and the Private Enforcement of Community Law' (2005) 64 *CLJ* 126

Beutler, B, 'State Liability for Breaches of Community Law by National Courts: Is the Requirement of a Manifest Infringement of the Applicable Law an Insurmountable Obstacle?' (2009) 46 *CML Rev* 773

Bickel, AM, *The Least Dangerous Branch: The Supreme Court at the Bar of Politics*, 2nd edn (Yale University Press 1986)

Biondi, A, 'Case C-253/00, Antonio Munoz y Cia, Superior Fruiticola SA v. Frumar Ltd, Redbridge Produce Marketing Ltd' (2003) 40 *CML Rev* 1241

Biondi, A and Farley, M, *The Right to Damages in European Law* (Wolters Kluwer 2009)

Blomberg, AB, 'European Influence on National Environmental Law Enforcement: Towards an Integrated Approach' (2008) 1(2) *Review of European Administrative Law* 39

Bobek, M, 'Why There Is No Principle of "Procedural Autonomy" of the Member States' in H-W Micklitz and B de Witte (eds), *The European Court of Justice and the Autonomy of the Member States* (Intersentia 2012) 305

——, 'Of Feasibility and Silent Elephants: The Legitimacy of the Court of Justice through the Eyes of National Courts' in M Adams et al (eds), *Judging Europe's Judges: The Legitimacy of the Case Law of the European Court of Justice* (Hart Publishing 2013) 197

——, 'The Effects of EU Law in the National Legal Systems' in C Barnard and S Peers (eds), *European Union Law* 3rd edn (Oxford University Press 2020) 154

Boch, C, 'The Iroquois at the Kirchberg; or, Some Naïve Remaks on the Status and Relevance of Direct Effect' in JA Usher (ed), *The State of the European Union: Structure, enlargement and economic union* (Longman 2000) 21

Bodansky, D, 'Legitimacy in International Law and International Relations' in JL Dunoff and MA Pollack (eds), *Interdisciplinary Perspectives on International Law and International Relations* (Cambridge University Press 2012) 321

Bogaart, M, 'The Emergence of the Framework Directive in EU Environmental Policy: An Exploration of Its Function and Characteristics' in M Peeters and R Uylenburg (eds), *EU Environmental Legislation. Legal Perspectives on Regulatory Strategies* (Edward Elgar 2014) 48

Bogojević, S, 'Judicial Protection of Individual Applicants Revisited: Access to Justice through the Prism of Judicial Subsidiarity' (2015) 34 *Yearbook of European Law* 5

——, 'EU human rights law and environmental protection: the beginning of a beautiful friendship?' in S Douglas-Scott and N Hatzis (eds), *Research Handbook on EU Law and Human Rights* (Edward Elgar 2017) 451

Bonelli, M, 'Effective Judicial Protection in EU Law: an Evolving Principle of a Constitutional Nature' (2019) 2 *Review of European Administrative Law* 35

Bossche, A-M van den, 'Private Enforcement, Procedural Autonomy and Article 19(1) TEU: Two's Company, Three's a Crowd' (2014) 33 *Yearbook of European Law* 41

Boyle, A, 'Human Rights and the Environment. Where Next?' in B Boer (ed), *Environmental Law Dimensions of Human Rights* (Oxford University Press 2015) 201

Brealey, M and Hoskins, M, *Remedies in EC Law: Law and Practice in English and EC Courts* (Sweet & Maxwell 1998)

Brkan, M, 'The Concept of Essence of Fundamental Rights in the EU Legal Order: Peeling the Onion to its Core' (2018) 14 *European Constitutional Law Review* 332

Broberg, M, 'Privates håndhævelse af EU-retten gennem præjudicielle forelæggelser' (2015) 128 *Tidsskrift for Rettsvitenskap* 455

Burbank, S, Farhang, S and Kritzer, H, 'Private Enforcement' (2013) 17 *Lewis & Clark Law Review* 637

Busch, D, 'The Private Law Effect of MiFID: The Genil Case and Beyond' (2017) 13 *European Review of Contract Law* 70

——, 'MiFID II: Stricter conduct of business rules for investment firms' (2017) 12 *Capital Markets Law Journal* 340

Büyüksagis, E et al, 'Punitive Damages in Europe and Plea for the Recognition of Legal Pluralism' (2016) 27 *European Business Law Review* 137

Cane, P, 'Accountability and the Public/Private Distinction' in N Bamforth and P Leyland (eds), *Public Law in a Multi-Layered Constitution* (Hart Publishing 2003) 247

Caranta, R, 'Judicial Protection against Member States: A New Jus Commune Takes Shape' (1995) 32 *CML Rev* 703

Caro de Sousa, P, 'Horizontal Expressions of Vertical Desires: Horizontal Effect and the Scope of the EU Fundamental Freedoms' (2013) 2 *Cambridge Journal of International and Comparative Law* 479

——, 'EU and National Approaches to Passing on and Causation in Competition Damages Cases: A Doctrine in Search of Balance' (2018) 55 *CML Rev* 1751

Chamon, M, *EU Agencies: Legal and Political Limits to the Transformation of the EU Administration* (Oxford University Press 2016)
Cherednychenko, OO, 'Public Supervision over Private Relationships: Towards European Supervision Private Law?' (2014) 22 *European Review of Private Law* 37
Claes, M, *The National Courts' Mandate in the European Constitution* (Bloomsbury Publishing 2006)
——, 'The European Union, Its Member States and Their Citizens' in D Leczykiewicz and S Weatherill (eds), *The Involvement of EU Law in Private Law Relationships* (Hart Publishing 2013) 29
Cleynenbreugel, P van, 'Transforming Shields into Swords: The Vebic Judgment, Adequate Judicial Protection Standards and the Emergence of Procedural Heteronomy in EU Law' (2011) 18 *Maastricht Journal of European and Comparative Law* 513
——, 'Judge-Made Standards of National Procedure in the Post-Lisbon Constitutional Framework' (2012) 37 *EL Rev* 90
——, 'The Confusing Constitutional Status of Positive Procedural Obligations in EU Law' (2012) 5 *Review of European Administrative Law* 81
——, 'National Procedural Choices before the Court of Justice of the European Union' in L Gruszczynski and W Werner (eds), *Deference in International Courts and Tribunals: Standard of Review and Margin of Appreciation* (Oxford University Press 2014) 175
Collins, H, 'The Unfair Commercial Practices Directive' (2005) 1 *European Review of Contract Law* 417
——, 'The Hybrid Quality of European Private Law' in R Brownsword et al (eds), *The Foundations of European Private Law* (Hart Publishing 2011) 453
——, 'Social Dumping, Multi-Level Governance and Private Law in Employment Relationships' in D Leczykiewicz and S Weatherill (eds), *The Involvement of EU Law in Private Law Relationships* (Hart Publishing 2013) 223
Comella, VF, 'The European Model of Constitutional Review of Legislation: Toward Decentralization?' (2004) 2 *International Journal of Constitutional Law* 461
Condon, R and van Leeuwen, B, 'Bottom Up or Rock Bottom Harmonization? Francovich State Liability in National Courts' (2016) 35 *Yearbook of European Law* 229
Craig, P, 'Legality, Standing and Substantive Review in Community Law' (1994) 14 *OJLS* 507
——, 'Formal and Substantive Conceptions of the Rule of Law: An Analytical Framework' [1997] *Public Law* 467
Craufurd Smith, R, 'Remedies for Breaches of EC Law in National Courts Legal Variation and Selection' in P Craig and G de Búrca (eds), *The Evolution of EU Law* (Oxford University Press 1999)
Cremer, H-J, *Human Rights and the Protection of Privacy in Tort Law: A Comparison between English and German Law* (Routledge-Cavendish 2010)
Curtin, D, 'Directives; The Effectiveness of Judicial Protection of Individual Rights' (1990) 27 *CML Rev* 709
Dam, C van, *European Tort Law*, 2nd edn (Oxford University Press 2013)
Damaska, MR, *The Faces of Justice and State Authority: A Comparative Approach to the Legal Process* (Yale University Press 1986)
Dannemann, G, 'Constitutional Complaints: The European Perspective' (1994) 43 *International Comparative Law Quarterly* 142
Darpö, J, 'Pulling the trigger: ENGO standing rights and the enforcement of environmental obligations in EU law' in S Bogojević and R Rayfuse (eds), *Environmental Rights in Europe and Beyond* (Hart Publishing 2018) 253
Dawes, A and Lynskey, O, 'The Ever-Longer Arm of EC Law; The Extension of Community Competence into the Field of Criminal Law' (2008) 45 *CML Rev* 131
de Búrca, G, 'The Language of Rights and European Integration' in J Shaw and G More (eds), *New Legal Dynamics of European Union* (Oxford University Press 1995)
——, 'After the EU Charter of Fundamental Rights: The Court of Justice as a Human Rights Adjudicator?' (2013) 20 *Maastricht Journal of European and Comparative Law* 168
Dedek, H, 'From Norms to Facts: The Realization of Rights in Common and Civil Private Law' (2010) 56 *McGill Law Journal* 77
Delicostopous, JS, 'Towards European Procedural Primacy in National Legal Systems' (2003) 9 *European Law Journal* 599

Della Negra, F, 'The Private Enforcement of the MiFID Conduct of Business Rules. An Overview of the Italian and Spanish Experiences' (2014) 10 *European Review of Contract Law* 571

Derlén, M and Lindholm, J, 'Three Ideas: The Scope of EU Law Protecing Against Discrimination' in M Derlén and J Lindholm (eds), *Volume in Honor of Pär Hallström* (Iustus 2012) 77

Dijk, P van et al (eds), *Theory and Practice of the European Convention on Human Rights*, 4th edn (Intersentia 2006)

Dougan, M, 'The Francovich Right to Reparation: Reshaping the Contours of Community Remedial Competence' (2000) 6 *European Public Law* 103

——, *National Remedies Before the Court of Justice: Issues of Harmonisation and Differentiation* (Hart Publishing 2004)

——, 'What Is the Point of Francovich?' in T Tridimas and P Nebbia (eds), *European Union Law for the Twenty-first Century*, vol 1: *Rethinking the new legal order* (Hart Publishing 2004) 239

——, 'When Worlds Collide: Competing Visions of the Relationship between Direct Effect and Supremacy' (2007) 44 *CML Rev* 931

——, 'Who Exactly Benefits from the Treaties? The Murky Interaction Between Union and National Competence over the Capacity to Enforce EU Law' (2009) 12 *Cambridge Yearbook of European Legal Studies* 73

——, 'The Vicissitudes of Life at the Coalface: Remedies and Procedures for Enforcing Union Law before the National Courts' in P Craig and G de Búrca (eds), *The Evolution of EU Law* (Oxford University Press 2011) 407

——, 'From the Velvet Glove to the Iron Fist: Criminal Sanctions for the Enforcement of Union Law' in M Cremona (ed), *Compliance and the Enforcement of EU Law* (Oxford University Press 2012) 74

——, 'Judicial Review of Member State Action under the General Principles and the Charter: Defining the Scope of Union Law' (2015) 52 *CML Rev* 1201

——, 'Addressing Issues of Protective Scope within the Francovich Right to Reparation' (2017) 13 *European Constitutional Law Review* 124

——, 'Primacy and the remedy of disapplication' (2019) 56 *CML Rev* 1459

Drake, S, 'More Effective Private Enforcement of EU Law Post-Lisbon: Aligning Regulatory Goals and Constitutional Values' in S Drake and M Smith (eds), *New Directions in the Effective Enforcement of EU Law and Policy* (Edward Elgar 2016) 12

Durant, IC, 'Causation' in H Koziol and R Schulze (eds), *Tort Law of the European Community* (Springer 2008) 47

Durovic, M, *European Law on Unfair Commercial Practices and Contract Law* (Bloomsbury 2016)

Dworkin, R, *Taking Rights Seriously* (Duckworth 1977)

——, *A Matter of Principle* (Harvard University Press 1985)

——, *Freedom's Law: The Moral Reading of the American Constitution* (Oxford University Press 1996)

Ebbesson, J, *Access to Justice in Environmental Matters in the EU* (Kluwer Law International 2002)

Edward, D, 'Direct Effect – Myth, Mess or Mystery?' in JM Prinssen and A Schrauwen (eds), *Direct Effect: Rethinking A Classic of EC Legal Doctrine* (Europa Law Publishing 2002) 3

Eidenmüller, H and Fries, M, 'Against False Settlement: Designing Efficient Consumer Rights Enforcement Systems in Europe' in H-W Micklitz and A Wechsler (eds), *The Transformation of Enforcement. European Economic Law in a Global Perspective.* (Hart Publishing 2016) 87

Eilmansberger, T, 'The Relationship between Rights and Remedies in EC Law: In Search of the Missing Link' (2004) 41 *CML Rev* 1199

Eliantonio, M, *Europeanisation of Administrative Justice?: The Influence of the ECJ's Case Law in Italy, Germany and England* (Europa Law Publishing 2009)

——, *Standing Up for Your Right(s) in Europe – A Comparative Study on Legal Standing (Locus Standi) before the EU and Member States' Courts* (Intersentia 2013)

——, 'The relationship between EU secondary rules and the principles of effectiveness and effective judicial protection in environmental matters: towards a new dawn for the "language of rights"?' (2019) 2 *Review of European Administrative Law* 95

Ellingsen, HK, 'Judicial Review of Administrative Decisions in Domestic Courts – Union Law requirements on the *locus standi* of individuals' in L Cadiet, B Hess and MR Isidro (eds), *Approaches to Procedural Law: The Pluralism of Methods* (Nomos 2017) 509

——, 'Effective judicial protection of individual data protection rights: Puškár' (2018) 55 *CML Rev* 1879

Emberland, M, *The Human Rights of Companies* (Oxford University Press 2006)
Engström, J, 'Rättsskyddsprincipens krav på talerätt i nationell domstol i ljuset av RÅ 2006 Ref 9 och C-216/02' (2006) 3 *Europarättslig tidsskrift* 511
——, 'The Europeanisation of Remedies and Procedures Through Judge-Made Law: Can a Trojan Horse Achieve Effectiveness? Experiences of the Swedish Judiciary' (PhD thesis, European University Institute 2009)
——, 'Effektivt Rättsskydd i Förvirring – Nationell prosess- och sanktionsrätt i ljuset av C-253/00 Muñoz' 2003 *Europarättslig tidsskrift* 167
Farhang, S, *The Litigation State: Public Regulation and Private Lawsuits in the United States* (Princeton University Press 2010)
Farnsworth, EA, 'Comparative Contract Law' in M Reimann and R Zimmermann (eds), *The Oxford Handbook of Comparative Law* (Oxford University Press 2006) 899
Fenger, N, *Forvaltning og fællesskab: Om EU-rettens betydning for den almindelige forvaltningsret: Konfrontation Og Frugtbar Sameksistens* (DJØF 2004)
——, *EU-rettens påvirkning af dansk forvaltningsrett* (DJØF 2013)
Fletcher, W, 'The Structure of Standing' (1988) 98 *Yale Law Journal* 221
Flynn, L, 'When National Procedural Autonomy Meets the Effectiveness of Community Law, Can It Survive the Impact?' (2008) 9 *ERA Forum* 245
Fornasier, M, 'The Impact of EU Fundamental Rights on Private Relationships: Direct or Indirect Effect?' (2015) 23 *European Review of Private Law* 29
Franck, J, 'Rights, remedies and effective enforcement in air transportation: *Ruijssenaars*' (2017) 54 *CML Rev* 1867
Fredriksen, HH, *Offentligrettslig erstatningsansvar ved brudd på EØS-avtalen* (Fagbokforlaget 2013)
Frese, MJ, *Sanctions in EU Competition Law: Principles and Practice* (Hart Publishing 2014)
Freund, B, 'Compensation for Remote Economic Losses Caused by Infringements of Art 101 TFEU – Otis and Others v Land Oberösterreich and Others (C-435/18)' (2020) 1 *GRUR International* 496
Fuller, L, *The Morality of Law* (Yale University Press 1965)
——, 'The Forms and Limits of Adjudication' (1978) 92 *Harvard Law Review* 353
Galetta, D-U, *Procedural Autonomy of EU Member States: Paradise Lost?* (Springer 2010)
Gallie, WB, 'Essentially Contested Concepts' (1955) 56 *Proceedings of the Aristotelian Society* 167
Garben, S, 'Sky-High Controversy and High-Flying Claims? The Sturgeon Case Law in Light of Judicial Activism, Euroscepticism and Eurolegalism' (2013) 50 *CML Rev* 15
Garth, B and Cappelletti, M, 'Access to Justice: The Newest Wave in the Worldwide Movement to Make Rights Effective' (1978) 27 *Buffalo Law Review* 181
Gaudet, R, 'Turning a Blind Eye: The Commission's Rejection of Opt-out Class Actions Overlooks Swedish, Norwegian, Danish and Dutch Experience' (2009) 30 *European Competition Law Review* 107
Gerven, W Van, 'Bridging the Unbridgeable: Community and National Tort Laws after Francovich and Brasserie' (1996) 45 *International Comparative Law Quarterly* 507
——, 'Of Rights, Remedies and Procedures' (2000) 37 *CML Rev* 501
——, 'The Emergence of a Common European Law in the Area of Tort Law: The EU Contribution' in D Fairgrieve, M Andenas and J Bell (eds), *Tort Liability of Public Authorities in Comparative Perspective* (The British Institute of International and Comparative Law 2002) 125
——, 'Substantive Remedies For the Private Enforcement of EC Antitrust Rules Before National Courts' in CD Ehlermann and I Atanasiu (eds), *European Competition Law Annual 2001: Effective Private Enforcement of EC Antitrust Law* (Hart Publishing 2003) 53
——, 'Bringing (Private) Laws Closer to Each Other at the European Level' in F Cafaggi (ed), *The Institutional Framework of European Private Law* (Oxford University Press 2006) 37
Gill-Pedro, E 'EU Environmental Rights as Human Rights: Some Methodological Difficulties Facing European Courts' in S Bogojevic and R Rayfuse (eds), *Environmental Rights in Europe and Beyond* (Hart Publishing 2018) 201
Glover, JM, 'The Structural Role of Private Enforcement Mechanisms in Public Law' (2011-2012) 53 *William & Mary Law Review* 1137
Godt, C, 'Enforcement of Environmental Law by Individuals and Interest Groups: Reconceptualizing Standing' (2000) 23 *Journal of Consumer Policy* 79
Gordon, R and Moffatt, R, *EU Law in Judicial Review*, 2nd edn (Oxford University Press 2014)

Görisch, C, 'Effective Legal Protection in the European Legal Order' in Z Szente and K Lachmayer (eds), *The Principle of Effective Legal Protection in Administrative Law: A European Perspective* (Routledge 2016) 29

Gormley, LW, 'Infringement Proceedings' in A Jakab and D Kochenov (eds), *The Enforcement of EU Law and Values: Ensuring Member States' Compliance* (Oxford University Press 2017) 65

Green, L, 'Two Views of Collective Rights' (1991) 4 *Canadian Journal of Law and Jurisprudence* 315

Gutman, K, 'The Essence of the Fundamental Right to an Effective Remedy and to a Fair Trial in the Case-Law of the Court of Justice of the European Union: The Best Is Yet to Come?' (2019) 20 *German Law Journal* 884

Gyselen, L, 'Liability of Supranational, State and Private Actors: Comments from the Point of View of EU Competition Law' in J Wouters, J Stuyck and T Kruger (eds), *Principles of Proper Conduct for Supranational, State and Private Actors in the European Union: Towards a Ius Commune: Essays in Honour of Walter Van Gerven* (Intersentia 2001) 135

Hækkerup, N, *Controls and Sanctions in the EU Law* (DJØF 2001)

Harding, C, 'Member State Enforcement of European Community Measures: The Chimera of "Effective" Enforcement' (1997) 4 *Maastricht Journal of European and Comparative Law* 5

Harlow, C, 'Access to Justice as a Human Right: The European Convention and the European Union' in P Alston (ed), *The EU and Human Rights* (Oxford University Press 1999) 187

——, 'A Common European Law of Remedies?' in C Kilpatrick, T Novitz and P Skidmore (eds), *The Future of Remedies in Europe* (Hart Publishing 2000) 69

Harris, D, O'Boyle, M and Warbrick, C, *Law of the European Convention on Human Rights* (Butterworths 1995)

Harris, DJ et al, *Harris, O'Boyle & Warbrick: Law of the European Convention on Human Rights* 4th edn (Oxford University Press 2018)

Hart, HLA, *Essays on Bentham* (Clarendon Press 1982)

——, *The Concept of Law*, 2nd edn (Clarendon Press 1997)

Hartkamp, AS, 'The General Principles of EU Law and Private Law' (2011) 75 *Rabels Zeitschrift für ausländisches und internationales Privatrecht / The Rabel Journal of Comparative and International Private Law* 241

Havu, K, 'EU Law in Member State Courts: "Adequate Judicial Protection" and Effective Application – Ambiguities and Nonsequiturs in Guidance by the Court of Justice' (2016) 8 *Contemporary Readings in Law & Social Justice* 158

——, 'Private Enforcement of Competition Law: Notes Regarding the Roles of EU and National Law on the Basis of Recent Preliminary Rulings' (2020) 2 *Europarättslig tidskrift* 193

Heidenhain, M, *European State Aid Law* (Beck 2010)

Heijden, J van der, 'The Long, but Promising, Road from Deterrence to Networked Enforcement' in S Drake and M Smith (eds), *New Directions in the Effective Enforcement of EU Law and Policy* (Edward Elgar 2016) 77

Hesselink, MW, *The New European Private Law: Essays on the Future of Private Law in Europe* (Kluwer Law International 2002)

——, 'The General Principles of Civil Law: Their Nature, Roles and Legitimacy' in D Leczykiewicz and S Weatherill (eds), *The Involvement of EU Law in Private Law Relationships* (Hart Publishing 2013) 131

Hilson, C, 'The Visibility of Environmental Rights in the EU Legal Order: Eurolegalism in Action?' (2018) 25 *Journal of European Public Policy* 1589

Hilson, C and Downes, T, 'Making Sense of Rights: Community Rights in EC Law' (1999) 24 *EL Rev* 121

Hjelmeng, E, *Privat håndhevelse av EØS-avtalens konkurranseregler* (Fagbokforlaget 2003)

——, 'Competition Law Remedies: Striving for Coherence or Finding New Ways?' (2013) 50 *CML Rev* 1007

——, 'Private Enforcement of Article 9 Commitment Decisions – "Objective" vs "Subjective" Direct Effect' in M Andenas and K Lilleholt (eds), *Remedies and Substantive Law – European Dimensions of Economic and Private Law. University of Oslo Faculty of Law Research Paper N. 2011-18*

Hodges, C, 'Objectives, Mechanisms and Policy Choices in Collective Enforcement and Redress' in J Steele and WH van Boom (eds), *Mass Justice: Challenges of Representation and Distribution* (Edward Elgar 2011) 101

——, 'Public and Private Enforcement: The Practical Implications for Policy Architecture' in R Brownsword et al (eds), *The Foundations of European Private Law* (Hart Publishing 2011) 437

——, 'Collective Redress: A Breakthrough or a Damp Sqibb?' (2014) 37 *Journal of Consumer Policy* 67

Hodson, D and Maher, I, 'The Open Method as a New Mode of Governance: The Case of Soft Economic Policy Co-Ordination' (2001) 39 *Journal of Common Market Studies* 719

Hohfeld, WN, *Fundamental Legal Conceptions as Applied in Judicial Reasoning*, ed WW Cook (Yale University Press 1964)

Holten, S van and Rijswick, M van, 'The Governance Approach in European Union Environmental Directives and Its Consequences for Flexibility, Effectiveness and Legitimacy' in M Peeters and R Uylenburg (eds), *EU Environmental Legislation. Legal Perspectives on Regulatory Strategies* (Edward Elgar 2014) 13

Ibáñez Colomo, P, 'EU Competition Law in the Regulated Network Industries' *LSE Law, Society and Economy Working Papers 08/2016*

Idema, T and Kelemen, RD, 'New Modes of Governance, the Open Method of Co-Ordination and Other Fashionable Red Herring' (2006) 7 *Perspectives on European Politics and Society* 108

Jacob, MA, *Precedents and Case-Based Reasoning in the European Court of Justice: Unfinished Business* (Cambridge University Press 2014)

Jacobs, FG, 'The Evolution of the European Legal Order' (2004) 41 *CML Rev* 303

Jacobs, FG and Deisenhofer, T, 'Procedural Aspects of the Effective Private Enforcement of EC Competition Rules: A Community Perspective' in CD Ehlermann and I Atanasiu (eds), *European Competition Law Annual 2001: Effective Private Enforcement of EC Antitrust Law* (Hart Publishing 2003) 187

Jans, JH, 'Legal Protection in European Environmental Law: An Overview' in H Somsen (ed), *Protecting the European Environment: Enforcing EC Environmental Law* (Blackstone Press 1996) 49

——, 'On Inuit and Judicial Protection in a Shared Legal Order' (2002) 21 *European Energy and Environmental Law Review* 188

——, 'State Liability: In Search of a Dividing Line between National and European Law' in D Obradovic and N Lavranos (eds), *Interface between EU Law and National Law* (Europa Law Publishing 2007) 281

——, 'Harmonization of National Procedural Law Via the Back Door? Preliminary Comments on the ECJ's Judgment in Janecek in a Comparative Context' in M Bulterman et al (eds), *Views of European Law from the Mountain, Liber Amicorum Piet Jan Slot* (Wolters Kluwer 2009) 267

Jans, JH and Duijkersloot, AP, 'State Liability' in JH Jans, S Prechal and RJGM Widdershoven (eds), *Europeanisation of Public Law*, 2nd edn (Europa Law Publishing 2015) 435

Jurgens, G, 'Introduction of a Relativity-Related Requirement in Dutch Administrative Law' (2007) 4 *Journal for European Environmental & Planning Law* 260

Kadelbach, S, 'European Administrative Law and the Law of a Europeanized Administration' in C Joerges and R Dehousse (eds), *Good governance in Europe's integrated market* (Oxford University Press 2002) 167

Kagan, RA, *Adversarial Legalism: The American Way of Law* (Harvard University Press 2003)

——, 'The "Non-Americanisation" of European Law' (2008) 7 *European Political Science* 21

Kakouris, CM, 'Do the Member States Possess Judicial Procedural "Autonomy"?' (1997) 34 *CML Rev* 1389

Kay, RS, 'Standing to Raise Constitutional Issues: A Comparative Analysis' in RS Kay (ed), *Standing to Raise Constitutional Issues: Comparative Perspectives* (Bruylant 2005) 1

Keessen, AM, *European Administrative Decisions: How the EU Regulates Products on the Internal Market* (Europa Law Publishing 2009)

Kelemen, RD, 'Suing for Europe Adversarial Legalism and European Governance' (2006) 39 *Comparative Political Studies* 101

——, *Eurolegalism: The Transformation of Law and Regulation in the European Union* (Harvard University Press 2011)

——, 'Eurolegalism and Democracy' (2012) 50 *Journal of Common Market Studies* 55

——, 'The Impact of the Court of Justice on the European Law Enforcement Architecture' in H-W Micklitz and A Wechsler (eds), *The Transformation of Enforcement. European Economic Law in a Global Perspective* (Hart Publishing 2016) 163

——, 'American-Style Adversarial Legalism and the European Union' (European University Institute) *EUI Working Paper RSCAS 2008/37*

Kelsen, H, *Pure Theory of Law* (University of California Press 1967)

Kilpatrick, C, 'The Future of Remedies in Europe' in C Kilpatrick, T Novitz and P Skidmore (eds), *The Future of Remedies in Europe* (Hart Publishing 2000) 1

Koch, C, 'Locus Standi of Private Applicants under the EU Constitution: Preserving Gaps in the Protection of Individuals Right to an Effective Remedy' (2005) 30 *EL Rev* 511

Komninos, AP, 'Public and Private Antitrust Enforcement in Europe: Complement? Overlap?' (2006) 3 *The Competition Law Review* 5

——, 'Civil Antitrust Remedies Between Community and National Law' in C Barnard and O Odudu (eds), *The Outer Limits of European Union Law* (Hart Publishing 2009) 363

——, 'Private Enforcement in the EU with Emphasis on Damages Actions' in D Geradin and I Lianos (eds), *Handbook on European Competition Law: Enforcement and Procedure* (Edward Elgar 2013) 228

Konstadinides, T, *Division of Powers in European Union Law: The Delimitation of Internal Competence Between the EU and the Member States* (Kluwer Law International 2009)

Koops, C, 'EU Compliance Mechanisms: The Interaction Between the Infringement Procedures, IMS, SOLVIT and EU-Pilot' (2011) *Amsterdam Centre for European Law and Governance Working Paper Series 2011–08*

Krommendijk, J, '"Open Sesame": Improving Access to the ECJ by Requiring National Courts to Reason Their Refusals to Refer' (2007) 42 *EL Rev* 46

——, 'Is There Light on the Horizon? The Distinction between "Rewe Effectiveness" and the Principle of Effective Judicial Protection in Article 47 of the Charter after Orizzonte' (2016) 53 *CML Rev* 1395

Lacchi, C, 'Multilevel Judicial Protection in the EU and Preliminary References' (2016) 53 *CML Rev* 679

Lahuerta, SB, 'Enforcing EU Equality Law Through Collective Redress: Lagging Behind?' (2018) 55 *CML Rev* 783

Lang, JT, 'Article 10 EC: The Most Important "General Principle" of Community Law' in U Bernitz, J Nergelius and C Cardner (eds), *General Principles of EC Law in a Process of Development* (Wolters Kluwer 2008) 75

Leczykiewicz, D, 'Private Party Liability in EU Law: In Search of the General Regime' (2009) 12 *Cambridge Yearbook of European Legal Studies* 257

——, 'The Constitutional Dimension of Private Law Liability Rules in the EU' in D Leczykiewicz and S Weatherill (eds), *The Involvement of EU Law in Private Law Relationships* (Hart Publishing 2013) 199

——, 'Effectiveness of EU Law Before National Courts: Direct Effect, Consistent Interpretation and Member State Liability' in A Arnull and D Chalmers (eds), *Oxford Handbook of European Union Law* (Oxford University Press 2015) 212

——, 'Conceptualising Conflict between the Economic and the Social in EU Law after Viking and Laval' in M Freedland and J Prassl (eds), *Viking, Laval and Beyond* (Bloomsbury Publishing 2015) 307

Leczykiewicz, D and Weatherill, S, 'Private Law Relationships and EU Law' in D Leczykiewicz and S Weatherill (eds), *The Involvement of EU Law in Private Law Relationships* (Hart Publishing 2013) 1

Leib, LH, *Human Rights and the Environment: Philosophical, Theoretical and Legal Perspectives* (Martinus Nijhoff Publishers 2011)

Lenaerts, K, 'The Court's Outer and Inner Selves: Exploring the External and Internal Legitimacy of the European Court of Justice' in M Adams et al (eds), *Judging Europe's Judges: The Legitimacy of the Case Law of the European Court of Justice* (Hart Publishing 2009) 13

——, 'Exploring the Limits of the EU Charter of Fundamental Rights' (2012) 8 *European Constitutional Law Review* 375

Lenaerts, K and Corthaut, T, 'Of Birds and Hedges: The Role of Primacy in Invoking Norms of EU Law' (2006) 31 *EL Rev* 287

Lenaerts, K, Gutman, K and Maselis, I, *EU Procedural Law* (Oxford University Press 2014)

Lianos, I, 'Competition Law Remedies in Europe' in D Geradin and I Lianos (eds), *Handbook on European Competition Law: Enforcement and Procedure* (Edward Elgar 2013) 362

——, 'Causal Uncertainty and Damages Claims for the Infringement of Competition Law in Europe' (2015) 34 *Yearbook of European Law* 1

Lindblom, PH, 'In dubio pro natura! Några civilprocessuella frågor inom miljöratten' (2000) 5 *Juridisk Tidsskrift* 805

Lindenbergh, SD, 'The Protection of Secondary Victims: A Comparative Overview', *Personal Injury Compensation in Europe Series: Fatal Accidents & Secondary Victims* (XPL Publishing 2005) 413

MacCormick, N, 'Rights in Legislation' in PMS Hacker and J Raz (eds), *Law, Morality and Society* (Clarendon Press 1977) 189

Maduro, MP, *We the Court: The European Court of Justice and the European Economic Constitution : A Critical Reading of Article 30 of the EC Treaty* (Hart Publishing 1998)

Mak, C, 'Rights and Remedies: Article 47 EUCFR and Effective Judicial Protection in European Private Law Matters' in H-W Micklitz (ed), *Constitutionalization of European Private Law* (Oxford University Press 2014) 236

Mak, V, 'The "Average Consumer" of EU Law in Domestic and European Litigation' in D Leczykiewicz and S Weatherill (eds), *The Involvement of EU Law in Private Law Relationships* (Hart Publishing 2013) 333

Martinsen, DS and Hobolth, M, 'The Effectiveness of Transgovernmental Networks: Managing the Practical Application of European Integration in the Case of SOLVIT' in S Drake and M Smith (eds), *New Directions in the Effective Enforcement of EU Law and Policy* (Edward Elgar 2016) 152

Mates, P and Bartoň, M, 'Public Versus Private Interest – Can the Boundaries Be Legally Defined?' [2011] *Czech Yearbook of International Law* 171

Meeus, R, 'Fill in the Gaps: EU Sanctioning Requirements to Improve Member State Enforcement of EU Environmental Law' (2010) 7 *Journal for European Environmental & Planning Law* 135

Mendes, J, *Participation in EU Rule-Making: A Rights-Based Approach* (Oxford University Press 2011)

Michaels, R, 'Of Islands and the Ocean: The Two Rationalities of European Private Law' in R Brownsword et al (eds), *The Foundations of European Private Law* (Hart Publishing 2011) 139

Micklitz, H-W, 'Administrative Enforcement of European Private Law' in R Brownsword et al (eds), *The Foundations of European Private Law* (Hart Publishing 2011) 563

——, 'Enforcement and Compliance: Editorial Introduction' in R Brownsword et al (eds), *The Foundations of European Private Law* (Hart Publishing 2011) 415

——, 'The ECJ Between the Individual Citizen and the Member States – A Plea for a Judge-Made European Law on Remedies' in H-W Micklitz and B de Witte (eds), *The European Court of Justice and the Autonomy of the Member States* (Intersentia 2012) 347

——, 'A Common Approach to the Enforcement of Unfair Commercial Practices and Unfair Contract Terms' in W van Boom, A Garde and O Akseli (eds), *The European Unfair Commercial Practices Directive. Impact, Enforcement Strategies and National Legal Systems* (Ashgate 2014) 173

Miles, J, 'Standing under the Human Rights Act 1998: Theories of Rights Enforcement & the Nature of Public Law Adjudication' (2000) 59 *CLJ* 133

Milutinović, V, *The 'Right to Damages' under EU Competition Law: From Courage v Crehan to the White Paper and Beyond* (Kluwer Law International 2010)

Mol, M de, 'Kücükdeveci: Mangold Revisited – Horizontal Direct Effect of a General Principle of EU Law: Court of Justice of the European Union (Grand Chamber) Judgment of 19 January 2010, Case C-555/07, Seda Kücükdeveci v Swedex GmbH & Co. KG' (2010) 6 *European Constitutional Law Review* 293

——, 'The Novel Approach of the CJEU on the Horizontal Direct Effect of the EU Principle of Non-Discrimination: (Unbridled) Expansionism of EU Law?' (2011) 18 *Maastricht Journal of European and Comparative Law* 109

Moor-van Vugt, A de, 'Administrative Sanctions in EU Law' (2012) 5 *Review of European Administrative Law* 5

Moor-van Vugt, AJ de and Widdershoven RJGM, 'Administrative Enforcement' in JH Jans, S Prechal and RJGM Widdershoven (eds), *Europeanisation of Public Law* (Europa Law Publishing 2015)

Nazzini R, 'Potency and Act of the Principle of Effectiveness: The Development of Competition Law Remedies and Procedures in Community Law' in Catherine Barnard and Okeoghene Odudu (eds), *The Outer Limits of European Union Law* (Hart Publishing 2009) 401

Nebbia, P, 'Damages Actions for the Infringement of EC Competition Law: Compensation or Deterrence?' (2008) 33 *EL Rev* 23

Odudu, O, 'Competition Law and Contract: The Euro-Defence' in D Leczykiewicz and S Weatherill (eds), *The Involvement of EU Law in Private Law Relationships* (Hart Publishing 2013) 395

Oliphant, K (ed), *The Liability of Public Authorities in Comparative Perspective* (Intersentia 2016)

Ortlep, R and Widdershoven, R, 'Judicial Protection' in JH Jans, S Prechal and RJGM Widdershoven (eds), *Europeanisation of Public Law*, 2nd edn (Europa Law Publishing 2015)

Ottow, A, 'Europeanization of the Supervision of Competitive Markets' (2012) 18 *European Public Law* 191

——, 'The New European Supervisory Architecture of the Financial Markets' in M Everson, C Monda and E Vos (eds), *European Agencies in between Institutions and Member States* (Wolters Kluwer 2014) 123

Ottow, A and Weers, K de, 'Towards a European Enforcement Toolkit?' (2011) 1 *The Europe Institute Utrecht Working Paper 01/11*

Pech, L, '"A Union Founded on the Rule of Law": Meaning and Reality of the Rule of Law as a Constitutional Principle of EU Law' (2010) 6 *European Constitutional Law Review* 359

Penner, JE, 'The Analysis of Rights' (1997) 10 *Ratio Juris* 300

Poelzig, D, 'Private or Public Enforcement of the UCP Directive? Sanctions and Remedies to Prevent Unfair Commercial Practices' in W van Boom, A Garde and O Akseli (eds), *The European Unfair Commercial Practices Directive. Impact, Enforcement Strategies and National Legal Systems.* (Ashgate 2014) 235
Póltorak, N, *European Union Rights In National Courts* (Wolters Kluwer 2015)
Posner, RA, 'Natural Monopoly and Its Regulation' (1968) 21 *Stanford Law Review* 548
Prechal, S, 'Community Law in National Courts: The Lessons from van Schijndel' (1998) 35 *CML Rev* 681
——, 'Does Direct Effect Still Matter?' (2000) 37 *CML Rev* 1047
——, 'Direct Effect Reconsidered, Redefined and Rejected' in JM Prinssen and A Schrauwen (eds), *Direct Effect: Rethinking A Classic of EC Legal Doctrine* (Europa Law Publishing 2002) 17
——, *Directives in EC Law* (Oxford University Press 2005)
——, 'Adieu à La Directive?' (2005) 1 *European Constitutional Law Review* 481
——, 'Member State Liability and Direct Effect: What's the Difference After All?' (2006) 17 *European Business Law Review* 299
——, 'Protection of Rights: How Far?' in S Prechal and B van Roermund (eds), *The Coherence of EU Law. The Search for Unity in Divergent Concepts* (Oxford University Press 2008) 155
——, '"Europeanisation" of the Law: Consequences for the Dutch Judiciary' (Raad voor de Rechtspraak 2005)
Prechal, S and Hancher, L, 'Individual Environmental Rights: Conceptual Pollution in EU Environmental Law?' 2002 *The Yearbook of European Environmental Law* 89
Prechal, S and Widdershoven, R, 'Redefining the Relationship between "Rewe-Effectiveness" and Effective Judicial Protection' (2011) 4 *Review of European Administrative Law* 31
Rabkin, JA, 'The Secret Life of the Private Attorney General' (1998) 61 *Law and Contemporary Problems* 204
Rathod, J and Vaheesan, S, 'The Arc and Architecture of Private Enforcement Regimes in the United States and Europe: A View Across the Atlantic' (2016) 14 *University of New Hampshire Law Review* 303
Ravo, LM, 'The Role of the Principle of Effective Judicial Protection in the EU and Its Impact on National Jurisdictions' in *Sources of Law and Legal Protection* (Edizioni Università di Trieste 2012) 101
Raz, J, *The Authority of Law: Essays on Law and Morality* (1979)
——, *The Morality of Freedom* (Oxford University Press 1988)
——, 'Rights and Politics' (1995) 71 *Indiana Law Journal* 27
Rehbinder, E, 'Locus Standi, Community Law and the Case for Harmonization' in H Somsen (ed), *Protecting the European Environment: Enforcing EC Environmental Law* (Blackstone Press 1996) 151
Reich, N, 'Public Interest Litigation Before European Jurisdictions' in H-W Micklitz and N Reich (eds), *Public Interest Litigation Before European Courts* (Nomos 1996) 3
——, 'The Courage Doctrine: Encouraging or Discouraging Compensation for Antitrust Injuries' (2005) 42 *CML Rev* 35
——, 'Horizontal Liability in EC Law: Hybridization of Remedies for Compensation in Case of Breaches of EC Rights' (2007) 44 *CML Rev* 705
——, 'The Public/Private Divide in European Law' in H-W Micklitz and F Cafaggi (eds), *European Private Law after the Common Frame of Reference* (Edward Elgar 2010) 56
——, 'The Interrelation between Rights and Duties in EU Law: Reflections on the State of Liability Law in the Multilevel Governance System of the Union: Is There a Need for a More Coherent Approach in European Private Law?' (2010) 29 *Yearbook of European Law* 112
Reiertsen, M, 'The European Convention on Human Rights Article 13: Past, Present and Future' (PhD thesis, University of Oslo 2017)
Renda, A, 'Private Antitrust Damages Actions in the EU: Chronicle of an Attempted Golpe' in H-W Micklitz and A Wechsler (eds), *The Transformation of Enforcement. European Economic Law in a Global Perspective.* (Hart Publishing 2016) 273
Robin-Olivier, S, 'The Evolution of Direct Effect in the EU: Stocktaking, Problems, Projections' (2014) 12 *International Journal of Constitutional Law* 165
Roeben, V, 'Judicial Protection as the Meta-norm in the EU Judicial Architecture' (2020) 12 *Hague Journal on the Rule of Law* 29
Ross, M, 'Beyond Francovich' (1993) 56 *MLR* 55
Roth, W-H, 'Transposing "Pointillist" EC Guidelines into Systematic National Codes – Problems and Consequences' (2002) 10 *European Review of Private Law* 761

Rubenstein, WB, 'On What a "Private Attorney General" Is – And Why It Matters' (2004) 57 *Vanderbilt Law Review* 2129
Ruffert, M, 'Rights and Remedies in European Community Law: A Comparative View' (1997) 34 *CML Rev* 307
Sadeleer, N de, *EU Environmental Law and the Internal Market* (Oxford University Press 2014)
Safjan, M and Düsterhaus, D, 'A Union of Effective Judicial Protection: Addressing a Multi-Level Challenge through the Lens of Article 47 CFREU' (2014) 33 *Yearbook of European Law* 3
Schiemann, K, 'Locus Standi' (1990) 35 *Public Law* 342
Scholten, M, 'Mind the Trend! Enforcement of EU Law Has Been Moving to "Brussels"' (2017) 24 *Journal of European Public Policy* 1
Semmelmann, C, 'The Public-Private Divide in European Union Law' in U Neergaard and R Nielsen (eds), *European Legal Method: in a multi-level EU legal order* (DJØF 2012) 183
Shelton, D, *Remedies in International Human Rights Law*, 3rd edn (Oxford University Press 2015)
Shuibhne, N Nic, *The Coherence of EU Free Movement Law: Constitutional Responsibility and the Court of Justice* (Oxford University Press 2013)
Smith, M, 'The Visible, the Invisible and the Impenetrable: Innovations or Rebranding in Centralized Enforcement of EU Law?' in S Drake and M Smith (eds), *New Directions in the Effective Enforcement of EU Law and Policy* (Edward Elgar 2016) 45
Smith, M and Drake, S, 'Introduction' in S Drake and M Smith (eds), *New Directions in the Effective Enforcement of EU Law and Policy* (Edward Elgar 2016) 1
Snyder, F, 'The Effectiveness of European Community Law: Institutions, Processes, Tools and Techniques' (1993) 56 *MLR* 19
Somsen, H, 'The Private Enforcement of Member State Compliance with EC Environmental Law: An Unfulfilled Promise?' (2000) 1 *Yearbook of European Environmental Law* 311
Sørensen, KE, 'Member States' Implementation of Penalties to Enforce EU Law: Balancing the Avoidance of Enforcement Deficits and the Protection of Individuals' (2015) 40 *EL Rev* 811
Spaventa, E, 'Seeing the Wood Despite the Trees – On the Scope of Union Citizenship and Its Constitutional Effects' (2008) 45 *CML Rev* 13
Storme, M, *Approximation of judiciary law in the European Union* (Nijhoff 2004)
Storskrubb, E, *Civil Procedure and EU Law: A Policy Area Uncovered* (Oxford University Press 2008)
Storskrubb, E and Ziller, J, 'Access to Justice in European Comparative Law' in F Francioni (ed), *Access to Justice as a Human Right* (Oxford University Press 2007) 177
Strand, M, *The Passing-On Problem in Damages and Restitution under EU Law* (Edward Elgar 2017)
Svetlicinii, A and Botta, M, '"Umbrella Pricing" in Private Enforcement of EU Competition Law and US Antitrust Law: Another Transatlantic Divergence?' (2016) 41 *EL Rev* 399
Szente, Z, 'Conceptualising the Principle of Effective Legal Protection in Administrative Law' in Z Szente and K Lachmayer (eds), *The Principle of Effective Legal Protection in Administrative Law: A European Perspective* (Routledge 2016) 5
Tamanaha, BZ, *On the Rule of Law: History, Politics, Theory* (Cambridge University Press 2004)
——, 'A Concise Guide to the Rule of Law' in G Palombella and N Walker (eds), *Relocating the Rule of Law* (Hart Publishing 2009) 3
Thio, SM, *Locus Standi and Judicial Review* (Singapore University Press 1971)
Thorson, B, *Individual Rights in EU Law* (Springer 2016)
Tountopoulos, V, 'Market Abuse and Private Enforcement' (2014) 11 *European Company and Financial Law Review* 297
Tridimas, T, 'Liability for Breach of Community Law: Growing Up and Mellowing Down?' (2001) 38 *CML Rev* 301
——, *The General Principles of EU Law*, 2nd edn (Oxford University Press 2006)
——, 'Bifurcated Justice: The Dual Character of Judicial Protection in EU Law' in A Rosas, E Levits and Y Bot (eds), *The Court of Justice and the Construction of Europe: Analyses and Perspectives on Sixty Years of Case-law* (TMC Asser Press 2013) 367
Trstenjak, V and Beysen, E, 'European Consumer Protection Law: Curia Semper Dabit Remedium?' (2011) 48 *CML Rev* 95
Trstenjak, V and Weingerl, P, 'Collective Actions in the European Union – American or European Model?' (2014) 5 *Beijing Law Review* 155

Türk, AH, *The Concept of Legislation in European Community Law: A Comparative Perspective* (Kluwer Law International 2006)
——, *Judicial Review in EU Law* (Edward Elgar 2009)
——, 'Judicial Review of Integrated Administration in the EU' in HCH Hofmann and AH Türk (eds), *Legal Challenges in EU Administrative Law: Towards an Integrated Administration* (Edward Elgar 2009) 218
Tyler, TM, *Why People Obey the Law* (Yale University Press 1990)
Tzakas, D-P, 'Effective Collective Redress in Antitrust and Consumer Protection Matters: A Panacea or a Chimera?' (2011) 48 *CML Rev* 1125
——, 'International Litigation and Competition Law: The Case of Collective Redress' in J Basedow, S Francq and L Idot (eds), *International Antitrust Litigation: Conflict of Laws and Coordination* (Hart Publishing 2012) 421
Varga, Z, 'National Remedies in the Case of Violation of EU Law by Member State Courts' (2017) 54 *CML Rev* 51
Visser, M de, *Constitutional Review in Europe: A Comparative Analysis* (Hart Publishing 2014)
Vitorelli, E, 'Collective Due Process of Law: Reconciling Representation and Participation' in L Cadiet, B Hess and MR Isidro (eds), *Approaches to Procedural Law: The Pluralism of Methods* (Nomos 2017) 345
Waldron, J, 'Is the Rule of Law an Essentially Contested Concept (In Florida)?' (2002) 21 *Law and Philosophy* 137
Wallinga, M, 'Why MiFID & MiFID II Do (not) Matter to Private Law: Liability to Compensate for Investment Losses for Breach of Conduct of Business Rules' (2019) 27 *European Review of Private Law* 515
Walkila, S, *Horizontal Effect of Fundamental Rights in EU Law* (Europa Law Publishing 2016)
Wallerman, A, 'Towards an EU Law Doctrine on the Exercise of Discretion in National Courts? The Member States' Self-Imposed Limits on National Procedural Autonomy' (2016) 53 *CML Rev* 339
Ward, A, *Judicial Review and the Rights of Private Parties in EC Law* (Oxford University Press 2000)
——, 'National and EC Remedies under the EU Treaty: Limits and the Role of the ECHR' in C Barnard and O Odudu (eds), *The Outer Limits of European Union Law* (Hart Publishing 2009) 329
Warin, C, 'Individual Rights and Collective Interests in EU Law: Three Approaches to a Still Volatile Relationship' (2019) 56 *CML Rev* 463
Weatherill, S, 'Breach of Directives and Breach of Contract' (2001) 26 *EL Rev* 177
——, 'The Elusive Character of Private Autonomy in EU Law' in D Leczykiewicz and S Weatherill (eds), *The Involvement of EU Law in Private Law Relationships* (Hart Publishing 2013) 9
——, *Law and Values in the European Union* (Oxford University Press 2016)
Weber, F and Faure, M, 'The Interplay between Public and Private Enforcement in European Private Law: Law and Economics Perspective' (2015) 23 *European Review of Private Law* 525
Wechsler, A and Tripković, B, 'Conclusions: Enforcement in Europe as a Market of Justice' in H-W Micklitz and A Wechsler (eds), *The Transformation of Enforcement* (Hart Publishing 2016) 377
Weiler, JHH, 'The Reformation of European Constitutionalism' (1997) 35 *Journal of Common Market Studies* 97
——, 'The Transformation of Europe' (1990) 100 *Yale Law Journal* 2403
——, 'Van Gend En Loos: The Individual as Subject and Object and the Dilemma of European Legitimacy' (2014) 12 *International Journal of Constitutional Law* 94
Wennerås, P, 'A New Dawn for Commission Enforcement under Articles 226 and 228 EC: General and Persistent Infringements, Lump Sums and Penalty Payments' (2006) 43 *CML Rev* 31
——, *The Enforcement of EC Environmental Law* (Oxford University Press 2007)
Weyer, H, 'Case C-426/05, Tele2 Telecommunication GmbH v Telekom-Control-Kommission, Judgment of the Court (Second Chamber of 21 February 2008, [2008], ECR-I-685' (2009) 46 *CML Rev* 1737
Widdershoven, R, 'The Principle of Loyal Cooperation: Lawmaking by the European Court of Justice and the Dutch Courts' in FAM Stroink and ECHJ Linden (eds), *Judicial Lawmaking and Administrative Law* (Intersentia 2005) 3
——, 'National Procedural Autonomy and General EU Law Limits' (2019) 2 *Review of European Administrative Law* 5
Wilhelmsson, T and Twigg-Flesner, C, 'Pre-Contractual Information Duties in the Acquis Communautaire' (2006) 2 *European Review of Contract Law* 441

Williams, R, 'Case C-47/07, Masdar (UK) Ltd v Commission, Judgment of the Grand Chamber of 16 December 2008, and Case C-446/04,Test Claimants in the FII Group Litigation v Commissioners of Inland Revenue, Judgment of the Grand Chamber of 12 December 2006 [2006]; ECR I-11753' (2010) 47 *CML Rev* 555

Wilman, F, *Private Enforcement of EU Law before National Courts: The EU Legislative Framework* (Edward Elgar 2015)

——, 'The End of the Absence? The Growing Body of EU Legislation on Private Enforcement and the Main Remedies It Provides For' (2016) 53 *CML Rev* 887

Wils, WPJ, 'Discretion and Prioritisation in Public Antitrust Enforcement, in Particular EU Antitrust Enforcement' (2011) 34 *World Competition* 353

Wind, M, 'Can Legal and Political Culture Explain the Success and Failure of European Law Compliance?' in H-W Micklitz and A Wechsler (eds), *The Transformation of Enforcement. European Economic Law in a Global Perspective* (Hart Publishing 2016) 69

Winter, JA, 'Direct Applicability and Direct Effect. Two Distinct and Different Concepts in Community Law' (1972) 9 *CML Rev* 425

Wrbka, S, *European Consumer Access to Justice Revisited* (Cambridge University Press 2014)

——, 'European Consumer Protection Law: Quo Vadis? Thoughts on the Compensatory Collective Redress Debate' in S Wrbka, S Van Uytsel and M Siems (eds), *Collective Actions: Enhancing Access to Justice and Reconciling Multilayer Interests?* (Cambridge University Press 2015) 23

Zakrzewski, R, *Remedies Reclassified* (Oxford University Press 2005)

Zekoll, J, 'Comparative Civil Procedure' in M Reimann and R Zimmermann (eds), *The Oxford Handbook of Comparative Law* 2nd edn (Oxford University Press 2019)

Zwart, T, 'Comparing Standing Regimes from a Separation of Powers Perspective' (2002) 53 *Northern Ireland Legal Quarterly* 391

INDEX

9 781509 937141

Printed by Libri Plureos GmbH in Hamburg,
Germany